RADICAL ROMANTICISM

RADICAL ROMANTICISM

Democracy, Religion, and the Environmental Imagination

MARK S. CLADIS

Columbia University Press

New York

W

Columbia University Press
Publishers Since 1893
New York   Chichester, West Sussex

Library of Congress Cataloging-in-Publication Data
Names: Cladis, Mark Sydney author
Title: Radical romanticism : democracy, religion, and the environmental imagination /
    Mark S. Cladis.
Description: New York : Columbia University Press, 2025. | Includes bibliographical
    references and index.
Identifiers: LCCN 2025010242 (print) | LCCN 2025010243 (ebook) |
    ISBN 9780231213325 hardback | ISBN 9780231213332 trade paperback |
    ISBN 9780231559836 ebook
Subjects: LCSH: American literature—19th century—History and criticism |
    Romanticism—United States | Social justice | Ecocriticism
Classification: LCC PS217.R6 C53 2025 (print) | LCC PS217.R6 (ebook) |
    DDC 810.9—dc23/eng/20250430

Cover design: Milenda Nan Ok Lee
Cover art: Albert Bloch (1882-1961), *Mountain*, 1916. Oil on paperboard, 25 1/8 × 31 3/4
in. (63.8 × 80.6 cm). Blanche A. Haberman Bequest. Inv.: 69.40; Whitney Museum of
American Art/New York, NY/USA; the Albert Bloch Foundation. Digital image @
Whitney Museum of American Art / Licensed by Scala / Art Resource, NY.

GPSR Authorized Representative: Easy Access System Europe, Mustamäe tee 50,
10621 Tallinn, Estonia, gpsr.requests@easproject.com

To my children, Sabine, Luke, and Olive

I will tell you something about stories. They aren't just entertainment. Don't be fooled. They are all we have, you see, all we have to fight off illness and death. You don't have anything if you don't have the stories.

—Leslie Marmon Silko

Contents

Preface; Or, How I Came to Write This Book and What Lies at Its Heart

Some years ago, my colleague Paul Kane and I traveled to the U.S. Southwest to gather material for a course we planned to teach the following semester, It's Only Natural: Contemplation in the American Landscape. The course would explore various philosophical, historical, and religious approaches to the natural world in North American traditions, including Indigenous cultures. Paul and I had come two thousand miles to learn from two people we believed could be of help: Lorain Fox Davis, a Cree and Blackfeet educator who lives in southern Colorado, and Benjamin Barney, a Diné (Navajo) educator who lives in Arizona. We were not disappointed. Both educators were bright, wise, and patient.

We brought with us such questions as: What are meaningful philosophical, religious, and aesthetic approaches to the land? What is the relation between inner and outer landscapes? How does the land nourish the environmental imagination, and how does the environmental imagination nourish a sense of the land? Ultimately, we asked such implausibly large questions as: What is home, beauty, and love, and how do these connect to the land? Lorain and Ben patiently listened to our questions, offering their own distinctively Indigenous perspectives. Eventually, we realized that most of our questions were clumsy and even insensitive. Our idea of "landscape"–with its sublime looming outside the self–was unhelpful. Home, beauty, and love are intimately connected to Indigenous lands, but given the criminal past and present dispossession of Indigenous lands, so are homelessness, despair, and resistance. And we discovered that Euro-American notions of "contemplation" are largely alien to Cree, Blackfeet, and Diné cultures. The land was not primarily a source of beauty and wonder, distant on the horizon, inspiring an elevated sense of life. Rather, it was a place of practical relations with the plants, animals, soil, and other entities of the more-than-human. Some of these relations were defined by kinship; some were not. But in every case the vast, intricate, and intimate relations with the land carried responsibilities and accountability. The land was a storied landscape, narrating people's identities and histories, witnessing sources of oppression and resilience—and yes, manifesting home, beauty, and love.

Not long after this research trip, I began some work on Romanticism, and I was surprised to see convergences between strands of Romanticism and Lorain's and Ben's Indigenous perspectives. I noticed aspects of Romanticism that I had been previously blind to. The Romanticism that I now viewed through an Indigenous lens was a Romanticism inextricably bound to practical action and intimate contact with the human and more-than-human worlds (and their always already relatedness). Lorain and Ben had given me insight into the practical environmental and political perspectives embedded within a subset of Romantic poetic and religious sensibilities—what I now call radical Romanticism.

Fundamentally, radical Romanticism is a less romantic Romanticism: It is focused not so much on sublime vistas but on poignant human encounters and events that bring attention to the experience of war, empire, misogyny, white supremacy, environmental degradation, and oppressive political and religious institutions. Radical Romanticism is an intellectual and aesthetic tradition, as well as a way of life. It seeks to cultivate perspectives, practices, and affect that bring dignity and justice to the human and the more-than-human worlds. It imagines ways in which the human and more-than-human are interdependent and mutually thriving and suffering. It acknowledges and brings witness (not voyeurism) to beauty and cruelty, hope and despair, wonder and uncertainty, mystery and knowledge, braiding these intricately together. It depicts life in times of personal and public crisis and fortifies our means of personal and public transformation. Radical Romanticism is rooted in the everyday experience of ordinary people, and it is as much about beauty and personal interiority as it is about catastrophe and sociopolitical institutions. Radical Romanticism interweaves the cultivation of personal resources (character, commitment, and interiority) and public praxis (solidarity, civic engagement, and transformation) to address such catastrophes as climate change and white supremacy. While confronting suffering and oppression among humans and the more-than-human, radical Romanticism also speaks of a beauty and hope that sustain those working for justice and flourishing.

This new understanding of a strand of Romanticism, in turn, challenged and opened up the traditional Romantic "canon." I came to see radical Romanticism as a dynamic, ongoing set of traditions that include, or at least are nourished and transformed by, such authors as W. E. B. Du Bois, Zora Neale Hurston, and Leslie Marmon Silko. Radical Romanticism allows me to interpret these authors in a new light, but more importantly, their work expands and transforms radical Romanticism. The book's conclusion considers additional radical Romantic voices, including those of queer and trans people. But the final interior chapter, "Leslie Marmon Silko and the Power of Indigenous Storytelling: Healing and Resistance in Defiance of Settler Colonialism," is in many ways the culmination of the book. It brings such catastrophes as settler colonialism, stolen Indigenous lands and children, and nuclear pollution and annihilation to the heart of radical Romanticism. This book, then, begins and ends in Indigenous traditions—with profound respect and in the mode of listening with humility.

The aim of this book is to show how radical Romanticism can contribute to the vitally important work of eco-democratic, spiritual worldmaking. To that end, the book offers a sustained argument for conceiving of radical Romanticism as an aesthetic tradition that embodies profound commitments to progressive democratic and environmental aims and that promotes those aims through literary art forms designed to move people to practical, transformational action. Although the book advances various paths and expressions of eco-democratic transformation, it ultimately seeks to invite practices of reading and engagement that assist the readers' own versions of eco-democratic, spiritual worldmaking. This entails, among other things, exploring radical Romanticism's contributions to the ongoing project of cultivating progressive democratic and environmental theory and practice in the context of catastrophe. In these pages, radical Romanticism—which began in and maintains revolution but is not limited to an era of European history—emerges as an ideology to be critiqued and an inheritance to be critically appropriated. From that inheritance and its various transformations over time and space, we stand to gain a dynamic, contemporary source of life-affirming beliefs, practices, and dispositions.

As in the traditional understanding of Romanticism, radical Romanticism often expresses the beauty and even holiness of the more-than-human. The moral imagination both discovers and co-creates with the more-than-human world in passages such as this:

Spreading trees spring from a prodigal luxuriance of undergrowth; great dark green shadows fade into the black background, until all is one mass of tangled semi-tropical foliage, marvellous in its weird savage splendor. Once we crossed a black silent stream, where the sad trees and writhing creepers, all glinting fiery yellow and green, seemed like *some vast cathedral,*—some green Milan builded of wildwood.[1]

These lines were composed by W. E. B. Du Bois, one of North America's greatest Romantic authors. Depicting the Chickasawhatchee swamp in Georgia, he continued his account:

And as I crossed, I seemed to see again that fierce tragedy of seventy years ago. *Osceola, the Indian-Negro chieftain.* . . . Their war-cry rang from the Chattahoochee to the sea. . . . Then the false slime closing about them called the white men from the east. Waist-deep, they fought beneath the tall trees, until the war-cry was hushed and the Indians glided back into the west. Small wonder the wood is red. *Then came the black slaves.* Day after day the clank of chained feet marching from Virginia and Carolina to Georgia was heard in these rich swamp lands. Day after day the songs of the callous, the wail of the motherless, and the muttered curses of the wretched echoed from the Flint to the Chickasawhatchee.[2]

Here, Du Bois is the master artist of the Romantic storied landscape, depicting the suffering and injustice, the beauty and holiness, the anger and silence carved into the land. This is not William Cronon's or Michael Pollan's characterization of "Romantic Nature" as that which is untouched by humans—as the pristine, the pure, and the ahistorical, as the strength of the Nation or the redemption of *le solitaire.* Rather, the more-than-human is intimately and explicitly related to culture and history. And in this regard, Du Bois is not alone among the Romantics.

Du Bois described a ruin at the edge of the swamp: Where once stood the grand bastion of the slave baron, now lies "such a ruin as this . . . a solitary gate-post standing where once was a castle entrance; an old rusty anvil lying amid rotting bellows . . . ; a wide rambling old mansion, brown and dingy."[3] The derelict plantation is a far cry from that standard Romantic trope, the picturesque ruin: a fragment of the past that is aesthetically and emotionally pleasing and ethically undemanding, producing a gentle nostalgia for a lovely or grand past. It is not so

Preface; Or, How I Came to Write This Book and What Lies at Its Heart xv

far, however, from Wordsworth's "The Ruined Cottage," a prophetic ruin that witnesses past suffering and oppression, unearthing the "untold stories" of the vulnerable and marginalized.

I have introduced Du Bois and the Chickasawhatchee swamp to suggest something about the complexity of Romanticism. When did it begin, and did it ever end? Does it include Wordsworth but exclude Du Bois? Does it pose a robust challenge to colonialism, imperialism, capitalism, war, racism, the subjugation of women, and the exploitation of the more-than-human? Or is Romanticism inextricably an escapist replacement for religion, complicit in genocide, exploitive colonialism, misogyny, slavery, and other forms of domination of people and place?

The ways and manners of Romanticism are legion. There are as many good and helpful portraits of Romanticism as there are authors wrestling honestly with the material broadly associated with it. In my case, I have interrogated a selection of this material and constructed my own portrait of Romanticism for the sake of advancing progressive democratic and environmental aims. I acknowledge that my selection of material is a constructive project, yet I also believe that I maintain an interpretive fidelity to the authors, texts, and events that I consider. While I bring to bear on my material such contemporary interpretive lenses as new materialism, postcolonial criticism, and queer, feminist, and critical race theory, I nonetheless seek to listen skillfully to what precedes me, to such British authors as William and Dorothy Wordsworth, Samuel Taylor Coleridge, and Mary Shelley and such North American authors as Margaret Fuller, Henry David Thoreau, Zora Neale Hurston, and W. E. B. Du Bois.

From these voices, I have both identified and reconstructed a set of progressive democratic, environmental traditions (historically embedded beliefs and practices, ideals and perspectives). These traditions are not stagnant: They are continuously nourished, challenged, and transformed by multiple authors, developments, and movements. For example, in the following pages I show how there is a close affinity between radical Romanticism and the work of Zora Neale Hurston and Leslie Marmon Silko. Their work in relation to radical Romanticism is excessive: They expand and transform radical Romantic traditions but are not limited by them. Intellectually and culturally, Hurston and Silko reside in many homes. Insofar as radical Romanticism is one of those homes, it must not be understood as a circumscribed European period of the past but rather as a set of flexible, dynamic traditions and living practices that remains with us today, constantly being renewed and transformed. This is the promise and hope of radical Romanticism.

Naming the content, context, and form of radical Romanticism is one way to limn it and suggest a family resemblance between such otherwise diverse authors as Jean-Jacques Rousseau, Dorothy and William Wordsworth, Coleridge, Mary Shelley, Fuller, Thoreau, Hurston, Du Bois, and Silko.[4] The *content* of radical Romanticism addresses a variety of socioeconomic, political, and environmental issues and frequently references religion as both a resource for beneficial change and an institution to be critiqued. The *context* are the crises and catastrophes that threaten to rip apart the social and natural fabric of existence, for example, the dispossession and injustice that comes from land enclosures and settler colonialism, the social and environmental wreckage caused by the Industrial Revolution and extractive capitalism, and the oppression and evil inherent in slavery, racism, patriarchy, and massive economic inequality. The aesthetic *forms* of radical Romanticism—its prose and poetry—are diverse, but they are crafted to convey the poignancy and urgency of the issues at hand and to move and shape readers into agents of social change. The forms seek to address the readers on many levels, engaging them as complex, cognitive-affective beings embedded in the webs of the matter and manners of life.

While I believe it is heuristically useful to distinguish content, context, and form, these three are in fact imaginatively interwoven in the rich, multifaceted literature of radical Romanticism. Taken together, they reflect an epistemology that refuses such destructive binaries as reason and emotion, culture and nature, and spirit and matter. Rather than assume there is an epistemological gulf between mind and the world, the assumption is that humans are profoundly intimate with the world (*pace* Cartesianism) but, at the same time, that the world is full of surprise, always ready to unsettle us with the unfamiliar amid the familiar. And rather than put a premium on rationality alone, radical Romanticism emphasizes vulnerability and interdependency. A person's worth is not measured by a capacity for rationality but by the simple fact of being human, understood in the most capacious manner possible. This is, in part, the humanism affirmed by radical Romanticism. At the same time, it also affirms an interdependent relationality to the more-than-human, challenging anthropocentric forms of humanism, displacing the human from the center of all things.

Radical Romanticism honors and cultivates a wide set of complex dispositions and affective responses, including hope, wonder, reverence, and love as well as despair, grief, irreverence, and rage. We are not asked to choose between "positive affects" and "bad feelings." William Wordsworth, Mary Shelley, and W. E. B. Du Bois, for example, expressed warranted despair when faced with (respectively) unjust war, patriarchy, and anti-Black racism. At the same time, they manifested a dispositional hope, working for change despite their reasonable despair and evidence that change, while possible, may not be likely. Such complex affective and dispositional responses are increasingly important as world populations confront such catastrophes as climate change, species extinction, white supremacy, fascism, and the possibility of nuclear annihilation. Engendering appropriate affects and dispositions is vital to radical Romantic efforts to promote forms of solidarity and life-affirming, progressive-democratic ways of life that resist the various faces of oppression.

A plurality of traditions and movements can contribute to achieving an environmentally responsive, progressive democracy. Radical Romanticism is one of them. It remains an open question whether a progressive democracy can be achieved or the extent to which it can be approximated—a society and form of government marked by justice, freedom, and equality and liberated from such harms as racism, patriarchy, homophobia, plutocracy, and wanton indifference to the more-than-human world. Hope, a prominent theme in this book, is a disposition and practice that nourishes efforts to work toward life-affirming practices in spite of obdurate obstacles. A progressive democracy requires arguments, principles, and public reasoning but much more as well. Radical Romanticism, as we will see in the following chapters, promotes what I call a *spiritual democracy*.[3] Think of spiritual democracy as a robust democratic *culture*: its practices and beliefs, institutions and laws, ideals and aspirations. *Spiritual*, here, connotes the complex integration of thought, skills, practices, dispositions, and emotions of diverse citizens as they pursue distinctively democratic, just relations among themselves and in relation to the more-than-human world.

Radical Romanticism seeks to bring attention to those who, for whatever reason, are not deemed worthy of care or grief. Racism and misogyny, transphobia and homophobia, anthropocentrism and fear of the "other" are only a portion of the ways that some are refused basic care and consideration. Insofar as the powerless and seemingly voiceless—among humans and the more-than-human— are excluded from democratic regard and care, a democracy neglects its responsibility to include and consider the *entire* community. Wordsworth, among other radical Romantics, sought to wake up his reader—the whole person—to the suffering and oppression of the marginalized, those whom many deem to be lowly or dangerously "other"—the unhoused, the refugee, the impoverished, the aged, the veteran, and the intellectually and physically disabled. This is a profound democratic aspiration: to help citizens witness the suffering and dignity of fellow citizens and of the more-than-human. The aesthetics of radical Romanticism can be summed up as various efforts to give sight to see, in Wordsworth's words, "souls that appear to have no depth at all / To careless eyes."[6]

The cultivation of democratic *enhanced attention* is wedded to the cultivation of radical Romantic *praxis-oriented empathy*. Praxis-oriented empathy is a form of affect and practice that both motivates and accompanies the witnessing of social harms and the practical work of social justice and transformation. Such empathy is a form of care but also a form of critique: Caring about suffering requires commitment to critiquing and dismantling structures and practices of injustice. Discerning critique, then, like democratic attentiveness and empathy, is a *practice* that radical Romanticism attempts to *inculcate*. Radical Romanticism, then, seeks to inform a people with a robust democratic way of life—a way of life that has the capacity to name unnecessary suffering and injustice, to work vigorously against it, and also to experience beauty and joy in individual, private ways and public, shared ways.

In the pages that follow, I often approach my sources in a mode of listening. This is especially true of my engagement with Mary Shelley, Margaret Fuller, W. E. B. Du Bois, Zora Neale Hurston, and Leslie Marmon Silko—authors whose life experiences were and are so drastically different from my own. Every listener, of course, is grounded and situated in a particular sociocultural context. I listen to my sources as the child of Greek immigrants; as a male U.S. citizen who is both complicit in and resistant to racism, misogyny, and white settler colonialism; and as an academic scholar who is engaged with a progressive form of Romanticism that I first began to perceive after having been influenced by Diné (Navajo), Cree, and Blackfeet instruction, specifically by their intimate, practical relation to place. I have learned that a profound form of alienation is to be severed from an intimate connection to place—to the land, the culture, the language, the stories, the more-than-human. This book, inspired by the Diné, Cree, and Blackfeet, is about what it might mean to reestablish just connections to people and place, to powerful stories and transformative ways of life.[7]

Storytelling is central to radical Romanticism, and it is central to my method and approach. Silko once claimed that "the only way to seek justice was through *the power of stories.*"[8] That claim could serve as the creed of radical Romanticism. In these pages, I often find myself as a curator or translator of powerful stories, creating something of a pluralist assemblage from master storytellers. To retell a story well requires the ability to listen well. That is the task I have set for myself. The storytelling in this book carries both critique and vision. We need both, and I am committed to both, though I might as well admit that I am more of a lover than a fighter.

I am drawn to the power of the literary arts, to their capacity to challenge, move, and change people and forge community. The art of the word has a profound capacity to name beauty and suffering and to thereby promote healing, solidarity, and activism. The literary arts and storytelling can be a form of ceremony, if ceremony is understood as revealing and generating transformational connections—connections that illuminate the intricacies of the world and our relations to it. Scholarship, too, can be a form of ceremony, especially if it includes a "responsibility to act with fidelity in relationship to what has been heard, observed, and learnt."[9] Ceremonies can heal and also disturb by revealing and attempting to address painful and destructive practices and illnesses in individuals and communities. In this way, ceremonies can be like a knife, seeking to cut away sources of suffering and oppression. Similarly, art—specifically, radical Romantic aesthetics—can draw its weapons in the service of social and political justice.[10]

Ceremony and storytelling seeking justice, then, are among my methods and approaches. The practice of hope is as well. As will become clear in the following pages, the form of hope manifested in the work and lives of radical Romantics is anything but Pollyannaish optimism. Rather, it is steeped in the pain and subjugation of humans and the more-than-human. Resistance to oppression—which entails reimagining and working toward just ways of being in the face of uncertainty—requires a dark, wild hope. This book will attempt to register and advance that peculiar form of hope.

In 1942, Eva Beatrice Dykes published her path-breaking book, *The Negro in English Romantic Thought.* Dykes, who graduated from Radcliffe College (now Harvard), was the first Black American woman to complete the requirements for a doctoral degree. The subtitle of her remarkable book on English Romanticism is *A Study in Sympathy for the Oppressed.* In this work she persuasively argued for interpreting Romanticism as a movement committed to "the amelioration of the condition of the lowly and oppressed." She understood, of course, that not all

Romanticism was committed to witnessing and resisting forces of oppression. But she identified a powerful strand of emancipatory Romanticism that does indeed carry that very commitment, and she lamented that most think of Romanticism simply as delightful "classics of English literature." It is appalling that this ahead-of-her-time author, powerful educator, and community leader has been all but forgotten.[11] In this regard, she has suffered the fate of countless dynamic, talented Black women.

I think of my book as a continuation of Dykes's powerful study of Romanticism. Like Dykes, I recognize that while Romanticism speaks in many voices, there is a salient radical Romantic subset of traditions that is dedicated to "the amelioration of the condition of the lowly and oppressed." With Dykes, I identify early British radical Romantics who sought to revolutionize society, honoring the dignity and transforming the conditions of the marginalized. Additionally, however, I also trace the subsequent development of radical Romanticism right up to the present day. For ultimately, I understand radical Romanticism not as a limited historical epoch of European culture that is frozen in the past but as a dynamic set of traditions—life-affirming beliefs, practices, and dispositions—that promotes justice, beauty, and flourishing in human and more-than-human worlds.

RADICAL ROMANTICISM

Introduction

"A LOUD PROPHETIC BLAST OF HARMONY": WHAT KIND OF WARNING IS REQUIRED?

In the *Prelude* (1805), Wordsworth wrote of a man who dreamt of awakening—awakening to urgency. In the dream, the man wakes up in a desert and sees another man holding a book in the form of a shell. He is enjoined to hold the shell to his ear, whereupon he hears not a recognized language but nonetheless "articulate sounds": "A loud prophetic blast of harmony / An ode in passion uttered, which foretold / Destruction to the children of the earth / By deluge now at hand."[1]

What kind of sound issues from a shell, a more-than-human book? A sound from the future, or perhaps a sound magnified, having been gathered from around the globe? Does it speak the language of rising seas? What kind of language, revelation, or forms of evidence would wake people and alert them to the impending emergency? Is that the "prophetic blast of harmony"? Perhaps the "articulate sounds" are a combination of the human and more-than-human, jointly forming an ode, a blast, a warning? After all, hearing the sound requires that the man bring his humanity to the shell-book. Yet could more people hear it? And when the man wakes up, does he take the dream seriously? Does he speak of it to others, and do they take him seriously?

The book in your hands asks what kind of warning is required to wake people up and alert them to the catastrophic. Fascism, white supremacy, patriarchy, homophobia, transphobia, and massive environmental degradation, including mass extinction and the climate emergency—these are some of the catastrophes of our age. For many, too many, these catastrophes are experienced as a daily reality. They do not need to be awakened. Yet others, too many, are not awake to the current catastrophes, or else they are in a dreamy state as they try to comprehend climate change and other massive crises. What would it take to wake them up?

I do not know what a shell as a book looks or sounds like. But I imagine that it resounds like the earth and seas. And I believe that the authors I listen to and discuss in this book create literary art *forms*—radical Romantic aesthetics—that approximate the sound of the shell-book. The form of their language attempts to sound—in both senses of that word—the varied and uneven topographies of world and life, issuing warning but also hope, witnessing disaster but also beauty.[2] The form and texture of their art palpably—*sensuously*—invites readers into their texts, seeking a strong alliance between author, reader, and world. In such an alliance, readers may hear the shell, wake up, and tend to the world with precision, grief, and care, working actively for beauty and against catastrophe.

SCOPE OF THE BOOK

The art and work of radical Romantics belong to an ongoing cluster of progressive traditions, beliefs, and perspectives that spring from the late eighteenth and early nineteenth centuries—European literary, philosophical, religious, and political movements—but they are by no means limited to European eras or authors. Exploring this dynamic constellation often requires a *triscopic* approach, that is, a methodology that involves careful attention to the interweaving of democratic, environmental, and religious (broadly understood) sensibilities. It also requires attention to forms of art that, like the shell-book, seek to in-*form* readers and inspire work for personal and social transformation.

Such an approach illuminates shared characteristics of the main figures in this book: Rousseau, Dorothy and William Wordsworth, Samuel Taylor Coleridge, Mary Shelley, Margaret Fuller, Henry David Thoreau, Zora Neale Hurston, W. E. B. Du Bois, and Leslie Marmon Silko. Chapter 1 is on radical Romantic aesthetics, specifically that of Wordsworth and Du Bois; the chapter allows me to develop the *engaged poetics and aesthetics* associated with radical Romanticism that I develop throughout the book. Moreover, by beginning with Du Bois and interpreting him as a radical Romantic, I am immediately challenging the traditional Romantic canon as well as many assumptions about Romanticism (e.g., it is escapist and unconcerned with political, racial, and economic injustice). Indeed, Du Bois emerges as the most prominent figure in the book given his distinctive position of being so firmly rooted in radical Romanticism even as he expands and transforms it. And just as the book begins with Du Bois to redefine Romanticism and its past, the book concludes with a chapter on Silko—the acclaimed Indigenous novelist, poet, and essayist—to reimagine Romanticism's future.

Radical Romanticism is unsettled and transformed by the work of such authors as Du Bois, Zora Neale Hurston, and Silko, even as the practice of unsettling and being unsettled is intrinsic to radical Romanticism. Such radical Romantics as the Wordsworths and Coleridge were unsettled by the French Revolution, were radicalized by it, and then sought to unsettle and challenge oppressive institutions, practices, and beliefs in Great Britain. Moreover, early radical Romantics sought to disclose and combat the socially and environmentally devastating practices of empire and the Industrial Revolution—including the dispossession of lands, child labor, the dangerous working and living conditions of laborers, the oppression of women, and extractive capitalism's massive destruction of the more-than-human. Early radical Romantics anticipated and critiqued the socioeconomic forces that would lead the world to "the Anthropocene" and the climate emergency. They anticipated the way empire and industrialization would dramatically transform and bring destruction to the world's ecosystems, and they critiqued forms of anthropocentrism and human hubris that exalted human sovereignty and domination over the more-than-human. While radical Romanticism does honor humans as worldmakers, such worldmaking refers to the power of the human imagination to co-create in a collaborative, reciprocal fashion with the more-than-human.

The sociopolitical and environmental work of radical Romanticism is performed in an embodied language that is thoroughly material, wonderfully queer, and powerfully poetic. Its interwoven politics and poetics seek to bring down borders that would establish harmful hierarchies between human and more-than-human, rich and poor, white and Black, men and women, straight and queer, able and disabled. It opposes the sovereign male, erect and isolated, and instead offers what it is to embrace—to think and feel—a life of relatedness: people in community, nourished by people and place, abiding by reciprocity and care, and all the while acknowledging vulnerability, uncertainty, and pain. Radical Romantic ways of thinking and feeling fashion lenses of attention and modes of being that illuminate what matters and why, where suffering and oppression has and does reside, and how to imagine and work toward ways of justice and sustainability, however uncertain and remote. Critique is at the heart of radical Romanticism, even as it itself has participated in destructive forms of hierarchies, racism, patriarchy, and settler colonialism. No author, tradition, nor society is innocent and outside critique.

TELLING STORIES TO WARN THE WORLD

At a recent meeting of the Association for the Study of Literature and the Environment, a guest speaker asked a guard at the convention hall, "Which way to the conference?" The guard replied, "You mean the conference about telling stories to save the world?" *Telling stories to save the world* is one way to think of the art of the radical Romantics, though *telling stories to warn the world* is more apt still. Storytelling is central to this book; it belongs to both its content and method. As I noted in the preface, I work as a curator of powerful stories. Stories have the capacity to meaningfully connect the present to the past and future, interweaving the reader's own story within a larger narrative and thereby providing a place to stand and witness the interrelatedness of past, present, and future oppression and justice, suffering, and beauty. Both critique and vision are powerfully conveyed via storytelling because stories can conjure provisionally holistic accounts of forms of oppression and paths forward. I write "provisionally" because, as is well known among Indigenous storytellers, the story told is never complete or static but rather is always contingent and contestable. Yet such provisionality does not render the story any less powerful or truthful. On the contrary, the story's strength is in its *becoming*—becoming more germane, more truthful, more revelatory.

Stories and ideologies are distinct from each other but also interrelated. Stories are particular and detailed, full of proper nouns, deeply rooted in place and time, and are usually associated with a particular storyteller or culture. Ideology, in contrast, tends to be anonymous even if it is associated with individuals or groups that manifest the ideology. Ideology informs the broad narrative—the cluster of stories—that we identify with and the kinds of stories we listen to and tell. Yet storytelling, given its specificity—its vivid depiction of a portion of life—has the capacity to enter the territory of a "foreign" ideology, reaching people who would not usually be drawn to and moved by the story, in large part because of the story's particularity: all the various "hooks," openings, and invitations that it offers. For example, imagine the reactionary who reads a moving story about a young lesbian, reflects on his own daughter who is a lesbian, and then proceeds to treat her with more understanding and empathy.

Storied landscapes figure importantly in radical Romantic storytelling. By *storied landscapes*, I mean places that have been endowed transactionally by human and more-than-human features.[3] Wordsworth's poems "The Ruined Cottage" and "Michael," Du Bois's *The Souls of Black Folk*, Hurston's *Their Eyes Were Watching God*, and Silko's *Ceremony* typify the process by which literature draws on and contributes to landscapes whose appearance and character are infused with history and culture, human sorrow and tenderness. "The Ruined Cottage" and "Michael," for example, are poignantly crafted storied landscapes that unearth "untold stories" of the vulnerable poor and the injustice that upended their lives. With the help of a guide, we come to understand the ruined cottage as a geophysical site inclusive of human and more-than-human stories—stories embedded in complex temporalities, physical processes, private human lives, and such public institutions as government, class, capitalism, and the politics of war. And in "Michael," again with the help of a guide, we come to see a heap of stones as carrying a tragic story of how the world of Michael, Isabel, and Luke came to ruins because of land enclosures and financial markets.

The radical Romantic authors in this book use storied landscapes to reveal histories and sites of oppression written in the land—histories and sites that might have remained silent if not for the storytellers' powerful witness and capacity to read and write the land. Whether protesting unjust land enclosures, settler colonial dispossession, industrial pollution, patriarchy, or anti-Black racism, radical Romantic storied landscapes disrupt the unjust status quo, offer alternative ways of being and remembering, and depict the land itself as a site of both relationality and contestation.

In the storied landscape, the more-than-human is typically both character and coauthor, for the storied landscape is a co-creation between the human and more-than-human. Beings and entities of the more-than-human are understood as having agency and the capacity to work on humans—to educate us, fashion us, to speak back to us. The more-than-human, in this radical Romantic perspective, is not a grandiloquent fiction created by poets but an autonomous presence that defies human efforts to systematically control and instrumentalize it. "Autonomous presence" should not imply that the land possesses something like a Kantian,

autonomous will. Rather, radical Romantics affirm varied and complex interconnections between the human and the more-than-human, a profound relatedness that nonetheless honors difference and distinctiveness among the world's
vast number of creatures, beings, and entities and their various forms of agency.

Some stories and storied landscapes, of course, can reinscribe domination and
oppression even as others reveal and combat such harms. Some stories injure while
others heal. The vision and content of the story determines its normative force.
I wish now to name the vision and some of the central content or themes of radical Romanticism, but first I will identify an exemplar of its vision and themes as
expressed in practice.

CENTRAL VISION AND THEMES

Dorothy Wordsworth's life, journals, and poetry express care for human community and its intimacy with the more-than-human. While on her walks, she often
observed and wrote about aspects of the more-than-human that could be described
as "outside her"—outside or different from humanity. Indeed, more than her
brother William, Dorothy wrote in a detached fashion to allow the creatures and
entities of the more-than-human to express their own natures. But she depicted
nature "outside her" neither as an alienating other nor as the transcendent sublime. Rather, she portrayed the more-than-human sometimes as neighbors, sometimes as strangers, but in every case honoring their integral being. Dorothy's
account of nature was typically bodily, relational, and close to home—in head-
aches and bowel pains, trees and plants, local gardens and fields. So, if William
on occasion depicted nature as sublime and transcendent, nature for Dorothy was
intimate, local, and included human community and culture.

In his "Tintern Abbey" ode (1798), a poem whose power and subject was revolutionary in the West, William described "plots of cottage-ground" and "orchard-
tufts"—sites of evident cultivation—as participating in "the *wild* green landscape."[4]
And here in that landscape, in still another site of wild culture, William introduced those "wild eyes" of Dorothy, offering his greatest tribute to her.[5] In
Dorothy—his home mate, his soul mate, his literary collaborator—he saw the
strength of culture and the wild fused in body and soul. She walked ten miles a
day, deep into the land with profound purpose but not narrow utilitarian aim
(she refused oppressive instrumentalism); wildly breaking from convention, she

read works deemed suitable only for men, including works considered scandal-ous; she wrote unconventional poems and journal entries that challenge such ways of being as the male "sovereign self" and that speak of the liberating interconnect-edness between humans and the more-than-human; she cared deeply for the desti-tute and sick even when she herself was poor; and she participated in the world with powerful attentiveness, discerning vibrancy in the winds and seas, the lands and trees, and the human connection to them.

Dorothy was a collaborator and source of support for William, but she was also an artist in her own right. Her poems and journals possess a distinctive voice, manifesting her remarkable powers of observation and expression, an astute everyday realism. She composed keen accounts of beauty and struggle, and she opposed all who sought to dominate humans or the more-than-human, advo-cating instead a practice of care. And unlike William, who often stressed the "oneness" of life, Dorothy tended to emphasize the diversity of life—even the diversity within a single self, as seen, for example, in her remarkable poem "Floating Island at Hawkshead" (1842). Her life options regarding education and career, among other things, were greatly limited, given the time's repressive gender roles. There can be no doubt that, in a less patriarchal culture, she would have achieved still more in the art of verse and prose. Nonetheless, she lived with a nonconventional wildness. Refusing to marry, she spent her days dwelling as a free spirit, encumbered by a host of domestic chores but also reading widely, speaking candidly, walking fiercely, and witnessing and recording the intimate connections among and between the human and more-than-human, with all its beauty and all its exploitation.

Dorothy Wordsworth's work and life exemplify such *central radical Romantic themes* as (1) salutary attention to an everyday realism, (2) noninstrumental modes of being, (3) the promotion of liberatory connections between people and place, (4) an ethics of care directed at both humans and the more-than-human, and (5) a rejection of the destructive culture/nature binary and the related idealism-empiricism polarity.

Radical Romanticism focuses on *everyday life as sites for the creation of art, rev-elation, education, and social critique.* Such creation is the result of the moral imagi-nation bringing critical attention, often via storytelling, to everyday realities. It is commonplace to juxtapose Romanticism with realism. After all, are not the Romantics interested more in imaginative than realistic things? What does Romanticism have to do with the practical, the objective, the concrete? Contrary to this conception, radical Romanticism is committed to a realism of the everyday. The imagination is not conceived as a form of fanciful self-expression but rather as a creative lens through which one might see the everyday more deeply, sharply, and richly and bring critical attention to the experiences of war, displacement, and the exploitation of humans and the more-than-human. While reading Milton's *Paradise Lost*, Wordsworth scrawled in the book's margin, "The real excellence of Imagination consists in the capacity of exploring *the world really existing*."[6]

Dorothy also manifested radical Romantic *noninstrumental modes of being*. This is not to say that radical Romanticism is indifferent to practical matters but rather that it critiques modes of being that systematically instrumentalize relations among humans and the more-than-human. Narrowly calculating ways of life wed to the rise of global capitalism encourage exploitive attitudes and practices, extinguish the capacity to experience wonder, surprise, and beauty, and fail to acknowledge aspects of life most worthy of care. If all beings and things are subject to control by calculation and instrumental rationality, then life in its fullness is rendered as inert and silent. However, the radical Romantic *wild*—that which (in humans and the more-than-human) is not subject to complete control— has the capacity to speak back and resist such attempted domination.

The promotion of *liberatory connections between people and place* is another central theme in radical Romanticism. Emancipatory interconnections between humans, place, and the more-than-human include practices and traditions that name, honor, and, in some cases, attempt to shape those interconnections. The examples are plentiful: Rousseau's Julie thrives in the eco-community, Clarens, an environmental, economic, and political alternative to prevailing oppressive, European sensibilities. The inhabitants of William Wordsworth's "Lake District" are at home in their place—dwelling as "co-partner[s] and sister[s] of nature"—but are threatened with displacement by new forms of capitalism and industry.[7] Mary Shelley's "Creature" strives his entire life to find and create a place of belonging, suffering as he pursues this unattainable goal. Du Bois's Zora, "child of the swamp" and powerful female leader, creates a home and community in cooperation with people and place, all the while working against the weighty forces of white supremacy. The theme of alienation caused by harmful disconnection and healing by way of liberatory connection runs deep in radical Romanticism. And as we will see, this radical Romantic theme will be developed and transformed profoundly by Silko. The depth of the development is in part attributable to the height of the ongoing crisis: *How does one establish home and belonging while simultaneously experiencing Indigenous dispossession?*

Anticipating the feminist ethics of care of such philosophers as Eva Kittay, Dorothy and William Wordsworth, among other radical Romantics, held that one's worth is not determined by measures of rationality but by the simple fact of being human and being in relation to others. And the scope of care extends to the more-than-human, as seen, for example, in the ecofeminist work of Mary Shelley, Margaret Fuller, and Zora Neale Hurston. A common theme in their work is opposition to hypermasculine individuality: the arrogance of thinking that one can "go it alone," erect and solitary. Shelley critiqued such masculinity with her character Victor Frankenstein, who perfectly embodies "the sovereign self"; and Fuller in *Summer on the Lakes* and Hurston in *Their Eyes* counter hypermasculine individuality with such practices as reciprocity, care, and mutual dependence among humans and between humans and the more-than-human.

Finally, Dorothy and her fellow radical Romantics rejected the *destructive nature/culture binary* and instead depicted an intricate relation between the two. Relatedly, radical Romantics mediated the *empiricism-idealism polarity*. There is a profound interconnection between empiricism—worldfinding, that is, being receptive to the world—and idealism—or world making, that is, creating or co-creating something new in the world. Radical Romantic storytelling is the art of openness to the world and, in response, of weaving something new in it, thereby co-creating with the world. In Silko's Indigenous storytelling, for example, she attends to Laguna Pueblo places and histories as well as other Indigenous and global places and histories, and in turn she creates a new story—a world of sorts. But this storied world is not an escape from worldfinding. It is the world found—with its pain and injustice, its beauty and love—portrayed with exquisite clarity and power. Indeed, it is thanks to the profound authenticity of the story that it can help one see the world clearly, as if for the first time. The power of storytelling is rooted in the meeting place of worldfinding and worldmaking—of receptivity and imagination.

CENTRAL METHODS AND APPROACHES

Having discussed some central themes in this book, I now turn to its core methods and approaches. Worldfinding and worldmaking are rooted in history and geography, and in this book I attend carefully to memories and traditions embedded in (but also exceeding) place. The role of tradition, memory, and witness is central to my approach and to radical Romanticism itself. Wordsworth, for example, turned to memory and history to help him navigate times of great personal and public crises: the promise and disillusionment of the French Revolution; the chaos and oppression of the British response to it; slavery; the increase in poverty, homelessness, and environmental degradation following the rise of industrialization and global capitalism; and the dispossession (enclosures) of common lands. In the face of political, environmental, and spiritual crises, Wordsworth asked: What can we learn from the ghosts and ruins of past hardship and sorrow? What sources of life and justice offer themselves? What is the relation between the present and past and between the current and former self? His claim, "The Child is Father of the Man," is a declaration of dependence.[8] For better or worse, the present is dependent on the past. It is a wellspring of nurturing vision and debilitating bias, of ethical guidance and brutal oppression.

Robin Wall Kimmerer, an enrolled member of the Citizen Potawatomi Nation, claims that "in order to walk forward on the path of life, we must first turn around and walk back along the trail that our ancestors followed and pick up what was left behind for us: fragments of land, remnants of stories, plant and animal relatives, and our languages and teachings."[9] She is referring to the "People of the Seventh Fire" and what they will need in order to bring change and protect life. But, as is her way, she is also generously articulating a fundamental lesson for an inclusive audience. In this book, I look back to radical Romanticism in search of "fragments of land, remnants of stories" in the hope that these may help in the "walk forward on the path of life." Radical Romantic traditions—fragments and stories—are like living beings: dynamic, responsive, changing, and conveying affect, perspectives, practices, and warnings. We can lose sight of past traditions and in doing so perhaps lose part of our selves, but the traditions do not necessarily disappear: They still live on in the hauntings of places and ancestors, pieces of language and culture. The traditions and stories lie waiting for us to return to them—to learn from them, retell them, expand and change them. To actively identify with a set of traditions is to seek them, name them, and in turn create them—to find and create their past but also their future. Again, worldfinding and -making are interdependent. In this fashion, in this book, I both find and make radical Romanticism.

Such finding and making is not a neutral or value-free endeavor. My principal objective is to critically appropriate ethical, social, and political resources for the sake of furthering progressive democratic and environmental aims. Yet while I critically appropriate what I find to be life enhancing and ethically discerning in radical Romanticism, I also recognize and bring attention to its inadequacies and ethical failures—some quite grave. Radical Romanticism initially arose in the context of a Eurocentric world of whiteness, patriarchy, colonialism, and anthropocentricism. Radical Romanticism was born out of resistance to these forms of oppression but has also perpetuated them. Of Romanticism more generally, it has been argued that its art and its production of "Romantic Nature" were shaped and ultimately supported by the socioeconomic conditions that maintained empire, colonialism, the oppression of women, and slavery. Additionally, vicious forms of nationalism have been associated with Romanticism, especially Romantic depictions of nature and the homeland. Nazi Germany, for example, can be viewed as a form or legacy of Romantic nationalism. The new historicists charge that "Romantic Nature" was an ideological form of escapist art that concealed oppressive economic and social structures.[10] In this view, nature is conveniently interpreted to allow empire and capitalism to exploit workers and natural resources while offering an elite culture the mind-numbing pleasures of the sublime, the beautiful, and the picturesque.[11]

While these critiques about Romanticism have been variously challenged, there is nonetheless truth in them, and radical Romanticism is not exempt from them. I will identify radical Romanticism's complicity in oppressive ideologies and institutions. Yet my primary efforts will be to disclose radical Romanticism as a progressive and emancipatory subset of traditions from within Romanticism more generally. In this subset of traditions, one finds penetrating critiques of empire, colonialism, capitalism, the oppression of women, slavery, socioeconomic inequality, and environmental exploitation. Additionally, I identify authors not usually deemed Romantic, and these authors, I have noted, powerfully transform the scope and shape of radical Romanticism. In my approach to radical Romanticism, then, while I register critiques *of* it, I mainly focus on the critical resources *within* it for the sake of combating oppressive systems of power and ideologies. This approach maintains that combating domination and exploitation requires locating oneself in ethical and spiritual traditions of excellence and political wisdom.

In addition to and in conjunction with such critical appropriation, I often pursue what I have called a triscopic approach, bringing attention to how progressive democratic, environmental, and religious sensibilities mutually inform one another. This approach yields fresh interpretations revealing democratic and environmental perspectives embedded within Romantic religious and poetic discourse. As a scholar of the academic study of religion, I often investigate the largely unexamined religious backgrounds, perspectives, and practices of what are otherwise considered secular thinkers, discourse, and institutions. Many conventional accounts of Romanticism neglect the religious aspects of Romanticism (Protestant and Catholic, orthodox and heterodox, deistic, pantheistic, and panentheistic), or they narrativize religion as belonging to a process of secularization and privatization. For the most part, however, Romantic authors did not eschew religion but rather dissociated it from strictly denominational church politics and engaged religion (broadly understood) in the service of sociopolitical aims. Romantic poetry has been similarly interpreted in a privatized fashion, reducing Romanticism's powerful environmental and political perspectives to nostalgic notions of the pastoral or to private gazes on the sublime. However, when we apply an interpretive lens that acknowledges the radical religious traditions that in fact permeate much of Romanticism, we gain insight into its religious as well as its political, economic, and environmental dimensions.

So, for example, in chapters 5 and 6 I show how secularized accounts of Wordsworth, Coleridge, and Du Bois fail to register the religion or spirituality that animates them and how these accounts thereby miss the close connections between religious, political, and environmental progressive thought. Secularized accounts of Silko hazard similar risks. The "spiritual" or the remarkable in Silko's authorship is central to it, and it bears directly on such *material* issues as Indigenous sovereignty, land justice, resilience, and continuance. In Euro-American scholarly environmental literature, the more-than-human is usually a *secular* concept that replaces "nature." Yet for Silko, among other Indigenous authors, the more-than-human includes not only "nature" but also ancestors, animal spirits, goddess creators, ghosts, and witches, among other beings or presences that settler cultures typically call "spiritual" or "supernatural." It is precisely here, on the "spiritual" or remarkable, that settler scholars often stumble or else secularize Silko.

Another approach in this book is to listen carefully to poetry and creative nonfiction for their various sociopolitical and environmental notes and tones—their lyrical quality. In *Narrative of the Life of Frederick Douglass*, Douglass writes of the power of the music of the enslaved: "They would make the dense old woods, for miles around, reverberate with their wild songs, revealing at once the highest joy and the deepest sadness. . . . Every tone was a testimony against slavery, and a prayer to God for deliverance from chains."[12] Like the radical Romantics, Douglass sought to wake people up not only with analytic arguments but with aesthetically crafted storied landscapes (in which history, brutality, struggle, and beauty, too, are inscribed into the land), thereby stirring a wide range of the cognitive-affective dimension in his readers and audience. While he was well versed in philosophy and employed it, he also recognized its limits. Hence, of those remarkable songs of the enslaved he wrote: "The mere hearing of those songs would do more to impress some minds with the horrible character of slavery, than the reading of whole volumes of philosophy on the subject could do."[13] Here Douglass brings attention to the potential power of aesthetics to change hearts and minds and bring transformative justice. In this book, I seek to do the same. Not wanting to elide the power and tragedy of sorrow songs—the songs of the enslaved—with radical Romanticism, I nonetheless seek to listen to the "music" of radical Romantic poetry and creative nonfiction, bringing attention to its capacity to warn, grieve, and surprise, to reveal the horrific and offer the salutary, to depict forms of subjugation and disclose life-enhancing possibilities.

A final comment on my approach and the use of the first-person plural pronoun "we." In an age of great divisiveness, I honor attempts to cultivate public languages, common projects, and diverse but related identities. The craft of the radical Romantics, I believe, can assist in cultivating public languages, shared projects, and forms of culture that facilitate the very conservations and changes that are necessary to make progress on *just transitions*—on the transformation of subjectivities, institutions, and practices for the sake of promoting justice and environmental care. The neoliberal language of self-interest is not adequate for providing rich, nuanced accounts of human motivation and action or for informing shared goals and how to achieve them. Making headway toward justice and care will require more than coordinated self-interests. It will require public languages and ways of life that nurture and put into practice powerful ethical commitments, beliefs, practices, and loves. Radical Romanticism, among other traditions and perspectives, can help us achieve this.

My commitment to shared public languages compels me on occasion to employ the first-person plural "we." I recognize that, given differences in race, class, gender, sexuality, and geographic location, people will respond differently to this book. I do not pretend to offer a universal argument that is convincing or edifying to all people everywhere. And at times I am quite explicit about differentiating between various audiences, for example, when and how Du Bois addresses Black readers as opposed to white readers. But at other times, the issues at hand are broadly inclusive, and I address readers accordingly as a "we."

Who is this "we"? This book brings together my areas of general expertise: environmental humanities, political theory, literary studies, and religious studies. The topic—the interrelation of progressive democratic, environmental, and religious traditions and perspectives in radical Romanticism—will be of interest to students and scholars of environmental humanities, political philosophy, literary criticism, religious studies, and those working at the intersection of critical race, feminist, and Indigenous studies. My hope, of course, is that some readers outside the academy will also be drawn to the matters in this book. Ultimately, the "we" is those who read these pages and who, regardless of their response to the book, are committed to justice and flourishing in worlds human and more-than-human.

"IF YOU WISH TO CONVERSE WITH ME, DEFINE YOUR TERMS"

The terms and concepts central to this book can be comprehended in the context of its specific arguments and narratives.[14] Still, some initial stipulations can help. Working at the juncture of political theory, literature, religious studies, and environmental humanities, *I discover, interrogate, and construct a cluster of radical Romantic traditions and perspectives that nourish ethical visions of an environmentally responsive and progressive eco-democracy embodied by citizens and embedded in its lands and institutions.* By "ethical visions," I mean linked yet diverse arrays of normative stories, perspectives, arguments, and insights that inform the ethos and practices of a people. By "embodied" and "embedded," I mean the ways eco-democratic beliefs, practices, and affect are enacted and reflected in the identities of individuals and in the lands and institutions in which they dwell. "Embodied eco-democracy" brings attention to the democratic *second nature* of citizens and to the cultural (not simply procedural) dimensions of democracy, including aesthetic, religious, and affective ones, highlighting the distinctive ways democratic citizens (broadly understood) move, dwell, and engage with humans and the more-than-human. "Embedded eco-democracy" also brings attention to the reciprocal relationships between democratic beliefs and practices and the *lands* that sustain them. Democracy informs the lands even as the lands inform democracy. By "lands," I refer not only to the soils and waters of the earth but to what Max Liboiron (Red River Métis/Michif) refers to as "the unique entity that is the combined living spirit of plants, animals, air, water, humans, histories, and events recognized by Indigenous communities."[15] By "environmentally responsive," I refer to an ever-evolving, dynamic set of beliefs, dispositions, and affects that dispose members of a democratic culture to see, think, feel, and act in ways that advance environmental justice and to treat with respect and care the various beings and entities of the more-than-human.

By "radical Romanticism," I refer to my selection and interpretation of Romantic material that highlights dynamic, ongoing *progressive* democratic and environmental commitments, ideals, institutions, beliefs, and practices. Romanticism is not a natural kind. It is a construction. Radical Romanticism, then, refers to my construction of (and faithful interpretations of) the progressive ways and manners of a Romanticism that is committed to exposing various forms of cruelty, callousness, and catastrophes as well as revealing forms of beauty, love, and goodness. "Radical," in this book, refers to both rootedness and critique, signifying that radical Romanticism is rooted in people, places, and traditions that cultivate critique. "Progressive" does not refer to linear progress in time; it is not, then, akin to Hegelian teleology or supersessionist notions of "things keep getting better." Rather, by "progressive" I refer to such aspirational goals as the eradication of racism, patriarchy, settler colonialism, homo- and transphobia, classism, and exploitive approaches to the more-than-human. Or, to put it positively, "progressive" refers to such aspirational goals as social and political equality and to justice and flourishing among humans and between humans and the more-than-human.

In this book, I refer to "spiritual democracy" and show how radical Romanticism can contribute to spiritual democracy—a lively, culturally specific, culturally contested, and progressive democracy that is both real and aspirational. Spiritual democracy is neither a mystical, nationalistic political body nor a democracy based on supposed transcendent or immutable ideals. "Spiritual," here, connotes the thought, skills, practices, dispositions, and affect of diverse individuals and communities as they pursue distinctively democratic relations, including relations to future generations and to the more-than-human. "Spiritual," in this context, refers to the integrative complexity of people and place—forms of knowledge and wisdom, practice and affect, gratitude and reciprocity: the whole person in ethical, democratic relation to people and place, now and into the future. Spiritual democracy is not primarily understood as a set of democratic procedures or legal codes, but neither is it *bereft* of procedural justice, legal codes, or of such democratic principles as "one person, one vote." But its scope is not limited to elections and procedures. It is informed by what Walt Whitman called "a sublime and serious Religious Democracy," the many and diverse cultural threads that form a complex, progressive democratic social fabric.[16]

People and place shape a spiritual democracy even as spiritual democracy shapes people and place. In this book, the shaping engendered by spiritual democracy is referred to as "democratic second nature": the cultivation of an ecologically responsive, democratic subjectivity. Second nature is the formative, dynamic process and condition of acquiring, in time and place, various beliefs, practices, and dispositions that become internalized. Progressive democratic second nature, while trustworthy, must be subject to constant critique and transformation. Indeed, *critique itself is a cultivated capacity in democratic second nature.* The implicit argument here is that progressive democratic thought and practice are not only compatible with ways of cultivation—tradition, practice, and exemplars—but require them. For some time now, I have been interested in models of democratic institutions, communities, and practice that do not rely on either (1) appeals to rational choice or market efficiency models, often purportedly derived from principles of universal, deliberative human rationality; or (2) political arguments based on natural reason or any other anchors in an ahistorical moral reality. My interest, rather, is in exploring models that describe progressive democracy as liberatory, sociocultural work, whether at the local, nation-state, or transnational level. To acknowledge the sociohistorical nature of democratic achievements (however limited) is also to acknowledge the fragility of these achievements. By acknowledging democratic forms of life that support just institutions and practices, we can purposefully attend to and cultivate a dynamic second nature—an identity or subjectivity—that combats such democratic threats as white supremacy, misogyny, and environmentally destructive forms of anthropocentricism.

"Praxis-oriented empathy" is a central disposition of democratic second nature. I distinguish praxis-oriented empathy from sentimental sympathy. Praxis-oriented empathy is a form of affect that both motivates and accompanies the witnessing of social harms and the concomitant practical work of social justice and transformation. In contrast, sentimental sympathy is a form of affect that treats the reader to "deep feeling" but entails no attending, practical consequences. It is what Oscar Wilde referred to as "the luxury of having an emotion without paying for it" and similar to what Saidiya Hartman and Xine Yao have referred to as the gaze of the voyeur or spectator.[17] There is nothing inherently wrong with sentimental sympathy, though it can be pernicious if readers credit themselves with helping the world merely via their profound feeling and concern. In addition to failing to produce practical results, which might be expected from apathetic readers, "sympathetic readers" may feel virtuous and experience personal self-fulfillment, having been "touched" by the suffering and oppression of others. Sentimental sympathy, then, must be differentiated from praxis-oriented empathy, the type of empathy radical Romantics seek to cultivate: an empathy that promotes forms of attention and engagement that include a wide range of emotional, bodily, intellectual, and practical political responses.

The work of praxis-oriented empathy does not collapse the profound difference between being a *witness* to pain and oppression and being a *sufferer* of such pain and oppression. Rather, praxis-oriented empathy nurtures accountability and action in those who seek to combat various causes of pain and oppression that they themselves have not necessarily experienced. In this regard, praxis-oriented empathy participates in the work inspired by such books as Rob Nixon's *Slow Violence*, Macarena Gómez-Barris's *The Extractive Zone*, and Paul and Scott Slovic's *Numbers and Nerves*. These books reveal to readers "slow" or "submerged" or other forms of violence and catastrophe and attempt to overcome readers' potential numbness, thereby mobilizing them to bring about urgent change.

THE JOURNEY: ARC OF THE BOOK AND BEARING OF ITS CHAPTERS

The journey in this book resists a strictly chronological arrangement of the chapters. While I am sensitive to and offer historical context for the chapters, the book is organized more by themes, topics, and authors. Various transformations to radical Romanticism—for example, by the work of Du Bois, Hurston, and Silko—appear throughout the book, intertwined with the radical Romantic work of Rousseau, the Wordsworths, Coleridge, Mary Shelley, Thoreau, and Margaret Fuller. While I often focus on the transformational moments in the development of radical Romanticism, I do not offer a triumphalist or supersessionist narrative in which earlier authors are necessarily eclipsed by later ones. I am more interested in gathering together the various liberatory strands of radical Romanticism than I am in perpetuating the idea that more recent work supersedes past work, even as more recent work critiques aspects of past work. For example, Du Bois is paired with Wordsworth and Thoreau in the first chapter in order to start the book with a robust account of radical Romantic aesthetics. The chapter reveals how Du Bois belongs to radical Romanticism even as he transforms it (and also how viewing Du Bois as a radical Romantic shifts the way we think of Wordsworth and Thoreau). While resisting a triumphalist narrative, the last three chapters of the book focus on progressive transformations of radical Romanticism, sharpening its lens of attention to anti-Black racism, patriarchy, and settler colonialism. Moreover, the book ends with Silko, an Indigenous author who exemplifies (and transforms) the best of the radical Romantics without herself necessarily being one.

Allow me now to provide the direction or bearing of the individual chapters. Chapter 1, "Radical Romantic Aesthetics: Wordsworth and Du Bois," brings us to the heart of radical Romanticism and the intricate relation between aesthetics, politics, and religion. I begin the chapter with a general account of radical aesthetics, addressing its nature, scope, and relation to ethics, the imagination, and taste. I then turn specifically to the radical aesthetics of Wordsworth and Du Bois. Finally, after comparing radical aesthetics to more traditional accounts of aesthetics, I conclude by extending the category of radical aesthetics to include such performative, nonliterary aesthetics as found in public celebrations and protests.

In chapter 2, "Into the Wild: Environmental and Racial Justice in Wordsworth, Thoreau, and Du Bois," I explore the environmental dimensions of radical Romanticism. In particular, I focus on the concept of the *wild*. My attention to the wild arises, in part, because of its historically complicated and troubled relation to both environmental thought and racial justice. Frequently in Western modernity, the wild is understood as that which is untouched by humans. The wild has also been understood as that which needs to be subdued insofar as it stands outside of civilization, whether as wild lands or wild (often Black or Brown) humans. These notions of the wild have been broadly and justifiably critiqued. I present an *alternative account* of the wild as found in radical Romanticism, paying attention to its ethical contributions to environmental and social justice—the wild as not only a place but also a condition and process: the wild as that which surprises and disorients and as that which contests longstanding (often oppressive) practices and conventions. The chapter concludes by portraying Du Bois as a powerful North American, radical Romantic author who wrote poignantly about the nexus of the human and the more-than-human, about its complex beauty and its equally complex suffering and injustice.

In chapter 3, "Rousseau's Garden as a World in Which to Live," I step back to the eighteenth century to look at a central figure who crafted profound environmental, economic, social, and political alternatives to prevailing European sensibilities—the very sensibilities that have greatly contributed to the current climate change catastrophe. Rousseau was one of the first modern Europeans to begin the work of dismantling the "nature as other" model. He understood the connection between the assault on the natural world on the one hand and social inequality and injustice among humans on the other. He saw that a reciprocal form of care for the land would entail reforming European institutions, practices, and perspectives—a thorough transformation of its politics and economics, its aesthetic and religious sensibilities. The intimate connection between the human and nonhuman is a central characteristic of radical Romanticism and a central focus of the chapter.

In chapter 4, "Romanticism, Religion, and Practice: Political and Environmental Implications," I show how secularized accounts of Romanticism belittle the significance of religion, tradition, and practice (cultivation and form). When we neglect the salience of religion, we fail to see the close, material connections between Romantic religious, political, and environmental radicalism. And if we discount tradition and practice, we fail to see the matter and manner—the culture and cultivation, including memory, stories, and the very *form* of art—by which radical Romantic authors conceived of and pursued sociopolitical and environmental aspirations. This chapter's investigation of Romanticism and secularization offers some broad lessons for ways to rethink the tangled relation between religion, modernity, and the secular.

Having shown the dynamic role of religion and form (including in-forming, or cultivation), chapter 5, "Dancing on a Flaming World: Du Bois's Poetry and Creative Fiction," turns to investigate these same aspects of Romanticism in Du Bois, yet "these same aspects" are now transformed in his work. Anti-Black racism is front and center, and the existential stakes are higher than what we find in Coleridge and Wordsworth. The struggle for life and freedom in the context of the brutalization and oppression of Black women, men, and children brings a mortal urgency and intensity not seen in the previous radical Romantic authors. The chapter focuses on how Du Bois crafted various forms of poetry and creative fiction to critique the unjust status quo and to vividly depict alternative, antiracist democratic politics and imaginaries. Furthermore, Du Bois portrayed the more-than-human not as existing outside humanity but as an integral feature of a shared and interconnected world. And by bringing attention to Du Bois the radical Romantic, we see religious thought employed as a vehicle to depict the pain, humiliation, and cruelty of racist oppression as well as sources of beauty, joy, and possibilities of social change; we see religion as an indispensable feature of Du Bois's artistic and moral imagination.

Chapter 6, "Ecofeminism and the Expansion and Transformation of Radical Romanticism," presents Mary Shelley, Margaret Fuller, and Zora Neale Hurston as ecofeminists crafting distinctive themes and forms of writing designed to reveal and combat patriarchy, racism, and anthropocentricism. Just as Du Bois expanded and transformed radical Romanticism by bringing to it the trauma and oppression of anti-Black racism, so too Shelley, Fuller, and Hurston expanded and transformed the tradition by powerfully addressing patriarchy and misogyny. Moreover, their resistance to patriarchy discloses the intersectional oppression of women, Black people, Native Americans, and the more-than-human. The chapter focuses on the distinctive *context*, *form*, and *content* of selected works (especially *Frankenstein*, *Summer on the Lakes*, and *Their Eyes Were Watching God*). I name the radical Romantic, ecofeminist form and content—and the connection between the two—and I characterize them as rooted in and responding to a catastrophic context. The ecofeminism of Shelley, Fuller, and Hurston, largely inspired by various religious and theological traditions, has wide implications for the radical Romantic aesthetic that seeks to cultivate such capacities as attention, care, reciprocity, and transformative justice between humans and between humans and the more-than-human. I interpret Shelley, Fuller, and Hurston as powerful feminist storytellers. As such, I see my role as a listener and a curator of their stories, as I seek to craft my own narrative about the ongoing traditions and ways of radical Romanticism.

In chapter 7, "Leslie Marmon Silko and the Power of Indigenous Storytelling: Healing and Resistance in Defiance of Settler Colonialism," I seek to listen to and learn from the work of Silko. In her novel *Ceremony*, suffering, healing, and resistance are embedded in Southwest storied landscapes, depicting such private crises as loss of identity, the trauma of war, and ruined friendships and such public crises as environmental disaster, racism, and extractive capitalism—the outcomes of settler colonialism. *Ceremony* depicts how Indigenous responses to personal pain and social injustice entail a dynamic interaction between Indigenous stories, ceremonies, lands, and a nonlinear (spiraling) understanding of time that interweaves past, present, and future. In Silko's novel *Almanac of the Dead*, we again find stories of suffering, healing, and resistance on both a private and public register. But this time the cast of subjugated characters is more diverse and transnational. Indigenous peoples of Mexico, Blacks, Latinx, and impoverished whites all seek in various ways to recover their stories and stolen lands and to restore health and justice to transnational communities through upheaval and revolution. In both novels, past and present events and oracles produce storied landscapes that speak of subjugated bodies, racial oppression, and broken relationships. Also in both novels, recovered stories, memories, and ceremonies work together to bring socioeconomic, ecological, and spiritual transformations. Jointly, the two novels present a vision of sovereignty reclaimed, cultural and personal identity reaffirmed, and lands (partially) liberated from settler colonialism.

In this chapter, I identify themes and practices that are shared by Silko and radical Romanticism—for example, storied landscapes as social critique and protest; the healing derived from the interconnection between people and place; the powerful otherness and agency of the more-than-human; and, most importantly, the pursuit of justice through the power of stories. Yet I also explore how Silko expands and transforms radical Romanticism, bringing to it powerful Laguna, Diné, and other Indigenous perspectives and ways of being, including an alertness to the catastrophes of settler colonialism, although she herself is not necessarily a radical Romantic. I contend instead that present and future iterations of Romanticism need to be deeply informed by her. Indeed, if radical Romanticism is to achieve its promise as a dynamic set of traditions and practices committed to sustainable, just relations among humans and between humans and the more-than-human, it must respectfully and humbly learn from those who have suffered most under the cruel subjugation of empire, white supremacy, and settler colonialism.

My conclusion, "The Work and Promise of Radical Romanticism in a World in Ruins" is a reflection on Silko's warning, "You don't have anything / if you don't have the stories."[18] What stories are circulating and being retold in the modern

West? In the United States, have white settler cultures in the past and present forgotten, suppressed, or ignored life-enhancing stories—stories that speak of justice and care for human and more-than-human communities? Settlers in the United States were drawn to and driven by destructive stories that spoke of white, male, human exceptionalism. The life-enhancing stories, however, have not died. They live in places and people, however marginally, waiting for a greater hearing to unleash their potential power. The stories I have identified in the dynamic traditions of radical Romanticism are potentially liberatory, providing ethical resources for living justly among human and more-than-human communities. These are stories that haunt, crying out so that their prophetic voice might be heeded, their emancipatory power released. The conclusion attends to Wordsworth's, Du Bois's, and Silko's *stories of ruins*—ruins that witness oppression and pain but also beauty and resistance. The topic of ruins necessitates the question of renovation: What might it mean to rebuild in the shadows of ruins? And even when the renovation is sound—good and just—how might we honor the enduring scar and grieve appropriately? The rest of the conclusion looks forward and asks: What new stories will be told and renovations attempted? To address this question, I explore new voices, for example, queer and trans authors who transform radical Romanticism with stories of pain and cruelty but also of dwelling justly among fellow humans and the more-than-human. The book then concludes with a final reflection on the nature and role of beauty, hope, and love in a world in ruins.

CHAPTER 1

Radical Romantic Aesthetics

Wordsworth and Du Bois

Thischapter focuses on the radical aesthetics of William Wordsworth and W. E. B. Du Bois. To learn about Wordsworth's and Du Bois's aesthetics is to learn about the intricate relation between aesthetics, politics, and religion in radical Romanticism. I begin the chapter by addressing radical aesthetics' features, scope, and relation to ethics, the imagination, and taste.[1] Next, I turn to the heart of the chapter: the radical aesthetics of Wordsworth and Du Bois. I then compare radical aesthetics to more traditional accounts of aesthetics, and I conclude by extending the category of radical aesthetics to include such performative, nonliterary aesthetics as found in public celebrations and protests.

RADICAL AESTHETICS

Scope

Radical aesthetics is radical both in its progressive approach and in its wide, non-traditional scope. It is an aesthetics that seeks to promote progressive, ethical perspectives, and its subject matter is not limited to the framed portraits in the museum or the picturesque on the horizon. Its sensibilities are seated in every-day justice and injustice, and thus its subject matter is more likely to pertain to the homeless population in eighteenth-century London or twenty-first-century Gallup, New Mexico, than to Leonardo da Vinci's *Portrait of a Man in Red Chalk* or the sunset over the Grand Canyon. This is not because the latter are unwor-thy of our attention but because our lives center primarily on everyday, pedestrian places and activities. The everyday includes the familiar and the surprising, anger and delight, horridness and beauty, despair and hope. In the manner of Wordsworth, Mary Shelley, Thoreau, Margaret Fuller, Zora Neale Hurston, Du Bois, Terry Tempest Williams, and Leslie Marmon Silko, radical aesthetics brings careful, critical attention to what is in plain sight as well as to what is hidden or concealed, while offering an appropriate ethical, political, and affective response to the social and natural quotidian world. In this chapter and book, I consider the radical aesthetics of the *art of the written word*—in poetry and prose—and its capacity to bring critical attention to such everyday ethical matters as the refugee's plight, the humiliation of racial discrimination, global warming, and the pain of economic inequality.

Given that radical aesthetics is located in the everyday, it is situated at the intersection of political, ethical, and religious spheres. Radical aesthetics acknowledges this dynamic amalgam and does not seek to impose artificial disciplinary boundaries that distort our everyday experience. Additionally, radical aesthetics acknowledges and embraces the intricate relation between the social and natural world—between the cultural materiality of language, practices, and institutions and the dynamic processes of land, sea, and sky. In particular, the art of the word can be understood as both a spiritual project engaged with a material universe and as a material project engaged with a spiritual universe. But rather than employ such binary terms as "spiritual" and "material," think of the art of the word—in the context of radical aesthetics—as a profoundly human project engaged ethically with the familiar and unfamiliar world in which we find ourselves.[2]

Radical aesthetics seeks to imagine what it would be like to *taste*—to experience ethically—the world in ways that are receptive to sensing the beauty and generosity, the pain and injustice in the otherwise familiar events, places, practices, traditions, and institutions that shape our lives. In order to focus on the everyday, radical aesthetics seeks to lift "the veil of familiarity," all those conventional, entrenched patterns of thought, sight, and practice that render invisible and voiceless those creatures, human or nonhuman, that lack power or agency to make their needs and desires apparent.[3] This critical, creative work requires a tutored moral imagination and the cultivation of a normatively penetrating sight—what I will call *democratic taste*.

The scope of radical aesthetics is as expansive as its engagement is deep and demanding. In this chapter, I will explore how the art of Wordsworth and Du Bois seeks to cultivate an ethical, democratic taste that engages our senses, emotions, judgment, and intellect. It seeks to nurture within us a particular kind of bodily-cognitive response to the everyday that surrounds us. The intent of Wordsworth's and Du Bois's art was to broaden our aesthetic response to the world.[4] The appropriate aesthetic responses to the intricate, complex world require much from us in the way of ethical, emotional, cognitive, and bodily sensitivity and discernment. The cultivation of such "appropriate aesthetic responses" is the work of radical aesthetics.

Radical aesthetics seeks to cultivate a fully engaged and attuned response to the natural and social worlds that moves people to delight in and decry the world in appropriate ways. There is nothing passive or docile about this aesthetic response, though a high premium is placed on *receptivity*—or what Wordsworth called "wise passiveness."[5] The radical aesthetic response is in part cognitive, because one needs to know something about the world to respond appropriately to a work of art or slice of life. For example, one needs to know something about poverty and farming to be appropriately *moved*—transformed—by Du Bois's prose about Black tenant farmers or Wordsworth's verse about unjust enclosures. But the aesthetic response entails more than cognition. It also requires a spiritual response, insofar as "spiritual" suggests that the whole person is called upon—that is, the integration of one's emotional life, bodily senses, moral judgment, and cognitive faculties.

In the view of Wordsworth and Du Bois, to be moved by a work of art (however modestly) is to *experience* the world differently and to *engage* with the world differently. While more traditional aesthetics features a viewer who quietly gazes upon the artwork or landscape for the sake of disinterested enjoyment (akin to the "male gaze"), radical aesthetics asks the observer to become an *active* witness to not only the artwork but the world. The witness seeks to alter the world, working for political change and conditions congenial to a progressive democracy that honors the dignity of persons and of the more-than-human and that seeks to abolish oppressive institutions and hierarchies such as systemic racism, patriarchy, homophobia, and extractive capitalism. Far from separating the observer from the everyday, radical aesthetics seeks to engage its participants in the world around them, and that broad, aesthetic engagement includes a wide range of emotional, bodily, intellectual, and political responses.

It is important to underscore that radical aesthetics embraces both "the ethical" and "the useful." By "ethical," I mean that radical aesthetics is unabashedly aligned with human and eco-emancipation.[6] By "useful," I mean that radical aesthetics includes such practical practices as food production, means of transportation, energy sources, and "crafts," which are conventionally excluded from the scope of aesthetics. Radical aesthetics, similar to some feminist aesthetics, brings attention to the art of cooking, tending to the sick and old, rearing children, growing food, making soaps and breads, and other such domestic arts while rejecting an essentialist identification of these arts with women. In this way, radical aesthetics is aligned with such authors as J. K. Gibson-Graham who seek to identify and explore diverse economic practices situated outside neoliberal economic institutions.[7]

By explicitly acknowledging the ethical and useful dimensions of aesthetics, radical aesthetics rejects most notions of the "disinterested gaze." Conventional aesthetics has frequently held that the object of art should be approached with objective disinterest. This distanced, contemplative approach is often deemed the ideal, lest the viewer have an unduly subjective or utilitarian approach to the work of art. Kant, for example, argued that we must approach art free of personal motivation or self-interest, never utilizing art as a means to an end. How else are we to see art for what it is, rather than as what we want it to be for our own sake? And how else are we to produce impartial, universal aesthetic judgments, if not by eliminating personal preference, desire, and goals? While there are strengths to this line of argument (for example, a high value is placed on our *receptiveness* to that which is outside us), conventional aesthetics pays dearly in espousing the disinterested gaze. By separating art from *interest*—from involvement, concern, desire, commitment, and love—it divorces art from ethics and politics. Radical aesthetics instead promotes active engagement and ethical critique.

It should be noted that progressive religious traditions have often supplied significant moral resources for radical aesthetics' engagement and ethical critique. Many radical Romantic authors, for example, identified with dissenting Christian traditions that put them into conflict with religious and political establishments. They routinely drew on Christian theology in efforts to condemn churches and clergy that supported slavery, unjust war, and practices that failed to provide aid and justice to the impoverished and vulnerable. One of their central religious tasks was to offer artistic, palpable accounts of the pain of poverty, disability, war, and unjust public policies. This literary aesthetic effort, which was often understood as a calling or vocation, was designed to cultivate the appropriate human emotions and praxis-oriented empathy in their fellow citizens.

The Moral Imagination

The imagination plays a large role in what I am calling radical aesthetics. The Romantic art of Wordsworth, Du Bois, and Mary Shelley, for example, often solicits from the reader an imaginative *empathy* for the stranger, the (otherwise) feared "other" or hideous "monster." Later in this chapter and in subsequent chapters, I will discuss in detail the particular devices and efforts that various radical Romantics employed to cultivate a moral imagination that would move people to care about the stranger, the "other," the "monster," near or far.

For now, however, I want to note that while it may seem intuitive that the concepts of the "moral" and the "imagination" travel together, there is in fact a long and complicated history that enabled these once disconnected and even antagonistic concepts to come together.[8] For much of Western history, reason and revelation were dependable sources of understanding, whereas the imagination was often perceived as being deceptive, seductive, and a source for unwarranted fears. Hobbes and Hume, for example, were suspicious of the imagination, believing it could enflame desire and distort one's perception of reality. In the mid- to late eighteenth century, however, the imagination started to be viewed more favorably. Even Hume linked the imagination to moral sympathy, claiming that "by the force of imagination," an otherwise abstract idea is transformed into robust impression.[9] This positive, moral reframing of the imagination culminates in such British radical Romantic authors as Wordsworth, Coleridge, and Mary Shelley and such American radical Romantic authors as Emerson, Margaret Fuller, and Du Bois.

I point to this history of imagination's reputation because I want to note that the concept of the *moral imagination* largely comes into being when the capacity for praxis-oriented empathy is linked to the imagination. Radical Romantics understood the moral imagination as that which can potentially lift the veil of familiarity (thereby interrupting habitual disregard) and lift the veil of otherness (thereby revealing the humanity of those dehumanized). The greater the invisibility or dehumanization, the greater the challenge and work of the moral imagination. And radical Romantics insisted that to recognize the humanity of the stranger or "monster" before us is to cultivate the humanity within us. Other-oriented love and respect enhance self-love and respect, and recognizing the vulnerability of those before us is to acknowledge our own vulnerability.

The work of the moral imagination, however, entails more than merely acknowledging the humanity of the dehumanized. It also makes concrete claims on us, our governments, and our political, social, and economic institutions. To varying degrees, the aesthetics of radical Romantics sought and seek to promote critical reflection *and action* to combat personal and institutional sources of oppression. One aim of radical aesthetics is to galvanize diverse individuals and populations—movements and groups of resistance—for the sake of generating enduring opposition to enduring domination. In the face of repression, radical aesthetics maintains a tempered hope in the work of imagining a more just future and working to achieve that future, however imperfectly.[10] Through aesthetics, the radical Romantics sought to cultivate a taste for a different future and therefore a different present.

Taste

Taste has been associated with aesthetics for over 250 years. By the late eighteenth century, it was commonly understood as the ability to judge excellence in art or beauty in the natural world. Someone with "good taste" could discern between the artistic genius and the mere amateur. Later, tasteful discernment was extended to distinguish between proper manners and base ones, correct etiquette and indecorum, the refined and the vulgar. When taste was understood primarily as a natural faculty, it was often associated with the aristocracy by virtue of their (supposedly) natural qualities. On the other hand, when understood primarily as an acquired faculty, taste belonged to the elite by virtue of their privileged education. In either case, taste could be perfected and cultivated, and those with access to wealth and privilege, usually white men, were afforded opportunities for such cultivation. Although the one whom the tasteful deemed a "genius" could presumably belong to any race, gender, or class, *he* in fact was typically white, male, and privileged, rendering taste a conduit for white supremacy, patriarchy, and elitism. Literary and social critics such as I. A. Richards and Pierre Bourdieu have shown how taste—aesthetic competence—is variously dependent on, and reinforces, a complex array of social, economic, and political power exchanges.[11] And feminist critics have demonstrated how taste historically has been gendered. Women, for example, supposedly had a limited taste and capacity for experiencing the sublime. Mary Shelley and Margaret Fuller, as we will see in chapter 6, thought otherwise.

Elitism, racism, and sexism have often traveled with "taste." But radical Romantics subverted this by identifying taste with ethical judgment and ways of living. "Having poor taste" is how Wordsworth, for example, described exploitative, wealthy real estate developers who refused to build and dwell in an economically just and environmentally sustainable manner.[12] In contrast, local inhabitants of modest means possessed "good taste," dwelling more justly and wisely. Later in this chapter, I will describe "taste" as an ethical feature of the radical aesthetics of Wordsworth and Du Bois.

Despite its pernicious, heavy baggage, I am attracted to the category of "taste" because of its association with *physical* taste and with the understanding that it can be *cultivated*. There is no scholarly consensus on exactly when taste expanded from a strictly physical category (e.g., involved with the tasting of food) to an aesthetic category.[13] As early as the fifteenth century, the Italian humanist Leon Battista Alberti used *gusto* to refer to judgment. By the mid-eighteenth century, the double meaning of taste had become commonplace. For example, under the entry *Goût* in Diderot and d'Alembert's *Encyclopedia*, Voltaire wrote:

> The preceding article has described taste in its physical meaning. This sense, this capacity for discriminating between different foods, has given rise, in all known languages, to the metaphorical use of the word "taste" to designate the discernment of beauty and flaws in all the arts. . . . In common with physical taste it is sensitive to what is good and reacts to it with a feeling of pleasure, it refuses with disgust what is bad.[14]

Aesthetic taste was eventually separated from its physical meaning. Kant, among others, worried that physical taste was too personal: It lacked the more universal disinterested interest required for making objective determinations about beauty and art. It was understood, then, that although taste had a double meaning, its physical meaning was to be shed when it came to works of art. Radical Romanticism, however, frequently sought a coalesced meaning. Coleridge, for example, connected the physical and intellectual meanings of taste, elevating taste as its own "intermediate faculty which connects the active with the passive powers of our nature, the *intellect* with the *senses*."[15]

Ultimately, I employ the term "taste" to refer to the normative manner in which people are trained to *ingest*—to take in, feel, experience—the world. From the start, taste was about making distinctions. I want to maintain this notion of judgment or discernment while expanding it beyond *making* wise distinctions (say, between a humane workplace as opposed to an oppressive one) to *feeling* those distinctions bodily or, better yet, holistically (affectively, cognitively, and ethically). Here, taste captures the cognitive-affective nexus of what it is to see and feel the world in a particular way. Whether we taste something pleasant or unpleasant, we have a strong response to it, which is precisely what practitioners of radical aesthetics seek to cultivate. Of course, they also seek to *shape* our responses, that is, to inform what it is that we taste as pleasant or unpleasant, what we experience as just or unjust.

When Du Bois wrote in vivid detail about the two summers he spent as a teacher serving in the impoverished, rural Tennessee community of Alexandria—bringing his readers into the concrete, everyday hardships of such lives as the resolute yet vulnerable Josie—he was seeking to honor that community but also to transform the taste of his white readers.[16] Likewise, when David Walker wrote his 1829 *Appeal to the Colored Citizens of the World*, he sought to transform the taste of his readers, Black and white. For his Black audience, Walker sought to help them to understand themselves as vital citizens courageously working to secure their freedom and rights. And although the white audience was not the principal audience, Walker understood the importance—and the formidable challenge—of transforming the taste of his white readers such that they, in the words of Melvin Rogers, "occupy a standpoint in which they see *and feel* the horror of black domination."[17] Both Walker and Du Bois sought to transform the taste of citizens such that they experience the appropriate righteous indignation—the appropriate rage—in the face of injustice. Taste—unlike judgment alone—expresses a physicality that I seek to retain.

But taste is not merely a subjective preference. Discerning judgment is central to it. Lewis Gordon notes that "critic and critique" are closely related to making critical judgments based on standards or criteria: "To make [critical] decisions requires *criteria*: standards and rules by which something is judged or decided upon."[18] Taste, then, entails both *judgment* as rule-governed critique and *expression* of informed, affective response.

My aim here has been to show why I find "taste" useful despite the justified critiques of it. And now that I have introduced radical aesthetics, noting its relation to ethics, the imagination, and taste, I turn to the aesthetics of the early Wordsworth.[19]

WORDSWORTH'S RADICAL AESTHETICS

To learn about Wordsworth's aesthetics is to learn about the intricate relation that radical Romanticism forges between aesthetics, religion, and democracy. Wordsworth believed in the social and political power of the well-crafted word. In a letter written in 1829, Wordsworth wrote, "Words are not a mere *vehicle*, but they are *powers* either to kill or to animate."[20] That is, the living power of a word can palpably contribute to life or to death. Wordsworth took this powerful claim seriously, dedicating his poetic aesthetics to life. In popular culture, however, reading poetry is often seen as a pleasant pastime, perhaps even as an escape from the "real" world. And even in academia, reading poetry is often seen as irrelevant to social, economic, or political "power"—either because poetry allegedly does not concern institutional power or else because, insofar as language itself is shaped by systems of power, the poetic does not critique power but rather serves as its "mere vehicle," perpetuating existing hierarchies.

I certainly do not dispute that various art forms, including poetry, can serve as mere pastimes. Nor do I dispute that poetry, like all language, is rooted in sociohistorical contexts and is therefore bounded by and often blind to social forces—some oppressive—that shape and cleave it. Nonetheless, poetry does not necessarily function as escapist entertainment or as a vehicle of power. Poetry can be a powerful educator in things private, such as how an individual handles a personal loss, and in things public, such as how citizens and their institutions see and treat the social "other" or "outcast" among them. Furthermore, a poem's "imprisonment" in language is no different, in principle, than that of a Marxist critique. All expressions—and all critiques—are bounded by sociolinguistic networks. Reformers and revolutionaries do the best they can with what they have, though some do considerably better than others. "Better," however, is not measured by the abstract notion of *escaping* sociolinguistic bounds but by working normatively *within them* to mitigate suffering and further justice. Poetry, then, *is* a power—for better or worse.

The early Wordsworth hoped that his radical aesthetics would contribute to the cultivation of a *democratic, aesthetic taste*. Wordsworth employed the term *taste* to refer to our capacity to experience the world normatively. When democratic taste has been suitably cultivated, one will see, feel, and apprehend the drama of life in a distinctive way. One will, for example, be empathetic toward those who are crushed by social and economic oppression. The characters that Wordsworth portrayed in his radical aesthetics were often located at the periphery of society, those that many deem to be lowly or dangerously "other"—the homeless, the refugee, the impoverished, the aged, the veteran, and the intellectually and physically disabled. Wordsworth vividly portrayed these characters so that we might see and feel their hopes and fears, their accomplishments and losses. We glimpse their humanity and, in turn, discover our own. This is a profound democratic achievement: to help citizens experience the dignity of their fellows. The aim of Wordsworth's radical aesthetics can be summed up as his various poetic efforts to give sight to see "souls that appear to have no depth at all / To careless eyes."[21]

Wordsworth's 1802 sonnet "The Banished Negroes" is one of his most significant attempts to present the dignity and humanity of one who is invisible—invisible in soul and human worth, though visible (even hypervisible) in body—to those with power, privilege, and membership in the majority culture.[22] In the summer of 1802, Napoleon had reintroduced slavery and instituted an ordinance that effectively expelled all people of color from France ("aucun noir, mulâtre, ou autres gens de couleur, de l'un et de l'autre sexe").[23] At the end of that summer, William and Dorothy Wordsworth traveled from Calais to Dover. A "fellow-passenger" on their ship was a Black woman who had been banished from France. As the head-note (added to the 1827 version of the sonnet) states, "Among the capricious acts of Tyranny that disgraced these times, was the chasing of all Negroes from France by decree of the Government: we had a Fellow-passenger who was one of the expelled."[24]

Much of the democratic and ethical work of the sonnet is done within the first three lines: "*We had a fellow-Passenger that came / From Calais with us . . . / A Negro Woman.*"[25] Here two subjects are placed in a complex relation. On one side there is the *we*—we, William and Dorothy; we, the other passengers; we, the white majority culture of the British nation and the (presumably) mostly white readers of the sonnet. On the other side is the solitary Black woman. These two sides appear asymmetrical and perhaps unequal: one Black woman up against multiple spheres of whiteness. Yet within the sonnet's first four words the asymmetry and potential inequality are troubled by the mediating term, *fellow-Passenger*, placing the woman among the *we*. Wordsworth's aim was to complicate the very notion of "we" such that there is now continuity—a shared humanity between Black and white, refugee and settled, French and British.

Wordsworth's inclusion, however, has not erased difference. He acknowledged both the woman's distinctive identity as well as her status as fellow traveler—as fellow human. This democratic move is accomplished by the employment of one of Wordsworth's more powerful aesthetic strategies: to reveal the unfamiliar in the familiar and the familiar in the unfamiliar. In this familiar event, the crossing from Calais to Dover, "careless eyes" are helped to perceive the unfamiliar—this Black homeless woman, a fellow human being, with depth of soul. In the face of her tangible presence, the travelers experience both distinctiveness and commonality.

In various ways, Wordsworth conveyed this woman as a both familiar and unfamiliar fellow traveler—"like a Lady gay / Yet silent," "from notice turning not away" yet "motionless in eyes and face." Perhaps when noting her unfamiliar way, Wordsworth himself participated in "othering" her. Mostly, however, he conveyed her humanity and depth of character. Understandably, she is dejected and keeping a low profile. And yet she will not turn away from her fellow travelers, being cowed into submissiveness. There is strength and dignity here, a refusal to be but an object of their gaze. She is not *rendered* silent; rather, silence, here, is a form of her agency. Later in the poem, when "on our proffer'd kindness still did lay / A weight of languid speech, or at the same / Was silent, motionless in eyes and face," her strong independence is depicted. She is not ready or willing to engage with the "proffer'd kindness." She has no interest in receiving the sympathy of those travelers around her. Self-possessed and fiercely her own person, she refuses to be easily captured by the onlooker's conceptual nets. After all, as the next lines dramatically indicate, she has experienced trauma and will not be easily consoled, for: "She was a Negro Woman driv'n from France / Rejected like all others of that race, / Not one of whom may now find footing there." Wordsworth then concluded the sonnet with explicit social criticism: "What is the meaning of this ordinance? / Dishonour'd Despots, tell us if you dare."[26]

When the poem was published in 1802, abolitionists in Britain were putting pressure on Parliament to end the transatlantic slave trade, even as Napoleon reintroduced slavery to Haiti, having captured and imprisoned Toussaint L'Ouverture. With "The Banished Negroes" (and other sonnets written around the same time), Wordsworth allied himself with the abolitionists.[27] Although his headnote and concluding lines express a clear political statement, the democratic and ethical work is mostly accomplished in the sonnet's earlier lines in which the Black woman is presented. Wordsworth's readers look into her eyes and her humanity, and they witness their own; he attempted to broaden both the category of being fully human and his readers' capacity for imaginative praxis-oriented empathy. Through an act of the moral imagination, his readers see what was once perhaps invisible to them.[28] Their eyes are no longer as careless as they once were. They have new sight. And to the extent that their recognition of who counts as fully human has grown, so has their own humanity.

Of course, Wordsworth's efforts were necessarily limited by his white and male experiences and perspectives. It is imperative that today, as one employs strategies to enhance the capacity of imaginative empathy, one not propagate what Lewis Gordon has called "the weight of colonial imposition: whether Black woman or Black man, the normative center is *white man*, not even white woman."[29] Indeed, one task of imaginative empathy is to disrupt the association of ethical worth with race, gender, power, and privilege.

Wordsworth's radical aesthetics, in making visible those who were relegated to the periphery of society, was thought by many to be unseemly, and accordingly his verse received much scorn and contempt. For example, in "The Idiot Boy" (1798), Wordsworth graphically depicts the love of a mother for her intellectually disabled child. Anticipating a feminist ethics of care such as that of Eva Kittay, Wordsworth implicitly argued that a human's worth is not to be measured by the capacity for rationality but rather by the simple fact of being human and in relation to others.[30] In the course of reading "The Idiot Boy," the reader is led to doubt the appropriateness of its title and to identify with the simple yet profound love that Betty Fox shows for her son, Johnny. Yet this demonstration of interdependent, vulnerable love between a mother and her intellectually disabled child drew disdain from Wordsworth's critics. As David Bromwich notes, "Wordsworth was felt to have abused the name and nature of human feelings by portraying the mother's affection for an aberrant instead of a normal person."[31] The work of radical aesthetics—the attempt to give sight to see "souls that appear to have no depth at all / To careless eyes"—is often unsettling.

Wordsworth never underestimated the challenge of cultural inertia. While often motivated by democratic commitments and reasoned principles, his radical aesthetics engaged with proper nouns—particular communities, people, places, and things—in order to make vivid ethical claims on our lives. As the 1790s progressed, Wordsworth became increasingly suspicious of the abstract—of things and ideas not rooted in the concreteness of time and space. This accounts for his eventual frustration with the abstract and impersonal nature of William

Godwin's political philosophy. Godwin had argued that people would inevitably become illuminated by the ways of reason and that the reformer's job was to help that enlightenment along, promoting impersonal truth and justice over private attachments and whim. His alternative was initially timely and attractive for Wordsworth, who had become disillusioned by the increasingly bloody and morally ambiguous French Revolution. Nonetheless, Wordsworth's faith in Godwin's philosophy was short-lived. Godwin's sanguine confidence in abstract reason, his strict impersonalism, and perhaps even his atheism became obstacles to Wordsworth, who had put much stock in the importance of concrete relations between people and place and in a "a motion and a spirit, that . . . / rolls through all *things*."[32]

Wordsworth expressed his doubts about the efficacy of abstract systems of thought in his 1798 "Essay on Morals":

> I know no book or system of moral philosophy written with sufficient power to melt into our affections, to incorporate itself with the blood and vital juices of our minds. . . . Bald and naked reasonings are impotent over our habits; they cannot form them; from the same cause they are equally powerless in regulating our judgments concerning the value of men and things. They contain no picture of human life.[33]

This passage reveals not only what Wordsworth took to be the limits of abstract systems but also the purpose and the high stakes of concrete, radical aesthetics. It was to be practical. It was to move and change people. It was to reach deep into the hearts and minds of citizens and produce new habits, political emotions, and ways of being. It was to present a robust "picture of human life."

Wordsworth's complaint about Godwin's abstract rationalism resembled Burke's critique of the French Revolution's faith in the Temple of Reason. In his 1789 "Letter to Charles-Jean-François Depont," Burke wrote, "You have *theories* enough concerning the rights of men. . . . It is with man in the *concrete*, it is with common human life and human actions you are to be concerned."[34] Unlike Godwin and like Burke, Wordsworth embraced the inevitable role of social traditions, habits, practices, and institutions. He did not spurn the idea of communities and individuals being rooted concretely in time and place. While Wordsworth shared with Burke the conviction that places inexorably shape communities and their members, Wordsworth also held that the reverse is true: that *the people* shape a place. True, Burke did believe that *some* of the people, namely, the elite, have or should have the power to shape and guide their communities. But Burke would not ascribe such agency to "the people"—the "unthinking public," as he referred to nonelites.[35] In contrast, the early Wordsworth believed in and depicted in his writing the agency of "the people" and their capacity to engage wisely with their social and natural environs.

In Wordsworth's poetry, certainly in the 1798 *Lyrical Ballads* and 1805's *The Prelude*, we see attempts to bring together Burke's emphasis on tradition and place with Godwin's emphasis on reason and principles. Like Burke, Wordsworth came to distrust abstract theories that hovered free of history or experience. Yet like Godwin, Wordsworth valued critical (and progressive) reflection and reasoned principles. In *The Prelude*, for example, Wordsworth mocked the idea of reason severed from time and place:

> How glorious!—in self-knowledge and self-rule
> To look through all the frailties of the world,
> And, with a resolute mastery shaking off
> The accidents of nature, time, and place,
> That make up the weak being of the past,
> Build social freedom on its only basis:
> The freedom of the individual mind,
> Which, to the blind restraint of general laws
> Superior, magisterially adopts
> One guide—the light of circumstances, flashed
> Upon an independent intellect.[36]

This passage, surely taking aim at Godwin's rationalism, challenges the idea that public well-being and freedom can be achieved by means of a rationality detached from experience rooted in place ("accidents of nature, time, and place"). Yet, wanting to be charitable toward those who put their hope in "human reason's naked self," Wordsworth went on to claim that many came to distrust tradition and practice because of powerful conservatives who refused to reform customs and laws even when circumstances (such as unjust policies) clearly dictated that change was needed. Here, Wordsworth was no longer taking aim at Godwin but rather at Burke and the other traditionalists who had given "tradition" and "second nature" a bad name. He noted that the French Revolution, despite its flaws, had nonetheless lifted "a veil" and "a shock had then been given / To old opinions." Yet in the name of "ancient institutions," many refused to acknowledge what the Revolution had revealed: the sight of human suffering and need for change.[37] The task and challenge for Wordsworth, ultimately, was *to employ a Burkean language of traditions, customs, and practices in service of a Godwinian, Rousseauian democratic vision*. A similar task and challenge are central to this book: namely, to employ traditions, customs, and practices in the service of an ecologically minded, progressively oriented democracy.

The early Wordsworth did not understand democracy chiefly as a set of formal political institutions but rather as a progressive culture or spiritual ethos that included the thoughts, skills, practices, dispositions, and emotions of diverse citizens. Wordsworth was committed to advancing an *embodied democracy* that emphasized the cultural dimensions of a democracy, including its religious and aesthetic ones. To achieve this goal, he sought to educate the *whole* person, rather than discursively addressing only the disembodied mind.

In sum, Wordsworth maintained that progressive political principles, such as those of Godwin, require more than abstract assent; they require the cultivation of humane *taste*, politically robust *emotions*, and a truly democratic *second nature*. The radical Romantic poem, in this view, is an institution—potentially as powerful as the church—capable of shaping and training individuals and communities in the ways of justice. The well-crafted poem is the Fourth Estate: felicitous power outside official state, clerical, and economic power. The poem participates in what Emerson, that American radical Romantic, called "the true romance which the world exists to realize . . . the transformation of genius [talents and gifts of the individual and community] into practical power [social reform]."[38] This was the work of the early Wordsworth, and as we will see now, it was the work of Du Bois as well.

DU BOIS'S RADICAL AESTHETICS

Du Bois and the Canon

In different ways at different times, Du Bois wielded aesthetics, sociology, history, economics, and philosophy to bear on such diverse subjects as religion, race, gender, class, justice, and the environment. Additionally, Du Bois was a nature writer and one of North America's first environmental justice authors. Du Bois's work can be legitimately framed or presented from different perspectives, yet I will suggest that there is a particular, radical aesthetic ethos that permeates almost all of his work. This Du Boisian aesthetic ethos can be understood in relation to Romanticism and to the tradition of powerful storytellers. For these reasons, I will put forward a portrait of Du Bois as a radical Romantic poet-sociologist-activist. Adding W. E. B. Du Bois to the Romantic canon of authors not only expands the canon but troubles and transforms it.

This section and much of the following chapter implicitly argue for Du Bois to be understood as one of North America's most important radical Romantics. To begin, however, it may be helpful to offer some explicit comments about Du Bois's place in a canon of radical Romantic authors.

By "canon" I do not mean a definitive and authoritative list of authors that all people must read if they are to be deemed educated.[39] I do not subscribe to this notion even if such a canon is expanded to include authors who have been shut out for centuries—for example, women, people of color, Indigenous people, and people in the Global South. By employing the term "canon of radical Romanticism," I mean to capture something of its original Greek etymology, namely, a measuring rod used in weaving and carpentry. Du Bois, among other radical Romantics, assists us in our own work *to weave or build something of liberatory excellence.* Insofar as authors in this dynamic canon share a form of excellence, they serve as exemplars of liberatory radical Romanticism. They have the potential to inspire and enhance our own emancipatory practices. Understood in this way, a canon is a practical tool.

There is, then, a resemblance between Du Bois's craft and that of such authors as the early William Wordsworth, Mary Shelley, Emerson, William James, and Terry Tempest Williams. In addition to this resemblance, there are direct, material connections. For example, Du Bois was influenced by such German Romantics as Schiller and Herder, such British Romantics as Wordsworth, Byron, and Carlyle, and such American Romantics as Emerson, Thoreau, and James. In *Black Is Beautiful: A Philosophy of Black Aesthetics,* Paul Taylor writes of Du Bois as "having been raised on Carlyle, Emerson, and Wordsworth, having taken the requisite course on 'self-realization ethics' at Harvard from George Herbert Palmer, and having spent his most crucially formative years studying under Rankean historicists at the University of Berlin."[40] And Christopher M. Stampone has argued that Wordsworth's ideals, forms, and lines of poetry permeate *The Souls of Black Folk* and inform Du Bois's efforts to create revolutionary Black art.[41]

Furthermore, Du Bois exemplifies radical Romanticism insofar as his literary art (his books, essays, novels, and poems) integrates the imagination, socioeconomic realism, "the everyday," and a prophetic ethical vision. Although Arnold Rampersad does not call Du Bois a Romantic author, he does state that Du Bois's "greatest gift was poetic in nature, and that his scholarship, propaganda, and political activism drew their ultimate power from his essentially poetic vision of human experience and from his equally poetic reverence for the word."[42] Du Bois's prophetic, "poetic vision" is seen in such aesthetically fashioned prose pieces as "Of the Passing of the First-Born" and "On the Coming of John" in *The Souls of Black Folk*, in such powerful novels as *The Quest of the Silver Fleece* and *The Dark Princess*, and in such finely crafted poems as "A Litany of Atlanta" and "The Song of the Smoke."

In Wordsworthian fashion, Du Bois perfected and employed the art of the storied landscape: the portrayal of landscapes whose appearance and character are infused with human history and culture. In such texts as "Of the Meaning of Progress" or "Of the Black Belt," Du Bois brought together realism, the imagination, culture, and the land for the sake of producing aesthetically forceful storied landscapes that protest racial and economic injustice and call for radical change. In Emersonian fashion, Du Bois's prose essays (for example, "Of Beauty and Death" and "The Souls of White Folk") bring together eloquence, critical inquiry, and prophetic pathos, demanding readers to think honestly and for themselves. In the fashion of other radical Romantics, Du Bois combined empiricism with idealism, realism with the imagination, romance with practical power.

Moreover, he sought to contribute to the transformation of the culture and institutions of the United States' deeply flawed democracy. Like Wordsworth before him and in anticipation of Dewey's later work, Du Bois was committed to advancing a vital, spiritual democracy: that is, a democracy that is a way of life—a robust set of customs, practices, and ideals—in addition to formal institutions. And, similar to other radical Romantics, Du Bois understood the power of offering exemplars for the sake of furthering a spiritual democracy; Du Bois put forward Harriet Tubman, Sojourner Truth, Alexander Crummell, and David Walker as well as unnamed enslaved Black women and men, who lived and died with dignity under horrific conditions. These exemplars offer not only transformative visions for the future of America but also sharp, vivid condemnation of past and present practices.[43]

The inclusion of Du Bois in the radical Romantic canon turns attention to the overwhelming whiteness of early radical Romanticism and, accordingly, to the absence of sustained discussions of race and diversity. Du Bois brings to radical Romanticism not only the topic of racism but the *experience* of racism. As he noted at the start of *The Souls of Black Folk*, "I who speak here am bone of the bone and flesh of the flesh of them that live within the Veil."[44] Unlike white Romantics, Du Bois directly experienced the injustice that he struggled against, giving him a perspective distinct from that of white radical Romantics. Relatedly, Du Bois contributes to radical Romanticism an abiding commitment to activism. This is not to say that radical Romantics before Du Bois were not involved in activism but that Du Bois's involvement was broader and deeper, especially later in his career as he sought to mobilize movements for substantive change—both institutional and cultural. Du Bois, then, belongs to radical Romanticism even as he added depth and breadth to it.

Du Bois and Spiritual Democracy

Du Bois argued that a genuine U.S. democracy would need to be based not only on an institutional but also a spiritual foundation—that is, on a substantive culture and cluster of practices that support (what I have called) *a progressive democratic second nature* and *aesthetic taste*. Importantly, in Du Bois's view, the cultures of the United States—especially the white ones—required educational, ethical, and aesthetic transformation. This was the path, at least in part, to achieving a spiritual, cultural democracy—a democracy in which justice is located not only in its laws and formal political institutions but also in the hearts and minds, the habits and practices of its citizens.

Throughout his long life, Du Bois wrestled with the question of how to achieve a progressive democracy in a racist nation. Around 1937, Du Bois worked on *A World Search for Democracy*, an unpublished book that compared fascism, communism, and democracy.[45] Notably, it was meant to be an epistolary treatise composed of letters between a professor at a Black college and a student. This aesthetic medium enabled him to express the cognitive and affective dimensions of political systems that greatly inform ways of life. The medium also enabled Du Bois to convey areas of doubt and uncertainty—dispositions rarely found in social science scholarship. At one point the student asks, "Professor, just what is democracy? . . . Where is democracy to be found?" The professor, accustomed to providing clear answers to students' questions, replies, "I do not know. I used to know. I was quite certain. But today I am puzzled."[46] In our own day, many share the professor's puzzlement. We must ask what we are *to do* with our puzzlement and whether we are to abandon the search for democracy. Du Bois's response to the uncertainty of democracy was to maintain a qualified "dark, wild" hope in its achievement, an achievement that would require a robust cultural transformation—a *spiritual* transformation that included dismantling oppression based on race, gender, and class via education, economics, religion, and aesthetics.

There was nothing Pollyannaish about Du Bois's hope and commitment to a radical Romantic spiritual democracy. What Joseph Winters wrote aptly of *Souls* could be said of Du Bois's work more generally: It "exists in the space between melancholy and hope, disappointment and possibility."[47] Du Bois lived through a U.S. era of unrelenting lynching, beatings, angry white mobs, Jim Crow laws, and other forms of cruel racism (an era still very much with us). His commitment to a robust spiritual democracy was not in spite of oppression but because of it, for he held that democracy was the most promising—even if doubtful and uncertain—path forward. In his view, material change such as the legislative undoing of Jim Crow laws was a necessary but insufficient condition in eradicating racism, among other devastating evils. A more comprehensive transformation—indeed, a new "*veritable Way of Life*"—was required.[48]

Sometimes Du Bois used the term *civilization* to capture what I mean by *spiritual* in the expression *spiritual democracy*. Although "civilization" is often narrowly associated with "high" and white Euro-American culture, Du Bois employed the term to capture the distinctive, historically constructed and embedded ethos and civic manners of a people. To him, "civilization" refers not to a people of "blood and soil" but rather to a people who share common aspirations, practices, and beliefs and who work toward a common future. As Carole Lynn Stewart has aptly claimed, "Without understanding Du Bois's consistent concern with specificities, local meanings, and dignities of the 'folk,' we cannot begin to appreciate his novel conception of *civilization as civil society*."[49]

British and American Romantics often explored the connections between a place and its inhabitants—including its nonhuman and deceased inhabitants. Wordsworth, for example, wrote much about the ways and manners of the Lake District; Thoreau did the same for Concord. And the German Romantics were preoccupied with *Das Volk* (the people) and its relation to place. While a student in Germany, Du Bois was exposed to the Romantic concept of *Das Volk* from such different German thinkers as Herder, Weber, and von Treitschke. Many have commented on this formative influence on Du Bois's notions of "the people" and "race."[50] For my purposes here, I simply want to note that Du Bois critically appropriated the idea of "the people" to demonstrate the various ways that Black Americans possessed a distinctive, robust heritage and culture that was worthy of pride and dignity. By promoting the idea of a distinctive people—a distinctive "civilization," if you will—Du Bois sought to underscore the distinctive gifts and talents that Black Americans bring to the U.S. democracy.

In doing so, Du Bois sought not simply to make a place for Black people in American democracy but to argue that American "Black folk" are needed to *transform* democracy in America. An aspect of the distinctive identity of Black Americans is "second-sight,"[51] the hard-earned capacity to see and protest inhumanity and injustice in a nation that is mostly blind or indifferent to the brutalities in its midst. As Lawrie Balfour writes:

> Even as African Americans contend with the alienating force of double-consciousness, however, they are also gifted with a form of "second-sight" through which it is possible to see "this American world" more clearly. Du Bois thus indicates how the vantage of the marginal affords possibilities for recognizing injustice and distortion that may not be readily available to the privileged.[52]

Even early on, and surely in his later work, Du Bois embraced a Boasian view of the social construction of race and "the people," in which a race or people is informed by its social experience over time and in space, and not by a racial biology. Moreover, Du Bois acknowledged the range of experiences and perspectives found *among* "Black folk." He documented such diversity empirically in his 1899 sociological study *The Philadelphia Negro*. In this groundbreaking work, Du Bois highlighted the heterogeneity among the Black population of Philadelphia, noting profound differences in class, religion, and politics.[53] In a tangible, concrete fashion, Du Bois sought to make it clear that there is no such person as *the* "Philadelphia negro." In a more philosophical manner, Du Bois explored the topic of diversity among Black Americans in various writings, including *The Souls of Black Folk*, *Darkwater*, *The Gift of Black Folk*, *Dusk of Dawn*, and in many essays and lectures. Again and again, in different modes and manners, Du Bois refused the homogenization of the lived experiences—in flesh and bones, hearts and minds—of Black Americans by the stereotypes produced by a racist United States.

Yet Du Bois also sought to identify common characteristics among different "folks"—Black folk, white folk, and at times human folk. He once spoke of "the greatest of human discoveries," namely, the recognition "of one's self in the image of one's neighbor; the sudden, startling revelation, 'This is another Me, that thinks as I think, feels as I feel, suffers even as I suffer'. . . . Here in this my neighbor stand things I do not know, experiences I have never felt, depths whose darkness is beyond me, and heights hidden by the clouds."[54] The neighbor is both "another Me" and "beyond me," both the same as me and different than me. But that is not the final revelation; Du Bois takes us a step further. If I am willing to push on, to wrestle with both the commonality and the difference that my neighbor presents to me, then I may receive "the faint yet growing comprehension of human likenesses that both transcend and explain the differences, and that reveal, in the realization, the essential humanity of all men,—that strange kernel of life, which, hidden though it be, . . . is yet for us and in us, the greatest fact in the world."[55]

This radical aesthetic work of "recognition" is shared by Du Bois and Wordsworth. In verse, Wordsworth sought to lead his readers to comprehend and respect the banished "Negro Woman" as a "fellow-Passenger" while still honoring her distinctiveness. In more philosophical but equally "poetic" prose, Du Bois, too, encouraged his readers to acknowledge—as a startling revelation!—both the distinctiveness and shared humanity of the neighbor—that is to say, *anyone* we may encounter. Wordsworth's "The Banished Negroes" was an abolitionist poem crafted to inspire (what Du Bois called) "startling revelations" to help shape public opinion and encourage the British Parliament to end the transatlantic slave trade. Du Bois's philosophical prose, too, had practical, normative goals in mind. Hence Du Bois insisted that after having received "the faint yet growing comprehension of human likenesses," concrete actions must come "without wavering, without compromise":

A consciousness of the humanity of all men, of *the sacred unity in all the diversity*, is not merely to lay down *a pious postulate*, but it is *the active and animate* heart-to-heart knowledge of your neighbors, high and low, black and white, employer and employed; it means a firm planting of human ideals; . . . and a reverent listening, not simply to the first line but to the last line of Emerson's quatrain:

> "There is no great, no small,
> To the Soul that maketh all;
> Where it cometh, all things are—
> And it cometh everywhere."[56]

In a powerful move, Du Bois insisted that the moral imperative embedded in "*the sacred unity in all the diversity*" not be allowed to rest quietly as a "pious postulate." And to that end, he brilliantly appropriated the Emersonian theological truth—Spirit is *everywhere*—as a prophetic indictment of the racism in America that denies the sacredness of Black Americans. To this prophetic indictment belongs the prophetic command to work for racial and social justice—in America and beyond.

Although Du Bois placed much hope in "the sacred unity," he was also clear-eyed about the tremendous obstacles that would need to be overcome to achieve even the first stage of the "startling revelation," namely, *This is another Me*. How do you open the eyes of white America when white Americans are convinced that they have already been enlightened? How do you dismantle bigotry and oppression when people do not recognize their bigoted and oppressive manners? Du Bois increasingly understood that racism in America was not a problem to be solved but a complex, pervasive cultural condition and set of institutional arrangements that would need to be challenged and dismantled with various tools, skills, and approaches.

My argument in this chapter is that a dominant approach of Du Bois was to "open the eyes" of his readers—to *move* them—by means of what I have called his radical aesthetics. Radical aesthetics, it should be clear, does not simply present "facts" or "arguments," as important as those are. Du Bois understood that "facts" and "arguments" would not be enough to startle people into a new revelation. Rather, radical aesthetics vividly and dramatically addresses the whole person—body and soul, affect and intellect, desire and imagination. Nourished by the long history of Black resilience as embodied in sorrow songs (Black spirituals), Du Bois's "dark, wild" hope was to move citizens, in all their appropriate heterogeneity, toward those shared ideals, beliefs, and practices that support a just, inclusive, and equitable society. From the start to the end of his career, Du

Bois never let go of this hope. In his final work, published in 1968, he wrote, "For this is a beautiful world; this is a wonderful America, which the founding fathers dreamed until their sons drowned it in the blood of slavery and devoured it in greed. Our children must rebuild it. Let then the Dreams of the Dead rebuke the Blind who think that what is, will be forever."[57] Du Bois understood, of course, that democracy in America has only existed as a dream, as an aspiration. But his hope in that vision and his work to realize it endured. That's not to say that his substantive positions did not change over time. Du Bois increasingly turned to socialism, to Marxist critiques of capitalism, and to global perspectives in order to better comprehend the United States' complicity in the international dimensions of slavery, colonialism, and economic oppression. But Du Bois never felt the need to choose between working on global and domestic issues, and working toward a vibrant, just democracy remained a worthy aspiration.

Du Bois's Radical Romantic Aesthetics

Du Bois's efforts to transform the hearts and minds—the habits, practices, and institutions of citizens—is the context for my broad argument that Du Bois can usefully be understood as a North American Romantic who employed radical aesthetics.[58] This broad argument tracks how Du Bois brought together aesthetic, political, and environmental insights in order to *wake up* his readers to the suffering of Black Americans laboring under Jim Crow laws and other forms of racism and economic exploitation. It also tracks how Du Bois employed a variety of tropes associated with "nature writing." With these tropes, he depicted both the complex beauty as well as the complex burden of the land to Black Americans toiling under distant landlords, unjust rents, and over-farmed fields— toiling under a "second slavery."[59] My broad argument notes how Du Bois's usage of radical aesthetic strategies enabled his readers to see—to *taste*, to *experience*— the humanity of those in front of them: *this* tenant farmer in semi-slavery, *that* field ruined by abusive exploitation, *that* Black child (Du Bois's) who died because no doctor would treat him.

Alexander Crummell, a courageous Black minister and activist, was presented vividly by Du Bois in *Souls* so that his readers might see and feel his humanity, his struggles, his oppression, his achievements. Du Bois's hope was that if he could open his readers' eyes and ears to *this* Black man, then perhaps some white readers would become open to receiving additional revelations about Black Americans.

As Melvin Rogers notes, "Crummell serves as a proxy for what goes unappreciated and unnoticed about blacks in America—their striving for success, the work of their lives, the character they model, and their frustrated attempt at self-realization."[60] Du Bois's white audience might begin to see Black Americans anew, with a recognition of their strength, their tenacity, and the tremendous obstacles set against them. And increasingly in Du Bois's writings this aesthetic effort was presented on a larger, global canvas that sought to capture the intimate connection between oppression in America and in other empires. To see one person in bondage in America was an opening to view the broader vista of the past and current effects of the international slave trade, colonial oppression, and other forms of systemic oppression and exploitation.

I have been employing the ocular, "to see," to capture Du Bois's effort to transform his readers' aesthetic experience of the world, specifically that they may perceive the many facets of racism *and* racial justice. This entails, among other things, genuinely seeing the human being in front of them as opposed to projecting racial stereotypes and bigotry. In this context, Lewis Gordon's account of hypervisibility is helpful. Hypervisibility, according to Gordon, "is a form of invisibility. For to be hypervisible is to be seen, but in a way that crushes the self under the weight of a projected, alien self ('Look, a *nègre!*')."[61] In light of these ocular concepts of "invisibility" and "hypervisibility" and the connection between them, Du Bois could be said to employ radical aesthetics for the sake of transforming his white readers' sight—but not *only* sight, of course. Radical aesthetics, in the hands of Du Bois, sought to transform his readers' multifaceted ethical taste or experience of the world.

As a social scientist, Du Bois could and did marshal powerful social scientific arguments. Moreover, he understood his sociopolitical work to be, in its own way, an aesthetic work designed to move and persuade people.[62] To this end, Du Bois created visually rich infographics to portray data and statistics that *graphically* illustrated the history of racial oppression in North America as well as the Black struggle against it. These colorful, dynamic, often spiraled charts and graphs present "the problem of the color line"—with all its detailed statistics on slavery, education, literacy rates, employment, and so on—visibly, palpably, aesthetically.[63]

Although Du Bois increasingly turned to an economic analysis of the cruel intersection of racism and capitalism both in the United States and globally, he recognized that the language of the social sciences could not always sufficiently convey such complex social and psychological circumstances as the oppressive life behind the veil—behind *the color line* (to employ the term that Du Bois appropriated from Frederick Douglass).[64] Indeed, it is telling that later in life he called his novel *The Quest of the Silver Fleece* "an economic study."[65] In *The Souls of Black Folk*, *The Quest of the Silver Fleece*, *Darkwater*, and elsewhere, he employed a radical aesthetics as a tangible way to *touch*—to move, inform, and transform—individuals for the sake of social and environmental justice. He considered such aesthetic work as a form of activist engagement. His skillful artistic depictions were to challenge his readers—confront them, wake them up—so that they might *see* more fully, *feel* more keenly the reality of the social and natural world around them.

Du Bois employed a radical aesthetics that included the art of the storyteller and of the storied landscape because he believed that social scientists, among others, often failed to convey an "intimate contact" with the social life and conditions of those whom they studied. How is one to convey such "intimate contact"? Not by being what he called the "car-window sociologist." Rather than practice a detached, abstract, drive-by sociology, Du Bois developed an empirically replete, aesthetic sociology that was designed to convey not only sociological information but also richly textured, aesthetically crafted portraits of social life that convey the quotidian struggles and victories—and the persistent racism and classism—that confront African Americans daily. And so, Du Bois often delivered his empirical accounts of the political, religious, and economic practices of various populations in an aesthetically rich language. How else could he offer what he claimed was most critical to our studies, namely, "the atmosphere of the land, the thought and feeling, the thousand and one little actions which go to make up life"?[66]

To be awakened to the world around us is to become aware of the cruel, salient past that has led to the present. Lawrie Balfour, glossing Du Bois's expression "present-past," notes that Du Bois "rebukes anyone who presumes that society can be healed without confronting the *living* legacies of its gravest crimes."[67] Balfour here cogently renders the theoretical lesson that Du Bois expressed by his radical aesthetics. Awareness of pain and oppression in the past brings knowledge of the same in the present and thereby conveys some understanding of the persistence of racism and the tremendous work required to combat it. An aspect of that work, on Du Bois's part, was to cultivate an empathy for the particular—for *this* face "black with the mists of centuries"—so that such empathy might be extended to others suffering from "present-past" oppression.[68] In this way, Du Bois worked his art to bring political and social change.

His radical aesthetics was not engrossed with that traditional aesthetic triad—the sublime, the beautiful, and the picturesque (though, as we will see in the next chapter, to some extent Du Bois employed these motifs, often to express a sense of loss and nostalgia for the sake of social critique).[69] That triad typically removes art from the everyday and renders the spectator distant and detached—a far cry from the *engaged* witness that Du Bois sought to create. Du Bois's radical aesthetics, in contrast to "traditional aesthetics," placed art at the center of an everyday realism and ordinary life, anticipating John Dewey's central argument in *Art as Experience*. For Du Bois, art is located in everyday living, and at the center of art is ethical critique. Du Bois's radical aesthetics, then, departs from what I earlier discussed as the traditional divide between aesthetics and ethics. Moreover, his aesthetics has close affinities with his democratic rhetoric, as portrayed by Melvin Rogers in his book *The Darkened Light of Faith*.

Rogers provides a helpful account of the descriptive and aspirational notions of "the people" in the context of democracy in America, and he uses this account to explicate powerfully what he calls "the rhetorical character" of Du Bois's *The Souls of Black Folk*. In Rogers's account, the descriptive notion of "'the people' refers to those individuals with rights and privileges of citizenship as enshrined in a constitutional structure," whereas the aspirational notion of "the people" "serves as a space for refounding the polity to be more inclusive, destabilizing the idea of homogeneity as a prerequisite for democratic stability."[70] The challenge is to move a democratic society from its exclusionary, status-quo, descriptive sense of "the people" to an inclusive, dynamic, aspirational form. Du Bois, in Rogers's view, takes up this challenge in *Souls*, and rhetoric for Du Bois becomes the means for calling the people to better visions of itself.

Radical aesthetics—which is closely aligned with Rogers's groundbreaking construal of Du Bois's rhetoric—seeks to move a people from the present land of injustice to the prospective land of justice, from how things are to how things could and should be. It contains within it hope for a more promising future, even in the absence of empirical grounds for such hope. Hope, here, offers an alternative stance to the fatalism of those "who think that what is, will be forever" (to quote again from Du Bois's last publication). This alternative stance—to be called to work for democratic, progressive change despite the tremendous obstacles set against such change—sustained Du Bois's vocation. How else are we to account for Du Bois's courageous appeals for change in the face of lynching, race riots, humiliating Jim Crow laws, and vast racial disparities in housing, criminal justice, health care, employment, and education? Du Bois's vocation as a radical artist was to make *vivid* the everyday suffering that is caused by racial injustice, and by means of that vivacity Du Bois hoped that humans might, in the words of Lewis Gordon, be moved "to organize a world in which they could actually live," that is, to construct "a liveable world."[71]

Du Bois's "Criteria of Negro Art": Du Bois as Theorist and Practitioner of Radical Aesthetics

In the "Criteria of Negro Art," a lecture given by Du Bois at the NAACP's annual conference in 1926, we find the powerful claim: "*All Art is propaganda and ever must be*, despite the wailing of the purists. . . . Whatever art I have for writing has been used always for propaganda for gaining the right of black folk to love and enjoy."[72] Du Bois's aesthetics, like Wordsworth's and other radical Romantics', carries a practical, ethical, and political purpose. Du Bois rejected the very idea of disinterested art—that is, art that is neither informing nor informed by the sociopolitical context of the artist. While Du Bois's statement that *all art is propaganda* is both an epistemological and an ethical claim, he mostly focused on the ethical. We saw how Wordsworth employed his art in an effort to assist his mostly white readers to *see*—to behold as a person of dignity—the Black human beings in their midst. Du Bois, in contrast, began by asking his mostly Black NAACP audience about a more fundamental issue: What is the purpose of art for a people who have suffered from horrific racial cruelty and are bravely fighting for radical change? How is it that "a group of radicals trying to bring new things into the world, a fighting organization which has come up out of the blood and dust of battle, struggling for the right of black men to be ordinary human beings—how is it that an organization of this kind can turn aside to talk about Art?" (993). Du Bois posed the essential question that Wordsworth and his readers could not: *What have we who are slaves and Black to do with art?* While much of Wordsworth's early audience wondered if his art was too political, none asked *what have we who are white to do with art?* White privilege made that a nonquestion. Du Bois, in contrast, did not have that luxury. For him and his audience, this is an authentic and primary question, to which his answer would be *everything*.

To those who see art as the great escape from the challenges and cruelties of life, Du Bois argued that art is in fact part of the great fight. But note how Du

Bois presented his *theory* of art in the very *medium* of art; that is, note how he *practiced* radical aesthetics as he *theorized* it:

> Let me tell you that neither of these groups is right [those who reject art as part of political struggle and those who embrace art as an escapist respite from such struggle]. The thing we are talking about tonight is part of *the great fight* we are carrying on and it represents a forward and an upward look—a pushing onward. You and I have been breasting hills; we have been climbing upward; there has been progress and we can see it day by day looking back along blood-filled paths. But as you go through the valleys and over the foothills, so long as you are climbing, the direction,—north, south, east or west,—is of less importance. But when gradually the vista widens and you begin to see the world at your feet and the far horizon, then it is time to know more precisely whither you are going and what you really want.
>
> (993; emphasis added)

Du Bois here engaged his audience on multiple affective-cognitive levels. He employed art to advance an argument about art and beauty as a form of political struggle. And his art prepared his audience for still another fundamental question: "What do we want? What is the thing we are after?" (993).

After decades of struggle, "looking back along blood-filled paths," had Black Americans reached a promised land? Made substantial change? Real progress? No. Rather, blood, suffering, and toil brought Black Americans to a *vista*, to a place where they could now see far enough to ask the fundamental question, *What do we want?* To this basic question Du Bois offered a simple, direct "answer" and a more penetrating follow-up question: "We want to be Americans, full-fledged Americans, with all the rights of other American citizens. But is that all? *Do we want simply to be Americans?*" (993; emphasis added). Du Bois understood, of course, the importance of civil rights. Yet he also understood the limits of rights granted by a white supremacist United States. As long as the white man is the normative center, Black Americans will remain at the periphery—with or without rights. The granting of rights is not sufficient, nor is becoming "Americans" unless America itself is transformed. A greater change, then, is required, and art has its place in that "pushing onward," in that "great fight."

But not any art will do. It must be progressively inflected art and, in particular, Black art. Why Black art? "Once in a while through all of us there flashes some clairvoyance, some clear idea, of what America really is. We who are dark can see America in a way that white Americans cannot" (993). The suffering and oppression of Black Americans have granted them, at great cost, the capacity to see America accurately: to witness its punishing racism and joyless capitalistic materialism. Black Americans, in other words, have a distinctively powerful *moral taste*. There is nothing mystical about this Black sight and insight. The blindness of the privileged is matched by the perspicuity of the oppressed.

It might seem obvious that Black Americans can see with clarity forms of ugliness in America—greed and materialism, callousness and xenophobia, aggression abroad and oppression at home. But why forms of beauty? *Whence Black Americans' distinctive capacity for beauty?* This question goes to the heart of Du Bois's argument in "Criteria" and in many ways to the heart of his life's work. Those who suffer behind the ugly veil seek not only their own escape from ugliness but the accessibility of beauty for all. Black Americans, given their position behind the veil, have a greater appetite and discernment for beauty. As Du Bois said to his audience on that night in 1926: "You realize this [that you do not want ugly materialism] sooner than the average white American because, pushed aside as we have been in America, there has come to us not only a certain *distaste* for the tawdry and flamboyant but a *vision* of what the world could be if it were really a beautiful world" (994; emphasis added). A distaste for ugliness is accompanied by a vision—as taste—for beauty. And what is this beauty?

> What is it? I remember tonight four beautiful things: The Cathedral at Cologne, a forest in stone, set in light and changing shadow, echoing with sunlight and solemn song; a village of the Veys in West Africa, a little thing of mauve and purple, quiet, lying content and shining in the sun; a black and velvet room where on a throne rests, in old and yellowing marble, the broken curves of the Venus of Milo; a single phrase of music in the Southern South—utter melody, haunting and appealing, suddenly arising out of night and eternity, beneath the moon.
>
> (995)

In *Souls* and elsewhere, he theorized Black resilience in the face of unspeakable oppression by ways of exemplarity, e.g., the historical Crummell or the fictional John Jones. In the passage just quoted, he employed a similar method, this time theorizing art by way of vivid, concrete example: a cathedral, a village, a sculpture, and a melody—European, African, Greek, and African American exemplars spanning "fine" art and the everyday. He wanted his audience to ask themselves: How can it be that we are surrounded by such beauty in the world and yet we experience such ugliness—such institutional, civic, and personal cruelty? Who shall vanquish ugliness and enthrone beauty?

After offering his four examples of beauty, Du Bois spoke these words:

Such is Beauty. Its variety is infinite, its possibility is endless. In normal life all may have it and have it yet again. The world is full of it; and yet today the mass of human beings are choked away from it, and their lives distorted and made ugly.... Who shall right this well-nigh universal failing? Who shall let this world be beautiful? Who shall restore to men the glory of sunsets and the peace of quiet sleep?

(995)

The activist desires everyday goods, everyday beauty, for Black Americans—for all Americans. The day when Black America can enjoy "the peace of quiet sleep"— this humble yet profound good—is the day when much in America will have changed. Lynching will have stopped. Discrimination will have disappeared. The veil will have been lifted. America's sight and taste will have been transformed: The Black man, woman, and child will no longer be seen as "problem" but as "fellow traveler" and citizen.

Again and again, in different ways, Du Bois sought to present his audience with these basic questions: "What has this Beauty to do with the world? What has Beauty to do with Truth and Goodness—with the facts of the world and the right actions of men?" (995). What does beauty have to do with such painful facts as the violence, unemployment, poverty, wage discrimination, and lack of health care and housing that Black Americans face, as well as the distinctive triple oppression of Black women? Du Bois knew that many in his audience, including many Black artists, would answer "nothing" to the question "What has beauty to do with the world?" But Du Bois courageously offered a different answer. After describing himself as "a humble disciple of art" and as one who "exposes evil and seeks with Beauty and for Beauty to set the world right," he put forward the creed shared by radical Romantics, namely, that "here and now and in the world in which I work they [beauty, truth, and right] are for me *unseparated and inseparable*" (995; emphasis added).

This was the creed professed by William and Dorothy Wordsworth, Coleridge, Mary Shelley, Margaret Fuller, Emerson, Thoreau, and Whitman. Each of these white Romantics believed in the "*unseparated and inseparable*" connection between beauty, truth, and justice. They believed in the connection, and they *made* it, creating art that truthfully named both the beauty and the ugliness in the world, both the just and the unjust ways of life, in the hope that beauty would wax and ugliness wane. They all took up, in different ways, the "great fight" against unjust wars; economic inequality; corrupt government and religious authorities; oppression based on class, gender, and race; harsh prison conditions; discriminatory educational practices; cruel treatment of animals; and extractive, exploitive approaches to the natural, nonhuman world. These radical Romantics, then, were committed to an art of everyday realism, revealing everyday beauty and exposing everyday ugliness and injustice.

However, white male Romantics did not suffer from systemic discrimination and oppression. Du Bois, in contrast, experienced firsthand the injustice that he fought against, an experience that provided him with a sight and insight not available to white male Romantics. Du Bois shared the creed of the radical Romantics and belongs among them, yet he also *lived* the creed, added depth to it, and thereby transformed the canon and the very nature of radical Romanticism.

Du Bois believed that Black artists and Black Americans more generally had within them "a new desire to create . . . as though in this morning of *group life* we had awakened from some sleep that at once dimly mourns the past and dreams a splendid future" (995; emphasis added). Du Bois's reference to the "group life" of Black Americans slips into a modest form of essentialism. But the rhetorical aim here is to promote a collective movement for the sake of social change. Moreover, he was challenging the pervasive racist view that Black Americans had little to contribute to the United States. Du Bois turned this view upside down, claiming that the hope of America is found in the vision and work of Black America. If America is to become a place of civic beauty, then white America must learn from the transformational sight, power, and art of Black America. Teaching white America, of course, should not be seen as still another burden on Black America, but Du Bois did see such transformational education as part of his "great fight" for racial justice.

Black Americans, in Du Bois's account, simultaneously *mourn* the absence of beauty caused by racial oppression and *dream* of a future replete with beauty. As Eric Watts writes of Du Bois, "the presence of injustice signifies the negation of beauty.... Du Bois argues that persons living in this 'civilized' world, due to widespread oppression, have 'their lives distorted and made ugly.'"[73] But Black America, thanks to its resilience, hope, and experience of oppression, is uniquely positioned to challenge ugliness and inaugurate beauty. Black Americans, in Du Bois's view, carry the light of the "romance of the world," namely, the creative, liberatory work for humans in the here and now (996). This work entails two central tenets of radical aesthetics, namely, the imagination in the service of truth and the ethical as a promoter of empathy—as Du Bois put it, truth as the "the highest handmaid of imagination, as the one great vehicle of universal understanding...[and goodness] as the one true method of gaining sympathy and human interest" (1000).

Du Bois here is employing what could be called the language of radical Romanticism: The moral imagination, in the hands of Black artists, is to bring about a transformational understanding and broad empathy. This is the true "romance of the world"—to create the revelation of human dignity and goodness as well as the social and institutional change that such a revelation would entail. Melvin Rogers writes, "When Du Bois weds truth and goodness to the artist's work and art to propaganda, he means for the reader to understand art as a vehicle for expanding the horizon of the recipient."[74] Art brings the potential, then, of "a wider view" as well as a different view, of an ethically transformed world. Du Bois held firm to the belief that the world was fundamentally fallen (an influence from his Calvinistic upbringing) but also to the belief that the world was always in flux and could potentially be progressively reformed (an influence from his Romantic background).[75] The romance of the world was to maintain both beliefs, including the tension between them, and to work creatively for the "wider view," "human sympathy," and "the great work of the creation of Beauty, of the preservation of Beauty, of the realization of Beauty" (1000). It might as well have been Du Bois but it was Emerson who, when wrestling with personal loss and public outrage, wrote the following: "Never mind the ridicule, never mind the defeat: up again, old heart! ... there is victory yet for all justice; and the true romance which the world exists to realize, will be the transformation of genius into practical power."[76]

We are now in a position to appreciate the radical nature of Du Bois's claim that "all Art is propaganda and ever must be, despite the wailing of the purists" (1000). There is no "art for art's own sake." All art, one way or another, is connected to a broader sociopolitical weave. Du Bois was implicitly asking, *What ends—what propaganda—will your art support?* Du Bois explicitly answered this question when he said, "Whatever art I have for writing has been used always for propaganda for gaining the right of black folk to love and enjoy" (1000). There was a strong, white consumer base that demanded "pure art" about Black subjects, that is, art that was (supposedly) apolitical and that depicted racialized, stereotypical Black life. Yet that art, too, Du Bois insisted, is propaganda however much it might be labeled "pure." In response to this white demand, Du Bois encouraged Black artists to challenge stereotypes and to create art that promotes truth and justice—especially truth and justice "for gaining the right of black folk to love and enjoy." Such artistic "propaganda," in Du Bois's view, is not antithetical to aesthetic beauty but is rather part of the great fight *for* beauty and against ugliness.

Du Bois took the side of the radical Romantics: Art does not betray itself when it portrays everyday beauty and ugliness for the sake of progressive social change. Listen to how Du Bois, in the middle of his argument for a theory of Black aesthetics, employs the tools of radical aesthetics—stirring the moral imagination, broadening human understanding and praxis-oriented empathy, creating an ethical taste, addressing the whole person cognitively and affectively, and fashioning a detailed, storied landscape in which one sees into the veil:

> There is in New York tonight a black woman molding clay by herself in a little bare room, because there is not a single school of sculpture in New York where she is welcome. . . .
>
> There was Richard Brown. If he had been white he would have been alive today instead of dead of neglect. . . . He was simply one who made colors sing.
>
> There is a colored woman in Chicago who is a great musician. She thought she would like to study at Fontainebleau this summer where Walter Darnrosch and a score of leaders of art have an American school of music. But the application blank of this school says: "I am a white American and I apply for admission to the school."
>
> (998)

In Du Bois's theory of art and in his own practice of the literary arts, the aesthetic is not seen as tainted by a connection to truth and justice.[77] Rather it completes itself. For while "somehow, somewhere" in an ethereal realm art might exist for its own sake, in the "here and now," art, truth, and justice are "unseparated and inseparable" (995).

Du Bois was the poet-sociologist-activist who was as at home in Romanticism as in history and economics. He practiced a radical aesthetics in various forms of literary arts—the stylistic revelatory essay, the engaging novel, the haunting poem—designed to transform people and their aesthetic *taste*: to open their eyes and to move them from one position to another, to a position that is aligned with social, racial, and economic justice. Du Bois deserves to be cherished and honored as one of North America's greatest radical Romantics.

RADICAL AESTHETICS IN LIGHT OF TRADITIONAL AESTHETICS

As should be clear by now, radical aesthetics departs in notable ways from what is commonly associated with aesthetics. Radical aesthetics does not insist on the traditional "Kantian divide" between aesthetics and ethics (a divide that Kant paved the way for even if he himself did not unambiguously insist on it).[78] While Kant did argue that the moral subject requires suitable training in order to grasp the sublime, thereby suggesting a relation between aesthetics and ethics, it is, nevertheless, a one-way relation. For Kant, aesthetics (the sublime) does not *shape* the moral subject; rather, it *requires* a (certain kind of) moral subject. Radical aesthetics, in contrast, maintains a two-way relation—a dynamic dialectic—between aesthetics and ethics: Art can ethically cultivate the subject even as the subject's ethical formation contributes to their apprehension of art.

This close connection between art and ethics informs an account of pleasure that signals another departure from more traditional aesthetics. Art and beauty may indeed, as traditional aesthetics would have it, bring pleasure. But the object of such pleasure, in radical aesthetics, is not unsullied beauty but rather an affecting, integrated depiction of a poignant slice of our social and natural world—for example, an apt, moving depiction of an impoverished tenant farmer, a mournful mother, or a fallow garden. Such skillful artistic depictions wake us up, helping us see more fully and feel more keenly the reality of the social and natural world around us. In this process of waking up, we do experience aesthetic pleasure. Such aesthetic pleasure, however, is primarily a consequence of ethical cultivation.

Although radical aesthetics participates in what Emerson and Du Bois understood as "practical power," it may still be understood as *disinterested*, capturing at least in part what Kant had in mind by the term. Radical aesthetics is disinterested insofar as it is not manipulated or produced for the sake of advancing narrow, private ends. The artist respects what is before them by listening to it, by treating it with fidelity. Radical aesthetics does not impose. It does not willfully distort. It seeks to witness accurately. Receptivity and responsiveness, then, are central to radical aesthetics. Disinterest, in this tradition, is Wordsworth's "wise passiveness" or Emerson's "All I know is reception."[79] Even that creative Romantic faculty, the *imagination*, is understood not as projection of fantasy but as a creative lens by which to bring clear-eyed attention to such experiences as war, racism, sexism, unemployment, and environmental degradation. The radical Romantic imagination exhibits a realism of the everyday as it engages in social criticism, bringing new (accurate, objective) sight to the social and natural worlds. Recall the note Wordsworth wrote in the margin while reading Milton's *Paradise Lost*: "The real excellence of Imagination consists in the capacity of exploring *the world really existing*."[80]

The "disinterestedness" of radical aesthetics, then, seeks to present the world faithfully, and the imagination is essential to this *creative, prophetic* task. It is a *creative* task insofar as perceptive discovery requires the imagination just as much as skillful creation. Creation requires receptivity even as receptivity requires creative attention. For this reason, radical aesthetics does not privilege the distinction between fiction and nonfiction but rather calls our attention to the contrast between the authentic and the inauthentic, the honest and the dishonest, between that which reveals "the world really existing" and that which distorts reality.

Presenting the world faithfully is a *prophetic* task insofar as it palpably brings into relief the normative gap between how the world is and how it ought to be. Once one becomes a witness and sees the world anew, one then *longs* for the world to become a different place—a place more just, less cruel. The term *longing* is important here, for it captures both the cognitive and affective aspects of radical aesthetics' prophetic task.[81] Radical aesthetics seeks not simply to convey information and content but also inspiration and motivation for its prophetic work. The "disinterestedness" of radical aesthetics, then, does not entail ethical indifference. Radical aesthetics is disinterested in narrow utilitarian aims, not critical, life-enhancing ones.

Furthermore, as I mentioned in my discussion of Du Bois, radical aesthetics is not preoccupied with the traditional aesthetic triad: the sublime, the beautiful, and the picturesque. This triad often renders art as an object for the detached spectator. It has been customary to think of Wordsworth as the poet of the glorious (and presumably *distant*) landscape. And indeed, in his verse we find some of the most moving, detailed, and powerful descriptions of landscapes ever crafted in the English language. But Wordsworth's poetry was not principally centered on a natural world divorced from the presence of humans. Wordsworth found most of his inspiration in the life, labor, and struggle of nonelites, and he presented their worth and dignity for all to see and feel. His poetry was above all about *people*—about people and the land, and about people and those public and private circumstances that comforted and confronted their lives.

Reading Wordsworth in this fashion—as a fundamentally democratic poet employing radical aesthetics—may not prima facie seem to cohere with what he is perhaps most famous for, namely, the "spots of time" in the *Prelude*. Wordsworth himself used the expression "spots of time" only once to refer to events in his childhood: "There are in our existence spots of time, / That with distinct preeminence retain / A renovating virtue, whence . . . / our minds / Are nourished and invisibly repaired."[82] Commentators, however, commonly employ the term to refer to a number of powerful, often revelatory incidents in Wordsworth's past. These incidents—vividly described memories—typically entail a solitary or isolated Wordsworth (even if he is in the company of others) encountering an evocative landscape (e.g., Snowdon). It is not clear, however, why an extended notion of "spots of time" cannot apply to transformative incidents in *the context of human communities and interactions* that had profound political and environmental implications for Wordsworth. Nicholas Roe, in fact, comes close to making this move. He interprets as "*almost . . . a spot of time*" a scene in the *Prelude* that depicts a poignant political event in Wordsworth's life in France during the Revolution.[83] Wordsworth and Beaupuy—his friend and political mentor—encountered on the road "a hunger-bitten Girl":

> and at the sight my Friend
> In agitation said, 'Tis against *that*
> Which we are fighting', I with him believed
> Devoutly that a spirit was abroad
> Which could not be withstood, that poverty,
> At least like this, would in a little time
> Be found no more[84]

In this spot of time, the impoverished girl became a palpable symbol of the Revolution and all that it stood for, and the symbol charged Wordsworth's life with a profound sense of purpose and meaning. An inner, Romantic transformation matched an outward, political orientation. Other such transformative moments that entail people and community could be plausibly cited as spots of time with compelling, explicit sociopolitical import (scenes, for example, from "The Female Vagrant," "The Old Cumberland Beggar," or "The Ruined Cottage"). All this is to say that neither Wordsworth nor the tradition of radical aesthetics is preoccupied with the solitary individual in the face of the distant, sublime landscape.

Radical aesthetics, in contrast to traditional aesthetics, aligns with the way Wordsworth and Du Bois placed an urgent concern for the everyday at the center of art. When Wordsworth offered his revolutionary description of *who* the poet is and *what* poetry is for, he highlighted the poet as a fellow human addressing fellow citizens and employing *everyday language*. And although that language was suitably transformed into poetic form (though not "ornately"), Wordsworth maintained that there is no fundamental difference between prose and verse (still another gesture toward the everyday).

Not only was the language of Wordsworth's poetry "everyday," but so were the characters, events, and places about which he wrote. In this regard, he revolutionized the scope or range of topics deemed poetic. Radical aesthetics, as I will illustrate in what follows, can take still another step toward the everyday. It affirms not only the everyday content of such art as a poem or sculpture but also the aesthetic quality of such everyday events and activities as "the zest of the spectator in poking the wood burning on the hearth" or the flowing movement of an interfaith unity walk to commemorate 9/11.[85] And the imagination—that capacity at the center of the production and reception of art—is a practical ability that permeates our everyday existence. Our very perception of the world depends on what Coleridge called "the primary imagination."[86]

My point is that radical aesthetics is often a *quotidian aesthetics*: It emerges from the everyday and largely remains there. It places a premium on presenting the ordinary and commonplace to move and touch citizens for the sake of promoting social justice and (as we will see) environmental practice. Ultimately, then, the aesthetics of radical Romanticism seeks to participate in "the true romance of the world," namely, the transformation of genius into practical power. Although I have focused on the literary arts of Wordsworth and Du Bois, I want to conclude by mentioning a nonliterary form of radical aesthetics, namely, *performative radical aesthetics*. For the power of the word is found not only in literary texts; it can be experienced in the streets. And the power of radical aesthetics is found not only in the word; it can be experienced in bodies and assemblies in such public spaces as a street or a roadside patch of grass. Here, of course, radical aesthetics is moving still further from traditional aesthetics. This wider view of aesthetics is championed in the work of Jacques Rancière, who describes "'aesthetic acts' as configurations of experience that create new modes of perception and induce novel forms of 'political subjectivity.'"[87] Aesthetics, in Rancière's account, should not be limited to what we typically think of as "works of art"—paintings, poems, and sculptures, for example. Rather, artistic practices are understood as salient aspects of everyday, human activity. "Artistic practices," Rancière writes, "are 'ways of doing and making' that intervene in the general distribution of ways of doing and making as well as in the relationships they maintain to modes of being and forms of visibility."[88] The everyday realism that Wordsworth and Du Bois championed is extended in this broad understanding of aesthetics.

Such an expansive, quotidian account of aesthetics can be seen in a variety of everyday activities, including performative, ceremonial ones that often mark religious "ways of doing and making." The following are three examples of what I call *performative radical aesthetics*:

- After the Orlando Pulse nightclub shooting, an interfaith council chooses to meet at a local "safe space" café in solidarity with LGBTQ and Muslim communities.
- After the Virginia General Assembly votes to stop accepting federal Medicaid funds for four hundred thousand Virginians, Jewish, Christian, and Muslim faith leaders stand with health care advocates, protesting the vote at the very podium in the State House from which the vote was announced.
- On the fifteenth anniversary of 9/11, an Interfaith Unity Walk takes place in a small town as about one hundred people join hands and form a human chain, linking together the sacred spaces of Jewish, Christian, Muslim, and Baha'i communities.[89]

These performative events exhibit aesthetic form as Dewey defined it: "*the operation of forces that carry the experience of an event, object, scene, and situation to its own integral fulfillment.*"[90] In these three cases, members of diverse communities unite to stand in solidarity against various threats to justice and democracy in the United States. There are, of course, many other poignant cases of *performative radical aesthetics* in which one particular community or movement organizes for the sake of justice. In each case, radical aesthetics is committed to justice and equity and to the cultivation of an expansive *taste* for justice and equity. While radical aesthetics does not require religious or theological sensibilities (such as those found in these three examples of performative events), in order to be called *radical*, it does require progressive democratic perspectives, practices, ideals, and beliefs—and progressive religious traditions and communities have often supplied such normative resources. Deep spiritual sensibilities informed and were expressed by the radical aesthetics of Wordsworth, Coleridge, Mary Shelley, Emerson, Margaret Fuller, Thoreau, Du Bois, Terry Tempest Williams, and Leslie Marmon Silko, among others, as well as by countless practitioners of performative aesthetics.

If the tradition of radical aesthetics is to flourish in the present and persist into the future, it must continue to be wed to substantive ethical webs of beliefs and practices, such as those found in progressive religious traditions but also in a variety of progressive secular traditions (and often, in fact, these traditions intermingle and mutually inform each other). The art of critique requires the vision of spirit. And that critical spirit, as I show in the next chapter, requires the wild.[91]

CHAPTER 2

Into the Wild

Environmental and Racial Justice in Wordsworth,
Thoreau, and Du Bois

In the last chapter, I explored the radical aesthetics of Wordsworth and Du Bois. I claimed that to learn about Wordsworth's and Du Bois's aesthetics is to learn about the tradition that I am calling *radical Romanticism* and the intricate relation it forges between aesthetics, politics, and religion. Among other things, we saw how radical aesthetics attempts to cultivate in readers a particular *taste*—a way of experiencing the world—such that they become more attentive and responsive to various forms of injustice. In this chapter, I explore the *environmental dimensions* of radical Romanticism, building on my earlier account of the ways and practices of its aesthetics. In particular, I focus on the concept of the *wild*. My attention to the wild arises given its historically troubled relation to both environmental thought and racial justice. In contrast to racist, "pristine," and ahistorical accounts of the wild, I present an alternative account of the wild as found in radical Romanticism, paying attention to its ethical contributions to environmental and social justice. After setting forth the wild as it is characterized by Wordsworth, Thoreau, and Du Bois, I conclude the chapter by considering Du Bois's "dark, wild hope" as a source of resistance and change for our present challenges.

THE WILD AS CONDITION AND PROCESS

Let's think for a moment about that American icon of wilderness, the Grand Canyon. As the Colorado River sinks and the Colorado Plateau rises, two billion years of the planet's history is revealed. The revelation of that history can bring the most cynical observer to sublime tears. I've seen it.

In a bus chartered by the organizers of the Association for the Study of Literature and the Environment conference, the professor on my right prepared me for the Grand Canyon as only an academic can. It turns out that the Romantics, feeling acute competition with the agents of the Industrial Age, attempted to accrue social capital by becoming experts in their own distinctive enterprise—the manufacturing of beauty and the sublime. The Romantics, I was told, sold the sublime in works of art to an uncouth middle class hungry for the status that accompanies culture and education. I was assured that the only way to *escape* the spell of the wild and beauty was to interrogate its bourgeois history.

And then, in the middle of this private lecture about the relation between tourism, postindustrialism, and the commodification of landscapes, the brilliant and ineffable Grand Canyon suddenly loomed out the bus window: a staggering wilderness of rock and light rising from the land in one organic surge. A deep silence filled the bus. After that, I didn't hear another word about producers and consumers of wild beauty.

Later, I asked the bus driver if he, too, had heard the silence. He had. He hears it most times as he approaches the rim of the canyon with his busloads of noisy tourists—groups of retirees, children, lawyers, Pentecostals, cooks, and academics, among others. Apparently, the wilderness is still being widely consumed. Yet I wonder if the wild and wilderness—for which I am using the Grand Canyon as a stand-in—does not in fact exceed the efforts of those who would trade in it, whether it be the attempt of poets to construct it or academics to deconstruct it.[1] The bus turns a corner, and our representations, however skillful, bow to the view out the window.[2]

And this can happen anytime, anywhere. On a bus to the Grand Canyon? Sure. But also on a bus through the canyons of New York City or along the canals of New Orleans. We need not travel to the Grand Canyon to learn that the view from our window is often larger than the art or theory that attempts to capture it. This is not at all to say that art and theory are somehow less real or astonishing than the world around us. Art and theory are part of our world. They can, I will argue, participate in the wild and add their own quality and insight to the land and our lives. Yet while art and theory can contribute to our world and help us see and understand it, they can also obstruct our sight and insight. We can be held captive by a narrow, highly domesticated theory or picture and thereby become blind to the world's vast intricacies and mysteries.

In this book, I have been arguing that understanding Romanticism as *artistic productions of the distant, removed, sublime landscape* is largely an academic construction. While that construct certainly does capture some aspects of Romantic work, it does not capture its dominant features—at least not those of such British Romantic authors as Dorothy and the early William Wordsworth, Wollstonecraft, Coleridge, and Mary Shelley and such American Romantics as Margaret Fuller, Thoreau, Whitman, and Du Bois. Nonetheless, Romanticism continues to be frequently depicted as fanciful art focused on the sublime and an escapist replacement for religion. Yet, I have argued, there is in fact a robust tradition of Romantic realism, especially *a Romantic realism of the everyday*—everyday suffering and injustice, everyday beauty and dignity, everyday lands and ecosystems and the human activities within them. In this tradition, wilderness or the wild is not sublimely looming *out there*, outside human dwelling and activity, but rather is found closer to home—in our lands, our cities, our communities, our bodies. I have named this tradition *radical Romanticism*, and I will argue in this chapter that it carries alternative notions of wilderness or the wild.

William Cronon has brought critical attention to "the trouble with wilderness," arguing that it can be dangerous to think of wilderness as that which is untouched by humans.[3] My disagreement with Cronon—and Michael Pollan, among others—is not with their critique of the "nature as other" model but with their placing the blame on the Romantics, specifically on Wordsworth and Thoreau. Pollan, for example, claims "the whole idea of nature being 'out there' . . . [is] an invention of . . . Thoreau and the English romantic poets."[4] I do not deny the existence of Romantic writing in which wilderness appears as distant or removed from everyday human experience (think of Wordsworth's nighttime ascent of Snowdon or Thoreau's climb up Katahdin). Some such depictions of wilderness can be profoundly problematic. Yet even many of these problematic accounts, if critically appropriated, can contribute favorably to an environmental ethic and ecocentrism. My principal endeavor in this chapter, however, is to show *alternative* notions of the wild and wilderness in what I am calling radical Romanticism. Within radical Romanticism, the wild is often understood as a part of our everyday lives, thereby challenging both the "domesticized" view that human community exists apart from wilderness and the "romanticized" view that wilderness and wildness exist as pristine, untouchable, or otherwise problematically "other."

In radical Romanticism, wilderness is understood not only as a *place* but also as a *condition* and *process*. For Mary Wollstonecraft, "wilderness" is a *place* that offers women a temporary retreat from patriarchal structures, a place in which they are free from oppressive constraints. But wilderness, for Wollstonecraft, is also a *condition*, a *rebellious state of being* that facilitates a positive freedom for radical action that challenges patriarchy and other forms of social and economic injustice. Additionally, in radical Romanticism, wilderness exemplifies that which cannot be subject to total control, that which surprises, awakens, disorients, and baffles. It gives birth to chaos and creativity—and to social justice.[5] Wilderness confronts and tests all things tame, domesticated, or highly controlled and regulated. It threatens to lift the veil of familiarity, revealing wonder and beauty but also unjust systems of power that govern our daily life. In the case of Du Bois, to lift the veil of familiarity is to lift the veil of racial oppression.[6] It is that which, potentially, fires the imagination and challenges longstanding (often oppressive) practices. Wilderness, in this alternative account, is not understood exclusively as unspoiled tracts of land (assuming there are such places). Like sunshine, wilderness suffuses town and country and everything in between: the mall, the farm, the housing development, the isolated forest, the tenements of New York City. And if the wild is, in part, defined by our inability to control it, then it is found in Acadia and Yosemite but also in hurricanes and cancer wards. The wild breathes life and also death.

None of this is to say that domestication and cultivation—the production of social conventions, laws, routines, and so on—are per se deadening, dangerous, or bereft of wilderness. Life-affirming and socially just conventions acknowledge wilderness and the vulnerability and lack of control that wilderness conveys. Harmful conventions, in contrast, disavow wilderness, perpetuating injustice and seeking radical control. Our choice is to embrace wilderness as the *vulnerable, interdependent selves* that we in fact are or else to attempt to conquer wilderness as delusional, *invulnerable sovereign selves.*[7] It is to move toward ecocentrism or else cling to anthropocentrism. To embrace the wild is not to substitute mindless spontaneity for mindless convention but rather to forswear sovereign invincibility, to challenge oppressive conventions and institutions, and to work together, as vulnerable selves, on the unending task of justice for exploited individuals and communities. Wilderness, as I will argue, is something we *find*, something we *make*, and something we ought to *cultivate* in our lives and culture. In radical Romanticism, it is not oxymoronic to wish that wilderness would become part of our second nature—specifically, our progressive democratic social nature. This alternative understanding of Romanticism's accounts of wilderness are legible in the work of Wordsworth, Thoreau, and Du Bois.

WORDSWORTH: "MINGLED WILDNESS AND CULTIVATION"

I will show that Wordsworth is not principally the poet of the distant or wild sublime but the poet of the everyday: the people and places close to home. And "close to home" is often where Wordsworth locates "the wild"—the wild dwells in the familiar and promises to enliven or upend it. Nonetheless, it has been customary to think of Wordsworth as the poet of the remote, sublime landscape—a form of problematic nature writing. Such writing can lure author and reader alike away from pressing sociopolitical issues and thereby thwart practical action. This is precisely the charge that the New Historicist Jerome McGann has launched against Romanticism in general and Wordsworth in particular.[8] While I am grateful to McGann for moving an entire generation of literary critics to give sociohistorical matters a central place in their interpretations, his critique does seem to rely on a rather romantic interpretation of Romanticism. The radical Romantic tradition that I am investigating, contra McGann, offers realistic accounts and critiques of a variety of sociohistorical developments and events. While I do not pretend that my account of Romanticism covers all that could fall under the term, I do claim that my account shows fidelity to many central Romantic texts and authors.

I read Wordsworth (at least the early Wordsworth) as a democratic and environmental poet who rejected a facile, dualistic relation between wilderness and culture. This portrait of Wordsworth, as I noted in the last chapter, may not seem to cohere with more mainstream readings of Wordsworth—the nature poet and his "spots of time." Yet, as I have argued, most of his poetry was situated in the context of various human communities, often in relation to the more-than-human. Again, none of this denies that Wordsworth is a poet of the magnificent landscape. He is that—but he is also much more. There is also Wordsworth the democratic-environmental poet who brought attention to the labors, struggles, and places of commoners. This Wordsworth wrote characters who were frequently deemed too wild and repellent to be suitable as subjects of poetry—the outcast, destitute, and sick. He placed people, often those at the periphery of "the conventional," at the center of his poetry. Land and place are central to his poetry, of course, but they are best understood as characters among other characters, informing and challenging readers in their mutual exchange.

Wordsworth's *A Guide Through the District of the Lakes* (1835) is one work, among many, that exemplifies his understanding of the connection between people, place, and the wild. Wordsworth had seen, first-hand, how urbanization, capitalism, and modern aesthetics had damaged erstwhile ecologically productive and beautiful lands by converting them into over-farmed enclosures or else into manicured gardens with imported species of plants and trees. Rather than put culture and nature in an opposing binary, he understood culture and nature as potentially working together for the sake of human flourishing and environmental sustainability. He described and celebrated England's Lake District not as a destination to be gazed upon but as a sustainable mode of dwelling that acknowledged and integrated the wild. The region's importance was rooted not in wild untouched lands but in its sustainable ways of living and working appropriate to the place. In Wordsworth's (no doubt idealized) view, the Lake District was ultimately an example of human communities marked by justice and a "perfect equality" and that were "incorporated with and subservient to the powers and processes of nature."[9] These communities exhibited both an *intimacy* with and *humility* toward the land and its wildness.

Wordsworth's hope was that his *A Guide Through the District of the Lakes* would reveal and cultivate a particular type of democratic, environmental, and aesthetic sense and sensibility—a particular *taste*. As we saw in the last chapter, *taste* expresses and fashions particular ways of seeing, dwelling in, and visiting a place. In Wordsworth's view, the Lake District offered embodied lessons in good taste—taste that promoted sustainable relationships between communities and the wild and the resultant tended lands that held them. These communities dwelled, as he put it, with "the character" and "the spirit of the place," in "*mingled wildness and cultivation*" (62 and 105; emphasis added). In these communities, Wordsworth saw living traditions and practices inscribed in and nurtured by the land—a way of life that was intimate with the wild.[10]

The Lake District, we need to keep in mind, was Wordsworth's home, and the nonelite who dwelled there, his neighbors. He did not visit these people as an admiring tourist but rather lived with and among them. He knew them, their strengths and limits, and he wrote of both. His great worry, however, concerned new forms of capitalism and industry (for example, enclosures, wage labor, and the establishment of a rural, landless proletariat subservient to the agrarian bourgeoisie) that threatened to undermine the sustainable practices, habits, and traditions of the Lake District and harm people and place. A sign and symbol of the threat to come were what we might call the new "McMansions": oversized luxury houses built on artificial summits and surrounded by newly planted non-native trees and plants ill-suited to the region. Wordsworth put in stark contrast the "unpractised minds" that built such gaudy edifices to the local inhabitants who built as "co-partner[s] and sister[s] of nature," thereby harmonizing "with the forms of nature" (54 and 56). These more local homes and lands were "blended all over the country under a law of similar *wildness*" (46; emphasis added). Indeed, their "humble dwellings" reminded one "of a production of nature, and may (using a strong expression) rather be said to have grown than to have been erected;—to have risen by an instinct of their own, out of the native rock—so little is there in them of formality, such is their wildness and beauty" (47). For Wordsworth, the wildness and beauty of the local homes were a powerful, symbolic condemnation of the "formalism"—that is, the instrumental rationalism—that was introduced by the Industrial Revolution and new forms of capitalism. Against the rapacious land enclosures and machines that would seek to control every aspect of one's life and land, Wordsworth championed the ethos of the Lake District and its culture of the wild.

If the Lake District was Wordsworth's favorite *wild culture*, his sister Dorothy—as we saw in the introduction—was his favorite *wild person*. In Dorothy, he saw the strength of culture and the wild united. And William's favorite wild person was a highly domestic person, taking care of every aspect of their home life (cooking; gardening; cleaning; shoe making; laundry; mending; caring for the young, the old, and the sick; and so on). Such domestic work is potentially good but is surely oppressive insofar as it is tied to repressive, gendered roles—as in Dorothy's case. The wild of the Lake District and of William was not sufficient to challenge the gendered codes that greatly limited Dorothy's life options. This patriarchal context with its gendered norms highlights William's conventional limits but also Dorothy's wild strengths. For Dorothy, in spite of gendered oppression, was an impressive literary collaborator, and she engaged wildly in such activities as exploring the countryside, writing poetry and remarkable journals, reading widely, and debating forcefully with a variety of literary figures. Refusing to marry, Dorothy courageously lived as a wild, free spirit, despite her being heavily encumbered by domestic chores and oppressive gendered codes. Surely not all "cultivation" is to be prized. Perhaps she would have recognized something of herself in Thoreau's bean field: cultivated and wild, both.

THOREAU: "HOPE IN THE QUAKING SWAMPS"

Immediately after Thoreau was released from jail, having been locked up for his civil disobedience, he was recruited to lead a huckleberry party.[11] The enlisted captain of the huckleberry party, then, was an ex-con—a nonconformist who refused to pay those taxes that supported slavery and the unjust war against Mexico. Wild spirits fill prisons.[12] Thoreau declared that prison is the only place in the United States that the free, wild citizen can "abide with honor." For it is in the prison—the place where "the State places those who are not *with* her, but *against* her"—that one finds "the fugitive slave, and the Mexican prisoner on parole, and the Indian come to plead the wrongs of his race."[13] In essence, Thoreau poses to us this question: With whom and where do you stand? Will you stand with justice and embrace the wild?

So Thoreau, that captain of the huckleberry party, participated in and was a leader in the wild—that which stands outside of and challenges capitalistic markets and imperialistic states, confounding oppressive customs and practices. He led a *party*. He was not the individual alone in the woods but a leader and member of a joyful, revolutionary guard. And consider what this wild, nonconformist leader was pursuing: *huckleberries*—a wild, heterodox fruit. You couldn't buy huckleberries in the Concord and Boston capitalist markets, markets powered by the "machine" that, in Thoreau's view, ran on oppression, robbery, and slavery. All societies have their "machines," but when "oppression and robbery" are central to the organized machine, "when a sixth of the population of a nation which has undertaken to be the refuge of liberty are slaves," it is time for wild citizens to "rebel and revolutionize" to bring the machine to a halt: "Let your life be a counter friction to stop the machine."[14]

We can think of Thoreau, then, as a wild leader who invites us to travel with him into the wild, into a condition and process that confronts mindless, tyrannical tradition and convention.[15] In the wild—whether in prison or the huckleberry field—we can gain critical distance on our society. In the wild, we are given the chance to participate in the dawn, in the possibility (not certitude) of newness. Thoreau, we may say, sought to awaken citizens to a more genuine, wild democracy. He sought to *cultivate* wild citizens.

Both "Civil Disobedience" (1849) and "Walking" (1851) seek to wake people from their slumbering citizenship—from their passive subservience to oppressive customs and laws. Both essays encourage citizens to become wild, self-reliant, critically thinking citizens. In the first sentence of "Walking," Thoreau announced that he wished to speak a word for "wildness" and to speak of the human "as an inhabitant, or a part and parcel of Nature." At the start of the essay, Thoreau located humans *in* and *of* nature and the wild. While Thoreau did not consistently differentiate "nature" and "the wild," he typically understood "nature" as the larger category that includes the wild. For example, he claimed that "Nature has a place for the wild clematis as well as for the cabbage." Nature, then, includes both the wild and the domestic, that which is out of human control as well as that which we intentionally cultivate. Note that although the wild is a subcategory of nature, it does not stand in contrast to humans. An inclusive understanding of nature as embodying and entangling both the domestic and wild in humans is central to such radical Romantics as Thoreau. How else are we to understand Thoreau's entreaty, "I would not have every man nor every part of man cultivated"?[16]

The wild, for Thoreau, is a human characteristic that one should aspire to and work to obtain. Not surprisingly, culture, too, can and should participate in the wild: "Give me a culture which imports much muck." In spite of the secondary literature that ascribes to Thoreau those standard binaries—human/nature, culture/nature, human/wild, culture/wild—he in fact troubled these binaries. Moreover, as with other radical Romantics, the wild for Thoreau is not simply a place but a disposition and process. The wild, for example, can be expressed in music and in the human voice, and the wild can (and should) be found in the citizen. Vital nations draw their "nourishment and vigor" from a "wild source," as do our ablest poets, philosophers, and reformers: from a wild nourishment "grew Homer and Confucius and the rest, and out of such a wilderness comes the Reformer eating locusts and wild honey."[17]

It should be clear, then, that wildness and wilderness for Thoreau are not located outside humanity and its cultures but are potentially close to home: in our cities and buildings, our music and voices, our swamps and poets, our bodies and our lives as *citizens*. The wild animates the democratic nonconformist, the one who—like Thoreau—refuses to pay taxes for vicious state pursuits such as wrongful wars, who stands up against unjust institutions and practices such as racism and economic exploitation, who harbors the innocent fugitive or refugee from the police, and who champions courageous insurrectionary abolitionists such as John Brown. Much of Thoreau's work is an invitation to cultivate the wild within us, to pursue a *wild second nature*. The cultivation of the wild in the human does not tame the wild but rather infuses it with an ethical orientation, thereby producing a wild spirit dedicated to the work of justice.

In his essay "Walking," Thoreau famously called a swamp the most valuable part of any property—"the jewel" of the land. Why lavish such praise on a quagmire? Because the swamp was resistant to narrow utilitarian ends: to capitalistic market and cultural forces that would tame it, domesticate it, and make it serve profitable purposes. "Profitable purposes" includes those aesthetic ones that would drain the swamp and replace it with "flower plots and borders, transplanted spruce and trim box," "gravelled walks," a "tasteful front-yard fence," and—we can add—a poison-perfect lawn. Thoreau's swamp stands as a wild presence, a valuable reminder that many things in life defy narrow, functional roles, cultural conventions, and susceptibility to control. Wilderness, then, is neither the reverential sublime that looms above us nor the "productive" wild that we seek to subdue and exploit. Wilderness, rather, is a condition and process that confronts the old, prepares for the new, and is a catalyst for hope. For this reason, Thoreau consistently associated wildness (including swamps) with the dawn and the dawn with the expectation and *possibility* of change. And thus the wild leader professed, "Hope and the future for me are . . . in the impervious and quaking swamps."[18]

Thoreau was wary of North Americans turning eastward toward Europe for such hope and light. "Eastward I go only by force, but westward I go free. . . . Mankind progresses from east to west." If the American task was to imitate the past, then the nation ought to look east. But if it sought "wildness" and "freedom," Thoreau urged the nation to face Oregon, not Europe.[19] We might be tempted to interpret "west" as a physical direction for Thoreau, perhaps even as a direction in support of Manifest Destiny. But from what we know of his critique of the westward railroad, the Mexican-American War, and the vicious treatment of Indigenous peoples, among other things, Thoreau was no friend of Manifest Destiny. If west served as a direction for Thoreau, it was a symbolic and ethical one.

Still, Thoreau could have pushed back harder against Manifest Destiny. Thoreau held that the United States' western expansion was inevitable. While he did strenuously critique that brutal expansion (especially the genocide of Indigenous populations and the violent annexation of northern Mexican lands), he did not push back sufficiently against what he considered to be the inevitable westward march of white settlers' civilization.[20] The same could be said of his condemnation of the violent and treacherous treatment of Indigenous populations. He held that Indigenous populations in the United States were destined to extinction, given the racism, greed, and exploitive ways of white settlers. Disastrously, such a sense of inevitability paves the way to its actuality.

Thoreau worried that the United States, for the sake of legitimacy, would seek to mindlessly import "Old World" opinion, custom, and tradition. This anxiety usually kept Thoreau from embracing the view supported by many British Romantic authors, namely, that freedom and wildness are as likely to issue from the past as from the present, that inheritance need not be a yoke of oppression but can serve as an accustomed, serviceable plow for uplifting new soil. This was surely the position of Wordsworth. Nonetheless, it was precisely Thoreau's suspicion of "the east" that enabled him to break free from the constraints of the past and to forge powerful stances against slavery, the extermination of Native Americans, and alienation caused by new market economies.

West is the direction of change and disruption, of challenging the way things are and hoping for what they might become. Daily, we are to travel west. Daily, we are to cultivate an openness to surprise, critique, and change. Yet after our daily journey into the wilderness, we are to return to the familiar, with "the sun on our backs . . . driving us home at evening."[21] This to and fro prescribes neither literal directions nor times of day. It is, rather, a dialectical process: an intermingling of the wild and the domestic, the unfamiliar and the familiar. We expose ourselves to the wild, and then we bring it home to illuminate our everyday practices, institutions, and lives. Of course, this dialectical process may *entail* a literal direction and time. Thoreau went to Walden to build a temporary home and to unsettle himself, his hope being that he would return from Walden made anew. Yet this process of leaving and returning can be a daily practice, *wherever* we are, even if we are standing still. By means of this process, we become like Thoreau's bean field: both cultivated and wild.

The wild and the domestic, then, are not two different places but rather are dialectical modes of being.[22] Thoreau worried that, in the absence of the wild, citizenship would become nothing but a mindless mechanism cranking along. Genuine democracy is not simply about the vote but about mindful, deliberate living—in both one's private and public life—that entails self-critique and social critique. Hence Thoreau wrote, "Cast your whole vote, not a strip of paper merely, but your whole influence."[23] What was ailing North American democracy was not so much a lack of democratic institutions but a dearth of wild democratic spirit. How else were citizens to confront the most profound, modern threats to a genuine democracy, namely, racism, capitalistic markets, consumerism, and the objectification and commodification of the natural world? The good news is that wilderness, as a resource for our challenges, is always close at hand.

As if to underscore the ubiquity of wilderness and to subvert the idea of the frontier as a place to be conquered, Thoreau wrote, "The frontiers are not east or west, north or south, but wherever a man *fronts* a fact . . . there is an unsettled wilderness between . . . him and the setting sun, or, further still, between him and *it.*"[24] Wilderness reminds us that the familiar is always subject to transformation—to revolution. It is in our home, if we want it to be, but it's often not comfortable. So why would we want to cultivate the wild, to work on practices that invite it into our lives? Thoreau answered, "In Wildness is the preservation of the world."[25] In the absence of wildness, we become the living dead: satisfied with being content in the familiar, status-quo present. We attempt total control of the social and natural world to prevent change, to keep out newness, and to silence the sounds of dawn. Yet the *preservation* of our world, ironically, requires openness to *change*—to disruption, to life, to the wild.

DU BOIS: "MUSIC OF A WILDNESS"

As I claimed in the previous chapter, adding W. E. B. Du Bois to the Romantic canon of authors not only expands the canon but transforms it. In particular, he complicates Romanticism by bringing to it an analysis of the racial and socio-economic forces that interact with land, labor, and the wild. Du Bois, in my view, is one of North America's most significant radical Romantics.

Michael Starkey notes, "Historical relationships between African Americans and wilderness have been largely overlooked by scholars. . . . Whites are almost exclusively the subject of the literature."[26] This is in part because many assume that there simply are no Black "nature writing" traditions. This assumption is patently wrong. Du Bois was well versed in Romantic genres of nature writing, and, as we will see, he employed many tropes and devices associated with these genres. Moreover, similar to such radical Romantics as the early Wordsworth and Mary Shelley, he crafted artistic accounts of the land not only to portray its beauty but also to depict various forms of injustice written in the land. Du Bois's vivid, detailed "storied landscapes" conveyed an often fraught relation between "the land" and African Americans toiling under unjust rents, distant landlords, and exhausted soil—toiling under a Reconstruction or Jim Crow "second slavery." As Michael Beilfuss has well expressed, Du Bois "employs [the familiar genres of pastoral and wilderness narratives] provocatively by offering bucolic descriptions of the rural South only to undercut them with irony, and by depicting a swampy wilderness only to complicate the image with a historical sense of its value as a place for alternative lifestyles and heroic resistance."[27]

Like Wordsworth and Thoreau, Du Bois usually understood the wild and wilderness not as sublime or pristine landscapes outside humanity but rather as a condition and process—a vitality and dynamism—that includes humanity. For Du Bois, the wild—and "nature" more generally—is neither limited to nor removed from place, history, and community.[28] This idea of the wild contrasts greatly with the ahistorical, extralinguistic depiction of "wilderness" found in many Euro-American traditions. While I disagree with some of Paul Outka's summary judgments about Romanticism and American transcendentalism, I agree that there is a dominant strand in Euro-American traditions in which, as Outka states, wilderness "marks a dehistoricized space in which the erasure of the histories of human habitation, ecological alteration, and native genocide that preceded its 'wild' valorization is, literally, naturalized."[29] In contrast to that intellectual and cultural strand, Du Bois understood the memory and experience of wildness as a potential source of dignity, cultural vigor, and social protest.

Michael Bennett rightly notes that the "main current within African American culture has, from Frederick Douglass to Toni Morrison, expressed a profound antipathy toward the ecological niches usually focused on in ecocriticism: pastoral space and wilderness. This fact challenges ecocritics to train our methods of reading and theorizing on African American cultural texts that question mainstream assumptions about the universal appeal of 'unspoiled' nature."[30] I do want to note, however, that there are a multitude of Black authors, present and past, who have crafted poignant texts that can broadly be construed as "nature writing," assuming that "nature" includes human nature, culture, and history. A good example of such Black nature writing is found in Camille Dungy's *Black Nature: Four Centuries of African American Nature Poetry*. In her introduction she writes: "Though these poems [in *Black Nature*] defy the pastoral conventions of Western poetry, are they not pastorals? The poems describe moss, rivers, trees, dirt, caves, dogs, fields: elements of an environment steeped in a legacy of violence, forced labor, torture, and death. . . . Even during the most difficult periods of African American history, the natural world held potential to be a source of refuge, sustenance, and uncompromised beauty."[31] What Dungy claims about the poems in her collection, I will claim about Du Bois: His writings offer an account of the natural world as a site of beauty and sustenance as well as violence and despair.

In particular, I am suggesting that Du Bois presented the wild as a place and a condition of resistance and hopeful transformation. This wildness and its concomitant hope are seen, for example, in his account of the Sorrow Songs. In *The Souls of Black Folk*, Du Bois claimed that "the *wild* sweet melodies of the Negro slave"–"the soul of the Sorrow Songs"–are distinctive African American contributions to the "American Republic."[32] What makes the Sorrow Songs *wild*? They are nurtured by a particular place *and* a particular cultural experience. In Du Bois's words, "Sprung from the African forests, where its counterpart can still be heard, it ['the music of Negro religion'] was adapted, changed, and intensified by the tragic soul-life of the slave, until, under the stress of law and whip, it became the one true expression of a people's sorrow, despair, and hope."[33] The Sorrow Songs were nurtured by African forests and were then intensified by the slave's experience of an oppression that was delivered by cruel public laws and brutal individual hands. The wild, then, is that which will not be subdued by unjust laws, chains, and whips. Challenging unjust public and private conventions that sought to control and manage every aspect of the lives of enslaved Black people, the wild nurtured the beauty, longing, and hope found in the Sorrow Songs and in the Black slaves who sang them. The wild permeated a slave culture that, against all odds, resisted practices of oppression and thereby produced the Sorrow Songs–songs of hope and loss, songs of resistance and suffering. Du Bois portrayed the African forests as contributing to the Sorrow Songs and, ultimately, to African American emancipatory traditions and practices.[34] This portrayal subversively challenges those various Western colonial accounts of Africa as a continent bereft of culture and liberatory resources. Du Bois honored Africa's forests, its traditions, and its contributions to the "American Republic."[35] Additionally, Africa and the Sorrow Songs nourished the wild, nonconformist aspects of Black religion, challenging oppressive religious traditions.

Du Bois was critical of much of conventional, organized Christianity and its metaphysics, but not of religion or spirituality per se. His writing manifested a spiritual stance that Jonathon Kahn has usefully characterized and brilliantly developed as "divine discontent" (Du Bois's own term). Think of "divine discontent" as a religious sensibility linked to critique and resistance—and to the wild. Or as Kahn so aptly puts it, divine discontent is "a promise, a covenant, and an urging toward a state of dissatisfaction with politics and society."[36] It is also a religious sensibility that galvanizes Black solidarity. As we will see later in this chapter, one site of this religiosity was woods or swamps adjacent to Southern plantations, places where slaves and free Black laborers could exercise some spiritual autonomy.[37]

In *The Souls of Black Folk*, Du Bois made it clear that this religion of protest was enlivened by a "soul"—an animating spirit or sensibility—that existed long before it came to the shores of North America. African religions didn't need America to become soulful any more than Black people needed Christianity to obtain souls. And when Black religions in America did mingle with Christianity, Du Bois implied that it was the wild soul of the African forests that fostered its distinctive "spirit of revolt."[38] Moreover, Du Bois's sociology of religion investigated the sociohistorical roots, institutions, and practices of a white supremacist Christianity that actively supported chattel slavery, oppressive Jim Crow laws, and segregationist, discriminatory practices beyond Jim Crow.

The wild of Africa, in Du Bois's account, is not an inhumane, bestial wild but rather a life-enhancing wild that sustains culture, heritage, and hope. For Du Bois, the lands, histories, cultures, and agencies found in Africa were a basis for freedom and equality for those outside of Africa—for all Pan-Africans. The wild of Africa, then, is not only a place but also a liberatory quality of being and a process of becoming. This wildness resists those oppressive practices and institutions that would attempt to subdue it and shackle its sources of hope. Like Thoreau, Du Bois linked hope to the wild, and like Thoreau, he linked the wild to the swamp.[39]

Du Bois's Swamps in The Quest of the Silver Fleece *and* The Souls of Black Folk

Thoreau had his wild swamp in the essay "Walking," and Du Bois had his in his first novel, *The Quest of the Silver Fleece* (1911). Thoreau's swamp was a nonconventional entity that resisted capitalist, market economies by its very nonproductive power. Du Bois's wild swamp, in contrast, became productive, but not to contribute to racist capitalist markets. Rather, Du Bois's swamp provided diversified food crops and cotton, a cash crop, enabling a Black community to become liberated from the white, capitalistic, and racist oppression of tenant farming.

For the Southern white culture that sought to subdue both Black bodies and swamp lands, the swamp was a wildness in need of taming. As Anthony Wilson has claimed, in Southern white culture "ideas of control, purity, and dominion over nature . . . were essential; in both literature and in the real world, the swamp always defied those ideas."[40] The swamp was hated insofar as it was perceived as difficult to subdue, and Black bodies were elided with the "savage" swamp and its wild lands. Indeed, the perceived proximity of Black humans to "nature" (to primitive, barbaric "wilderness") signaled their distance from culture and civilization.

Du Bois, in contrast to this Southern white culture, portrayed the swamp as a place of beauty, wild resistance, and survival, as an alternative land and way of life that offered some modest protection and hope for Black populations. Moreover, as Beilfuss skillfully notes, this alternative account of the swamp and wildness also stands in contrast to the standard account of the Romantic sublime: "For many African Americans, these wilderness spaces [Southern swamps] were not forlorn territories divorced from humanity, *nor were they sublime landscapes that could empower the subject who sought them for temporary escape from the burdens of 'civilized life,'* they were arenas of resistance, self-determination, ownership, and alternative societies."[41] For Du Bois, the swamp and its Black inhabitants participated in a wildness that did not stand outside of culture but instead assisted in its transformation.

It is not uncommon for dominant colonial perspectives to portray "border" areas such as "inaccessible" swamps and forests as uncivilized places of savagery. In *Slow Violence*, Rob Nixon describes how the British colonizers in Kenya understood the Mau Mau's forest as "a place beyond reach of civilization, a place of atavistic savagery." This stands in stark contrast to the view of the Kenyans who resisted colonial oppression, for whom "the forest represented something else entirely [different from atavistic savagery]: it was a place of cultural regeneration and political refusal, a proving ground where resistance fighters pledged oaths of unity, above all, an oath to reclaim, by force if necessary, their people's stolen land."[42] These two contrasting perspectives on the forests—the colonial view and the anticolonial one—are similar to those that Du Bois identified in his depictions of Southern swamp lands. Struggling against a distinctive form of settler colonialism, Du Bois represented the swamp as neither the stereotypical Romantic sublime bringing spiritual nectar to the solitary wanderer nor as the uncivilized land in need of subjugation. Rather, he depicted the swamp as a place of cultural nourishment, wild resistance, and hopeful change. These themes are vividly portrayed in *The Quest of the Silver Fleece*.

In *The Quest*, Zora—a child of the wild—leaves her swamp in Alabama to gain an education in New York City. When she returns home, she and her swampland are mutually transformed. Both become Thoreau's bean field: cultivated and wild, both. Her education in the North does not destroy within her the wild "vigor and life" of the swamp culture in which she was raised; rather, the wild becomes infused with new ideas and perspectives. Zora returns home from the North with a wild idea, "a plan of wide scope—a bold regeneration of the land": clear a portion of the swamp and on it create "a free community," namely, a collective cotton farm that would protect local African Americans from cruel, white economic power.[43] For years white landowners had been exploiting Black tenant farmers and the land on which they worked. As Brett Clark and John Bellamy Foster note, white "landowners built their wealth on the exploitation of the laborers and the exhaustion of the soil. At harvest time, they stole the silver fleece [the cotton] from the tenant farmers, buying the cotton at bargain prices, subtracting rent, food, and supplies, leaving the farmers with little money for a year's work."[44] Zora's swamp farm would provide a liberatory alternative to the cruel "second slavery" of tenant farming.

The white farming practices of cotton monoculture both abused laborers and degraded the soil. Zora, a "child of the swamp" and its "music . . . of a wildness," understood that the liberation of her people and the land depended on the creation of a just community built on and in the wild—the very wild land that was considered worthless by the white racist landowners.[45] This revolutionary idea and its implementation are portrayed as the work of a powerful woman, *a genius of the wild*: someone who is vital, nonconformist, and practiced in the ways of freedom. Not only are the crops of the collective farm nourished by the swampland, the people, too—their spirits—are nourished by it. The swamp, then, is not only a place. It is a culture, a condition, and a process of transformation: a wild way of being that challenges a variety of institutions and conventions, including racist and exploitive, capitalist ones.[46] And Zora, open to the wild, imaginatively and skillfully leads her people against unjust laws, virulent corruption, and violent mobs. Bles—her friend, lover, and finally husband—admits that, while he had once thought of himself as Zora's patriarchal guide, he now understands himself as her coworker, nay, her "follower."[47] With Zora, Du Bois, in the spirit of the wild, challenges racist and sexist conventions about the capabilities of Black women.[48]

This fertile ground of Zora's swamp stands in sharp contrast to the "gloomy soil" of a desolate town of African Americans that Du Bois described in *The Souls of Black Folk* (1903). Because of the white practice of over-farming and the falling price of cotton, "the whole land seems forlorn and forsaken." In the wake of white flight, the remaining Black population must struggle with "the half-desolate spirit of neglect born of the very soil." Owing to the sins of the previous white population, people and place now suffer together. Du Bois began *The Souls of Black Folk* by stating the unasked question: "How does it feel [for the person of color] to be a problem?"[49] Mary Shelley, as we will see in chapter 6, posed a similar question in her novel *Frankenstein*: How does it feel (for the creature) to be a problem? What is it like to move through life being perceived as an "other" who is a problem to life—that is, a problem to the life of the dominant culture? Yet both Du Bois and Shelley also added this question: What does it mean that the nonhuman is perceived as a problem, as an "other" to be subdued? For is not the more-than-human, too, behind the Veil? This is not, in my mind, a misappropriation of Du Bois's powerful metaphor. As Bénédicte Boisseron has powerfully argued, there is a connection between anti-Black racism and white supremacist anthropocentrism.[50] How else are we to interpret Du Bois's account of plantation farming as "the hard ruthless rape of the land"?[51] How else are we to understand Du Bois's environmental justice, as when he linked Black and environmental exploitation in this line, "The harder the slaves were driven the more careless and fatal was their farming," or in these lines, "The poor land groans with its birth-pains, and brings forth scarcely a hundred pounds of cotton to the acre, where fifty years ago it yielded eight times as much. Of this meagre yield the tenant pays from a quarter to a third in rent, and most of the rest in interest on food and supplies bought on credit"?[52] Land, buildings, and Black laborers share an exhaustion and ruin under white oppression. Black people and Black land are problems to be exploited or else, once expended, left to languish. How can hope and vitality return to such a community and its land?

One answer to the questions posed by *The Souls of Black Folk* comes eight years later with the publication of *The Quest of the Silver Fleece*, in which Du Bois offered the wild as a prospect and strength embodied by a people and place. Spiritual resilience, political resistance, and economic transformation flowed from Zora's swamp not by exploiting it but by identifying with its sources of life.[53] But *Souls*,

I should note, has its own swamp, which also responds to questions of hope and despair: You may remember the Chickasawhatchee swamp in Georgia from the preface. It is a wild place—wild in the radical Romantic sense—and a storied landscape. The swamp is both land and culture, an ecosystem and an archive of history, a site of oppression and of hope. Listen to how Du Bois prepared his readers to hear his account of the swamp: "How curious a land is this,—how full of untold story, of tragedy and laughter, and the rich legacy of human life; shadowed with a tragic past, and big with future promise!" Inscribed in the land are stories of Black and Indigenous tears and oppression as well as resistance and hope. Similar to Wordsworth's work in his poems "The Ruined Cottage" and "Michael," Du Bois lends us sight to read the land and to hear in it an otherwise "untold story"— lives crippled by oppressive social and economic forces as well as lives sustained by sources of hope and resistance. Du Bois's Chickasawhatchee swamp stirs the imagination with flashes of the sublime, a "weird savage splendor."[54] But this wild sublime is not removed from history or humankind; rather, it is intertwined with both, speaking in a varied language of sacred beauty, ruined plantations, Indigenous struggle and slaughter, and Black slaves and chain gangs.

Hope is found in the wild, in the swamp, and even in the former plantation lands connected to the wild. As Scott Hicks maintains, "Juxtaposed against the richness and fertility of the swampland soil stands the decayed and wasted richness and fertility of the archetypal Southern plantation. Like the swamp, this place remains a site of fertility; a sense of optimism for the possibility of renaissance appears to pervade it."[55] But this hope is not facile and optimistic but dark and somber. Even Zora's wild, fertile swamp carries with it precarity, suffering, and uncertainty. Ultimately, Du Bois portrayed hope as a virtue and social practice that does not ignore anguish but remembers and anticipates it.

The Need for the Wild

There is a serious challenge for the project of critically appropriating the wild. Euro-American colonizers have employed "the wild" derogatorily to characterize Indigenous populations and, more to the point in this chapter, white Americans have used the term to dehumanize and demonize enslaved Black people and African Americans more generally. Black people and Native Americans were frequently stigmatized as "wild savages," that is, as dangerous creatures that stood outside of civilization and culture given their lack of moral formation—or even lack of innate capacity for moral formation. In this racist, derogatory usage, the wild is not that which is *sublimely* distant from humans (as in William Cronon's and Michael Pollan's mischaracterization of Romantic wilderness).[56] Nor is the wild, in the derogatory usage, the radical Romantic alternative account of the wild, that is, the wild as a condition and process that is beneficial to humans. Rather, this pejorative wild conjures a bestial, mulish force that needs to be dominated and controlled lest it become a menace to white civilization.[57] Here, Black bodies and their swamps are a threatening wild that requires subjugation. Again, this stands in stark contrast to the wild as a site of complex beauty, refuge, and resistance.

What, then, are we to do in light of this racism associated with "the wild"? The task, as I see it, is twofold. First, we should critically appropriate and construct helpful notions of the wild and wilderness, accounts that assist us in our pursuit of environmental and social justice. Second, we must critique and censure problematic notions of the wild, specifically those that separate humans and their histories from the wild and those that denigrate the racialized other—and women, particularly women of color—by associating this "other" with an inhuman wild. It would be a mistake not to embark on this reconstruction of a beneficial notion of the wild. Yes, the concept of the wild carries much deleterious baggage. But the promise of the wild remains great, and it must be kept for *all* North Americans. It must contribute to the eradication, not the reinscription, of "the color line."[58]

The United States needs the wild for the sake of democratic transformation. In the previous chapter, I noted Du Bois's commitment to a *spiritual* democratic culture, a democracy in which justice is located not only in its laws and institutions but also in the hearts and minds, the habits and practices, of its citizens. An aspect of that spiritual democratic culture is its *wildness*: its capacity to challenge and unsettle and to incite hope and transformation. In Du Bois's account, we hear the spirit of a genuine democratic culture in that "*wild* voice" of the courageous abolitionist David Walker, as he boldly condemned the atrocities of slavery to an audience of Southern legislators.[59] And we hear it as well in Zora's voice as she stood in front of her congregation, "with the *wild* yearning to help," and proposed the wild idea of a collective farm, imploring, "Oh, my people! . . . Rescue your own flesh and blood—free yourselves—free yourselves!"[60]

Linking the wild and democratic transformation is vividly illustrated by the Niagara Movement, an activist group and forerunner to the NAACP cofounded by Du Bois in 1905 and dedicated to aggressively challenging racial discrimination in America. Niagara Falls, the source of the group's name and its first meeting place, was suggestive of the wild and mighty "current of change" that was needed to transform American democracy. Du Bois honored the power and beauty of the falls as linked to liberatory, transformative change. Yet at the same time, he suggested that the United States had betrayed the freedom that the falls symbolizes; the United States was busy erecting white supremacist Confederate monuments even while it was revering Niagara Falls as an icon of American liberty. Against the oppression of the newly erected Confederate monuments, Du Bois lifted up the beauty and freedom of (a newly reappropriated) Niagara Falls, thereby engaging in a form of immanent critique.[61]

Although I have been focusing on Du Bois and the concepts of the wild and wilderness, a broader argument can be made about Du Bois as an American Romantic environmental writer who employed a political aesthetics. Du Bois brought together aesthetic, political, and environmental themes and insights to bring attention to "the beauty of the world"—a beauty "not to be denied."[62] Appropriately acknowledging and honoring beauty was, in Du Bois's view, an ethical task, and this view informed his aesthetic work. This aesthetic and ethical sensibility produced compelling descriptions of the grandeur and loveliness of the natural world, the built world, and the social world—and their complicated intersections. And this same commitment to "beauty" fueled his detailed accounts of "the ugly," that is, of how those with the power and privilege of race and class dominate Black laborers—women, men, and children—and the land and places in which they work, making the explicit connection between the exploitation, exhaustion, and rape of people and the land. Du Bois, then, was one of the first to see the connection between racial and environmental justice more broadly, and he conveyed that connection by means of radical Romantic aesthetics. In *Darkwater*, for example, we find some of the most glorious environmental writing found in the Romantic tradition. And we find not only "nature writing": Du Bois's accounts of *urban* beauty rival those of Whitman and anticipate second-wave environmental writing. Yet these lovely, uplifting passages alternate, without warning, with graphic descriptions of the cruelty of racism. The beautiful and the ugly (as he called it) are presented with all their unresolved tension.

Sometimes, however, Du Bois did provide connections and segues between his moving accounts of beauty and his equally heartrending accounts of moral ugliness. After limning the most resplendent portrait of Acadia National Park ever written, he added, "God molded his world largely and mightily off this marvelous coast and meant that in the tired days of life men should come and worship here and *renew their spirit.*" Immediately after this account, Du Bois, the narrator, is in a Black, Southern home and wonders why those who suffer from oppression don't travel to such "places of beauty and drown themselves in the utter joy of life." The response comes from "the little lady in the corner": Did you ever see a Jim Crow waiting room, a Jim Crow train? "No," she says, "no, we don't travel much."[63]

In this terse reply, Du Bois offered an incisive critique of those "nature traditions" and of (what would become) those national parks that assume the privileged mobility of the white wanderer, the one who enjoys spiritual rejuvenation in the splendor of the natural world. The same critique is made implicitly in *The Souls of Black Folk*. In the chapter "Of the Meaning of Progress," for example, Du Bois, a young Black man in search of a summer teaching job, must walk the rural Southern countryside: "I see now the white, hot roads lazily rise and fall and wind before me under the burning July sun; I feel the deep weariness of heart and limb as ten, eight, six miles stretch relentlessly ahead." In his account of walking through the countryside, Du Bois also crafted gentle passages that are reminiscent of Thoreau's sauntering in his essay "Walking": "Next morning I crossed the tall round hill, lingered to look at the blue and yellow mountains stretching toward the Carolinas, then plunged into the wood."[64] But mostly, Du Bois made it clear to the reader that as a Black man walking the rural roads of America, he had not the safety, means, or leisure of someone like Thoreau. And by such masterful, artistic juxtaposition ("no, we don't travel much"), Du Bois issued one of the earliest critiques of racist environmentalism: white privilege and Black disadvantage written not only in the laws of the land but in the land itself. Just as racist Jim Crow laws restricted where and how Black Americans could move, live, and work, one's experience of the land reflected those racist laws, making it painfully clear where Black Americans belonged and where they did not.

In his fiction and nonfiction prose, Du Bois emphasized how the lack of mobility for Black people in white America has dire economic consequences. But as we have seen, for Du Bois such lack of mobility also has profound spiritual and aesthetic ramifications. In his view, it is a spiritual and aesthetic crime to deprive Black Americans access to American lands. As Kimberly Smith so eloquently states:

> The impact of racial prejudice on blacks' relationship to the land was not merely economic, however. Du Bois was equally concerned with how racism could affect a community's moral and spiritual relationship with the natural

world. Indeed, the relationship between politics and aesthetics—a central concern for romantic philosophers such as Rousseau and especially Burke—is also a major focus of Du Bois's thought. That nature held moral, spiritual, and aesthetic value was, for Du Bois, a claim needing no defense.[65]

I do not want to say here that restrictive Jim Crow laws and oppressive socioeconomic conditions completely blocked African Americans' connection to and enjoyment of American lands. As we have seen, Du Bois wrote of African Americans' diverse aesthetic, spiritual interactions with the land. Nonetheless, racist laws and practices erected a variety of obstacles that rendered the experience of the land more problematic for Black Americans than for white Americans. And those racist obstacles persist. For example, "Black farmers have historically faced race-based lending discrimination when applying for loans from the United States Department of Agriculture (USDA), which often denied loan applications from Black farmers, delayed the loan process or allotted them insufficient funds." This, no doubt, explains in part why only 1.34 percent of American farms are Black-owned.[66]

Whether depicting a swampland or national park, a plowed field or city street, a view out of the Jim Crow train car or a ruined plantation, Du Bois employed the Romantic craft, creating aesthetically complex accounts of the beauty and joy, the suffering and injustice that are etched into that nature-culture matrix known as "world." But unlike the early Romantic authors, Du Bois also demonstrated the various ways that racism can render the land as a site of punishing labor, anguish, and painful exclusion. We see, then, Du Bois as a practitioner in the tradition of radical Romantic aesthetics even while he transformed it. He is one of North America's first and most gifted environmental authors and ecocritics, one who took an intersectional aesthetic, sociological, economic, and historical approach to race, justice, and the natural world. Still more, he is a moral and religious philosopher wrestling with the question of hope in times of despair.

A Dark, Wild Hope

The question of hope and its relation to despair looms all around us—in private conversation and in public discourse. In the humanities, one finds a pervasive pessimism as various fields grapple with such catastrophes as climate change and white nationalism. Du Bois's responses to the catastrophes that he faced are instructive as we attempt to respond robustly to our current catastrophes: to climate change, yes, but also to the white supremacy that Du Bois had to contend with and that continues to inflict suffering on people of color and that is entirely intertwined with environmental catastrophe. Resilience and vulnerability, resistance and uncertainty—these all informed Du Bois's dark, wild hope. And this hope—not sunny and Pollyannaish but rooted in suffering, trial, and grief—is a powerful resource for us today.

In the previous section, I began to explore Du Bois's account of the wild as a source of hope and change. We saw, for example, that in *The Quest of the Silver Fleece* the wild swamp is not only a place but a process of hopeful transformation that challenges racist and exploitive capitalist institutions and practices. The struggle against persistent racism (among other oppressive structures and conventions) is a feature of the wild. Such struggle is a practice of hope, specifically a form of hope that is rooted in an agonizing present and colored by an uncertain future—and by the relation between such agony and uncertainty.

So, although ultimately I am going to argue for hope—to conclude with hope—it is important to note straightaway that dark, wild hope does not deny but rather acknowledges and bears witness to the multiple forms of oppression and risk that various world populations currently face. The hope that I find in Du Bois is not a cheerful denial of cheerless facts, nor is it faith in inevitable progress. It is, rather, hope as a social practice that is informed by suffering and loss, by uncertainty and vulnerability.

Now, words can be hollow and facile, especially theoretical ones. This is, in part, why Du Bois employed a radical aesthetics. Rather than writing abstractly about Black suffering, he constructed vivid prose to convey graphically this and other forms of suffering. In *The Quest of the Silver Fleece*, the struggle against white oppression is bloody, costly, and uncertain. As Zora and her community bravely create their cooperative farm, white mobs destroy their crops, burn their buildings, and lynch community members ("two red and awful things" hang from a tree). In its detailed, palpable, aesthetic discourse, the language of the novel delivers the horror of Black strife and suffering. But it also delivers a hope that sustains resilience and resistance. In the last lines of the novel, Zora proposes marriage to Bles as they stand ready to keep up "the great fight" in the presence of the wild swamp and the beauty of the moon: "[Zora] stood very still and lifted up her eyes. *The swamp was living, vibrant, tremulous.* There where the first long note of night lay shot with burning crimson, burst in sudden radiance the wide beauty of the moon."⁶⁷ In the poetics of the novel, Du Bois expressed a hope forged in fire and grounded in the wild of swampland.

Dark hope is also found in "Of the Passing of the First Born," that poignant chapter in *The Souls of Black Folk* where Du Bois gave a moving account—a threnody—of the death of his eighteen-month-old child. No white doctor would tend to the child sick with diphtheria. The chapter reads like a song of mourning. "Unto you a child is born"—thus begins the chapter like a trumpet proclaiming the birth of a biblical prophet.⁶⁸ But what does this birth bring, of what does it speak—of hope or doom? It's a difficult question, and Du Bois did not provide a simple answer. Back and forth, Du Bois moved between past, present, and future sorrows as well as past, present, and future sources of hope.⁶⁹ From this complex motion across temporal geographies of suffering and hope, of injustice and expectation, there emerged "*a hope not hopeless but unhopeful*":

> And thus in the Land of the Color-line I saw, as it fell across my baby, the shadow of the Veil. Within the Veil was he born, said I; and there within shall he live.... Holding in that little head—ah, bitterly!—the unbowed pride of a hunted race, clinging with that tiny dimpled hand—ah, wearily!—to *a hope not hopeless but unhopeful*, and seeing with those bright wondering eyes that peer into my soul a land whose freedom is to us a mockery and whose liberty a lie.⁷⁰

Unhopeful hope? Yes, for even as Du Bois and Nina Gomer, his wife, traveled down the street to bury their child, the white city folks glanced at them and uttered the n-word. *Unhopeful* hope? Yes, for Du Bois would lament, "'Not dead, not dead, but escaped; not bond, but free'.... Well sped, my boy, before the world had dubbed your ambition insolence, had held your ideals unattainable, and taught you to cringe and bow. Better far this nameless void that stops my life than a sea of sorrow for you." Yet Du Bois was not content to stop at "unhopeful hope" alone. His meditation on the death of his son demanded of him something more intricate, something more difficult. It demanded of him "a hope not hopeless." And so, at the conclusion of his threnody, he exclaimed, "Surely this is not the end. *Surely there shall yet dawn some mighty morning to lift the Veil and set the prisoned free....* A morning when men ask of the workman, not 'Is he white?' but 'Can he work?' When men ask artists, not 'Are they black?' but 'Do they know?'"⁷¹

In this remarkable passage, Du Bois maintained a "hope not hopeless" for a "mighty morning," a transformed future. His dead child is not Edelman's "the Child," embodying a reproduction of the present in the future.[72] Rather, Du Bois's child dies as a condemnation of the present and as a forged-by-fire, wild hope for a different and more just future. A transformed future requires a present-minded focus on current injustice, which itself requires "*a hope not hopeless but unhopeful.*" Without denying the immense suffering caused by persistent racism in America, indeed, by acknowledging it, Du Bois articulated a hope in and for the current struggle and work.

There is a resemblance between Du Bois's chapter on the passing of his son and Emerson's essay on the passing of his son. In what is perhaps Emerson's most difficult and important essay, "Experience" (1844), he offered an account of his grief—or an account of the inadequacy of grief—for the death of his son. The essay weaves between modes of power and vulnerability, of hope and despair. Yet it concludes with a chastened form of hope. It is a hope that has emerged from death; it is scathed but not ruined. For Emerson, as for Du Bois, our true vocation and journey is to acknowledge grief and despair, inequality and injustice, and at the same time to work courageously with hope for social transformation. It could have been Du Bois, but it was Emerson who, when wrestling with personal loss and public injustice, concluded "Experience" with these lines: "Never mind the ridicule, never mind the defeat: up again, old heart! . . . there is victory yet for all justice; and the true romance which the world exists to realize, will be the transformation of genius into practical power."[73]

However, the character of hope is different for Emerson and Du Bois. While Emerson's hope is chastened, it does not carry the weight of Jim Crow's lynching, humiliation, and discrimination—a discrimination that would deprive a Black child from receiving urgent medical attention. Emerson's hope is not as dark as Du Bois's "hope not hopeless but unhopeful." In reference to Du Bois, among other Black writers, Joseph Winters speaks of a *hope draped in black*: "This melancholic hope . . . suggests that a better, less pernicious world depends partly on our heightened capacity to remember, contemplate, and be unsettled by race-inflected violence and suffering."[74] We cannot find *that* form of melancholic hope in Emerson. We need Du Bois and other authors who are more explicit in their invitation for us (in the words of Joseph Winters) "to think hope and melancholy together."[75] So both Emerson and Du Bois, *but especially Du Bois,* offered a hope rooted in trial and suffering, a wild hope presented as a radical practice of present-minded resistance.

I now wish to ask: What can we learn from Du Bois's dark, wild hope, which emerged in resistance to racism, to help us reflect on a hope in the context of today's white nationalism as well as climate change and other environmental disasters? The first, most fundamental lesson is this: While it is tempting to dismiss hope as naïve or even delusional, lack of hope is a dangerous scenario. Du Bois never lost sight of the importance of keeping hope of some form alive. The absence of hope may foster passive nihilism and moral paralysis.[76] If we stop hoping for a more just future, we may stop working to achieve it. Rather than thinking of hope as a naïve or *unrealistic* stance, Du Bois would have us conceive of hope as a way to open our eyes to the reality around us. As Teresa Shewry has noted, "Hope involves orientation of the critical eye to what in the present world might otherwise escape notice; such an orientation allows a relationship with an uncertain, promising future."[77] Hope, then, does not deflect our sight from unpleasant realities but rather brings critical attention and active engagement to them for the sake of imagining and working toward a more promising future.

The hope that we find in Du Bois does not deny suffering and loss but includes them. Climate change has already brought tremendous suffering and loss. It is not a future event alone. Nor is it merely a recent event. A disastrous change in climate ought not to be understood simply as carbon-induced climate change but rather as a variety of anthropogenic environmental changes in which Black and Indigenous populations have experienced a home in ruins. When Native American communities were forcibly removed from one region of the United States to another, they experienced climate change.[78] So did the roughly 12 million enslaved Africans who were forcibly transported to the Americas. There are numerous forms and causes of what we might call climate change and the attendant ruined homes. Some populations are living in them presently and have for some time now. Loss and injustice, then, haunt our past and present—and they haunt our future. But lest one become paralyzed over such loss, Du Bois would recommend a dark, wild hope that remembers loss for the sake of both mourning and morning—for both grief and transformative change.[79] Hope and despair, then, should not be understood as a binary: We do not need to choose between them.

Sunny hope will not serve our needs. Much good work in affect studies has investigated and critiqued various forms of hope and optimism. For example,

Lauren Berlant describes how attachment to hope in the American Dream can sabotage public and private flourishing, rendering one blind to systems of domination.[80] Bladow and Ladino write of the importance of "recuperat[ing] bad feelings" and note that "straightforward emotions like hope are of dubious efficacy."[81] And yet, in a reparative mode, Berlant also writes of "having adventures and being in the impasse together, waiting for the other shoe to drop, and also, allowing for some healing and resting, waiting for it not to drop."[82] And Bladow and Ladino claim that "both climate and social justice activists require altruistic emotions as a foundation for action."[83] We need, then, not only to recuperate "bad feelings" but to honor and cultivate a wide, complex set of affective responses. As Catriona Sandilands wisely states, "A monolithic diet of fear starves more complex feelings. It does not touch the difficult heart of what so many people are currently experiencing in their everyday lives in these climate changing times: grief, rage, hope, wonder, perplexity, even love."[84] My claim is that Du Bois's dark, wild hope belongs precisely to a rich catalog of complex affects that are needed for these difficult, challenging times.[85]

Wild hope is a vocation—a virtue or cultivated disposition to continue the work for beneficial change despite one's reasonable mood of despair and evidence that amelioration, while possible, may not be likely.[86] It looks at reality with clear-eyed vision and announces *wildly*: we have work to do. This wild hope, ever practical and realistic, is a living reality in our world today. Macarena Gómez-Barris complains that our academic conception of the "no future" Anthropocene fails to register the resilience and resistance of Indigenous populations dwelling in extractive zones so oppressive that they are already living in the so-called no future.[87] Others, too, such as J. K. Gibson-Graham, reveal living pockets of resistance within capitalistic societies that oppose extractive economies and politics.[88] Gómez-Barris and Gibson-Graham surface the submerged work of hope. As Catherine Keller has argued, resistance requires that we embrace uncertainty and risk and reimagine our ways of being with the human and more-than-human.[89] Such risky reimagining requires a wild hope. Without it, we cannot take even the first step. This is surely the view of the Potawatomi author and activist Robin Wall Kimmerer when she writes, "It is not enough to weep for our lost landscapes. . . . I choose joy over despair." Kimmerer goes on to note that she is not naïve to the oppression of land and people, but she worries that when "environmentalism becomes synonymous with dire predictions and powerless feelings," it breeds "despair when it should be inspiring action."[90]

The metaphor of the step is a not a simple one. Hopeful work does step *forward*, but not into preordained progress. Rather, hopeful work steps *into* the present struggle, ever-seeking to understand those past ways that led to the struggle, ever-seeking to imagine and work toward a more just future—a justice that includes the more-than-human world. Hopeful work resists the problematic futurism that queer theorists such as Edelman and Ensor have so ably critiqued.[91] Taking steps forward does not deny present harms or seek to save the unjust status quo from future catastrophe. Stepping forward, the work of hope embraces Ensor's environmentalism, namely, an environmentalism that takes "its cues from queer theory . . . seek[ing] less to save the planet from a single, cataclysmic end than to embrace the ethical and practical demands posed by the multiple endings that condition our experience of the everyday."[92] The work of hope does not ask us to choose between being attentive to current *or* future suffering and injustice. Rather, the work of hope acknowledges the connections between the two. It also includes the vulnerability and uncertainty that the present and future mutually bring to us. Indeed, *vulnerability and uncertainty are the context and argument* for dark, wild hope. No doubt it is tempting to resign to extractive and racist capitalism, lament it, and assume alternatives are impossible. But the more difficult, radical act is to imagine a desirable and just future.

Imagining future dystopias can also be a radical, powerful act, but the normative force of such dystopias is to highlight present and possible future injustice and suffering in *the hope* that they might be mitigated.[93] Indeed, Du Bois's dystopia "The Comet" (1920) vividly depicts future forms of hope and love when the apparently sole survivors of an apocalypse—Jim, a Black man, and Julia, a white woman—become the new Adam and Eve and the categories "high and low, white and black, rich and poor" evaporate.[94] Such hope and love are tender seeds found in the present but overwhelmed by systemic racism. The precarity of such seeds is made clear at the end of "The Comet," when it becomes apparent that Jim and Julia are not in fact the sole survivors: When whiteness reappears (via Julia's father and a white mob), so too comes the return of anti-Black racism and hatred—these powerful "seeds," like hope and love, that are also rooted in the present.[95] The continuity between the present and future, with all its hope, despair, love, and hatred, are perfectly expressed in "The Comet," and "The Comet" perfectly expresses Du Bois's dark, wild hope.

In either case, then, whether imagining a brighter future or warning of a dark dystopia, hopeful, wild acts are always rooted in present, everyday reality—with all its suffering and, yes, with all its undeniable beauty. This is the work of the dark, wild hope that Du Bois made into a lifelong practice—one we should cultivate within ourselves and our institutions as we imagine a future built on social and environmental justice.

In this chapter, I have explored some environmental dimensions of radical Romanticism, building on the ways and practices of its aesthetics. In different ways, Wordsworth, Thoreau, and Du Bois all portrayed the wild not as that which stands outside humans but rather as a liberatory condition and process that includes humans. Additionally, Du Bois challenged the notion of the wild as uncivilized lands and vulgar Black bodies that need to be subdued for the sake of white civilization. As we saw, Du Bois presented the wild as a place and a condition of resistance and hopeful transformation. Jointly, Wordsworth, Thoreau, and Du Bois provide what I have called radical Romanticism's alternative account of the wild. And of the three, Du Bois brings to radical Romanticism critical perspectives of environmental and racial justice.

In the next chapter, I take a historical step back to look at Rousseau, one of the first modern Europeans to begin the work of dismantling the "nature as other" model. Rousseau understood the intimate connection between the degradation of the natural world and social injustice. This connection is a central characteristic of radical Romanticism and a primary focus of the next chapter.

CHAPTER 3

Rousseau's Garden as a World in Which to Live

This chapter is about a land—its gardens and Alpine geography—and its accompanying culture in Rousseau's bestselling novel *Julie; or, The New Heloise* (1761). This epistolary novel probably sold more copies than any other book in the eighteenth century. Publishers could not keep up with demand, so for the first time in history, a book was rented out by the hour. The aesthetic craft of *Julie* gripped the minds and bodies of its readers, leading them to "choke with emotion," to weep and convulse, to experience extreme joy (when, for example, Julie's garden is portrayed) and intense sorrow (when, for example, Julie dies). The affective response of its readers matched Rousseau's concrete, detailed portraits of the characters—which includes the land itself. Indeed, many readers refused to believe that *Julie* was a work of fiction.[1] If radical aesthetics is the art of moving people profoundly, both affectively and cognitively, especially toward ethical aims, then one of its first practitioners can be said to be Rousseau.

However much the French Revolution is associated with Rousseau, it was the *garden* revolution, as found in *Julie*, that captured his heart and announced his most acerbic social, economic, and political critique. In *Julie*, Rousseau not only critiqued the European developments that would eventually lead to climate change, but he also offered a rich, detailed way of life that provides us with imaginative resources for combating environmental and social calamities today.

Rousseau is central to the story that I want to tell about radical Romanticism. At a time when many were celebrating the Age of Enlightenment and industry for the sake of human progress, Rousseau crafted a nineteenth-century countercultural narrative. In this narrative, human progress—the advancement of ethics, science, technology, and the arts—is a tragedy. It is the story of the human departure from a sustainable relation to the more-than-human world—from Nature's original Garden—and of the rise of *amour-propre* (excessive self-regard), private property, social inequality, and the exploitation of humans and the natural world by the wealthy and powerful.[2]

In this Rousseauian countercultural narrative, to be close to the natural world is not to be *subhuman* but to be *fully human*—in contrast to many European anthropocentric, racist, and misogynist accounts. It is hard to exaggerate what a profound shift this represents. Up until Rousseau, a variety of intellectual and cultural Western traditions had associated *men* with spirit, mind, and high culture. The spiritualized, intellectual man represented the height of humanity, the one made in the immaterial, transcendent image of God or Plato's Forms. Meanwhile, women and enslaved people, among others, were associated with materiality, the bodily, and the uncultured—in other words, with nature or the natural world. In this view, *nature is other and inferior*, as are women and enslaved people. In particular, the Black woman's body in the Euro-American imagination was frequently connected to the primitive, the anticultural, the "natural."[3] In various Western narratives, women, along with the rest of the natural world, needed to be subdued in order to be made safe and useful.[4] Historically, the connection between women and the natural world often went hand in hand with that destructive dualism that severed the natural world from culture, mind, and spirit.

This association of the ideal of humanity with the immaterial, the disembodied, and culture-sans-nature has contributed greatly to ecological crises. Many aspects of Euro-American cultures tend not to honor dirt or labor that pertains, for example, to food or food production. They tend not to honor bodies or the materiality of the natural world—except as a "natural resource" to be exploited. Hence, they can burn, pillage, trash, and poison nature and still remain spiritual, intellectual, cultural beings. In order to prevent this wanton destruction, humanity and spirituality must not be conceived of as disembodied and disconnected from the more-than-human.

Ecocriticism encourages humans to identify with and have affection for the natural world. Yet, as long as the pervasive dualism that severs the natural world from culture, mind, and spirit persists, it will be difficult for women and people of color to affirm their association with the natural world, for it risks inadvertently perpetuating the oppressive construction of women and people of color as fundamentally uncultured creatures who need to be restrained. In order for women and people of color to be appropriately identified with nature, their association with nature as that-which-must-be-subdued must be overturned, as must the elitist identification of white men with spirit, intellect, and culture.

In sum, then, the idea of *nature as other* must be dismantled.[5] And Rousseau was one of the first modern Europeans to begin this work. For Rousseau, human identification with the natural world was ethically and spiritually beneficial. And Rousseau challenged not only the "nature as other" model but also the harmful nature/society binary.

Now, it might seem that Rousseau's remedy for our fall from "Nature's Garden"—that is, from the normative "state of nature"—would be a return to that state. But such a return, in Rousseau's view, is not possible.[6] As it turns out, the departure from the state of nature was itself *natural*. Various human capacities made the departure out of the asocial, prelinguistic state of nature entirely predictable.[7] Since Edmund Burke, it has become commonplace to claim that, in Rousseau's account, humans are born good—born natural—and then society corrupts them.[8] And Rousseau did say as much on occasion in a few pithy phrases. But the fuller Rousseauian account is that the propensity to depart from the state of nature is part of the human natural condition. It's only natural to fall. The so-called fall, in Rousseau's view, led to the potential for humans to enjoy a new social form—a Second Garden or second nature—that is itself necessarily part of nature and entirely embedded in the natural world.

Rousseau proposed a variety of ways or paths to cope with our "fallen" condition. I will refer briefly to some of these in what follows. For now, what is important to note is Rousseau's acknowledgment that (1) there is no escaping the social condition, that (2) our social condition is embedded in nature and nature remains normative (but in complicated ways, e.g., ethical commands are not written in nature), and that (3) a central ethical task is to integrate the social and the natural in ways that sustain just human societies and healthy ecosystems. And as I have claimed, there is no radical gulf between the natural and the social: Nature led to and remains present in the social.

There have been and continue to be environmentalists whose focus is primarily on protecting the natural world from degradation caused by humans. While these approaches have some merit, they have been justifiably criticized by such scholars as Macarena Gómez-Barris, Rob Nixon, and Kyle Whyte.[9] The general critique is that environmental approaches that focus on "protecting the natural world" tend to operate within the nature/society binary and thereby preclude a sustainable integration of human society and the more-than-human world.

Insofar as this is the case, they neglect the broader geopolitical, economic contexts that bring mutual damage to place and people—especially vulnerable populations. If we could call Rousseau an early protoenvironmentalist, he would be in a different, more holistic category than those who focus on the natural world alone. He understood the intimate connection between the degradation of the natural world and social inequality; he understood that caring for the health of the natural world would entail reforming the social one—which would require a holistic reformation of its politics and economics, its aesthetic sensibilities and religions. In sum, Rousseau discerned a connection between human and nonhuman health and sickness, and this connection is a central characteristic of radical Romanticism and a focus of this chapter.[10]

Rousseau's most important political, aesthetic, and environmental vision is found not in the social institutions of *The Social Contract* (1762) but rather in *la terre*—the gardens, lands, and Alpine geography—of *Julie.* By means of imaginative gardens, lands, and socioeconomic relations, Rousseau crafted in *Julie* an environmental, economic, and sociopolitical alternative to prevailing European sensibilities—the very sensibilities that have greatly contributed to the current climate crisis and other social and environmental harms. In this chapter, I focus on Julie's eco-community, Clarens, and her private garden, the Elysium. In *Julie,* Alpine geography (nature) and Clarens's mountain manners (culture) do not fight and struggle against each other but rather support and augment each other. In this fusion of land and culture, Rousseau challenged the nature/culture binary and introduced alternative Western aesthetic sensibilities and notions of labor, economy, and the land in response to modernization, industrialization, and nascent capitalism.[11] The land and culture of *Julie*'s gardens produce an environmental vision of a household or community economy embedded in a larger "natural economy"—within the workings of the more-than-human. In the imagined lands and gardens of Clarens—its own microuniverse—Rousseau brought together the useful and the beautiful, the public and the private, and the natural and the social. This complex fusion offers an alternative garden ecology to prevailing exploitive market economies. I wish now, then, to focus on *Julie*'s lands and gardens, one of our earliest examples of an environmentally sustainable household economy that provides resources to reflect critically on cultural and socioeconomic institutions and practices that exploit laborers and the land.

CLARENS ON THE PATHS TO REDEMPTION

The question of redemption—of rescuing humans from exploitive social arrangements and from potentially destructive aspects of human nature—preoccupied much of Rousseau's thought. Throughout his works, he proposed a few different paths to redemption. Two of these paths are in stark contrast: an extreme public path and an extreme private path.[12] The public path, as found in *Considerations on the Government of Poland* (1772), recommends that individuals snugly ensconce themselves within a highly nationalistic, educative civic body; the private path, as found in *The Reveries of the Solitary Walker* (1782), recommends that individuals— *les promeneurs solitaires*—cultivate a spiritual, interior life and extricate themselves from commitments and other social entanglements that exacerbate the human propensity to inflict harm. The one calls for the loss of the private life, the other the loss of the public. Both are effective if the goal is to live undividedly; both are inadequate if the goal is to live a full, flourishing human existence. Rousseau understood as much.

Rousseau's most famous path to redemption is what I call his *middle way*— that of the Flourishing City as depicted in *The Social Contract*.[13] This is his attempt to bring together the two paths, public and private. This middle way demonstrates how to balance or integrate the duties and prerogatives of the individual with those of the body politic. There is, however, another option, which is the focus of this chapter. It is what I call *the way of the eco–mountain community* as found in *Julie*. This is the way of friendship, love, marriage, community, and just and agreeable labor. It is also the way of intimate and ecological relation to the natural world. And, unlike the other proposed paths to redemption, this one—as we will soon see—is expressed by women and, in salient ways, depends upon women.

This path runs, conceptually speaking, between the private path and the middle way, and hence it can be called the *moderate public-private* path. "Moderate" because it does not revolve around the *solitaire* or a larger collective such as the nation-state; "public-private" because at its center stands the *household* or *community*. This path incarnates Rousseau's deepest political and environmental fantasy and attempts the precarious balance between solitariness and sociability and between "nature" and art or culture. Clarens, then, is the name of Julie's household but also the name of Rousseau's *political-domestic, environmental vision*.

Rousseau's ideal home was never Nature's Garden inhabited by the *solitaires*, those barely human creatures. Rather, his ideal was this *second* garden, the ecological community.

Clarens, of course, is more than a home. It is a way of life, held together by a multitude of miraculous balancing acts. Clarens's mountain manners (its culture) and Alpine geography manage to keep everything in place, at least provisionally. The severe Alpine geography brings natural necessity (such as keeping warm and being nourished) into the daily life at Clarens, encouraging social interdependence rather than frivolous or destructive sociability—vain gamesmanship or economic antagonism, for example. Together, the land and the manners jointly form Clarens: a place where the self is neither extinguished nor puffed up but lives in accord with itself, others, work, the divine, and the natural world.

THE LAND AND THE MATERIALISM OF THE WISE

In *Julie*, Rousseau embedded the idea that the land informs ethical, aesthetic, and spiritual dispositions. Before the publication of *Julie*, Rousseau had drafted or outlined what he thought would become one of his most important works, *The Materialism of the Wise*.[14] As it turns out, materialism—the materiality of the natural world—has been central to Romanticism from its beginnings. In *The Materialism of the Wise*, Rousseau wanted to show that human character, practices, and ways of life are informed not only by *sociolinguistic* environments but also by the *physical* ones: "Climates, seasons, sounds, colors, darkness, light, the elements, food, noise, silence, motion, rest, all act on our machine and consequently on our soul."[15] It is no coincidence that Clarens is located high in the Alpine mountains. The mountains and the hardy way of life that they demanded in the eighteenth century endowed the residents with a particular type of character and intimate relation to the nonhuman world—or so Rousseau argued.

He was one of the first to ascribe such agency to the land, that is, to the material, physical world. In his view, the physical world shapes humans even as humans shape the physical world. He held that this "dialectic" was true of such urban sites as Paris, but in the case of Paris, the human socioeconomic craft of worldbuilding had become corrupted by ruthless capitalism and cruel power grabs. Human ethical formation, for Rousseau, is produced not only by culture (including sociolinguistic practices) and biological inheritance but by the physical environment as well—or, rather, by the physical environment *in relation* to other sources of human life.

The salutary aspects of Clarens are not, of course, attributable to geography alone. Alpine geography works dialectically with Clarens's mountain manners. Functioning in a way similar to the tutor in *Emile* (1762) or the Great Legislator in *The Social Contract*, mountain manners at Clarens nourish selves and institutions that mitigate false needs, anomic desires, and structural social and economic inequality. The mountain manners also serve to cultivate social dispositions, practices, and institutions that work with and demonstrate a just gratitude toward a central source of life, the Alpine land itself.

Subsequent Romantic authors such as Dorothy and William Wordsworth in Britain and Margaret Fuller and Thoreau in the United States would continue this practice of ascribing agency or "autonomous presence" to the physical environment, especially to natural ecosystems variously delimited. Like Rousseau, they presented a portrait of something like a shared agency, as the human and the nonhuman reciprocally engage and produce—or co-create—that which we commonly call "the world." *The materialism of the wise* is to acknowledge and honor the materiality that sustains us—that *is* us. Rousseau powerfully portrayed that form of wise materialism in *Julie*'s eco-community.

AESTHETIC AND RELIGIOUS SENSIBILITIES

Rousseau, in *Julie*, revolutionized Western aesthetic and religious sensibilities. Travelers used to shutter their carriages when crossing the Alps to protect themselves from the ugly, barbarian landscapes—those uncouth, godforsaken, jagged peaks. Rousseau turned this negative aesthetic upside down: He would get out and walk to experience more intimately the wild, Alpine landscape.[16] In Rousseau's imagination, the Alps represented the starkest contrast to the world of corrupt human institutions—not a contrast to humanity or social institutions per se but to unjust, exploitive, and capitalistic ways of life. His praise and descriptions of the Alps introduced a new aesthetic that shaped the Romantic imagination and inaugurated the genre of *nature writing* (and in particular, pedestrian nature writing).[17] This new understanding of what *counted* as beautiful—the tortuous, irregular, Alpine landscape—produced a new vision for the form and ethos of the ideal *garden*. For Rousseau and subsequent generations, the formal, "artificial" garden with its "unnaturally" shaped trees and geometric, regular design came to be viewed as a deformation of nature. The now celebrated "natural" garden, in contrast, was planned to be unplanned: asymmetrical, overflowing, and irregular. The natural garden was to be crafted as an "artificial wilderness."[18]

This new Rousseauian aesthetic had a profound religious dimension. If you want to worship, he said, go outside. That which had once been considered grotesque was now a church of reverence and a setting for revelation and religious education. The Alps were not simply the *context* for spiritual edification; they were the *text* itself. Rousseau's religious aesthetic declared that in the natural world we are most likely to receive spiritual revelation. And no Rousseauian figure expresses this new religious aesthetic better than Julie. Her husband, Wolmar, is driven to atheism, having been raised in a dogmatic, ritualistic, and artificial Christian tradition (482). Julie, in contrast, possesses a lively, dynamic faith that is directly connected to the beauty of the earth as well as to the goodness—and the suffering—of fellow humans and nonhumans (484-85). Her faith does not sever her from the meaning of the earth and its relationships but connects her to life—both human and more-than-human. Hers is a worldly religion. Wolmar, however, is unable to sympathize sufficiently with the suffering of his fellow creatures because, without the benefit of a spiritual connection to the natural world, his moral reasoning is cold and detached (483-84).

So, Rousseau transformed that which was considered ugly and godforsaken into that which is beautiful and divine. His ethical and spiritual accounts of the natural world would greatly influence such British Romantics as the Wordsworths, Mary Wollstonecraft, and Mary Shelley and such North Americans as Emerson, Margaret Fuller, and Thoreau. I should note that although Rousseau extolled Alpine landscapes in *Julie* and elsewhere, he also wrote poignantly of the human relation to a variety of lands, including diverse lands worked by humans.

Rousseau's religious aesthetic is found throughout *Julie* but also in his bestselling educational treatise and novel *Emile* (published a year after *Julie*). When the pupil Emile is ready for his religious education, a wise Savoyard priest becomes his spiritual guide. What is significant, however, is not only *who* offers the spiritual guidance but *where* it takes place. The sagacious guide leads his pupil up a high hill from where he and Emile witness a beautiful valley "crowned by the vast chain of the Alps." Of this place and time, Emile states that it was "the fairest picture which the human eye can see. You would have thought that nature was displaying all her splendour before our eyes to furnish *a text for our conversation*. After contemplating this scene for a space *in silence*, the man of peace [the priest] spoke to me."[19]

A common mistake is to assume that the *creed* of the Savoyard priest is found exclusively in the priest's *words*. This is a serious error. Emile's spiritual education starts and ends in *the land* that presents itself to him and in *the silence* that is reverently offered and in which the revelation is received. There is a close connection between the Savoyard priest's central lesson and the idea of receiving revelation in and through the land. Emile's spiritual guide counsels him to seek an inward authority—the voice of conscience—that is supported by the voice of nature. The ultimate revelatory guide for life, then, consists in *an attunement* between the inner and outer—the inward authority of the self and the outer authority of "nature." Emile is to look inward, or as Emerson would later say, "Obey thyself."[20] But Emile is also to look outward, or as William Wordsworth would later say, look to "the round ocean, and the living air, / And the blue sky," to that presence that "rolls through all things"—look for and see signs of Spirit in the world around us and within us.[21] This form of subjective universality—this harmonizing dance between inner and outer—is distinctively Romantic and distinctively Rousseauian. The Savoyard priest channels this view when he says, "I perceive God everywhere in His works. I sense Him *in* me; I see Him all *around* me."[22] With this notion of God or Spirit in humans and around humans in the natural world, Rousseau challenged the rigid binaries of outer/inner, Spirit/human, and Spirit/nature. Instead, he advanced a vision of a dynamic interrelation between humans, Spirit, and the natural world, and that perspective would greatly influence British and North American Romantics.

Rousseau inaugurated, then, an aesthetic form of revelation and knowledge that is still very much with us today. Additionally, he crafted a particular practice for receiving revelation and knowledge. Rousseau (and later Wordsworth, Emerson, and Thoreau, among others) instructed us to step back from the noise, chaos, and oppressive ways of industrial, capitalistic life in order to gain both personal equanimity and public perspective. This "stepping back" may seem purely private or even escapist, but it possesses a public purpose oriented toward social justice. One "withdraws," thus moving *forward* into alternative ways of being, for the sake of an enhanced private life as well as a public vision and critical perspective.

Rousseau's religious aesthetic is also noteworthy for what it declares about human nature and its relation to the more-than-human world. In *Julie* and elsewhere, Rousseau brought attention to the continuity between humans and more-than-human creatures. Rationality, for Rousseau, was not the mark of a supposed human exceptionalism that radically separated humans from other-than-human creatures. Indeed, in *Discourse on the Origin of Inequality* (1754), Rousseau went so far as to claim that "Nature" never intended humans to be creatures of reflection (a human "who meditates is a depraved animal"!).[23] This claim is quite the rebuke to Descartes's "I think, therefore I am." Of course, as humans become social creatures, reflection and self-consciousness become part of the human condition—for better and for worse. Reflection enables humans to become ethical creatures, but it also contributes to a host of social and personal woes, such as inequality, exploitation, and alienation. For present purposes, however, I simply want to note that Rousseau troubled the idea that rationality is a mark of human exceptionalism.

This move is significant for thinking about the human relation to the more-than-human. Rousseau argued that we should view ourselves chiefly as *suffering* creatures rather than *rational* ones; therefore we can identify with nonhuman animals as mutual sufferers. Rousseau placed a great premium on *pitié*—the capacity to empathize with others, humans and nonhumans alike. His insistence on treating nonhuman animals with care sprang from his *minimizing* the distinction between nonhuman animals and humans, or rather *emphasizing* the shared identity between the two.[24] In this regard, Rousseau provided a radical critique of those before him—Plato, Aristotle, Descartes, Augustine, Aquinas, and Calvin, for example—who championed human exceptionalism and thereby severed humans from the rest of the natural world.

Additionally, Rousseau's religious aesthetic, as found in *Julie*, portrayed the natural world not as a static, passive machine to be exploited but as a dynamic, active expression of Spirit to be honored and treated with respect. The natural world moves and evolves, and it includes human animals who, as seen in the *Second Discourse* and other writings, are also dynamic and evolving, often in response to the natural world. This idea was revolutionary. And as we will soon see, Rousseau insisted that there is a potential, achievable accord between dynamic "nature" and its dynamic humans. But dissonance is also a possibility—indeed, a likelihood.

WORK AND HOME ECONOMICS AT CLARENS

When Euro-Americans think of the term "landscape," they often imagine the *solitaire* contemplating the distant sublime or picturesque vista. And Rousseau, to some extent, contributed to this often unhelpful association. But he and others in the radical Romantic tradition frequently employed the term "landscape," or simply "the land," to refer to a wide range of lands—commercial sites and farmlands, jagged peaks and gentle valleys, dry deserts and lush gardens, large cities and small communities. I now wish to turn to Rousseau's most revolutionary landscape, namely, that small eco-community known as Clarens—Julie's home, *Julie's eco-republic.*

Work lies at the heart of Clarens. Alienation from labor was an abiding concern for Rousseau: He feared that workers would be increasingly exploited and find limited meaning and satisfaction in their work, as capital in international markets became more fluid, profit dominated all other goals, and the division of labor grew. Labor at Clarens challenged these unhappy trends. St. Preux (Julie's former tutor and lover) summed up Clarens's alternative way of life and work in a single sentence: "Everything one sees in this house joins together the agreeable and the useful; but useful occupations are not limited to activities that yield a profit" (386).

At Clarens, the very idea of work is redefined. Reduced neither to profit nor to efficiency, work is wed to that which is purposeful and agreeable. Rousseau, like Marx, sought to remind us that we are sensuous, tactile creatures who find purpose in congenial work. In Rousseau's fantasy, Clarens's sustainable labor practices, working in accord with the natural and social world, stood in stark contrast to the exploitive economic and political institutions on which more and more laborers were dependent. At Clarens, one is actively connected to the land, and there is an intimate, beneficial connection between people, place, and practices; outside Clarens in such capitalistic cities as Paris, one is reduced to working passively within oppressive social structures, and one experiences alienation from the social and natural world.

It is tempting to interpret Rousseau's fantasy as pitting "town" against "country." However, it would be more accurate to see it as juxtaposing *corrupt sociability* with *ethical sociability.* Rousseau attempted to find social, cultural ways of life that worked agreeably with the natural world and in conjunction with such natural human dispositions as *pitié* (empathy) and *amour de soi* (healthy self-care). In Rousseau's view, large European cities were competitive centers that produced oppressive, capitalistic practices, institutions, and even character types. In such an environment, it would prove difficult to sustain one's own integrity, much less participate in ethical social institutions. Clarens—an imaginary eco-community that exemplified sustainable, just, interdependent relations between and among humans and their nonhuman environment—was Rousseau's answer to the problem of how to dwell justly and sustainably in the social and more-than-human world.

The home and lands of Clarens are simple, practical, and agreeable. Clarens's residents bring beauty and utility together, trading luxury and opulence for sustainability and joy in the natural and social world. As St. Preux notes, the house is altered to match the newly devised sustainable practices of Clarens: "It is no longer a house made to be seen, but to be lived in" (363). The grounds, too, are transformed. The old billiard room, for example, was converted to a useful wine press and a dairy room. The property is adorned with practical but beautiful vegetable gardens: "The vegetable garden was too small for the kitchen; the flower bed has been turned into a second one, but so elegant and so well designed that this bed thus disguised is more pleasing to the eye than before" (364). Vineyards are planted, and exotic, decorative trees are replaced by local fruit, nut, and shade trees. All in all, "everywhere they have replaced attractive things with useful things, and attractiveness has almost always come out the better" (364).

Now, it may seem as if Rousseau intended to present Clarens as entirely "natural," as if it emerged directly from its mountain soil. In fact, however, *every aspect of Clarens is shaped by human imagination and hands in cooperation with the natural world.* This mingling of wildness and cultivation—this "natural" sociability—is best captured by Rousseau's portrayal of Julie's garden, her Elysium. The garden is physically connected to the heart of Clarens (it is "quite close to the house," a mere "twenty paces" [387]) but also spiritually connected, for Julie's garden expresses the spirit of Clarens: a place where the natural and the social are in accord.

JULIE'S GARDEN, THE ELYSIUM

Upon entering the Elysium, whose gate would have been impossible to find without Julie's assistance, St. Preux is struck by the dense foliage, the abundance of flowers, the sound of a running brook, and the singing of birds: "I thought I was looking at the wildest, most solitary place in nature, and it seemed to me I was the first mortal who ever had set foot in this wilderness" (387). Following along the "tortuous and irregular alleys" of the garden, St. Preux is struck by how the garden appeared to be "without order or symmetry" (389, 388). It appears to St. Preux as "rustic and wild" (388). So, when Julie declares that the Elysium is entirely under her direction, St. Preux balks, "I see no human labor here," and he insists that the garden "cost [Julie] nothing but neglect" (388). As is her way, Julie is patient yet firm with St. Preux: "It is true . . . that nature did it all, but under my direction, and there is nothing here that I have not designed" (388).

Who or what is the central author of the garden—Julie or the natural world? There is no simple answer. With the Elysium, Rousseau troubled the idea of a singular, sovereign agent. We are always *co-creators* with and within the natural world. In this way Rousseau anticipated the Anthropocene: All places are now co-created by humans and nature, together, for better and for worse. Rousseau asks of us whether our co-created place will be a work of life-enhancing justice and art (such as Clarens and its Elysium) or a work of injustice and destruction.

When Julie asserts that "Nature did it all," she acknowledges a fundamental environmental principle: to recognize that all that we have and are is the result of nature's matter and manners, while also affirming that humans work nature, alter nature, and belong to the natural world. She also articulates a statement of piety—to honor this foundational source of life, the natural world. Julie's Elysium *is* natural insofar as only nature, not Julie, can create a flower or a bird. It is also natural insofar as Julie—like the local residents of Wordsworth's Lake District— chooses not to import "exotic plants or fruits" but rather to utilize those that are "local" (388). Still, it is Julie who planted and cultivated the raspberries, currants, lilac bushes, wild grapes, hops, jasmine, and hazel trees. And it is Julie who diverted the water from an ornamental, superfluous fountain to make a brook and who enticed the birds to reside in her sustainable garden. Julie's garden, like the rest of Clarens, is Rousseau's imaginary model of nature's ways and the human imagination working together sustainably and wisely. This model challenges the idea of human ownership of the earth. When St. Preux sees birds in the Elysium, he first thinks they were captured as if in an aviary, but he later declares, "Now I understand it: I see that you want [the birds as] guests not prisoners" (391). His comment is meant to compliment Julie on her generous approach to the birds. But Julie pushes back—once again correcting St. Preux's limited vision—"Who are you calling guests? . . . It is we who are theirs" (391). In this ecological reversal, humans are not sovereigns lording over the land but rather guests who must tread with respect.[25]

And Rousseau creates still another kind of reversal—a reversal of gendered power and nonhuman power. In the garden, Julie educates St. Preux: She becomes the teacher to her former tutor, the male philosopher. Her empowerment comes, in part, through her work in the garden and her management of Clarens's ecological community. As the garden grows and flourishes, so does Julie. There is a reciprocal, bidirectional cultivation at work here: Julie's work with the garden equips her with a new sight for and relation to the more-than-human world. In the traditional Western model, white men are at the top of the great hierarchy of life, with the more-than-human at the bottom. In contrast, in the Elysium, Julie and the garden are St. Preux's teachers, and plants, trees, and birds are not merely "natural resources" to be exploited but species to be respected. Once again, then, *Julie* troubles the rigid boundaries and hierarchies between the human and the more-than-human.

Manfred Kusch and Lester Crocker, among others, have argued that in the work of Rousseau and the Western imagination more generally, the garden stands as the antithesis to wilderness, disorder, and chaos.[26] Of Julie's garden in particular, Kusch claims that "it establishes . . . the binary opposition of inside/outside, garden/wilderness, civilization/Nature." I have argued, however, that precisely through Julie's garden, Rousseau rejected such binaries as "order and disorder, harmony and chaos, the garden and the non-garden."[27] Julie's garden does not exclude wilderness nor even disorder and chaos. Indeed, Julie labors to *import* wilderness, disorder, and chaos into her garden (hence St. Preux's account of the garden as "uncultivated and wild; I see no human labor here"). Like Kusch, Crocker claims that there is a binary between Julie's garden and wilderness—the wilderness of the pristine forests outside Clarens.[28] But there is, in fact, great *continuity* between Julie's garden and the forests and the greater Valais. The garden is fashioned to reflect the irregularity, complexity, and tumultuous variability of the life of the forests.

The garden also possesses its own distinctive identity and role. The chapter that describes the garden in great detail begins with a reflection on the role of "agreeable leisure" and good work: While the agreeable and the useful come together in good work, the "alternation of labor and enjoyment is our genuine vocation" (387). The distinctive purpose of the garden is to provide "agreeable leisure." This is not to deny that labor is required to maintain the garden but to emphasize that Rousseau went to great lengths to emphasize the relative self-sufficiency of the garden. Indeed, part of the wonder of Julie's art in crafting her Elysium is how it is both a full and lush "artificial wilderness" and a low-maintenance garden. Even the initial making of the garden is inexpensive; indeed, as Julie notes, "It cost me nothing" (388).

The garden, then, is presented more as a place of repose than of labor, precisely as our "genuine vocation"–the art of sustainable living–requires a special kind of repose or enjoyment. There are forms of repose, what Rousseau called "indolent idleness," that do not contribute to the art of living (387). In contrast to indolent idleness, Rousseau inaugurated a major theme in Romanticism, namely, *purposeful idleness*, or what William Wordsworth would later call "wise passiveness," or what Thoreau would seek to express by the practice of sauntering.[29] Julie's garden most fully expresses Rousseau's opposition to a way of life systematically structured for the sake of maximized, capitalistic profit and opulent indulgence. The garden is a symbol of the nonutilitarian, countercultural practice of purposeful idleness.

With the garden, Rousseau declared a revolution, and central to this Garden Revolution is the "wild." Many commentators have justifiably remarked on the artifice of Julie's garden. Julie's artfulness, however, is not principally one of deception but of creation–better still, of *co-creation*. In the end, the garden does not only *look* wild; it *is* wild. This is why Julie feels the need to correct St. Preux, who initially thinks the garden is "all natural" and then subsequently concludes that it is "all artifice." Correcting his later view, Julie declares, "Everything you see is *wild* . . . it's enough to put [robust plants] in the ground, and they grow on their own" (394; emphasis added). Ultimately, of course, Rousseau–via Julie–sought to challenge St. Preux's binary insistence that the garden must be either wild or artful–the garden is wild and cultivated, *both*.[30]

This brings me to a second, related sense in which the garden is wild, employing the expansive sense of the wild as described in chapter 2. The garden–and Clarens more generally–is wild insofar as it challenges destructive economic, social, and environmental conventions. The wild, cultivated garden is the work and symbol of a wild, subversive culture. In this wild culture, contrary to capitalist convention, workers are treated with dignity. Work is understood as participation in the art of living, not the maximization of economic utility and the accrual of social status. Domination is replaced with community. The natural world is understood not as an unlimited resource made to satisfy endless human desire via extraction, production, and consumption but rather as a practical and beautiful home shared by humans and the more-than-human. A revolutionary alternative, the garden offers a capacious home that sustainably integrates culture and nature such that humans may live simply and justly in both the social and natural world. It thereby provides a profound set of ethical beliefs and practices that are helpful as we face such social and environmental challenges as climate change, the bioaccumulation of industrial toxins, soil erosion, deforestation, and the marginalization and displacement of communities for the sake of "development" and resource extraction.

Rousseau's literary garden participated in a tradition of revolutionary utopian thought and forged a new tradition of physical revolutionary gardens that serve as a "symbol for political resistance."[31] Whether literary or physical, "the garden" incarnates a just state of affairs, thereby demonstrating how things *could be* outside the garden. Although establishing a sustainable community—socially and environmentally—is a significant achievement, such local projects are not sufficient in and of themselves to tackle today's global socioeconomic and environmental challenges. Gardening as a radical, political act cultivates sustainable and ethical practices in one place, now, in the hope that such practices will propagate elsewhere, in the future. The revolutionary vision is planted and grown in the garden, and it then must escape the confines of the garden. Planting "seeds for radical change" is the gardener's hope and goal.[32]

"Seeds for radical change" was certainly Rousseau's hope. He was also interested in cultivating a *taste* for change. Almost 20 percent of the "Elysium chapter" is a discussion of taste (394–98). Those eager to display their wealth or their pedantic botanical knowledge exhibit a "false taste" (394). The former seek "grandeur" by cultivating showy lawns and straight avenues of perfectly erect, bald trees; the latter seek acclaim by ripping plants from their native environments and displaying them like a jumbled display of jewels in a museum, an attempted testimony to European global supremacy (394–95). Such false taste is contrasted with an "uncorrupted taste" that shuns boastful ostentation and the unjust institutions that support wealthy and powerful braggarts (396–97). Genuine, ethical taste delights in neither the purchased "formality" of the elitist's garden nor the colonized plants of the collector but rather in the simplicity of the everyday, in the "common grasses, common shrubs, [and] a few trickles of water flowing without frills" (397). "Uncorrupted taste," of course, pertains to making skillful judgments about not only the art of gardening but also about the art of living—simply, justly, and sustainably. By making do with less—by escaping the quagmire of the capitalistic culture of overextraction and consumption—those with good taste cultivate rebellious gardens and lives that challenge the aesthetic and political status quo. By means of his craft in radical aesthetics, Rousseau's ultimate goal was to cultivate a taste for the kind of *culture* that supports the social, political, and environmental justice found in Julie's Clarens and garden.

WOMEN, ECOFEMINISM, AND JULIE

Just as Julie's secret garden appears wild and purely natural but instead is the result of much labor and transformation, so, too, is Julie herself the result of much labor and transformation. Her virtue and character must be cultivated, fought for, and won. Like the garden, Julie is the combination of nature and art. She becomes *second* nature perfected. Again, then, we see that Rousseau's transformative scheme is not a return to nature but a progression to second nature.

What is the result of this transformation? Does Julie become the silent, submissive housewife relegated to the private sphere? Or the dynamic, independent woman who challenges gender stereotypes and enjoys a robust public life? Neither account captures her. On the one hand, standard feminist critiques apply. Julie becomes the complete and virtuous woman as she becomes a wife, a mother, and the emotional center of her family. Her life and duty are completed only in death—in sacrifice for one of her children. On the other hand, Julie speaks her mind openly; she challenges prejudices; she is a working woman with many significant responsibilities. Unlike *Emile*'s Sophie (that "ideal woman" who is passive and weak and seeks to please men), Julie is strong and independent. At Clarens, women's lives are not radically relegated to the private sphere, because there is no strict distinction between public and private. Julie is self-possessed: She "know[s] and follow[s] rules other than public judgments, [her] principal honor is the one [her] conscience renders [her]" (518). It is Julie, therefore, who sees through the pretensions of a patriarchal society that places status and wealth above intelligence and character. In sum, Julie is Rousseau's model of the virtuous human—male or female: She is candid, sincere, and authentic. She pursues friendship, character, and wisdom, not wealth, power, and status. She is practical and uninterested in frivolity or luxury, yet she seeks beauty and simple pleasures. She is spiritual but not religious; that is, her love of God is expressed by service to humanity and not by the recitation of dogmas and participation in baroque rituals. Her God is enjoyed not in a suffocating church but in expansive nature.

Moreover, of all the admirable friendships at Clarens, that of Julie and Claire is the most commendable. What Montaigne once said of his best friend, La

Boétie, could be said as well of Julie and Claire: "Our souls mingle and blend with each other so completely that they efface the seam that joined them." In fact, Julie and Claire's friendship resembles in most ways Montaigne's description of the ideal friendship. One wonders if Rousseau was inspired by Montaigne's essay "On Friendship" and if he meant to challenge Montaigne's claim that women do not have the capacity for that sacred bond, for Julie and Claire exhibit all the virtues of friendship.[33] They even seem to compensate each other for the inadequacies of their male friends—St. Preux's hurtful rashness, for example, or Wolmar's narrow logic and cold reserve.

There is a way, then, to interpret Rousseau's Clarens as implicitly advancing the dignity and rights of women. By portraying a marriage based on friendship and compatibility, it challenged the notion that women were property subject to contract. By displaying the vivid interior lives of Julie and Claire, it defied the idea that women were docile and unimaginative. And by depicting the strong friendship between Julie and Claire, it contested the view that women were incapable of such relationships.

Nonetheless, Rousseau's utopia was no utopia by contemporary feminist perspectives—or by those of such nineteenth-century critics as Mary Wollstonecraft. In spite of her independence, Julie yields to patriarchal authority, first to her father, then to her husband. Julie is a companion to Wolmar, but she is also a subordinate helper. Although all matters are discussed together, Wolmar is clearly the head of the household. It turns out that in the Second Garden, at Clarens, some oppressive social conventions are firmly in place, conventions that Rousseau supported. Men's authority remains supreme. Rousseau would have us believe that such conventions are rooted in a "natural" second nature.[34] Julie is not Sophie, but neither is she a woman liberated from patriarchy. Ultimately, she trades her father's overbearing dominance for Wolmar's patriarchy.

Clarens remains androcentric, and this androcentrism is secured by, perhaps even requires, Julie's death. After diving into icy waters to save one of her children, Julie contracts and eventually dies of pneumonia. It is as if Julie, the one who exemplifies a life fashioned by the natural and the social in the Alpine geography, must be sacrificed so that life, duty, and love can perfectly converge in this one instance and in this one individual. The delicate balance between the natural and the social is eventually upended and demands Julie's life. In the end, Rousseau's augmentation of the Western imagination—the construction and gift of Julie—appears to require her silencing.

Clarens cannot survive the death of Julie, yet its patriarchy requires it. On the final page of *Julie*, Claire names some of the central features of Clarens and declares them demolished: "Confidence, friendship, virtues, pleasures, frolics, the earth has swallowed all" (612). As for her relation to friends and community, Claire confesses, "I am alone amidst everyone" (611). The only voice she hears is that of the dead—the ghost of her best friend, Julie, "Claire, O my Claire, where art thou? what doest thou far from thy friend?" (612). With this final sentence the novel ends: Julie's "coffin does not contain all of her . . . it awaits the remainder of its prey . . . it will not wait for long" (612). The redemption that Clarens has to offer is ultimately precarious and partial (incomplete *and* biased). Clarens alone, then, cannot serve as an adequate model for us.

THREE GARDENS FOR THE ANTHROPOCENE: THE FANTASTIC, THE QUEER, AND THE CIVIC

Rousseau's utopian garden can be usefully compared to two real-world political gardens: Derek Jarman's queer garden in Dungeness, England, especially as depicted in Jarman's film *The Garden*; and the urban community garden of Roxbury, Massachusetts, as described by William Shutkin in *The Land That Could Be*.[35]

The redemptive power of Clarens and its Elysium requires isolation from the socioeconomic corruption that radiates from European centers of power. Jarman's garden, too, is located at the periphery of centers of power. Yet in contrast to the Elysium, Jarman's garden does not highlight repose and harmonious cooperation, although those characteristics are present. Rather, it emphasizes the vulnerabilities of humans and the more-than-human. Unlike the Elysium, it is not enclosed and protected by a hidden gate. Instead, it is porous to the world and thereby subjected to such environmental harms as air and water pollution and such social harms as homophobia, racism, and consumerism. The garden is not lush or especially picturesque in the traditional sense, though it does contain beauty; it is rocky, scrappy, and dry, located in the only desert in the United Kingdom, and contains such objects as broken glass, rusty nails, and barbed wire (objects that have no place in the Elysium).

In addition to Rousseau's Elysium and Jarman's garden, I wish to bring attention to the Roxbury urban garden described by Shutkin. This urban garden is an intentionally mobilized, public collective designed to bring socioeconomic change to Roxbury, an area marked by environmental degradation (including the presence of fifty-four *known* hazardous waste sites), middle-class white suburban flight, and discriminatory banking and real estate practices.[36] Unlike the Elysium and Jarman's garden, the Roxbury urban garden is an explicitly political project designed by local residents to address food insecurity and empower socioeconomically disadvantaged people of color through civic and environmental engagement.[37] Neither utopian fantasy nor expression of beauty embedded in vulnerability, the Roxbury urban garden project is a significant but small-scale attempt to assist a community that has experienced massive environmental and socioeconomic harm. In sum, these three gardens are noteworthy sites that feature the intersection—the mutually shared ways of flourishing and destruction—of the human and more-than-human.

All three gardens are "redemptive," but in different ways. Shutkin describes the Roxbury garden as an "urban village model. . . . Gardens, orchards, greenhouses and bioshelters, and street trees will give the Dudley neighborhood [in Roxbury] the appearance of a thriving natural area. . . . At the same time, these ecological assets will be the drivers of the area's economy, providing jobs and creating wealth for local residents."[38] It is redemptive in its civic environmentalism and through the practice of community building. Similarly, the Elysium is redemptive in its transformation of social relations (human to human) and relations to the natural world (human to nonhuman), as well as transformation within the self (curbing alienation and fostering gentle *amour de soi*). Finally, the redemptive power of Jarman's garden is both palpable and ambiguous. On the one hand, the garden is a powerful witness to the unceasing vulnerability and subjugation that occurs in the social and natural world. There is undeniable beauty in the garden and its gardeners, but that beauty is matched by the dying and death of those suffering from AIDS, the injustice at the hands of the intolerant, and the needless destruction of the natural environment. Jarman's garden is a wilderness of failure and terminality; solutions and future aspirations are not offered. Still, there is a redemptive ray in the belief that the garden will "come back next year"—a modest but hopeful vitality that remains alive in an otherwise damaged and damaging world. So, while Jarman's queer garden displays mourning, grief, and vulnerability rather than any explicit political action, it nonetheless implicitly calls for political change.[39] Like the Elysium and Roxbury, it, too, plants seeds of transformation.

Of the three gardens, Rousseau's is the most fantastic and utopian. His garden community is his vision of a just, sustainable set of relationships and practices among humans and the natural world. It is an Eden largely free of vulnerability and injustice. It offers a vision of how things *could* be and thereby condemns how things are. Roxbury's community garden, in contrast to Rousseau's Eden, is a highly limited but actual urban oasis, a concrete experiment and endeavor in civic environmentalism. Like Rousseau's Eden, however, it, too, imagines *the land that could be*. It offers aspirational, ecological democracy. Jarman's garden, like Rousseau's, is an Eden of sorts—a place filled with beauty, wonder, and much love. And like Shutkin's garden, it could be understood as a place of aspirational, ecological democracy: a place where the dignity of persons and the life of the natural world are respected and honored.

But there is more. Life in Jarman's garden, whether human or more-than-human, is deemed sacred, and the sacred plays a powerful role in every aspect of the garden. Perhaps for that reason, Jarman links his garden not only to Eden but also to Gethsemane. The sacred, for Jarman, is not only found in beauty and wonder but also in vulnerability and pain. His garden announces: Our redemption—however partial—is found in both beauty and suffering. That declaration, so absent from Rousseau's Clarens, is a powerful creed for life in the Anthropocene.[40]

OUTSIDE THE GARDEN: CULTIVATE A WORLD IN WHICH TO LIVE

Clarens, Rousseau's flawed fantasy, remains one of his most important statements of social protest. Julie's Alpine eco-community and its inner sanctum, the Elysium, together form Rousseau's most sustained attempt to craft a vivid, self-contained world that serves as a striking alternative to the rapacious order of his time. In the garden and in the social, institutional, and physical form of life that supports it, we find Rousseau's central religious, political, aesthetic, and environmental vision and fantasy. The world of Clarens and its garden palpably illustrate Rousseau's hope for how we can live peaceably and justly with fellow humans and the natural world that sustains us.

Clarens was Rousseau's protest against those market economies that encouraged avarice, a brutal division of labor, and alienation from self, work, community, and the more-than-human world. Moreover, the family and friendships at Clarens condemned the utilitarian character of the marriages and friendships of Rousseau's age, in which spouses and friends were deemed useful in the effort to amass public status and wealth. The realms of intimacy at Clarens opposed the cold, calculating, public world of Hobbesian market relations, personal exploitation, and social climbing. Clarens, then, has much to teach us about the symptoms and causes of modern alienation. It also has much to contribute to contemporary environmental and democratic critique. In constructing Clarens, Rousseau identified one of the most important threats to the environment and to progressive democracy: the ways of *amour-propre*, which fuels nationalistic and individual anomic desire and the quest for wealth and power and thereby contributes to unsustainable environmental practices and structural social inequality. Rousseau's critique suggests that while science, technology, and policy help address environmental problems, we also need to address those fundamental dispositions and practices that determine our relation to the natural world. Learning to live sustainability, in other words, is a spiritual and cultural challenge—not just a technical one. This is one of Rousseau's chief lessons.

Some deep ecologists of the "happy-minded type" (to employ William James's term)[41] seem to say: "Just recognize your true nature—just listen to nature—and you will see that your true self is really an expanded Self that includes all things. Once you come to this realization, you simply will not *want* to live in an environmentally destructive fashion anymore. You don't need to strive to radically reshape yourself and the institutions in which you are embedded. It will just happen naturally once you and everyone else recognizes their true Nature." Rousseau offered a different approach: The self *and our social institutions* need to be fundamentally transformed in ways that acknowledge that we are embedded in the natural world and in social worlds and that there are ethically better and worse ways to live in them. Flourishing ways of life will, among other things, honor the natural world and blunt *amour-propre*.[42] Our environmental *and* cultural crises require a radical transformation of self and society. We live outside the Garden—we live in the Anthropocene or, more appropriately, given Rousseau's critiques, the Capitalocene. Rousseau was clear about this. We need, then, to *cultivate* democratic environmental virtues and institutions. Clarens offers us Rousseau's best approximation of a sustainable society outside the Garden, thereby providing imaginative, ethical resources to help us as we address such challenges as climate change and environmental justice.

CHAPTER 4

Romanticism, Religion, and Practice

Political and Environmental Implications

I n this chapter, I argue that secularized accounts of Romanticism belittle the significance of religion, tradition, and practice for such British Romantic authors as Wordsworth and Coleridge.[1] This belittlement exacts a heavy toll. When we neglect the salience of religion, we fail to see the close, material connections between Romantic religious, political, and environmental radicalism. And if we discount tradition and practice, we fail to see the matter and manner—the *culture* and *cultivation*, including memory, stories, and the very form of art—by which Romantic authors conceived of and pursued their sociopolitical and environmental aspirations. We fail to grasp the moral psychology that animated much radical Romantic thinking about such fundamental matters as the formation of the self and associations, sources of moral authority and critique, and the human relation to the more-than-human world. In this chapter, I highlight the role of religion, tradition, and practice in radical Romanticism in order to better explore its ethical and liberatory dimensions. However, I do not reject all accounts of secularization. It is worthwhile to identify which aspects of these accounts to let go of and which to keep—for surely some aspects should be kept. This chapter's investigation of Romanticism and secularization offers some broad lessons for ways to rethink the tangled relation between religion, modernity, and the secular.

After characterizing what I mean by theories of secularization and how these theories have dominated accounts of Romanticism, especially British Romanticism, I focus on two poems—one by Coleridge, the other by Wordsworth—that problematize secularized accounts of Romanticism and the place of tradition and practice in modernity.[2] The poem by Coleridge, "The Eolian Harp" (1796), suggests that we take religion, and even traditional Christianity, as an authentic

Romantic expression. The poem by Wordsworth, "Nuns Fret Not at Their Convent's Narrow Room" (1802), suggests that we take discipline, cultivation, practice, and form as authentic Romantic motifs. Together, the poems disrupt the view that British Romanticism replaces God with nature and discipline and form with unencumbered freedom. I conclude by suggesting that when we disclose the language and ways of religion, form, and practice in radical Romanticism, we also make more apparent its progressive political and environmental dimensions. To develop this claim, toward the end of the chapter I have a separate section on *democratic second nature* and its relation to critique and progressive politics.

In this chapter, then, I indicate the political and environmental dimensions of radical Romantic religious sensibilities.[3] My focus, however, is on a foundational issue: how the very real presence of religion, tradition, and practice in radical Romanticism disrupts theories of secularization.[4] Until we gain clarity on this, we will be unable to appreciate the public—political and environmental—aspects of Romanticism, whether in past or present forms. My aim is to complicate secularized views of Romanticism and offer a more plural account of radical Romanticism, one that acknowledges the dynamic presence of religion, tradition, and practice.

HELD CAPTIVE BY A THEORY AND WORLDVIEW

Despite the various challenges to simplistic accounts of secularization, whether by Saba Mahmood, Talal Asad, or Jeffrey Stout, the deep-seated dispositions and presumptions of these simplistic accounts persist in academia and beyond.[5] There are, of course, many conceptions of secularization. In this chapter, "secularization" refers to the view, roughly stated, that religion in the world is both declining and privatizing.[6] This view can further be characterized by three positions: (1) Religion is a discrete, sui generis phenomenon, (2) religion is not self-critical or open to critique and exchange (because, it is held, religion is radically subjective or based on dogmatic authority or both), and therefore (3) religious citizens can and should accept the privatization of religion; that is, they should keep their religion out of politics.

These three positions presuppose a narrow, parochial view of religion that is unconvincing in the face of actual, lived religion. Generally speaking, religion is a culturally complex, historical institution or set of practices (whether formal like a church or informal like deism or religious *nones*—that is, those who do not affiliate with organized religion) that cannot be separated easily or radically from other institutions and practices, whether they be moral, aesthetic, economic, or political.[7] Religions dynamically change in response to and in dialogue with individuals, communities, events, and developments both within and outside a given religious tradition. A religion is a pervasive aspect of a person's identity, informing and informed by one's various beliefs, practices, and loves—all of which are embedded in and respond to local, national, and global sociohistorical and physical circumstances.

Actual, lived religions, then, undermine the narrow, parochial way that religion is understood by the theories of secularization I have identified and defined. The social history of this narrow, parochial view is complex. One explanatory narrative points to various eighteenth- and nineteenth-century Enlightenment and Romantic thinkers who (supposedly) promoted the view that religion is ultimately subjective and private—a narrative that I will soon turn to and challenge.[8] Another explanatory narrative argues that the narrow, parochial way of conceiving religion was strategically forged in the nineteenth century when it was tactical for European nations to conceive of religion as a discrete, private arena separate from the state and from science. Jointly, these explanatory narratives suggest that in modernity it was convenient for many European constituencies to establish a pact of nonaggression between "religion" and "the secular"—privatized religion would not interfere with politics and science, and a laicized public would not interfere with religion.[9]

While these accounts have *some* merit, they often fail to investigate the ways in which they operate with—and help create—a concept of religion that has little connection with actual lived religion. Moreover, there is a darker side to some theories of secularization. It is one thing to promote a privatized view of religion to foster a pact of nonaggression; many religious believers themselves have contributed to this pact. It is another thing to aggressively promote the view that religion per se is a destructive, superstitious relic that has no place in modernity. In this view, secularism is the essence of modernity and religion is the antithesis of all that is modern.[10] This is potentially vicious secularism. It is not only historically incorrect—it fails, for example, to acknowledge the frequent connection between religious practitioners and modern liberatory movements—but it also risks demeaning the moral integrity of religious practitioners en masse.

If we are to move beyond an aggressive secularism that promotes empirically questionable historical narratives and judgments, and if we wish to develop a judicious response to questions of religion in modernity, we need to acknowledge and investigate the ways in which religion, modernity, and the secular are plural, dynamic, and interrelated. To that end, it is helpful to revisit Romanticism, for depictions of it have played a key role in narratives of secularization.[11]

RELIGIOUS VISION AS PUBLIC VISION

In many accounts of Romanticism, its religious aspects (Protestant and Catholic, orthodox and heterodox, deistic and panentheistic) are neglected or, if included, are narrativized as part of a secularization process.[12] While it is convenient to claim that Romantics eschewed religion in lieu of secularized thought, it is more accurate to say that they often dissociated religion—understood as normative beliefs, practices, and perspectives pertaining to Spirit or the Divine—from strictly denominational church dogmatics and social structures. Moreover, they engaged religion, broadly understood, in the service of progressive social and environmental aims—both national and global.[13] By applying an interpretive lens that acknowledges the religious traditions that permeated much of Romanticism, we gain insight into not only its dynamic religious dimensions but its political, economic, and environmental dimensions as well.

Although scholars, highly influenced by secularization theories, routinely assume that religion was waning during the height of British Romanticism (roughly 1790–1850), participation in formal religious institutions was actually increasing during this time.[14] More importantly, close readings of salient Romantic texts manifest robust religious traditions, themes, and images.[15] Only an opaque lens, such as a prior interpretive commitment to secularization and its worldview, would obscure the sight of such palpable signs of religion. Not all Romantic texts, of course, look alike or have a similar commitment to or concept of religion. Yet much religion was present, and its diverse forms often supported the progressive politics of its time. The writing and reading of texts like Wordsworth's *Prelude* or Coleridge's "Religious Musings," for example, were conceived as a form of religious and political practice that shaped author and reader alike.

Religion contributed importantly to both the content and expression of Romantic *public* visions. Romantic authors frequently identified with dissenting Christian traditions that put them at odds with the religious and political establishment of the day. Their radical religious views were understood as a political stance and practice, and they were thereby frequently deemed enemies of the state and suffered accordingly. Theologically, they were a diverse group, but many tended to advance a theology that was part panentheistic, part Christian orthodoxy. Spirit, it was commonly held, is infused throughout nature, endlessly sustaining and creating. And social protest was itself understood as a religious practice. The poetic, religious vocation of many Romantic authors was to offer vivid descriptions of the horrors of war, poverty, and various unjust social and environmental policies, thereby evoking the appropriate human affect and praxis-oriented empathy in otherwise prejudicial hearts.

Political agitation, then, tended to go hand in hand with religious agitation. More often than not, political and religious revolutions were championed by the same characters. This is not surprising. At the turn of the nineteenth century, the Church of England was intimately connected to the government. Opposition to the church was considered opposition to the government and vice versa. Because of their nonconformist religious status, deists, Catholics, and Protestants of various stripes—Baptists, Congregationalists, Presbyterians, Quakers, and Unitarians—experienced oppression at the hands of the church and the state. Moreover, the church was increasingly seen as callous regarding the plight of those who suffered from war, slavery, poverty, and the grueling changes brought by urbanization and the Industrial Revolution. Many religious dissenters, then, from different religious backgrounds and socioeconomic strata—and also members of the Church of England itself, including Thomas Clarkson and William Wilberforce—challenged the moral authority and actions of the church and state for their injustice, intolerance, coercion, and ruinous public policies concerning war, slavery, industry, and social justice.

Indeed, it's important to understand the significant role that religion played in British politics at the start of Romanticism. Before the French Revolution and the progressive political movements that it spawned in Britain, religious activism had already laid the groundwork for progressive British politics of the 1790s and beyond.[16] *Religious* protest, in other words, paved the way for more explicitly *democratic* protest. Religious and political liberty traveled together as aspirational ideals, social movements, and progressive art.

In general, then, radical Romantic aesthetics can be understood as belonging to an enterprise that seeks to cultivate in individuals and communities the ways of Spirit and justice. Ironically, the radical Romantic work of literary art can be thought of as the embodiment of Burke's philosophical anthropology—highlighting the formative role of traditions, practices, and virtues—but in the service of a progressive democratic, religious, and environmental vision.

COLERIDGE'S "THE EOLIAN HARP"

In order to concretize the dynamic presence of religion, practice, and tradition in radical Romanticism, I consider two poems: Coleridge's "The Eolian Harp" and Wordsworth's "Nuns Fret Not at Their Convent's Narrow Room." "The Eolian Harp," first composed in 1795 and then worked on for the next twenty-three years, is a love poem, a nature poem, and a religious poem—all three, intertwined. It begins with Coleridge addressing his then fiancée, Sara Fricker: "My pensive Sara! thy soft cheek reclined / Thus on mine arm, most soothing sweet it is / To sit beside our cot, our cot o'ergrown / With white-flowered jasmin, and the broad-leaved myrtle."[17] In this lovely opening, Coleridge introduces us to Sara, thoughtfully and erotically reclining on the poet's arm. Accompanying Sara are the wild characters jasmin and myrtle, unkempt and penetrating, overrunning the human-made cottage. Jasmin and myrtle are emblems of innocence and love, but they are also a presence in their own right, a visual and fragrant reminder of the wild that is always with us, even when close to home. As evening descends, other characters of the more-than-human world inhabit the poem: Clouds darken, stars shine, a local bean field scents the air, and the murmuring sea "tells us of silence" (line 12).

In the Euro-American imagination, the wild is often associated with uproar—the sound of crashing waves, clapping thunder, or in racist nineteenth-century anthropology, shrieking wild humans. But in this poem, Coleridge, who in the late 1790s had been poetically investigating the multiple facets of the natural world and how it shapes and educates humans, presents us with *the silence of the wild*. Coleridge suggests here and elsewhere that our ability to hear the silence—to hear "the world so hushed!" (line 10)—increases our capacity to be attentive and receptive to the world around us, both human and more-than-human.

Immediately after enveloping us in silence, Coleridge introduces the subtle yet wild melodies of the Eolian Harp:

> How by the desultory breeze caressed,
> Like some coy maid half yielding to her lover,
> It [the harp] pours such sweet upbraiding, as must needs
> Tempt to repeat the wrong! And now, its strings
> Boldlier swept, the long sequacious notes
> Over delicious surges sink and rise,
> Such a soft floating witchery of sound
> As twilight Elfins make, . . .
> Footless and wild, like birds of Paradise,
> Nor pause, nor perch, hovering on untamed wing!
>
> (lines 15–26)

Eolian harps are stringed instruments strummed by the wind. The harp, here, is seduced by the wild—the "desultory breeze"—as its mysterious music sinks and rises, "footless and wild," "hovering on untamed wing!" The harp itself is human-made: It has structure, and the arrangement and tuning of the strings is formal. Yet the resulting music is like that of the Greek god Pan: haunting, seductive, and dangerous—half-human, half-wild.[18] "Hovering on untamed wing," the music of the Eolian harp intimately links artifact to the natural, human to the divine. It is Spirit incarnate, and the poem is a species of incarnational theology. The harp's melodies profess "the one Life," a central and shared religious tenet that inspired and animated much of Coleridge's and Wordsworth's poetry and philosophy.

With no need for a transition, then, Coleridge can move within the same stanza from "untamed wing!" to

> O the one Life within us and abroad,
> Which meets all motion and becomes its soul,
> A light in sound, a sound-like power in light,
> Rhythm in all thought, and joyance every where—
> Methinks, it should have been impossible
> Not to love all things in a world so filled;
> Where the breeze warbles, and the mute still air
> Is Music slumbering on her instrument.
>
> (lines 27–34)

In this panentheistic vision, the *one Life*—which is within us and without—inspirits and animates all things, connecting even apparent opposites—"a light in sound, a sound-like power in light"—including humans and the more-than-human world. Humans are radically intimate with the natural world because "the one Life," or Spirit, pervades everything above, below, about, and within us. If we were searching for one candidate for the quintessential Romantic religion, we could stop here with Coleridge's "one Life theology." Anticipating such North American Romantics as Emerson and Terry Tempest Williams, Coleridge's one Life theology declares that humans are fully at home in Spirit *and* in the more-than-human world, for there is no fundamental alienation between Spirit and humans and no abiding gulf between humans and the more-than-human. This theology and philosophical anthropology is a long way from eighteenth-century views that were greatly informed by Francis Bacon's *man over nature, God over man* or Rene Descartes's *mind over matter.*[19]

When Coleridge pens "Methinks, it should have been impossible / Not to love all things in a world so filled," he maintains that the natural world is not an adversary or "Other" to be subdued but rather a home to be loved. If only we had the capacity to attend to the particular intricacies of this world—*this* cottage, *these* flowers, *this* bean field—and if only we had ears to hear the melodies of the wind, it would be impossible "not to love all things in a world so filled." Such irrepressible love is a far cry from Godwinian abstract rationalism and Benthamite leveling calculation. Although the early Wordsworth and Coleridge shared Godwin's commitment to social equality and political critique, they increasingly resisted his severe first-order impartiality, his view that individuals should not be motivated by local attachments or private considerations.[20] Coleridge's and Wordsworth's storied landscapes, in contrast to Godwin's "rational" philosophy, implicitly argued for the moral importance of all those proper nouns that make claims on our lives—particular communities, people, places, and things.

Yet rootedness in the particular need not be equated with narrowness of the parochial. On the contrary, we move from a particular evening (the eve of Samuel and Sara's marriage), in a particular place (a cottage in Clevedon, Somersetshire), near a particular sea and bean field, to "the one Life within us and abroad," that is, to a global, spiritual vision that elicits love and calls for justice in our relations to the natural and social worlds. The particular leads us to the expansive, and back again. In the process, we experience an irresistible love of this world—or at least what "*should* have been" (emphasis added) an irresistible love.

The conditional here suggests that the lovability of a world "so filled" has its requirements, its conditions. It requires *work*. One must work to be attentive and receptive to the graceful ways of the world. To have grace and love in one's life, one must train.[21] There are lots of exercises within reach: Open your eyes and try to see something, and see it well. Read a poem. Read *this* poem. Look at a friend or a stranger. Love them. Comfort them. Being attentive to the world also enables us to see more clearly sites of injustice and suffering, and with such sight comes a praxis-oriented empathy and participation in transformative solidarities. That, at least, was the hope of Coleridge and Wordsworth. In this poem, Coleridge is mostly focused on the need to work on being attentive and receptive to see and experience the grace and love that sustain us and surround us.

Thoughts, too, can be instances of grace and love. In the next stanza, Coleridge tells Sara of his experience earlier that day, when, delighting in the beauty of the moment, immersed in the more-than-human, there occurred to him "many a thought uncalled and undetained," reflections "as wild and various as the random gales" (lines 39 and 42). As the wild wind sweeps and plays his mind, he speculates:

> And what if all of animated nature
> Be but organic harps diversely framed,
> That tremble into thought, as o'er them sweeps
> Plastic and vast, one intellectual breeze,
> At once the Soul of each, and God of all?

(lines 44–48)

Coleridge depicts all of nature as diverse, organic Eolian harps, enlivened and sustained by that dynamic, vast, intellectual breeze, that "Soul of each, and God of all." Contrary to many commentaries on this passage, this is not Coleridge's foray into pantheism but rather into pan*en*theism.[22] God, here, is radically immanent yet is not—as in pantheism—reduced to or totally identified with "all of animated nature."[23] The "God of all" suffuses creation yet remains more than its summation. A powerful doctrine of creation is at work in this model of "organic Harps diversely framed." The divine breeze enlivens all material things and is not alien to them. Matter—Eolian harps of all kinds—is not a mere frame to be filled with Spirit. There is, rather, an intimate interconnection between all material things, including humans, and the breath, spirit, wind that stirs them. And creation, in this model, is not static—having occurred only once upon a time, "in the beginning"—but rather is "plastic," that is, dynamic and continuous.

Now, it might be tempting to see Coleridge's Eolian theology as a poetic expression of David Hartley's theory of associationism. The concept of the Eolian harp, after all, was used by Hartleyan associationists as a metaphorical illustration of the material process by which vibrations of sensory intuitions are translated into human cognition. This early form of cognitive science, inspired by Locke, was extremely popular in the late eighteenth and early nineteenth centuries. Both Coleridge and Wordsworth were attracted to aspects of associationism throughout their lifetimes. For them, the appeal of associationism was its insistence on the materiality and embodiment of cognition, its affirmation of a nondualistic relation—an intimate *association*—between the imaginative faculties of the human mind and the manner and matter of the nonhuman, natural world.

Yet Wordsworth and Coleridge also had their reservations. In Coleridge's poem, the fundamental cause of animation, whether in the music of the harp or the thought of humans, is not simply vibrating, sensory data. Rather, the fundamental cause of animation is that vast, spiritual breeze stirring within and without. The breeze is the fusion of Spirit and the material. But the material is not "the profane" holding the sacred—the superfluous body holding the divine soul. The breeze is sacred in its entirety. On the one hand, Coleridge is expecting his readers to connect the Eolian harp in the poem with the theory of associationism— that is, with an argument for a radical, empirical connection between humans and their home, the natural world. Yet, on the other hand, he wants to introduce the plasticity and dynamism of the one Life—the divine breeze that is fully immanent yet remains more than the summation of all material things.

As I noted earlier, if there were one candidate for British Romantic religion, it would be Coleridge's one Life, panentheistic, Eolian theology. But there is more than one candidate. The candidates are legion: Multiple forms of religion (as well as atheism) inhabit Romanticism.[24] Romanticism is neither a religious nor a secular monolith. And in the next, concluding stanza of the poem, Coleridge offers an alternative to the one Life religion. Immediately after the inspired supposition that "what if all of animated nature / Be but organic Harps diversely framed," Coleridge surprises us by abruptly presenting the commanding face of Sara, whose "more serious eye a mild reproof / Darts" (lines 49–50). Sara stalks Samuel with a formidable gesture that expresses disapproval of his speculations. Her expression alone, it would seem, is enough to bid Coleridge to "walk humbly with [his] God" (line 52). But Sara, in fact, does not merely frown. Of Sara, that "daughter in the family of Christ," Coleridge writes: "Well hast thou said and holily dispraised / These shapings of the unregenerate mind; / Bubbles that glitter as they rise and break / On vain Philosophy's aye-babbling spring" (lines 53-57).

Sara has a voice, and with it she powerfully reminds Coleridge that "philosophy," that is, speculative metaphysics, is simply not equipped to speak so unreservedly of "the Incomprehensible" (line 59). Under the guidance of Sara, Coleridge grasps that one may speak of "the Incomprehensible" only with "awe" and a "faith that inly *feels*" (lines 59-60; emphasis added). He offers thanks, then, to the God who with "saving mercies healed [him]" and who now provides him with graceful particulars at this time, in this place—*this* cottage, *this* peace, *this* partner, Sara (see lines 58-64).

Most commentators curse these lines.[25] Sara, the nag, beats down one of the boldest Romantic thinkers with the staff of stale, Christian orthodoxy. The concluding stanza, in this view, is nothing less than a moral backslide. The poem begins with Romantic eroticism, moves seamlessly to creative, Romantic "secular spirituality," and then ends, miserably, in anti-Romantic Christian orthodoxy, with the full oppressive weight of original sin and blind faith.

This standard account, however, is perhaps more telling of the commentators' commitment to theories of secularization than of the poem itself. "The Eolian Harp," a well-known Romantic poem, indisputably concludes with orthodox Christianity. Why, then, should one not conclude that Christianity, among other religious positions, is central to Romanticism? Why not assume that Sara's voice is Coleridge's as well? Perhaps Coleridge is presenting two appealing religious stances and the tension between them. On the one hand, he puts forward "the healthy-minded," Eolian religion that promises a natural harmony in the world and within each creature. In this religion, the exercise of poetic and philosophical imagination is itself a form of divine practice. On the other hand, he presents "the sick-soul," "Faith-that-inly-feels" religion that promises grace in a world where sin and misery abound.[26] In this religion, the exercise of piety—gratitude to God—is a more worthy practice than engagement in speculative inquiry.

Perhaps the poem is, among other things, an exploration or expression of the strengths of each religious stance and even of a possible tense reconciliation between them. In dialogue with "pensive Sara"–thoughtful, reflective Sara–Coleridge presents two lively religious options and perhaps wonders if he must choose between them. Can organic, Eolian religion and orthodox Christianity be held, practiced, and cherished by one person? Would that not be one form of authentic Romantic religion?

Both Coleridge and Wordsworth were preoccupied with articulating an intimate, theologically sound interrelationship between God, humans, and the more-than-human world. Both were eager to see the divine in the everyday—in the physics of light, the ecosystems of the land, the kindness of strangers, in the cry of the outcast and oppressed. They struggled, however, with how to express this complex relationship among Spirit, humans, and the natural world. God the Person seemed too anthropomorphic; God the Force seemed too abstract. Coleridge attempted the formulation of God as "plastic and vast . . . / At once the Soul of each, and God of all." Was that formula adequate? He and Sara had their doubts. But the quest continued. Indeed, it could be said that to this Romantic religious quest Coleridge and Wordsworth dedicated much of their life's work.[27] They struggled to articulate a fitting sacramental view of the world: a world in which divinity is radically present and to which humans respond by caring for justice and for the common good of diverse, overlapping communities—communities big and small, local and international, of humans and of stone, and everything in between. Of such a sacramental world one could say, "methinks, it should have been impossible / Not to love all things in a world so filled." In such a sacramental world, one could see how a love poem, a nature poem, and a religious poem could be organically interwoven as one.

One could also say, as did Coleridge, "From east to west / A groan of accusation pierces Heaven! / The wretched plead against us; . . . / . . . we [have] gone forth / And borne to distant tribes slavery and pangs."[28] Those lines are from Coleridge's social protest poem "Fears in Solitude," written in 1798—three years after "The Eolian Harp"—when Britain was on the brink of war. The social protest poem, as we will see, is closely connected to the sacramental poem "The Eolian Harp." "Fears in Solitude" begins with the goodness and beauty of the sacramental world, "a quiet spirit-healing nook / Which all, methinks, would love" (lines 12–13). Here, again, as in "The Eolian Harp," Coleridge presents a world that he deems irresistibly loveable. From the prospect of this sacramental dwelling, he sternly censures his nation—its citizens and leaders—for its support of war, slavery, and religious intolerance. His critiques are especially remarkable given the fierce patriotism gripping his native Britain in anticipation of a French invasion. After crying out, "Oh! my countrymen! / We have offended very grievously, / And been most tyrannous," Coleridge declares it is the warmongers, the supporters of slavery, and the religiously intolerant who are in fact the unpatriotic—the "enemies / Even of their country" (lines 41-43, 174-75). They transgressed the nation's heart and soul, its laws and its professed religion. Their prayers became cries for victory, "all our dainty terms for fratricide" (line 113). In doing so, "We join no feeling and attach no form! / As if the soldier died without a wound; / As if the fibres of this god-like frame / Were gored without a pang" (lines 116-19).

Affect is corrupted, ethical sight is lost, and the "godlike frame"—an in-spirited frame, not unlike that of the Eolian harp—is desacralized, now seen as lifeless thing. The poet's job, in Coleridge's view, is to cultivate in citizens the appropriate affect in response to the horrors of war and slavery. Such affect includes shame, horror, outrage, and repentance but also something akin to Du Bois's dark, wild hope. This hope acknowledges the reprehensible realities of the present world while also registering a sacramental world that points to beauty, justice, and goodness. Hence the poem concludes with the same sacramental land in which it began: "O my Mother Isle!" whose "lakes and mountain-hills," "clouds . . . [and] quiet dales," "rocks and seas," inspire "ennobling thoughts" and adoration of "all lovely and honourable things" (lines 177-89). The land—this complex, integrated relationship among Spirit, humans, and the natural world—is itself an agent that provides ethical bearings that point to inclusion, peace, and justice. While the land includes a record of Britain's actual, flawed past and present state of affairs, it also offers a sacramental, aspirational vision, judging and inspiring.

Perhaps the tension between the sacramental and the actual is captured by the tension between "Eolian religion" and "orthodox Christianity," that is, by a religion that speaks of "the one Life within us and abroad / . . . and joyance everywhere" and by a religion that speaks of a world marked by human fallenness: cruel injustice, love of war, and hatred of fellow creatures. This same tension speaks not only to our political condition but to our environmental one as well. Indeed, as is usually the case, the political and the environmental interconnect in radical Romanticism. Coleridge wrote of a more-than-human world that is free from destructive, human exploitation and one that suffers greatly from precisely such exploitation. He depicted matter as lively and vibrant ("organic Harps diversely framed"), and he would have shared Jane Bennett's view that "the image of dead or thoroughly instrumentalized matter feeds human hubris and our earth-destroying fantasies of conquest and consumption."[29] He celebrated the beauty of the natural world, including pedestrian, everyday beauty (for example, "This Lime-Tree Bower My Prison").[30] But he also wrote of forms of beauty that are often scorned by a narrow, constricted human aesthetics (for example, the water snakes in "The Rime of the Ancient Mariner").[31] He brought attention to the desires and well-being of more-than-human creatures, and he also decried cruel human actions that frustrate those desires and tyrannize their vulnerable lives (for example, "To a Young Ass").[32] His Eolian, sacramental, aspirational world is one in which humans honor and care for the more-than-human; his orthodox Christian world is one in which sinful humans are condemned for their disregard and exploitation of the more-than-human. His poetry captured both worlds, with all their tension, promise, and destruction. Unfortunately, standard theories of secularization have failed to take seriously both worlds, and therefore these theories have been blind to the religious, political, and environmental complexity of the poem.

The culmination of the poem is the two religions, with all their political and environmental implications, lingering and intermingling, in the mind and life of author and reader alike—in all who seek to interweave love, nature, justice, and religion (broadly understood). I have identified the two religions in the poem as the Eolian one Life theology and orthodox Christianity. But we can think of other religious or ethical stances that roughly correspond with the poem's two religions—one emphasizing the glorious sacramental, the other the fallen, limited human. Today, for example, there are forms of deep ecology and new materialism that resonate with Eolian one Life theology. These highlight the nondualistic, holistic relation between the human, the more-than-human, and the spiritual. They tend to emphasize the goodness and beauty of the world, if only humans would choose to recognize their place in the sacred, interconnected fabric of life. In contrast to this worldview, there are forms of environmental and political pessimism that resonate with orthodox Christianity insofar as they emphasize vicious human ways—inescapable neoliberal capitalism, systemic racism, and extractive exploitation—and produce apocalyptic scenarios that rival those of the book of Revelation.

We can think of the sacramental vision as a source of hope—a hope that justice and care between the human and more-than-human can be achieved. At the very least, the vision inspires a hope that such justice and care are dynamic aims worthy of pursuit. But how are we to pursue them? Coleridge held that we participate in a "one Life" that animates all, that joins all. Yet is it enough merely to educate people about the existence of Eolian, one Life theology? The Romantics are often *portrayed* as advocating the following optimistic view: As we pursue unencumbered individuality—being spontaneous, free, and creative, each in our own way—we will effortlessly recognize unity among the various parts of the Universe or the one Life. This spontaneous, Romantic spirituality is often juxtaposed with traditional religion, especially Christianity with its prescribed beliefs and practices—with its emphasis on *cultivation, discipline,* and *form.* But Coleridge, as we have seen in "The Eolian Harp," was not ready to dismiss traditional Christianity. Nor was he willing to dismiss cultivation, discipline, and form.

In his "A Moral and Political Lecture," the radical Coleridge of 1795 sounds like a (counterfactual) progressive Edmund Burke, emphasizing the importance of traditions, practices, and habits for the sake of achieving the true ideals of the French Revolution—equality, liberty, and solidarity—but without the bloodshed. In the lecture, Coleridge condemns corrupt government policies, the war with France, and slavery and calls for the abolition of private property. If genuine reform is to be achieved, he maintains, it will in large part be thanks to the practices and discipline of the "friends of freedom," a potentially treasonable term synonymous with Jacobean revolutionary sympathies. Freedom requires, among other things, *political friendships* dedicated to advancing ethical, social practices as justice for all. Coleridge calls for a bloodless revolution that will come by way of political friendship, education, principles of justice, and a "taste" for reform.[33] From Rousseau and Godwin, he had learned about the evils that come from private property and social inequality. But unlike Godwin, Coleridge offers an approach that emphasized *bildung,* that is, the *cultivation* of the civic self, specifically the democratic citizen. Radical democratic reform, in Coleridge's view, requires the cultivation of democratic friendships, practices, habits, and affect. The early Coleridge did profess a faith in the Eolian, one Life spirituality, maintaining that humans and the more-than-human were united in Spirit, love, and justice. But he also maintains that *cultivation, discipline,* and *form*—notions typically associated with traditional religion—are indispensable for the realization of the Eolian vision. As we will see in the next section, Wordsworth shared this conviction.

WORDSWORTH'S "NUNS FRET NOT AT THEIR CONVENT'S NARROW ROOM"

I now turn to a poem by Wordsworth to further this investigation of the dynamic presence of religion, practice, and cultivation in radical Romanticism.

Throughout his lifetime, Wordsworth wrote poems that were influenced by and expressed religion (for example, "The Ruined Cottage," "Tintern Abbey," "Home at Grasmere," "Michael," "Ode to Immortality," and the various versions of his epic poem *The Prelude*). In spite of this abundance of religion, there is a dominant interpretive tradition, emerging especially after World War I, that reads these poems as instances of secularization by which Nature comes to replace religion. Yet if we can escape this narrow interpretive tradition, we see in Wordsworth's poems diverse traditions and perspectives, including religious ones, brought together in novel ways.

While there are many examples of explicitly religious poems penned by Wordsworth, I have chosen to focus on a poem in which the topic is not religion per se but rather the place of tradition, discipline, form, and freedom in modernity. This cluster of topics pertains to our broad themes of religion, modernity, and the secular. In many standard accounts, Romanticism frees itself from the yoke of religious tradition, discipline, and form and thereby soars, unshackled, to the lofty heights of subjective expression and unrestrained imagination.[34] Yet it is precisely this narrative of Romanticism, modernity, and secularization that is questioned and undermined by Wordsworth's "Nuns Fret Not at Their Convent's Narrow Room." In this poem, Wordsworth juxtaposes the potential happiness of encumbrance, discipline, and form to a painful, entirely unmoored freedom. A disciplined, cultivated form of life, one that brings together usefulness and beauty, labor and purpose, offers relief to those suffering from what Milan Kundera has named "the unbearable lightness of being."[35] Wordsworth wrote a sonnet to justify the *form* of the sonnet but also to justify the very idea of forms and practices that cultivate—that in*form*—our lives. At the heart of Romanticism, then, we find a defense of cultivation, form, and discipline. This is not what most portraits of Romanticism lead us to expect.

Allow me now to quote the poem, written in 1802, in full:

> Nuns fret not at their Convent's narrow room;
> And Hermits are contented with their Cells;
> And Students with their pensive Citadels;
> Maids at the Wheel, the Weaver at his Loom,
> Sit blithe and happy; Bees that soar for bloom,
> High as the highest Peak of Furness Fells,
> Will murmur by the hour in Foxglove bells:

> In truth the prison, unto which we doom
> Ourselves, no prison is: and hence to me,
> In sundry moods, 'twas pastime to be bound
> Within the Sonnet's scanty plot of ground:
> Pleased if some Souls (for such there needs must be)
> Who have felt the weight of too much liberty,
> Should find short solace there, as I have found.[36]

Nuns do not worry about their tiny rooms, hermits and students are happy in their solitude, and skillful laborers such as the spinner or weaver "sit"—*work*—contentedly. The disciplines or forms of life that cultivate these individuals and the communities are not oppressive but liberating. They experience a positive freedom: the capacity to realize their fundamental passions and purposes. Just as bees "soar for bloom," these individuals live and work with focus and intention. Cultivation, vocation, and life are gracefully united and thereby constitute a form of human flourishing.

Like most virtues and commitments, practiced work will at times feel like a burden. Nonetheless, practiced work ranks as one of the greatest gifts. It can save your life. Emerson and the Wordsworth who influenced him agreed about this: "Every man's task is his life-preserver. The conviction that his work is dear to God and cannot be spared, defends him."[37] Those lines are from Emerson's essay "Worship," but they might as well be a gloss on Wordsworth's sonnet. For both radical Romantic authors agree that good work and the cultivation that it requires can preserve your life against such threats as despair and rootlessness, heartless politics and unhappy change, thoughtless neighbors and bad luck.

To those, then, who would deem cultivation, practice, and discipline as repressive, as anti-Romantic, Wordsworth declared, "In truth the prison, unto which we doom / Ourselves, no prison is." Wordsworth understood, of course, that there are many kinds of prisons or cells. Some *are* oppressive.[38] But we ought not to assume that *any* cell—any encumbrance, restraint, or form—is despotic or inauthentic. To inhabit a form that is useful and beautiful can be as elevating and natural as the bee in flight. It can also bring comfort to those "who have felt the weight of too much liberty."

"The weight of too much liberty"—this is that modern disease that Rousseau, a founder of Romanticism, called *mal de l'infini* and that Durkheim, a founder of the social sciences, subsequently developed as the concept of *anomie*. Anomie is a form of collective unhappiness in which individuals suffer from a dearth of—a "*freedom*" from—life-enhancing social ideals, practices, public goals, and commitments. Lacking meaningful associations and commitments, individuals suffer, because detachment wounds. With the phrase "the weight of too much liberty," Wordsworth looked back to Rousseau and forward to Durkheim, and he named—from the heart of Romanticism—the human suffering that flows from the dearth of meaningful and ethical social practices and associations.

From what we know of the sociohistorical context in which he wrote the sonnet, along with the poems "Written in London" and "London," Wordsworth understood "the weight of too much liberty" as a social disease with a specific historical narrative. It emerged from a constellation of such events as the Industrial Revolution, population displacements, and global capitalism. "The weight of too much liberty" was principally understood as a public, not a private, disease. And the public consequences were potentially grave. Insofar as citizens are unanchored in traditions, practices, and institutions that promote equality and justice, they are susceptible to destructive social crazes that can place power in the hands of those unworthy of it.

For example, in "Written in London" and "London" (a pair of poems composed at the same time as "Nuns Fret Not," in 1802) Wordsworth complained of the recent growth of isolated, "selfish men"—now "the wealthiest man among us is the best."[39] "Rapine, avarice, expence, / . . . these we adore."[40] These anomic, unjust social trends must be countered by the cultivation of "*manners*"—that is, such forms, practices, and habits as "virtue, freedom, power."[41] The "manner of freedom" must be distinguished from "the weight of too much liberty." The former entails the forms and practices of nondomination; the latter refers to the lack of such forms and practices. To be clear, Wordsworth was not championing *all* forms, practices, and disciplines. There are "narrow rooms" that bring domination and tyranny, and these must be resisted with a different set of "narrow rooms," that is, with traditions, practices, and forms that promote freedom, equality, and justice.

As a countermeasure to "the weight of too much liberty," Wordsworth proposed "to be bound / Within the Sonnet's scanty plot of ground." Confinement to poetic *form*, the constraint of the sonnet—its "scanty plot of ground"—brings solace and a type of freedom. It is a comfort and freedom that comes from belonging to a poetic tradition, community, discipline, and practice. It is the freedom to labor and create within the form of a (dynamic) cultural set of goods and practices. The *form* of the sonnet, then, is a condition of liberty—liberty for poet and reader who embrace and work within the form. Wordsworth, however, was not only addressing the writing and reading of poetry. He and Coleridge were explicit about their efforts to join others and contribute to the creation of local, national, and even global democratic *forms* of life. This shared work entailed shaping the *taste* of their readers, that is, cultivating in them a discerning capacity and longing for beauty, justice, and solidarity. This, ultimately, was their poetic and religious calling. Yet that social current, anomie, "the weight of too much liberty," was a tide turned against beauty, justice, and solidarity. What was needed, in part, was a different tide, a current that carried life-enriching, democratically progressive practice, discipline, and belonging.

For some time now, many have characterized Romanticism, and Western modernity more generally, as the *flight* from "the narrow room"—the flight from tradition.[42] The Romantic ideal, supposedly, is to be free of social cultivation and discipline so that one can discover one's authentic self and create spontaneously. Yet at the peak of Wordsworth's authorship in 1802, we hear in the sonnet a commanding Romantic voice that speaks of the good work and satisfaction that come from tradition, cultivation, and discipline and also of the collective pain and self-indulgence that come from "the weight of too much liberty." Wordsworth the Romantic assumed an *apparently* anti-Romantic stance.

Foucault, of course, would famously challenge the very idea that Western modernity can be characterized by the absence of cultivation and discipline. Hence his claim that "the 'Enlightenment,' which discovered the liberties, also invented the disciplines."[43] Modernity, especially in the view of the early Foucault, is fraught with normalizing discipline and practice that deprive us of freedom, cause pain, and bring oppression.[44] Wordsworth, in contrast, worried about the pain that comes from the absence of discipline and practice, or at least from the absence of suitable ones. Yet despite what appears to be their conflicting positions, perhaps we do not need to choose between Foucault and Wordsworth. Wordsworth told us the truth about the potential benefits that flow from social cultivation and practices. He rejected the very idea of a *fundamental* antagonism between cultivation and discipline, on the one hand, and flourishing individuals and just communities, on the other. In spite of his opposition to Burke's politics, Wordsworth affirmed Burke's notion of second nature, that is, of the formative, normative role of traditions, practices, and virtues.[45] Yet Foucault told us the truth about the human suffering that flows from oppressive social discipline. Mechanisms of discipline, supposedly "intended to alleviate pain, to cure, to comfort . . . all tend, like the prison, to exercise a power of normalization."[46] This is not to say that Foucault failed to note any affirmative aspects of social discipline or that Wordsworth ignored all deleterious ones. It is rather to say that we need both perspectives to acquire a fuller account of the potential good and harm that comes from humans engaged in social cultivation, practice, form, and association.

Yet the Foucauldian perspective, both in the academy and in popular culture, has gained ascendency over the Durkheimian-Wordsworthian one. We typically talk of social forces or power as disciplining the individual and thereby producing oppression and suffering. This focus reflects a tacit and persistent reverence for the sacrosanct interiority of the self and its presumed right to create itself freely, autonomously, without normative encumbrance. It reflects secularized accounts of Romanticism that portray religion as the chief representation of all things traditional and as the source of practices and disciplines, which—in these accounts—thwart individuals from freely shaping their art and lives. If we accept these interpretations of Romanticism, we ought to dismiss Wordsworth's sonnet as an anomaly. But if we acknowledge Wordsworth's voice in the sonnet as an authentically Romantic one, we need to revise and enlarge our accounts of Romanticism and modernity. The end result would not be to replace one monolithic Romanticism with another but to arrive at a more multifarious, less static, account.

Aspects of what we call secularization would belong to a more pluralistic account of Romanticism, as would other Romantic innovations—some of which are signaled by Wordsworth's sonnet. Note the lines "the prison, into which *we doom / Ourselves*, no prison is" (emphasis added). We have chosen our cell, the form that shapes us. The idea of *choosing* our traditions and disciplining practices is a parallel innovation to what we found in Coleridge's "The Eolian Harp," where we are implicitly asked to wrestle with and perhaps combine religious options. In both poems we confront two seemingly contradictory Romantic ideals: (1) to belong to—and be informed by—a place, a set of social practices, a tradition; and (2) to employ one's imagination, critical inquiry, and autonomy. While both Coleridge and Wordsworth grasped the potential tension between these ideals, neither viewed them as irreconcilable. Indeed, both usually understood the ideals as mutually enabling. To Wordsworth and Coleridge, it's only natural that individuals *find* themselves in a variety of overlapping communities, traditions, and social practices and also that individuals *make* choices within them, including, evidently, the choice to highlight the very role of particular social practices of the flourishing life. "Choice" entails critically evaluating those traditions, social practices, and habits that inform us, determining what is to be kept, what is to be discarded, and what is to be reformed—the very approach to Romanticism I exemplify in this book.

Needless to say, there are practices that warrant critique. Wordsworth and Coleridge decried, for example, painful social, economic, and political inequalities that were deemed "natural." Yet they were also blind to many unjust practices that were considered "normal." For example, they were not sufficiently aware of the demeaning and oppressive "narrow rooms" to which women were consigned. William Wordsworth's own sister, Dorothy, was an avid reader, keen observer, and skilled poet, yet pervasive patriarchy limited her life options. Practices and forms that enforced patriarchal, racist, classist, and homophobic practices were ubiquitous (as they are today). But the ubiquity of unjust practices and forms is not an argument to disparage practices and forms entirely. Wordsworth and Coleridge rejected the idea that we must choose between the way of tradition, practice, and discipline and the way of imagination, reform, and autonomy. Their verse and prose attempted to reveal the logic of the close connection between social training (cultivation and practice) and social revision (critique and reform).

I claimed that some aspects of secularization would belong to a more capacious, plural account of Romanticism. The sonnet, for example, speaks of choosing our cell, electing our practice. This allows for choosing a nonreligious practice, and we see the birth of agnostic and atheist options among the Romantics. Atheism, as we understand the term today, was not prevalent during the Romantic era, and it certainly was not Wordsworth's or Coleridge's practice at any stage of their careers. But we can see how the necessity of choosing one's practice, always in the context of one's sociohistorical milieu, could and would introduce new forms of religious diversity, including those of private spirituality as well as agnostic and atheist forms.

Colin Jager, an excellent scholar of Romanticism who is attentive to religion, claims that Wordsworth's sonnet is profoundly secular because religious forms of life are seen as "a pleasant respite from the business of wrestling with modern freedom."[47] Jager, drawing explicitly on Talal Asad's account of the Protestantization and secularization of religion, interprets Wordsworth's lines "In sundry moods, 'twas pastime to be bound / Within the Sonnet's scanty plot of ground" as an example of religion "practiced in one's spare time."[48] He claims, then, that these lines refer to a "transfer of power—from disciplined knowledge to optional pastime."[49] But Wordsworth, a poet who mainly composed in blank verse, was specifically referring to the "brief solace" of inhabiting the sonnet—a particular, earlier poetic form that continued to hold relevance for him. And his larger claim is that there are assorted forms and disciplines worthy of critical appropriation. If the form of the sonnet can assist the poet of blank verse, what other traditions and practices are available to us to supply solace and life-enhancing freedom? In the end, Wordsworth's sonnet acknowledges earlier forms of discipline and practice and the necessity of maintaining some such discipline and practice, variously and critically, in the present. It does not systematically reduce religion or other forms of practice to an "optional pastime." *That* anomic scenario—"the weight of too much liberty"—is precisely the state of affairs that Wordsworth wished to challenge and forestall. Moreover, religion for the Wordsworth of 1802 was hardly an optional pastime. It was a substantive and enduring aspect of his identity and poetic vocation.

Jager also claims that "the sonnet offers a familiar secularization narrative" as it moves from "nuns and hermits" to "student to maid to weaver to bee": "Choosing the constraint of the sonnet is here rendered as a natural culmination of the process of secularization enacted by the transformation from nuns into bees." In Jager's view, the sonnet moves from the nuns' *religious* "submission to artificial constraints" to the bee's *natural* observance of nature itself.[50] The assumption, here, is that there is something of a ranked order or movement in the sonnet, a progression that moves from the old religious order to the modern natural order. But if this is the case, why is the student ranked above the hermit and below the spinner? Does the student belong to an order of the past when compared to the spinner or weaver? And why does the poet come after nature's bee? Is the poet somehow more natural than the bee?

More likely, Wordsworth began the sonnet with nuns, hermits, and students as paradigms of a disciplined life. He then broadened the very idea of the disciplined life by naming the laborers, acknowledging the dignity of their skill and craft. Next, he evoked the bees to illustrate that good work and discipline are found in all creation: More-than-human creatures, too, labor expertly. Finally, he presented the poet not as the culmination of a movement from the religious to the natural but as a self-reflexive act in which the poet within the poem reflects on the form of the poem and labor of the poet. He thereby offered a defense of the discipline of the sonnet and, more broadly, a defense of the disciplined, skillful life that potentially promotes beauty, justice, and freedom.

In the sonnet, then, we do not find "a familiar secularization narrative" moving from the religious to the natural but rather a complex account of *the naturalness of second nature*: the human propensity and need to be shaped by tradition, practice, and form. Moreover, the supposed *juxtaposition* of religion to nature, which characterizes so many portrayals of Romanticism, in fact belies a central feature of many of its leading authors: the effort to link intimately the divine and the natural.

SECOND NATURE, DEMOCRACY, AND CRITIQUE

Wordsworth's verse, especially his early work, can be understood not only as *forms of poetry* but as *forms of democratic practice*. Part of that practice entailed offering portraits of the various forms of democratic character. Wordsworth sought to convey a democratic ethos through his verse, insofar as it reveals the everyday, common human dignity found in fellow citizens' practices, manners, and beliefs. As noted in chapter 1, Wordsworth's characters are often located at the periphery of society—the impoverished, the homeless, the disabled, the refugee, the beggar, the wounded veteran. In Wordsworth's vivid portraits we glimpse the selfhood of the person who is, or should be, the recipient of democratic rights; the one who is, or should be, protected by the state from such harms as exploitation by the wealthy and powerful; the one who is, or should be, seen as a person of worth and a fellow citizen.

To portray the dignity of common people was a radical act. Wordsworth was not alone in supporting the formal, democratic equality of the people, but he was rather singular in his championing of a *spiritual democracy*: a supportive culture that promoted the *social equality*—the mutual humanity—of the people, *all* the people, including the powerless, the neglected, the despised, and the rejected. He understood democratic culture as an ethos, a set of practices and customs, and the appropriate political and social affect. It pertained to *forms* of life and not only formal institutions. Wordsworth was committed, then, not only to political but also to cultural transformation, and he doubted whether the former was possible in the absence of the latter.

To say that Wordsworth was committed to democracy as forms of life is to say that he was committed to the formation of a *democratic second nature*. The early

Wordsworth sought to bring together second nature and progressive politics. By second nature, I refer to the process and condition of our acquiring dispositions, habits, practices, beliefs, and perspectives that become so thoroughly internalized that they seem "natural" to us. Our *first* nature, then, might be understood as a set of capacities and dispositions with which we are born; our *second* nature, in contrast, is a *formative process* and a dynamic product of our experience of living over time. By means of this formative process, our capacities and dispositions develop, and our habits, practices, disciplines, and beliefs are forged. Wordsworth held that second nature, while often trustworthy, must be subject to critique and transformation. Much of his early work was dedicated to cultivating a *democratic* second nature among his fellow citizens. Although Rousseau, Burke, and Wordsworth had different views on the relation between nature and second nature, all three acknowledged the dominance and power of second nature in the life of the individual and society.

James Chandler argues that Wordsworth moved away from Rousseau's exalted notion of *nature* to Burke's *second nature* around the year 1798.[51] My account is different. From the start of his writing career, Wordsworth had an elective affinity for the very idea of *second nature*, whether or not he had ever read Burke's treatises and essays. His early verse, "An Evening Walk" (1793) or "Salisbury Plain" (1795), for example, intimates his future emphasis on how place—a land, an association of people, and the history and stories that they mutually produce—inform its inhabitants' emotions, dispositions, practices, beliefs, and habits. Early on, Wordsworth was sympathetic to the view that an array of past emotions, events, and dispositions fuse with a place, comingling with the land and informing a robust second nature in its inhabitants.

In addition to his natural affinity for the general features of Burke's notion of second nature, Wordsworth was also attracted to and influenced by Rousseau.[52] This began at least by 1791, when Wordsworth was radicalized in France and became familiar with the Rousseau of the French Revolution. *That* Rousseau—the Revolutionaries' interpretation of Rousseau—was a champion of "Nature" and "Reason," not of second nature. It was around this time when Wordsworth most likely read Burke's *Reflections on the Revolution in France*. Burke, of course, opposed the Revolutionaries' Rousseau, specifically his support for democracy and his (alleged) faith in reason and theory divorced from history and experience. And Wordsworth opposed Burke, as seen in his *Letter to the Bishop of Llandaff*. The "letter" was as much a reply to Burke as it was to the bishop, and it was informed by Rousseau as much as by the progressive political activist Thomas Paine. Still, Wordsworth's *Letter to the Bishop of Llandaff,* which is his only explicit treatment of Burke during this time, is mute on the topic of second nature. Wordsworth was explicit about his opposition to (1) blind, oppressive custom, (2) slavish obedience to "dead parchment," and (3) thwarting the establishment of liberty and equality. But such opposition is not in itself a challenge to the concept of second nature. And indeed, unlike other progressive thinkers, Wordsworth chose not to criticize Burke on the powerful and potentially beneficial role of second nature.

Wordsworth learned much from his fellow radical republicans, lessons that he never entirely forgot.[53] He learned of the political implications that flow from having one's sympathies aligned with "the people," specifically with the disenfranchised and disempowered. This commitment to "the people" is a pervasive feature of Rousseau's actual authorship and not just of the Revolutionaries' caricature of him. *This* Rousseauian commitment had a profound influence on Wordsworth. Yet as the French Revolution became more violent and as Wordsworth's sympathies with it became more equivocal, Wordsworth entered a personally difficult period during which he produced arguably his best work. Much of his verse in this period can be characterized as bringing together second nature—with its emphasis on tradition, practice, form, and place—with the progressive political ideals of Rousseau and the Revolution.

Democratic second nature would surely have been an oxymoron for Burke. In his view, democracy, with its leveling aspirations, undermines the established ruling hierarchies that have organically emerged over time and bring stability to society. To Burke, democracy spawns a self-interested form of individualism that destroys generous, life-giving traditions, customs, and habits. Democracy, an experiment inspired by perilous, abstract theory, would eventually erase our second nature and thereby render us exposed and vulnerable, bereft of moral and social instincts and protection.

For Wordsworth, democracy was not an abstract theory bereft of lived experience. In the Lake District, for example, he perceived democratic forms of life— traditions, practices, and beliefs—that supported the dignity and respect of individuals as well as the natural world in which they were embedded. This ethical view—to see the humanity in each neighbor and citizen, including the unhoused, the disabled, and the destitute—had roots in this culture. That same culture, of course, also endorsed many antidemocratic practices and beliefs. But with imagination and his own cultivated ethical perspectives, Wordsworth championed and fashioned a distinctively democratic vision. He understood that democracy required *novel* political developments. Democracy was not simply a hermeneutical selection and then affirmation of assorted, local democratic manners—it was also a *transformation* of social and political manners and institutions. A truly democratic second nature must remain dynamic. Critique and openness to change must be inculcated.

Closely related to the concept of "second nature" are "taste" and "place," and unsurprisingly these terms play significant roles in the work of Wordsworth. As we saw in chapter 1, Wordsworth employed the term *taste* to refer to our capacity to experience the world normatively. One's taste is nurtured by *place*—place being understood geographically, culturally, and socioeconomically. This proposition links Wordsworth back to Burke and forward to Foucault. Like Burke, Wordsworth held that one's capacity for civic affections and duties has its roots in one's local attachments and education (broadly understood). For Wordsworth, the local is where democracy and economy have a human face—in daily activities, close to home. Without strong attachments to local communities, one's wider civic existence risks becoming abstract and hollow. A local sense of place is an indispensable step toward a more expansive one. Yet like Foucault, Wordsworth also grasped that disciplines and practices that are rooted in a place can inflict harm. For example, in the poems "Expostulation and Reply" and "The Tables Turned," Wordsworth disclosed how a prevailing local culture's emphasis on industry, book-learning, and scientific "dissection" make it difficult for one to engage in such counterpractices as nonutilitarian "wise passiveness," experiential learning, and envisioning the interconnectedness of things. In this case, the "local culture" is most likely the academic culture of such places as Cambridge University.

Usually, however, Wordsworth worried about the harm that flows when industrial capitalistic practices and forms of discipline—such as those that come with wage labor and the establishment of a rural proletariat—destroy the practices, habits, and traditions that had emerged over time in a place. To battle such invasive forces, Wordsworth understood that one must not only seek to protect local practices but also to cultivate strong, broad civic practices rooted in democratic manners and processes. So while Wordsworth was indeed a champion of local democracies informed by their distinctive geographies and cultures, he, along with Coleridge, also maintained the necessity of cultivating broad cosmopolitan sensibilities.

Wordsworth desired that his art would both *express* and *nurture* something like a "civic" or democratic second nature. On the one hand, he frequently claimed that his life and poetry were nurtured by the place and taste in which he was raised. An interlaced weave of geography and culture—a spiritual inheritance of rocks and streams, manners and habits—had shaped his life and poetry. His art was an *expression* of his second nature. Yet his art also sought to *nurture* in readers a distinctive form of a democratic second nature. He sought, in other words, to cultivate a robust democratic taste in his readers.

Yet it is important to note that whether Wordsworth was expressing or nurturing a second nature, this activity was not simply a process of mirroring or replicating some static, received set or form of habits, beliefs, and practices. Wordsworth, as we have seen, held that one must *choose* one's inheritance and critically engage with it. In his view, there is always a dialectical relation between inheritor and inheritance. Neither remains static. And so Wordsworth actively fashioned his inheritance even as it fashioned him. This active participation in one's inheritance—a well-known process in many Indigenous communities, as we will see in chapter 7 on the Laguna Pueblo author Leslie Marmon Silko—was a goal Wordsworth set for himself as well as for his readers.

We can think of Wordsworth's poetry, then, as the result of an active relation between inheritor and inheritance: as the labor of a dynamic second nature. The potentially dynamic character of second nature is worth emphasizing, since second nature is often associated with conservatism, that is, with an unchanging status quo. Yet second nature is acquired over time, and it is potentially responsive to changes in culture, geography, and the human imagination. Indeed, *responsiveness* itself—the work of reflection and critical inquiry—is a trait and capacity supported by a democratic second nature. Responsiveness, critical inquiry, and second nature pull together in radical Romanticism.

Second nature, then, is subject to assessment and revision. But critique of this kind is neither disembodied nor wholesale, as if one could step outside of one's self and world and put to doubt everything at once. Sounding remarkably similar to Wittgenstein in *On Certainty*, Wordsworth described the futility and ultimately the despair in his own past attempts to drag "all passions, notions, shapes of faith / Like culprits to the bar, suspiciously." But this should not suggest that recovery from global doubt and its attending despair are to arrive by means of a blind affirmation of tradition, practice, and custom. Recovery from paralyzing doubt comes, rather, from "a power / That is the very quality and shape / And image of *right reason*" and the "*intellectual eye*."[54] "Right reason" and the "intellectual eye" refer to judgments, evaluations, and critiques that are informed by one's embeddedness in the social and natural world. They reflect experience even as they reflect *on* experience. Second nature, properly acquired, is a deposit of past insight and wisdom that, with the aid of "right reason" and the "intellectual eye," is constantly negotiating new circumstances and revising itself in response to them.

My larger argument is that *second nature* (along with form, discipline, and practice) and *critique* (as an ethical and valued social practice) are not incompatible. Theorists of second nature can acknowledge the roles of both social formation and moral autonomy (what Wordsworth called the "*intellectual eye*" and what Emerson would call "self-reliance"), depicting moral autonomy as the cultivated capacity to reflect critically on one's culture, history, location, and circumstance. Human character and action, in this view, are understood to be as much a matter of social formation as of something like self-legislation—the imperative that one must *adjudicate* and not simply *conform* to past conventional adjudication and practice. Democratic second nature entails, among other things, a cultivated capacity for discerning critique.

Pace Burke, democratic forms, virtues, and practices are a flourishing society's most promising grounds. To bring attention to the relation between democracy and second nature is to bring warning as well as hope. For that which has been made can also be remade, enhanced, and fortified—for better and for worse. Yet by acknowledging progressive democratic forms of life, we can purposefully attend to and cultivate this dynamic second nature in order to strengthen and further such achievements as the safeguarding of human dignity and the promotion of social and environmental justice and to combat such democratic threats as white supremacy, misogyny, and transphobia. Our hope and our duty, as Wordsworth understood it, is the cultivation of a robust cultural democracy—a *democratic second nature*.

RADICAL ROMANTIC RELIGION, DEMOCRACY, AND ECOLOGY

Read together, Coleridge's and Wordsworth's poems exemplify the strengths and limits of secularized interpretations of Romanticism. Both poems place a premium on individual choice or discerning, ethical judgment—what Emerson would call "self-reliance." Both poems also honor the integrity and inherent value of the more-than-human world. These two stances—the elevation of the individual and of "nature"—are precisely what standard secularized accounts would predict that we would find. Yet contrary to secularized accounts, Coleridge's "The Eolian Harp" also highlights the ethical role of religion, both panentheistic religion and traditional Christianity. And Wordsworth's sonnet emphasizes the abiding, ethical role of that which secularism associates with religion— namely, tradition, discipline, form, and practice.

When our secularized narratives become more nuanced, when we become aware of the salient role played by religion and practice in Romanticism, we find ourselves in a better position to grasp radical Romantic efforts to contribute to a progressive democratic and ecological culture: an environmentally responsive democracy embodied by its citizens and embedded in its lands. The early Wordsworth and Coleridge did not understand democracy only as a set of formal political institutions but rather as a progressive culture that included the practices, habits, and emotions of its diverse citizens. They were committed to advancing an *environmentally responsive* democracy that emphasized an evolving set of virtues and practices that dispose citizens to see, think, feel, and act in ways that uphold the "the integrity, stability, and beauty" of the planet's interrelated natural and social communities.[55] And this vision of an embodied, environmentally responsive democracy was informed by and an expression of various religious traditions, especially panentheistic, Christian ones. In particular, Wordsworth and Coleridge understood a connection between (1) a divinity that permeates and affirms an intimate association between humans and the more-than-human world and (2) a robust democratic ethos that champions justice among humans and respect and care for the more-than-human.

The ecological impact of industrialization, urbanization, empire, and unbridled capitalism was significant for radical Romantic authors. The poetry and prose of the radical Romantics conveyed an unprecedented sensitivity to the interdependent relation between people and place, between things social and natural. And the language and perspectives of religion and progressive politics greatly informed their ecological responses. Religious, panentheistic perspectives, for example, challenged various toxic, dualistic models that implied an exploitive relation between humans and the more-than-human. These perspectives encouraged the virtue of paying attention to the diverse voices in the land: to the voice of fellow citizens, especially those whose voices are rendered faint, and to the word-less voices of creatures and ecosystems.

Water and air pollution, deforestation and land enclosures, urban slums and disrupted local economies—these are but some of the ways that the world of the Romantics was being altered by empire, capitalism, industrialization, and urban-ization. It has become commonplace to characterize the Romantic response to these changes as a retreat into nostalgic longing for the past ways of the pastoral English village and countryside. Deprecating "the city" and exalting "the coun-try" is considered a key motif in the Romantics' supposed withdrawal from the harsh realities of their time. Yet ascribing "retreat" and the facile *country-over-city* paradigm to the Romantics has greatly distorted their complex responses to the changing world around them. Their critiques did not amount to a censure of "the city" per se. Rather, they addressed specific deleterious practices and develop-ments. For example, although such poets as Wordsworth and Coleridge deplored London's connection to exploitive imperial power and its cruel disparity between rich and poor, they celebrated aspects of its aesthetic beauty and cultural diversity.

Urban centers, of course, were more likely than rural communities to suffer from certain types of grief caused by the Industrial Revolution and urbanization. Most factories and mills were concentrated in cities, and many of their workers had recently fled the poverty-stricken countryside—a poverty largely caused by public policies in support of economic "development." Industries in the city drew their workers from the country and, in turn, spewed their pollution into the water and air of the newly arrived residents. The sight and stench of floating industrial waste and sewage, the dark, killing smog and soot from burning coal, the squalor of overcrowded living conditions, the cruel child labor, and the mistreatment of animals—in such conditions as these many radical Romantics saw the links between environmental, political, and economic developments.

Informed by the ways and beliefs of progressive religious traditions, radical Romantics conveyed apocalyptic warnings in visionary verse and prose, issuing prophetic caution about the fragility and interconnectedness of the social and natural worlds and about the need for social, political, economic, and environ-mental change. Their active involvement in such campaigns entailed traveling at the crossroads of religious, democratic, and environmental thought, practice, dis-cipline, and habit.

CHAPTER 5

Dancing on a Flaming World

Du Bois's Poetry and Creative Fiction

I n this chapter, I present Du Bois as a radical Romantic poet and speculative fiction author who employs religious forms and motifs to reveal and
combat anti-Black racism, among other forms of oppression. This portrait
of Du Bois will no doubt surprise many. Romanticism, as we have seen, is usually
understood as a specific, delimited period of artistic and intellectual history—a
period that Du Bois does not belong to either chronologically or (as most would
assume) ideologically. But by bringing attention to Du Bois the radical Romantic,
we see religious thought employed as a vehicle to depict the pain, humiliation,
and cruelty of racist oppression as well as the possibilities of social change; we see
religion as an indispensable feature of Du Bois's moral and artistic imagination.
Moreover, by reading Du Bois as a radical Romantic, we again expand our understanding of Romanticism as well as our accounts of the religiously informed
moral aesthetics that Du Bois brought to his work as a social critic—work that
both denounces racist oppression and imagines postracist futures. My strategy
in constructing radical Romanticism is to reinterpret some "standard" Romantics but also to introduce new Romantic authors and themes: to critically appropriate the existing tradition but also to enlarge and enrich it. In the previous
chapter, I sought to show the dynamic role of religion and form in Romanticism.
I now turn to Du Bois to investigate these same aspects of Romanticism—the
role of religion and form and their implications for progressive thought and
practice.

Yet, in Du Bois these same aspects are transformed. Anti-Black racism and
misogyny are front and center, and the existential stakes are higher than those of
Coleridge and Wordsworth. The struggle for life and freedom in the context of

brutalized and oppressed Black women, men, and children brings a mortal urgency not seen in the previous Romantic authors. For example, Du Bois's work contains a spirituality comparable to Wordsworthian and Emersonian panentheism. But Du Bois's panentheism includes a divine permeating not only the beauty of the natural world but a Black Christ lynched and a Black female Moses dying before experiencing the freedom that she brought to her people.

This chapter will place special emphasis on Du Bois's poetry and speculative fiction published in his book *Darkwater* (1920). My main intervention is to show how Du Bois used various forms of poetry and creative fiction to critique the unjust status quo and to vividly depict an alternative, antiracist democratic politics. Furthermore, utilizing the forms of poetry and creative fiction, Du Bois depicted the more-than-human not as outside humanity but as an integral feature of a shared and interconnected world. Similar to Coleridge and Wordsworth, Du Bois worked in a creative, aesthetic medium that allowed him to (1) express profound affect and pathos, (2) make robust declarations and judgments, and (3) craft forms of expressions that acknowledge uncertainty, ambiguity, or a lack of resolution. Stirring affect, astute ethical judgment, and authentic uncertainty about future outcomes all mark Du Bois's poems and speculative fiction, as he brings together his vision of change with the cruel reality of racism in the United States.

We have already seen how *The Souls of Black Folk*, Du Bois's most famous work, can also be read as a radical Romantic text that plies aesthetics, pathos, ethical judgment, and uncertainty as it names and critiques racism in the United States. The success of *Souls*, unfortunately, has in many ways eclipsed the brilliance of *Darkwater*. And insofar as it is treated, it is the discursive essays—not the poetry and fiction—that receive the most attention. In contrast, in this chapter I focus on the poetry and speculative fiction, noting its religious, radical Romantic dimensions and its work as social criticism. Moreover, I explore how the very rhetorical form of *Darkwater*—the alternation of critical essays with religiously informed poetry and fiction—creates arenas for uncertainty, indeterminacy, and alternative futurities as Du Bois seeks to work against white supremacy.

I begin with a general account of the role of religion, tradition, and practice in Du Bois's poetry and creative fiction. I then offer specific readings of poems and speculative fiction in *Darkwater*, focusing on "The Prayers of God," "Jesus Christ in Texas," "The Comet," and "A Hymn to the Peoples."

RELIGION, FORM, AND PROGRESSIVE POLITICS

When discussing Coleridge's "The Eolian Harp" and Wordsworth's "Nuns Fret Not," we discovered that we miss much if we fail to attend to religion in Romanticism. The same lesson applies to Du Bois, who has frequently been described as a secularist or an agnostic who showed little interest in religion.[1] Yet as recent scholarship has shown, Du Bois was keenly attuned to and interested in religion, and he himself had profound religious sensibilities. For example, Jonathon Kahn has convincingly argued that it is wrong to think of Du Bois as "hostile to religion, as uninterested in religion and its rhetoric, concepts, narratives, and practices, and most important, as bereft of something recognizable as religious faith."[2] Religion, of course, is a capacious term that refers to many different forms of beliefs and practices. As Aptheker has rightfully claimed, "Du Bois was not religious in a conventional sense.... He was, however, deeply religious in that he believed in a kind of ultimate mystery in life, guided by some Creative Force."[3]

When Aptheker refers to Du Bois as "not religious in a conventional sense," we probably have a sense of what he means. As an adult, Du Bois was not a regular churchgoer and was critical of many aspects of "organized" religion, yet he persisted in maintaining some form of religious (or spiritual) beliefs and sensibilities. Du Bois was not an orthodox or traditional Christian but instead was highly interested in the prophetic or ethical aspects of Christian traditions, especially those that galvanized Black solidarity. He also studied the sociohistorical roots, institutions, and practices of white supremacist Christianity. Moreover, Du Bois maintained a personal religiosity that largely resembled a panentheistic, Romantic spirituality, a form of religiosity that I have alluded to throughout this book. A genealogy of it could plausibly begin with Rousseau's Savoyard priest, in which the revelatory guide for life consists of an attunement between the inner and outer—the inward authority of the self and the outer authority of "nature" or "spirit"—later manifested in Wordsworth's and Coleridge's one Life theology, and subsequently inherited and transformed by such North American Romantics as Margaret Fuller and Ralph Waldo Emerson and then again by such American pragmatists as William James and John Dewey. This Romantic spirituality, broadly understood here, challenged the rigid binaries of Spirit/human and Spirit/nature. Instead, it supported a vision of a dynamic interrelation between humans, Spirit, and the more-than-human world.

Du Bois manifested aspects of this Romantic spirituality in his life and work. We saw many examples of this in chapter 2. Yet, as we also saw in that same chapter, there were additional spiritual influences in his life. The Sorrow Songs—"the wild sweet melodies of the Negro slave"[4]—profoundly influenced and shaped Du Bois. In them he discovered a distinctively Black religiosity that spoke of hope and loss, resistance and suffering, Black solidarity and a "spirit of revolt."[5] In *Divine Discontent: The Religious Imagination of W. E. B. Du Bois*—arguably the best book we have on Du Bois and religion—Jonathon Kahn argues that Du Bois launched a form of African American pragmatic religious naturalism:

> Du Bois drinks fully from both streams—from pragmatist and African American traditions. In drawing on these two traditions—in creating a race-imbued pragmatic religious naturalism—Du Bois transforms both the American philosophical tradition and African American religious thought. By using pragmatist tools . . . Du Bois creates a new black faith: a radical version of pragmatic religious naturalism that displays a grasp of the sociopolitical implications of pragmatist thought that is more powerful than the pragmatists themselves.[6]

Kahn skillfully draws attention to the way Du Bois brought together the sensibilities of both American pragmatism and a distinctively Black spirituality. For my part, I want to note the close connection between radical Romanticism and such pragmatists as John Dewey, George Santayana, and William James.[7] My point is not to claim that we ought to see Du Bois as a Romantic and not a pragmatist but rather that Du Bois, who powerfully contributed to diverse academic fields through various forms of discourse, was influenced by a wide range of intellectual and spiritual traditions. Du Bois was influenced by Romanticism and pragmatism, but his reception of these traditions was always highly informed by distinctively Black intellectual and spiritual traditions and by Black responses to white supremacy and other forms of oppression. Du Bois fashioned a discerning amalgam of intellectual and faith traditions, and from that emerged a prophetic or religiously inspired progressive politics, one that included penetrating critiques of white America. And Du Bois's religiously inspired, prophetic engagement is most clearly seen in his poetry and creative fictional work.

Like Wordsworth and Coleridge—and Rousseau, for that matter—Du Bois's poetry and creative fiction broke down unhelpful, rigid binaries between the human, the divine, and the natural. He did not relegate Spirit to outside or above the human and more-than-human realm. Instead, his panentheistic, Romantic spirituality understood Spirit as working intimately in humans, history, and the natural world. Also, like Wordsworth and Coleridge, Du Bois employed "form" and "cultivation" for the sake of liberatory aims. As Wordsworth celebrated and employed the power of the form of the sonnet, so too Du Bois employed *forms* of poetry—psalms, hymns, biblical stories, among other forms—to produce powerful social critique and an embodied progressive politics. He both honored the forms and innovated within them, composing a body of work that portrayed the shapes and shades, the struggles and hopes, of life behind the Veil—life under the conditions of anti-Black racism.

The very shape of *Darkwater* illustrates both Du Bois's awareness of and skillfulness in literary forms. By interspersing powerful prose essays with his lucid, intense poems and short stories, Du Bois created a text in which the nonfiction and "fiction" pieces respond to each other, echoing but also augmenting the arguments, affect, and pathos of each text. Allison Blackmond Laskey has convincingly argued that Du Bois employed the ancient, oral story technique of the ring composition, a form of narrative structure in which a central theme is announced, developed, and then returns to its original starting point.[8] I wish here not to make a purely aesthetic remark but to emphasize the larger ramifications of the forms and the process of *in-forming* in Du Bois's work.

Of course, Du Bois understood that form—cultivation, discipline, and tradition—can also enforce an oppressive status quo. But he sought to use form to advance an embodied, antiracist democracy. As Wordsworth sought tangible means to contribute to shaping a progressive democratic second nature, so too Du Bois employed a variety of forms (cultural, religious, and aesthetic) to cultivate progressive, democratic sensibilities that exposed and challenged white supremacy, gender inequality, and colonialism.[9] Du Bois understood the power of *forms* in the art of social critique as well as in the production of transformative visions for the future. My main intention, here, is to note that Du Bois used various forms of poetry and creative fiction to critique the unjust status quo and to vividly depict alternative anti-Black democratic politics. Social scientific research and publications, in Du Bois's view, contributed to social change, but more was required. Ignorance was not the only or central obstacle to change. Social practices, affect, and stubborn bias also needed to be addressed.

For this reason, Du Bois claimed, "Not simply knowledge, not simply direct repression of evil, will reform the world. In long, indirect pressure and action of various and intricate sorts, the actions of men which are not due to lack of knowledge nor to evil intent, must be changed by influencing folkways, habits, customs and subconscious deeds."[10] Du Bois's poetry and speculative fiction belong to "actions of various and intricate sorts" designed to influence "folkways, habits, customs, and subconscious deeds." Society and culture at large require a profound democratic transformation in their practices and affects, their habits and manners. They require a spiritual—and not only a formal institutional—transformation. Religion and form, in Du Bois's poetry and creative fiction, are at the heart of that transformative effort.

AFFECT/REASON, EXISTENTIAL INTENSITY, AND UNCERTAINTY

In *Darkwater*, Du Bois attempted to address the *whole* person: one's mind and heart, reason and affect (to employ these somewhat problematic binaries). Yet it would be a mistake to assume that in *Darkwater* the fictional writings address the "heart" whereas the essays address the "mind." Heart and mind are addressed in both forms of writing. The prose pieces, for example, elicit strong affective responses, and the poetry and fictional pieces often respond to and even extend arguments from the essays. Indeed, one function of the creative fictional pieces is to advance an argument in the prose essays by taking readers beyond empirical realities and allowing them to imagine, for example, a world free of racism and classism.[11] The creative pieces vivify—in graphic detail—the very pain and suffering that the prose arguments seek to identify and combat. The creative pieces, together, elucidate both a fully realized, just democracy and the formidable obstacles to achieving such a society.

Du Bois anticipated what we now call the genre of speculative fiction, a genre that often clarifies present issues by situating them in imaginative settings—the fantastical, the futuristic, the magical, the supernatural, the cataclysmic. It presents us with what is and what may be, and the unknown between the two. And it is precisely this tension or uncertainty between what is and what may be that has been put to great use by various Black, Indigenous, and Latinx authors.[12] Du Bois is one of those authors. He employed the genre of speculative fiction to present both a vision of a genuinely postracial world and the obdurate realities of anti-Black racism.

One might be tempted to ask: Which form of writing was more important to Du Bois, the scholarly essay or the poetry and creative fiction? In his "Postscript" to *Darkwater*, he mused, "In my mind, now at the end, I know not whether I mean the Thought [scholarly essays] for the Fancy [poetry and creative fiction]—or the Fancy for the Thought."[13] It seems clear that, in spite of Du Bois's social scientific training and commitments, he valued both types of writing, acknowledging their differences but also their interrelatedness. Again, the relevant distinction is not between heart and mind, affect and reason. No, the distinction between "Thought" and "Fancy" is more about how argument and affect are expressed differently in the different genres. For example, the prose essay "The Souls of White Folk" powerfully and discursively names the national and international harm that flows from white supremacy. In the essay's companion poem following it, "The Riddle of the Sphinx," we find the same topic, but this time it is addressed with greater pathos and intensity: "I hate them [the white world's vermin and filth], Oh! / I hate them well" (26). But again, the presence of "greater pathos and intensity" should not imply that "thought" or "argument" is not present. The poem *argues* for the dignity of Black women in light of their heavy burdens and their "Wild spirit of a storm-swept soul, a-struggling to be free" (27).

Du Bois's poetry and creative fiction pieces are, above all, powerful forms of social critique. Take the first poem in *Darkwater*, "A Litany at Atlanta." This prayer boldly critiques God, religion, and white America. It begins by accusing God of silence: "O Silent God, Thou whose voice afar in mist and mystery hath left our ears an-hungered in these fearful days— / . . . . / *Keep not Thou silent, O God!* / Sit no longer blind, Lord God, deaf to our prayer and dumb to our dumb suffering" (12–13). God's silence and indifference are intolerable given the injustice and suffering inflicted on innocent Black people. The accusation and outcry are global, participating in the long tradition of protest against a removed, distant divinity. Yet the protest is also decidedly local: Du Bois accuses God of allowing lawless white mobs to brutally batter and kill innocent Black citizens during the three-day 1906 Atlanta Race Massacre.

After addressing God as blind and deaf, Du Bois lodges still another charge and possible explanation for God's callous inaction: "Surely Thou, too, art not white, O Lord, a pale, bloodless, heartless thing!" (13). Is God a white supremacist who turns a blind eye to the torture and murder of Black humans? Yet immediately after posing the frightful question, without waiting for an answer, Du Bois recants: "Forgive the thought! Forgive these wild, blasphemous words" (13). This recantation is reminiscent of Coleridge in "The Eolian Harp," as is the way that Du Bois, like Coleridge, goes on to declare faith in God: "Thou art still the God of our black fathers and in Thy Soul's Soul sit some soft darkenings of the evening, some shadowings of the velvet night" (13). Du Bois professes a Black faith in the Black-souled God of Black ancestors. And it is this God that Du Bois then beseeches: "But whisper—speak—call, great God, for Thy silence is white terror to our hearts! The way, O God, show us the way and point us the path!" (13). Ultimately, the poem offers no resolution regarding God's silence or Du Bois's own personal struggle between faith and despair.[14] Rather, the poem deftly poses profound questions and accusations, matches them with apt affect and pathos, and then concludes with the same silence with which it began:

> We bow our heads and hearken soft to the sobbing of women and little
>   children.
> *We beseech Thee to hear us, good Lord!*
> Our voices sink in silence and in night.
> *Hear us, good Lord!*
> In night, O God of a godless land!
> *Amen!*
> In silence, O Silent God.
> *Selah!*
>
>   (14)

When Coleridge wrote "Fears in Solitude," he struggled to make sense of the chaos, injustice, and war—justified in the name of God—that his country was determined to wreak on the world. Coleridge cried out to his God for understanding and accused his country of fervently supporting unjust war, slavery, and religious intolerance. When Du Bois wrote "A Litany at Atlanta," he, too, struggled to make sense of a cruel world, but above all, he strove powerfully to *name* the cruelty: "A city lay in travail, God our Lord, and from her loins sprang twin Murder and Black Hate. Red was the midnight; clang, crack, and cry of death and fury filled the air and trembled underneath the stars where church spires pointed silently to Thee. And all this was to sate the greed of greedy men who hide behind the veil of vengeance!" (13). Here racial hatred, economic greed, and their horrid consequences are named. But Du Bois, as is his way, also felt compelled to name concrete particulars: "Behold this maimed and broken thing, dear God; it was an humble black man who toiled and sweat to save a bit from the pittance paid him" (13). *This* man, who did all that was expected of him, struggling to make a living, abiding by both written and unwritten laws, "lieth maimed and murdered, his wife naked to shame, his children to poverty and evil" (13). "A Litany at Atlanta" exemplifies what Du Bois's poetry and fiction pieces accomplish: a creative, affective form of social critique that is rooted in an unassailable logic and that resists easy resolutions or closure.

Resistance to easy resolutions or closure is especially noteworthy in Du Bois's creative fiction pieces. These short stories often transport the reader to an alternate time or place, suggesting how this world could be—what it would look like, how it would feel—if racial and economic justice were achieved. In "The Princess of the Hither Isles," for example, a princess rejects the oppressive gold and power of the white colonial king who pursues her and instead longs for a "black beggar man" (38). The Black man, "set 'twixt Death and Pain," is revealed in his "grave majesty"—he is a person of justice, beauty, and courage (38-39). To him the white Princess offers her "bleeding heart," which she literally rips from her breast (39). In anger, the king strikes with his sword "that little, white, heart-holding hand until it flew armless and disbodied up through the sunlit air" (39). A great chasm appears— "wide as heaven from earth, deep as hell, and empty, cold, and silent"—separating the warm, blissful "Empire of the Sun" from the cold, gloomy Hither Isles (39). The Princess, peering into the abyss, issuing "a cry of dark despair," hears from the depths, "Leap!" "And the Princess leapt," and thus the story concludes (39).

But what kind of conclusion is this? Does she reach the Empire of the Sun, "the warmth of heaven's sun" (39)? Is she united with the noble Black beggar man? Does the offering of her bleeding heart bring about redemptive change, or does it simply disappear into an "empty, cold, and silent" abyss? These specific questions point to fundamental, daily questions for those who witness all manner of suffering and sorrow caused by unbending racial and economic injustice yet continue to hope and work for change.[15] Does their struggle and blood merely vanish into a silent void? Du Bois intentionally leaves these questions unanswered, underscoring both the indeterminacy of the future and the durability of white supremacy.

Analytic, discursive prose can articulate the logic of Du Bois's fictional writings' skillful inconclusiveness, but it cannot elicit the appropriate affect, convey the existential intensity, or parse the various threads of ambiguity, uncertainty, and open-endedness. Genres have strengths and limits. A strength of Du Bois's fiction is its ability to express a wide range of the human drama that is not easily captured in sociological, political, or economic discourse. "Racial inequality" is a necessary but abstract term. Du Bois's radical aesthetics sought to transform the abstract term and all that it means into vivid experiences with richly textured events and characters.

Like Wordsworth, he did this in part by introducing characters not commonly found in the standard texts of his readers. As we saw in chapter 1, Wordsworth introduced characters who at the time were considered unsavory as topics for poetry: the "beggar," the "idiot boy," "the banished negro," the wounded veteran, the unhoused, and the refugee. Wordsworth vividly portrayed these characters so that we might see and feel—intellectually and affectively—their suffering, challenges, and occasional victories. Du Bois introduced his own set of atypical characters: the Black farmer struggling under Jim Crow; the Black woman molding clay who is refused admission to any school of sculpture; the young Black woman, Josie, who faces myriad obstacles and dies without medical attention; the (fictional) Black man who, after a global catastrophe, finds himself in a new, hopeful world as a Black Adam with a white Eve, only for racism to come rushing back upon him.

Wordsworth and Du Bois both introduced nonstandard characters into their genres to reveal and name a world to their readers. But the task for Du Bois was a more complicated one. Wordsworth's readership was economically diverse but solidly white. Du Bois, in contrast, was addressing both Black and white readers, and this entailed a different set of challenges. For his Black readers, Du Bois sought to *name* an anti-Black racist world that was already intimately known. In the act of naming came a palpable, compassionate, mutual understanding and mourning, as if to say, "Yes, this is the world that we encounter daily." For white readers, Du Bois's task was perhaps still more difficult. First, there was the challenge of a Black author addressing a white readership. How is the perceived "problem" to address the actual problem? Does he assume a minimally shared sense of justice, integrity, honor, and decency? Does he assume solidarity or at least pretend that it is present? Does he assume that truth and beauty will prevail if depicted honestly and compellingly? Or does he simply seek to speak the truth to his white audience, regardless of consequence? Du Bois occupied all these stances. But there is an additional one. Du Bois sought to work on his white readership, to subtly cultivate and change them, such that they could see and feel—to some extent—the world of anti-Black racism, with all its suffering, cruelty, and injustice. Like Wordsworth, Du Bois sought to create a reader not formerly present: someone whose body and soul could be exposed—not temporarily transported into but opened up—to life behind the Veil, and thereby experience a praxis-oriented (not sentimental) empathy. We see this powerful endeavor—what I have called his radical aesthetics—in most of his writings but especially in such essayistic texts as those in *Darkwater* and in his poetry and short stories. Having introduced Du Bois's fiction and poetry, I now wish to linger with a few pieces from *Darkwater*.

THE POETRY AND SHORT STORIES OF *DARKWATER*: SPIRITUAL VISION AND HOPE STAINED IN BLOOD

The Prayers of God

The poem "The Prayers of God" mingles heaven and earth to such an extent that it seems impossible to distinguish between them. The poem repudiates white supremacist Christian ideology and asserts a religiosity that breaks down the rigid binaries that would separate the Divine from humans and the rest of the world. In contrast to a high white Divinity that rules over humanity while sanctioning white lords over Black people, "The Prayers of God" speaks of a Divine that suffers with and in a cruel, racist, and war-torn world. "The Prayers *of* God" expresses *God's* prayers, pain, and hope.

We saw how Wordsworth and Coleridge employed a one Life worldview that articulated a nondualistic, holistic relation between the human, the more-than-human, and the Divine. That ethical and spiritual stance often highlighted the beauty and goodness of the world and the need for humans to recognize their home in the interconnected fabric of the one Life. In "The Prayers of God," Du Bois articulated his own version of one Life theology. But unlike that of Wordsworth and Coleridge, this Du Boisian spirituality begins with the death and ugliness of the world, not its life and beauty. "Death" and "the ugly" are the companion terms to "life" and "beauty" in Du Bois's powerful chapter "Of Beauty and Death," which immediately precedes "The Prayers of God." The two compositions are related. "Of Beauty and Death" oscillates between moving accounts of life and beauty in the natural and social world and equally moving accounts of death and the (ethically) "ugly," especially that of racism and war. The chapter concludes with the mournful notion that while evil exists eternally in its incompletion, beauty triumphs only in death: "All is not beauty. Ugliness and hate and ill are here with all their contradictions and illogic; they will always be here—perhaps, God send, with lessened volume and force, but here and eternal, while beauty triumphs in its great completion—Death" (120).

"The Prayers of God" begins where "Of Beauty and Death" ends. Like beauty, God, too, is present in the finite that is near at hand, not in some distant eternality. And it is in war and hatred, in racism and greed, that revelation occurs. God, as it turns out, is in fact closer than we thought. For God is the victim of every murder and every form of racism, hatred, and economic exploitation. Spirit is not separate from the world. Spirit is fully present—and suffers accordingly.

Du Bois was attentive to the form of "The Prayers of God," which resembles the psalms of lament in the Bible, wherein the beseecher begins by invoking God and then complains to God and pleads for help in light of a particular crisis or injustice. Thus the poem starts with a white man praying to God: "Name of God's Name! / Red murder reigns; / All hell is loose; / . . . / Thou sittest, dumb" (121). As war, greed, despair, and death are covering the earth, the suppliant calls on God to no longer remain silent:

> Stand forth, unveil Thy Face,
> Pour down the light
> That seethes above Thy Throne,
> And blaze this devil's dance to darkness!
> Hear!
> Speak!
> In Christ's Great Name—
>
> (122)

And then, for the first time in his life, the white man hears and grasps a truth that turns his world upside down:

> This gold?
> I took it.
> Is it Thine?
> Forgive; I did not know.

Blood? Is it wet with blood?
'Tis from my brother's hands.
(I know; his hands are mine.)
It flowed for Thee, O Lord.

War? Not so; not war—
Dominion, Lord, and over black, not white.

(122)

The psalm of lament is suddenly interrupted by the shocking, profound revelation that the unjust wars, vicious colonial trade, and murderous oppression
were not, in fact, licensed by God for the benefit of the supposed white chosen
people. The one who started by asking God for help in the midst of a bloody catastrophe is learning that he in fact is responsible for the bloodshed. God has heard
his prayer and has spoken, and the white man responds:

I hear!
Forgive me, God!
Above the thunder I hearkened;
Beneath the silence, now,—
I hear! . . .

We murdered
To build Thy Kingdom.

(122)

But more revelation is to come. The man's *earth* has now been turned upside down:
His white supremacist worldview is exposed as vicious and categorically ungodly.
Next his understanding of *heaven*, or the divine, is turned upside down. The man
confesses:

and in Thy Name,
I lynched a [n-word]—

(He raved and writhed,
I heard him cry,

I felt the life-light leap and lie,
I saw him crackle there, on high,
I watched him wither!)

(123)

The revelation that follows announces that this horrid murder of a man is also a lynching of God:

Thou?
Thee?
I lynched Thee? . . .

That black and riven thing—was it Thee?
That gasp—was it Thine?
This pain—is it Thine?

(123)

The Divine is here, present in the finite, lynched, over and over again. The Divine is every Black innocent person who has been lynched. The religious ideology that supported white supremacy is turned on its head. The white man who prayed for God's intervention against sinners discovers that he and his kind are the sinners committing the most grievous crimes. These crimes certainly include anti-Black racism but also other forms of oppression, colonialism, and concomitant wars:

Are, then, these bullets piercing Thee?
Have all the wars of all the world,
Down all dim time, drawn blood from Thee?
Have all the lies and thefts and hates—
Is this Thy Crucifixion, God . . .
Is this Thy kingdom here, not there . . .?

(123)

The kingdom of God is here on earth, and in it, God is repeatedly crucified. This is the Divine revelation that the white sinner has been granted. He started by asking God not to sit "dumb" but to "speak!" (122). God grants his petition. What does the white man hear?

Who cries?
Who weeps?
With silent sob that rends and tears—
Can God sob?

Who prays?
I hear strong prayers throng by,
Like mighty winds on dusky moors—
Can God pray?

(123)

The white man asks to hear the voice of God, and his prayer is answered. He now hears God not as a booming voice from some faraway heaven but weeping and praying close at hand. There are two revelations at the end of the poem. God weeps, suffering with humanity and all wounded creation. But also this: God *prays*, and hence the title of the poem, "The Prayers of God."

What might God pray for? And *to whom* does *God* pray? "Prayest Thou, Lord, and to me? / *Thou* needest me? / Thou *needest* me? / Thou needest *me*?" (123). If the reader is shocked by the prayer of God, so is the white supremacist in the poem. The three italicized words express three revelatory astonishments: (1) God has *needs*, (2) God needs *humans*, and (3) God needs the *white supremacist*. I will address this surprising turn in what follows, but first I should note that to imagine a God in need of humanity and the rest of creation is, in many ways, to be in the company of Wordsworth and Coleridge and all those who would insist on an intimacy between Spirit and earth. To imagine such a God is to envision a panentheistic partnership, a universe in which Spirit and matter are radically intertwined, evolving, changing, and growing together. That is the God of Wordsworth and Coleridge and of such North American Romantics as Emerson, Fuller, and Whitman. It is an affirmation of both Spirit's material immanence and of earth's sacredness.

All this can be seen in Du Bois. God is present in the here and now ("Thy kingdom here, not there"). God is not divorced from humans and the rest of creation but is instead radically immanent, so much so that God is in the world and needs it. The earth, then, is a sacred place. Yet, for Du Bois, the proximity of God and the sacredness of the earth should make us tremble. For, insofar as the earth is sacred, Du Bois insists that it is desecrated. It is despoiled by anti-Black racism and all other forms of hatred, oppression, bigotry, and economic exploitation. We have desecrated the earth, and hence God weeps.

But "The Prayers of God" does not principally address a *generalized*, sinful humanity—a sinful "we"—but rather a particular white supremacist. And it is this white supremacist that God needs. In this remarkable turn, Du Bois declared that Spirit—justice, truth, honor, beauty—seeks out the transformation of the anti-Black racist. The corollary to this is that as long as racism persists, the earth remains desecrated. The oppressed populations of the world and their allies can perhaps create pockets of hope and justice and home, but the earth and its Spirit will mourn and suffer as long as racism persists. Hence God needs the white supremacist, transformed, to join the struggle for a just and truly beautiful earth.

What is the white supremacist's response to the prayers of God? The poem closes with: "*Courage, God, / I come!*" (123). These two concluding, optimistic lines would seem out of place in any of Du Bois's writings, but perhaps especially in a book that contains such scathing essays on white culture as "The Souls of White Folk" and "The Damnation of Women." My own view is that, in the context and form of this poem, Du Bois sought to startle the imagination by posing at the end of the poem a final astonishment: *Imagine, just imagine, the white supremacist is awakened by Spirit and seeks to become its ally. Just imagine.* Perhaps Du Bois's fierce struggle against—and despair over—anti-Black racism required, on occasion, such flights of the moral imagination. The imaginative, here, provides not only modest hope but also a resounding and instructive counterfactual to the world as we know it.

"Jesus Christ in Texas"

Like "The Prayers of God," "Jesus Christ in Texas" exposes white supremacist Christian ideology and offers an alternative version of Christianity that associates Spirit with the downtrodden, specifically with Black people suffering under white oppression. In "The Prayers of God," the white man, because of the Veil, fails to recognize Spirit for most of his life. This same theme is found in "Jesus Christ in Texas." For above all, "Jesus Christ in Texas" is a story about *recognition*: about how some and not others are able to recognize the humanity in front of them, the divinity in front of them, and the close connection between the two.

The short story begins in Waco, Texas, with four men in the twilight: a recently captured convict, the convict's guard, the colonel, and "the stranger." The Black convict is breaking up stones with a heavy hammer. The white guard convinces the white colonel that it would be in their financial interest to force the Black convict to build a new railroad line rather than pay for his room and board in prison. All the while, the stranger quietly listens and then poses the rhetorical question: "This will be a good thing for [the Black convict]?" (59). The colonel rationalizes the exploitation of the convict while also sensing something compelling and mysterious about the stranger. He offers him a ride to town and eventually invites him into his home. As they are about to get into the car, the eyes of the stranger and those of the convict meet, and "the hammer fell from his hands" (60). This is the first recognition of the stranger as divine. Jesus Christ, apparently, is in Waco, Texas.

During the next few hours, there is a series of recognitions, partial recognitions, and misrecognitions. When the stranger enters the colonel's home and is introduced to his wife and their minister, he is shown gracious hospitality, until the light is turned on: "The woman stared in amazement and the colonel half rose in anger. Why, the man was a mulatto, surely; . . . He was tall and straight and the coat looked like a Jewish gabardine. His hair hung in close curls far down the sides of his face and his face was olive, even yellow" (60). The colonel, his wife, a minister, and the guard—all these white people recognized something of importance in the stranger until their captivation turned to indignation when his complexion and race were revealed. Only in the dark—in the absence of color—can they achieve a partial recognition of the humanity and divinity in the Christ figure, the person of the stranger.

There is an exception: The colonel's young child is immediately drawn to the stranger, and she continues to desire his company even with the lights on. Could it be that this child, thus far, has not been thoroughly trained in the ways of the Veil? She embodies that trope of Romanticism so prominent in Wordsworth, Emerson, and now Du Bois—the Child who has a fresh relation to the world and has yet to be corrupted by vicious habits, practices, and beliefs, that is, corrupted by a vicious *second nature*. The child, then, still has the capacity to recognize the humanity and divinity of those around her and innocently wishes to spend time with and play with the stranger.

There are examples of partial recognition of the stranger. The minister, even with the light on, says to the stranger, "Surely, I know you, I have met you somewhere" (61). But the stranger responds, "I never knew you." For a passing moment, a guest in the home thinks that she sees "the shadow of great, white wings" behind the stranger (61). These are fleeting glimpses of recognition that generate no appropriate response. The Black adults in the story, however, exhibit a full recognition of the stranger and respond robustly. The colonel's Black butler, for example, upon seeing the stranger, feels a "sudden gladness," drops to his knees, and whispers, "My Lord and my God!" (60). The Black nurse in the household runs down the staircase, clutches the stranger's cloak, and "kneeled in the dust" (61). He blesses her, and with a glad cry, she leaves the house and "turned north, running" (61). *Running to freedom* is one of many examples of what I mean by a "robust response" to a full recognition of the stranger.

Full recognition, here, goes both ways: the Black adults recognize the Christ figure, while the Christ figure recognizes the Black people's humanity. Such mutual recognition has intrinsic value. It appropriately honors and does justice to the parties involved. But this Christ figure, who is at the heart of facilitating such full recognition, is no miracle worker in the traditional or sentimental sense of the term. Social and racial justice, for example, do not pour down from Heaven and set all right. Does the nurse who runs to freedom obtain it? Does the butler escape his servitude? And what of the convict? Does the Christ figure save him from cruel captivity?

As the stranger leaves the colonel's home, to the great relief of his hosts, bloodhounds are heard. The minister comments casually, "Another one of those convicts escaped. . . . Really, they need severer measures" (62). The convict has escaped, and the stranger seeks and finds him just as the bloodhounds do: "A greyhound shot out of the woods behind him, howled, whined, and fawned before the stranger's feet. Hound after hound bayed, leapt, and lay there; then silently, one by one, and with bowed heads, they crept backward toward the town" (62). The bloodhounds honor the Christ figure and stop their pursuit of the convict. This is an act of recognition with a robust response. The dogs, these more-than-human creatures, join the ranks of those able to recognize the stranger. In doing so, the rigid binaries that would radically separate the human, the nonhuman, and the divine are torn down, or at least blurred.

After the Christ figure bathes the head of the convict, unfetters him from his chains, and conceals "the prison stripes" by wrapping him in his own cloak, the convict finds employment on a farm. It is a new day, and the convict works with great integrity (62). But circumstances quickly turn against him. Later that night, the white wife of the farmer and the Black convict accidentally collide in the dark on a path. The white farmer yells to the convict guard and his mob: "He— attacked—my wife,' ... The mob snarled and worked silently. Right to the limb of the red oak they hoisted the struggling, writhing black man" (63-64).

Immediately before this, the farmer's wife is in conversation with the stranger. Like the other white adults in the story, she is initially attracted to the stranger in the night. There is a partial recognition. But when he begins to press her to extend Christian neighborly love to local Blacks living in destitution, she lights a lamp, sees his "dark face and curly hair," "shrieked in angry terror," and runs away into the dark (64). And that is how she happens to collide with the Black convict. It is one blind act of racism, among many, that braids the rope of the Black man's death.

At the end of the story, the white woman is afforded a full recognition of the Christ figure. Recovering inside her home, she feels compelled to look out the window. Behind the dead, lynched Black convict, she sees "hung the stranger on the crimson cross, riven and blood-stained, with thorn-crowned head and pierced hands" (64). In an agony of tears, she proclaims, "Despised and rejected of men"—a biblical passage from Isaiah 53:3 that Christians commonly associate with Jesus as the suffering servant. What is her robust response to this gift of revelation? All we are told is that she "stretched her arms and shrieked" (64). There is little hope here of repentance and change. As for the hope of a better life for the tortured, Black convict, the final words of the story are from the stranger on the cross to the dead convict: "This day thou shalt be with me in Paradise!" (64).

Paradise has historically played an important role in Black religious traditions in the United States. It has offered some comfort and hope to a people who had little comfort or reason for hope in a cruel world. Du Bois, of course, knew of this form of religious solace so prevalent in the Sorrow Songs, and he honored it (even if he himself took no or little metaphysical comfort in an otherworldly paradise). Yet there is another function of *paradise*, or the *kingdom of God*, that is found in Black spiritual traditions, one that Du Bois frequently utilized. The Kingdom of God stands in judgment of the racial injustice in the world. The Black convict and the mixed-race stranger are associated with the Kingdom of God and its justice, while those who, in one way or another, crucify them are associated with divine condemnation. "This day thou shalt be with me in Paradise!" are not only words of comfort but of fierce critique.

As in "The Prayers of God," so in "Jesus Christ in Texas": White supremacists have lynched the divine and those associated with the divine.[16] The Christ figure and the oppressed Black humans are tortured and murdered. They share Spirit and they share crucifixion—that is, humiliation, oppression, torture, and murder. They mutually recognize Spirit in each other. Indeed, Spirit breaks down the divide between the Christ figure and Black humans. Again, then, in the work of Du Bois, the rigid binary between humanity and divinity is challenged.

The essay that immediately precedes and is paired with "Jesus Christ in Texas" concludes with these words: "In fine, can we not, black and white, rich and poor, look forward to a world of Service without Servants? A miracle! you say? True. And only to be performed by the Immortal Child" (58). "The Immortal Child" signifies Du Bois's this-worldly, heavenly hope: a liberatory, bright future for this world.

The chapter in *Darkwater* titled "The Immortal Child" begins with these words: "If a man die shall he live again? We do not know. But this we do know, that our children's children live forever and grow and develop toward perfection as they are trained. All human problems, then, center in the Immortal Child and his education is the problem of problems" (95). Du Bois argued that Black children deserve a broad, high-quality liberal arts education to help them flourish as individuals and democratic citizens. Such an education would, among other things, address institutional racism and how to dismantle it. It would include practical skills, but the emphasis would not be on how to train students "as servants and laborers and mechanics to increase the land's industrial efficiency" (102). Ultimately, it would "aim to develop human souls; to make all intelligent; to discover special talents and genius" (101). This is the education that Black children are denied yet deserve.

But about two-thirds of the way though the chapter, Du Bois asks, "But why am I talking simply of 'colored' children? Is not the problem of their education simply an intensification of the problem of educating all children?" (103). Du Bois concludes the chapter by stating that if the world is to make the "future safe," then it must educate "the Immortal Child. And that child is of all races and all colors. All children are the children of all and not of individuals and families and races" (106). It's clear, then, that the "Immortal Child" is all children and the "infinite possibilities"—alternative futures—that they represent.

And so, in "The Immortal Child," Du Bois asks, "Is democracy a failure? Train up citizens that will make it succeed. . . . Train [women] as workers and thinkers and not as playthings, lest future generations ape our worst mistake. Do we despise darker races? Teach the children its fatal cost in spiritual degradation and murder, teach them that to hate [Black and Chinese people] is to crucify souls like their own" (104). In these lines, Du Bois implored his readers to honor the child, to acknowledge the child's spirit, and to educate the child to love justice, work for democracy, and abjure misogyny and racism. Anything short of such humane training is to inflict on them "spiritual degradation."

The white daughter of the colonel is among "the immortal children." She is yet to be fully trained in the ways of racism and hatred. Her spirit is relatively intact, and hence she can still recognize the divine, discern the everyday miracle of the presence of Spirit in the world. For the daughter, whiteness is not the definition of divinity. It is easy and natural for her to see the dark stranger as love and Spirit. Du Bois's hope is in this child and all children, that is, in the future that they *potentially* represent. This hope is not in a replication of the present but an alternative future in which humanity is at one with Spirit and in which white supremacy, racism, and misogyny have no place. "The Immortal Child" was Du Bois's hope, but it was a dark, wild hope. It nurtured his work and vision, and it was rooted in a world where a Black Jesus Christ is lynched by a white mob. The hope offers no answer to the question: Will the white colonel's daughter eventually join the lynching mob? Hope does not answer questions; it only asks them.

"The Comet"

In Du Bois's speculative fiction piece "The Comet," there is another "white daughter" on whom some hope rests, at least momentarily, before that hope is shattered by the realities of white supremacy. "The Comet" begins with *how things are* (that is, with the solidity of anti-Black racism), moves to *how things could be* (a new age in which racism and anthropocentricism dissolves), and concludes abruptly by returning to *how things are*. Hope is located perilously between the first and third moment of *how things are*—that is, hope between the hard, cruel facts of racism in North America. Drawing on religious and biblical themes, Du Bois depicted a world free of racism and anthropocentrism. We are presented with a new Eve and Adam in a postanthropocentric world created by a great catastrophe. The agency of the more-than-human appears to be the only means to eradicate racism, but at a terrible price. By means of a fictional primordial couple and new world, Du Bois offered a glimpse of Spirit, humanity, and the more-than-human coming together at the end of history, or at least at the end of racist history.

"The Comet" starts with a Black man who is both invisible and hypervisible: "Few ever noticed him save in a way that stung" (124). His name is Jim, but the narrator initially refers to him as "the messenger." Angels are messengers, and this particular messenger will bring a message to the world not with trumpets blaring but with a quiet integrity. Having descended into the dark depths of New York City, he will emerge in the light of a new age and earn his place as the new Adam.

He works in a bank, and the president of the bank sends him into "the lower vaults" to look for some records (124). The narrator notes that this task is "too dangerous for more valuable men." The vaults are dark, damp, dirty, and rickety. And so Jim descends into "the bowels of the earth, under the world." While Jim is below, the tail of a comet passes over the earth and poisons it with its gases. Underneath the city, Jim hears a "boom" and eventually notices a strange odor (125).

After much struggle, Jim finally emerges from the depths and discovers dead bodies wherever he looks and goes. It is the first time in his life he can move freely through the city without the scourge of racism. At one point he realizes that he is hungry and enters a restaurant to find some food: "'Yesterday, they would not have served me,' he whispered" (126). His freedom from racism, however, comes at a heavy price: He is all alone, and everywhere he hears only silence.

Yet the silence is suddenly broken by a woman's voice: "The human voice sounded in his ears like the voice of God" (127). In the midst of cataclysm, when all of humankind and history seem to be suspended or erased, Jim hears the woman's voice as divine, subtly registering the interconnectedness of the human and Spirit. But that subtle recognition is short-lived. Jim runs to the aid of the woman who is screaming, "Hello—hello—help," but when they come face to face, silence returns: "They stared a moment in silence. She had not noticed before that he was a Negro. He had not thought of her as white. . . . Yesterday, he thought with bitterness, she would scarcely have looked at him twice. He would have been dirt beneath her silken feet. . . . Of all the sorts of men she had pictured as coming to her rescue she had not dreamed of one like him" (127).

Eventually, the two of them—Jim, the Black man, and Julia, the white woman—drive around the city in search of life, but "everywhere was silence and death—death and silence!" (128). They go to the central telephone exchange in an attempt to contact someone, anyone: "'Hello!'. . . . Would the world *answer*?

Was the world—Silence!" (129). A terrible silence is how they hear a world without humans: a dreadful, anthropocentric silence. The comet, the natural agency of the more-than-human, silences the anthropocentric world.

And then it happens: The anthropocentric silence, death, and despair subtly shift or give way to a more ecocentric world of silence, reverence, and hope. The anthropocentric world is gone, but a new, more inclusive world is preparing to welcome the new human couple: Jim and Julia now "seemed to move in a world silent and asleep,—not dead. They moved in quiet reverence.... All nature slept until—" (130). The more-than-human is quiet, resting, and waiting *until* Jim and Julia fathom "the vision of a mighty beauty": The couple, Black and white, can begin humankind anew in a freshly awakened, nonanthropocentric world. And they are now able to hear more than silence in the new world. They hear "the lapping of the waters," "where the water called below," the waters that speak of a new world and that swallowed up the old one that "lies beneath the waters now" (130). They perceive the "mighty beauty"—spirit, humanity, and the more-than-human intertwining and conspiring for the sake of a new beginning, vision, and hope. The more-than-human is not depicted as outside humanity but as an integral feature of the human/divine drama. The announcement of the new bridal couple and fresh beginning for humanity is proclaimed by a star: "Low on the horizon lay a long, white star—mystic, wonderful!" (132).

This more-than-human agent, the bright star, brings the message of a new beginning—a message of hope. The agency of the star thereby joins the agency of the comet. Nothing less than the end of human history is required for the white woman to grasp the senselessness of racism and the humanity—and spirit-filled nature—of Jim. And the agency required to erase racism is located in the more-than-human, namely, in the comet and the star, among other entities. Sometimes called an act of God, the comet brings both justice and a fresh start. The more-than-human bestows on Jim the recognition of his humanity. Now that the anthropocentric world has been destroyed, Julia has new perspective: "How foolish our human distinctions seem—now," and Jim responds, "Yes—I was not—human, yesterday" (131). It is the new, ecocentric world that allows Jim to be fully human. Ecocentrism is not antihuman.

When Jim notes that death is "the leveler!" Julia responds, "And the revealer":

A vision of the world had risen before her. Slowly the mighty prophecy of her destiny overwhelmed her. Above the dead past hovered the Angel of

Annunciation.... She was neither high nor low, white nor black, rich nor poor. She was primal woman; mighty mother of all men to come and Bride of Life. She looked upon the man beside her and forgot all else but his manhood.... She saw him glorified. He was no longer a thing apart, a creature below, a strange outcast of another clime and blood, but her Brother Humanity incarnate, Son of God and great All-Father of the race to be.

(131)

Before the comet erased human history, the enactment of this spiritual vision—a Black man marrying a white woman—had been a felony. Until as recently as 1967, sixteen states still deemed interracial marriage a crime.[17] But with the sudden erasure of such cruel laws and all that they mean, the union of Jim and Julia is "a thought divine, splendid" (132).

Here Du Bois reached for and employed religious images and themes to show not only the *injustice* of racism but also the *beauty* of a postracist, postanthropocentric world, crafting a utopian futurity that inspires ethical possibility by imagining profound social, political, and environmental transformation. In "The Comet," justice and beauty unite in what Du Bois considered to be the truth of "the mighty human rainbow of the world," a phrase from the concluding poem of *Darkwater* (134). Justice was always Du Bois's first priority, but he also sought, by means of aesthetics, to portray the beauty of a world free of racism, patriarchy, economic oppression, and anthropocentricism. Spirit, or the divine, is depicted as the *earthly* locus for both justice and beauty, just as Jim is described as "Son of God"—as "Humanity incarnate"—and the more-than-human is depicted as a vital agent and integral feature of the divine-human drama.

Yet the promise of the new couple and an antiracist world is dashed with the arrival of Julia's father and a group of white men. As it turns out, the anthropocentric world did not come to an end—"only New York" (132). Jim is called the n-word and is almost lynched. Julia does state, quietly, that Jim rescued her, but she "did not look at him again" (133). As Jim makes his way past the mob, a bystander cries out, "Well, what do you think of that? ... of all New York, just a white girl and a [n-word]!" So much for Julia's revelation and transformation. It lasted only as long as the comet had temporarily eclipsed racism's grip on the present. There was a brief moment of freedom, beauty, and justice as the Veil was lifted and removed. But the cataclysm was not total, history and the status quo returned, and the Veil fell back to earth.

"The Comet" is the last chapter in *Darkwater*, and it is the only chapter that does not pair a discursive essay with a short story or poem. Clearly, as Du Bois sought to bring his book to a conclusion, he looked to the future—a speculative, fictional future. He employed the moral imagination to create something new: a postracial and postanthropocentric world. This imaginative act fashions a titanic conditional: "Imagine, just imagine, if *this* were to happen." By means of this fantastical story, Du Bois intimated that humanity could perhaps overcome racism if given a fresh start. He crafted a utopian futurity that inspires ethical possibility by imagining profound social and political transformation. This speculative fiction is an exercise in hope. The story is an exercise in the education of the "Immortal Child," for each birth, however modestly, represents humanity's chance at a fresh start. To those who will populate the next generation, the story announces—as might a biblical angel—this could be your future.

The form of this hope, however, is but another example of dark, wild hope—hope rooted in death, vulnerability, and despair. After all, the hopeful vision requires a cataclysmic event. The immensity of the catastrophe is but an indication of the immensity of "the Veil"—that catastrophe—and the challenge to overcome it. And the hopeful vision of a postracial, postanthropocentric world is situated precariously between the racist world before and after the comet's destruction. The hope is provisional, conditional, vulnerable, even "fantastic." This is not to discount the work and practice of such a precarious, dark hope. It is only to make clear that when Du Bois looks to the future, the sight is neither clear, nor certain, nor optimistic. A postracist world is far from an inevitable future. "The Comet"—the culminating chapter of *Darkwater*—looks forward, offering a powerful vision of justice and beauty. Yet in the end, the future looks gravely like the present and the past.

"A Hymn to the Peoples"

Du Bois chose to conclude *Darkwater* with his poem "A Hymn to the Peoples." As an aesthetic form, hymns are religious songs or poems that express a people's praise of the divine but also their profound sorrow and joy, their despair and hope. Hymns are built on and create solidarity—even when sung in private, as when the slave moved alone in the woods to run an errand, singing "wild songs, revealing at once the highest joy and the deepest sadness," to quote Frederick Douglass.[18] Du Bois's concluding poem is no different from other hymns, except that it is a hymn *to the peoples*. It is not a hymn of one people or religion but a hymn of many peoples and their many faiths. Moreover, although the hymn is at times addressed to "Lord of Lands and Seas!" and to "World-Spirit," it is also addressed "to the Peoples" and concludes with these lines: "Help us, O Human God, in this Thy Truce, / To make Humanity divine!" (135). The hymn, then, is addressed to both an immanent divinity and a divine humanity.

This ambiguity is fitting of a spirituality that does not conform to the rigid divine/human binary. The poem also refuses the simplistic, religious/secular binary. Once again, Du Bois's poetry and fiction resist the facile impulse to categorize complex human belief and practice into one of two categories, secular or religious. Neither an orthodox Christian nor a conventional atheist, Du Bois intricately interwove religious and secular language, yielding a spiritual sensibility that speaks of a "World-Spirit"—a spirituality not unlike the Romantic panentheistic one Life. But if this Du Boisian sensibility is akin to one Life spirituality, it also breaks from it. For "World-Spirit," found in the last lines of a book that details the pain and sorrow of anti-Black racism, would seem to repudiate the gentle, "healthy-minded" presence of Wordsworth's and Coleridge's one Life spirituality.

"A Hymn to the Peoples" is a plea for the diverse peoples of the world to join in solidarity and confess their sins, repenting of them in order that war, hatred, and racism would cease. This Promethean task—that humans change their ways—requires that humans become godlike. Once again, as in "The Comet," the measure of the vast challenge (to overcome oppression) is shown by the immensity of what is required (to become godlike). The hymn is an appeal to both the divine and humans to "make Humanity Divine!"

The poem begins:

> O Truce of God!
> And primal meeting of the Sons of Man,
> Foreshadowing the union of the World!
> From all the ends of earth we come!
> Old Night, the elder sister of the Day,
> Mother of Dawn in the golden East,
> Meets in the misty twilight with her brood,
> Pale and black, tawny, red and brown,
> The mighty human rainbow of the world,
> Spanning its wilderness of storm.

(134)

The "truce" is *the break from suffering*—the radical, transformative *disruption*—that is to come at dawn, at the potential beginning of a new era. As in "The Comet," the new era is a postracist time, its harbinger being when "Pale and black, tawny, red and brown / The mighty human rainbow of the world" comes together, "spanning its wilderness of storm," and prefigures the solidarity of a possible New World. *That* is the vision, the conclusion, that Du Bois offers in *Darkwater*.

Religiously, it is ecumenically in the spirit of the one Life: "So sit we all as one. / So, gloomed in tall and stone-swathed groves, / The Buddha walks with Christ! / And Al-Koran and Bible both be holy!" (134). The temporal tones of the poem are futuristic, centering on the light that shines at dawn and the starlight that pierces the dark night, announcing the daylight that is to come: "And on the darkest midnight blaze the stars— / The far-flown shadows of whose brilliance / Drop like a dream on the dim shores of Time, / Forecasting Days that are to these / As day to night" (134). There is in the poem, then, much future light—"*Forecasting Days*" that will bring humanity out of the present darkness. But this future light is matched by the present pain and despair caused by moral evil—by cruel human deeds. The poem accuses humans of murder, greed, hypocrisy, tyranny, and of despising "*the Soul that breathes within*" (134; emphasis added). The accusation is that humans have departed from their Soul-full, spirit-filled status, bringing destruction and ruin to fellow humans.

It is noteworthy that Du Bois begins "Of Our Spiritual Strivings," the first chapter in *The Souls of Black Folk*, with these lines from Arthur Symons: "O water, voice of my heart . . . All night long crying with a mournful cry."[19] He then pairs *the mournful cry* with musical notation from the Sorrow Song, "No Body Knows the Trouble That I've Seen." For Du Bois, a mournful cry is central to religion and to Black spiritual striving. It is a characteristic *form* of the hymn, especially of the Sorrow Songs and what William James described as "sick-soul" religion (see chapter 4, note 26).

Hence the poem closes with these lines: "We see . . . the poverty of Wealth, / We know the Anarchy of Empire, . . . / . . . / Save us, World-Spirit, from our lesser selves! / Grant us that war and hatred cease, / Reveal our souls in every race and hue! / Help us, O Human God, in this Thy Truce, / To make Humanity divine!" (135). This is a plea for "World-Spirit" to raise humans up from their criminal ways and deliver them from racism, hatred, and war. "World-Spirit," we have seen, is in many ways resonant with Wordsworth's and Coleridge's "one Life within us and abroad / . . . / At once the Soul of each, and God of all."[20] Spirit is immanent, belonging to humans, yet also somehow transcends humans, at least transcending their "lesser selves." Spirit, then, is neither identical to nor alien to humankind: Both alterity and commonality are present. This "World-Spirit" that troubles the strict human/divine binary is powerfully expressed in the final two lines: "Help us, O Human God . . . To make Humanity divine!" The divine *in* and *of* humanity is called on to assist humanity in achieving their status as Spirit-filled, soulful creatures. Perhaps only when humans gather together in a revolutionary truce—in a disruptive break from violence and hatred—will the divinity of humans be revealed. In that event, we perceive the "Human God"—a phrase that radically upends the secular/religious binary.

"A Hymn to the Peoples" is clearly a plea for global peace and racial harmony—that "the mighty human rainbow of the world" would prevail over hatred and bigotry. The poem was initially written for the occasion of the 1911 Universal Races Congress, an international event held in London that was dedicated to combating racism and fostering mutual understanding between "the peoples of the West and those of the East."[21] Knowing the occasion for which the poem was written elucidates the "universal," ecumenical nature of the poem, including such lines as: "The Buddha walks with Christ! / And Al-Koran and Bible both be holy!" It would be a mistake, however, to limit the significance of the poem to the event that initially occasioned it. Du Bois *chose* to conclude *Darkwater* with it. He ended *Darkwater* with a vision of—and an entreaty for—hope and unity. We must acknowledge Du Bois's choice here.

We must also, however, consider another context of "A Hymn to the Peoples," and that is the entirety of *Darkwater* itself. The poem concludes the chapter "The Comet," a short story that shoots troubling arrows through "the mighty human rainbow of the world." "The Comet," too, offered a vision of hope and unity, only to abruptly shatter it. Du Bois's hopeful visions—as well as his Romantic spirituality—are always tempered and forged in realities of pain and injustice. In *Darkwater*, such realities are powerfully depicted when Du Bois writes of how Black women are abused and oppressed variously by white men and women but also by Black men. In the essay chapters "Of the Ruling of Men" and especially "The Damnation of Women," Du Bois mounts arguments for the dignity and rights of women in light of unjust oppression. These arguments are greatly enhanced by the short stories that accompany the chapters' essays. In "The Call," the short story that accompanies "Of the Ruling of Men," a solitary Black woman courageously answers the call of God (and God, it turns out, is also Black). In the short story "The Children of the Moon," which accompanies "The Damnation of Women," we again have a brave Black woman who skillfully leads Black men to their freedom. These short stories, in conjunction with the essays, depict not only the suffering and oppression of Black women but also their wisdom, strength, and mighty achievements. The essays and short stories *move* readers to grasp this imaginative horizon: If Black women can achieve such leadership and accomplishments under conditions of brutal oppression, think of how the world would benefit from them should they be released from their unjust chains and burdens.

Again, however, reality runs up against vision. In the "The Children of the Moon," for example, the powerful Black woman leader works to liberate her people, but she herself can only glance from afar at the freedom for which she fought. The vision of freedom and hence hope is rooted in the liberatory work of this Black, female Moses figure, but racist and misogynist reality determines the story's conclusion. This tense, tragic commingling of vision and reality is perhaps most powerfully displayed in the poem "The Riddle of the Sphinx." This poem accompanies the trenchant essay "The Souls of White Folk" in chapter 2 of *Darkwater*. In that essay, Du Bois crafts a persuasive and moving account of Euro-American white people systematically oppressing people of color globally. White empires claim global privilege and possession: "Then always, somehow, some way, silently but clearly, I am given to understand that *whiteness is the ownership of the earth* forever and ever, Amen!" (16; emphasis added). The intensity of the critique of whiteness in the essay continues and flows into the accompanying poem, "The Riddle of the Sphinx." The white empires—"The white world's vermin and filth"—are "spoilers of women" and "unarmed men" (26). This empirical reality, so forcefully described and judged ("I hate them, Oh! / I hate them well"), will one day be challenged when "the black Christ be born!" and "daughters of evensong" sing, "Black mother of the iron hills that ward the blazing sea, / Wild spirit of a storm-swept soul, a-struggling to be free, / Where 'neath the bloody fingermarks thy riven bosom quakes, / Thicken the thunders of God's Voice and lo! a world awakes!" (27). The Black mother with her *wild* spirit, "a-struggling to be free," and the Black Christ will jointly awaken the world. "God's Voice" announces hope, newness, and change, but in the midst of "the bloody fingermarks." Again, Du Bois deliberately brings together, tensely, two sets of existential affect: the despair and anxiety of struggle and oppression and the resilience and hope of new, liberatory ways of life. A religious vocabulary is employed to capture both sides of this tragic equation. Romantic, panentheistic, one Life spirituality is engraved and stained by bloody finger marks.

The white empire has brought and will bring suffering to the four corners of the earth, "Till the devil's strength be shorn" by the Black mother and the Black Christ (27). In the context of the poem's simultaneous holding together of hope and despair, vision and reality, the final lines of the poem seem less about a *future* time than a *continuous process* of suffering, struggle, and "awakening." That process, among other things, relies on a cooperation between the human and the divine, or perhaps on a divine understanding of the human and a human understanding of the divine. In either case, Du Bois rejected the rigid human/divine binary as well as the despair/hope binary. In its place, we find a dark, wild hope animated by an immanent spiritual vision in the context of struggle and suffering.

DANCING ON A FLAMING WORLD

In this chapter, I have focused on the role of religion and form in Du Bois's poetry and short stories. Like Wordsworth and Coleridge, Du Bois defied destructive binaries that radically separate the human from the divine and the human and the divine from the natural world. His "naturalistic," Romantic spirituality conceived of the divine as working immanently in humans, history, and the natural world. Moreover, like the Romantics before him, Du Bois used *form* and *cultivation* in pursuit of liberatory aims. He employed and uniquely inhabited the forms of poetry, hymns, psalms, and biblical stories, producing vivid, striking social critique that revealed the shape and horror of white supremacy. When faced with deep-seated, persistent anti-Black racism that was immune to "reason" and other forms of "enlightenment" via social scientific or scholarly arguments, Du Bois employed literary forms in an attempt to address both the mind and heart, the reason and affect, of his white readership. Like Wordsworth, he sought to cultivate in his readers a range of pathos, affect, and praxis-oriented empathy. This attempt was for the sake of social change but also a powerful form of *truth telling*. Whether or not his white audience would listen or understand, Du Bois would speak the truth to them in a language full of powerful imagery, concrete characters, and compelling narratives. At the same time, for his Black readers, Du Bois would honor their struggle and suffering, their victories and achievements with poetry and short stories that centered their experiences under white supremacy—behind the Veil. He would also offer them a complex, dark, wild hope.

Du Bois offered his art to promote existential understanding, social critique, and social change. As we saw in chapter 1, Du Bois was adamant that art—and specifically Black art—should have a robust role in civic engagement. Further, Du Bois celebrated not only various forms of Black art but *Black lives* as works of art. Consider this passage from his autobiography, *Dusk of Dawn*: "Art is not simply works of art; it is the spirit that knows Beauty, that has music in its soul and the color of sunsets in its headkerchiefs; that can dance on a flaming world and make the world dance, too. Such is the soul of the Negro."[22] Here, Du Bois described art as the matter and manners of daily lives. The everyday courage, struggle, beauty, and spirit of Black lives are honored as forms of art. Du Bois's own art—in the written word—attempted to convey the richness of this day-to-day, living Black art. It is an art that experiences and expresses the "flaming" world—a world on fire with such infernos as racism—but also that dances "on a flaming world" and even makes "the world dance."

Art that dances in morning and mourning, that honors the everyday and every-day people, that reaches hearts and minds, that critiques and transforms—such is the aesthetic of radical Romanticism. Du Bois belongs to this tradition even as he transforms it.[23]

CHAPTER 6

Ecofeminism and the Expansion and Transformation of Radical Romanticism

In this chapter, I present Mary Shelley (1796–1851), Margaret Fuller (1810–1850), and Zora Neale Hurston (1891–1960) as ecofeminists who craft distinctive themes and forms of writing designed to reveal and combat patriarchy, racism, and androcentrism. I interpret Shelley and Fuller as radical Romantics and Hurston as having a strong family resemblance to radical Romanticism. As noted in previous chapters, radical Romanticism is an ongoing, dynamic set of traditions. It does not belong to one era in European history. Moreover, just as Du Bois expanded and transformed radical Romanticism beyond its commitment to abolitionism, by bringing to it the trauma and oppression of anti-Black racism, so too Shelley, Fuller, and Hurston expand and transform it by addressing patriarchy and misogyny. Du Bois certainly brought more attention to the oppression and resilience of women, especially Black women, than did such Romantics as Rousseau, Wordsworth, or Coleridge. Nonetheless, Du Bois's analysis and depiction of the suffering, oppression, dignity, and power of women is limited in comparison to that of Shelley, Fuller, and Hurston. Moreover, their resistance to patriarchy discloses the shared, interrelated oppression of women, Black people, Native Americans, and the more-than-human.

This chapter focuses on the distinctive *context*, *form*, and *content* of selected works, specifically Shelley's *Frankenstein* (1818) and *The Last Man* (1826), Fuller's *Summer on the Lakes* (1844) and *New York Tribune* reviews and essays, and Hurston's *Their Eyes Were Watching God* (1937). I name the radical Romantic, ecofeminist form and content—and the connection between the two—of these texts, and I characterize them as rooted in and responding to a context of catastrophe. While I do bring attention to the continuities between their work and other radical

Romantics, I mostly explore the innovations that their work introduces. Such innovations include pushing back against patriarchal *forms* of writing (e.g., the linear argument yielding a tidy, determinate conclusion) by creating ecofeminist forms that are variegated weaves of genres, temporalities, and spatialities that produce robust critique and life-affirming ways of being. The innovations also include such themes or *content* as the confluence of nature, women, and other marginalized people such as Black and Indigenous peoples as targets of patriarchal oppression and exploitation.

As we will see, the ecofeminism of Shelley, Fuller, and Hurston has wide implications for the radical Romantic aesthetic that seeks to cultivate such capacities as attention, care, reciprocity, and transformative justice between humans and between humans and the more-than-human. In the pages that follow, I begin by discussing the *context, form, and content* of their writings. It is heuristically helpful to distinguish context, form, and content, yet these three are in fact interwoven in our authors' multifaceted literature. Next, I discuss each author separately, allowing me to selectively highlight central aspects of their radical Romantic ecofeminism. I interpret Shelley, Fuller, and Hurston as powerful feminist storytellers. As such, I see my role largely as a listener and curator of their stories as I seek to craft my own narrative about the ongoing traditions and ways of radical Romanticism.

CONTEXT, FORM, AND CONTENT: THE MANNER AND MATTERS OF RADICAL ROMANTIC ECOFEMINISM

Catastrophe is the setting or context of the central works of Shelley, Fuller, and Hurston. Each author crafts compelling storied landscapes rooted in and responding to the crises and ruins that come from patriarchy, pandemic, extermination, deluge, racism, war, and assaults on the natural world.

Shelley's *The Last Man* depicts a plague that kills off every human except for Lionel Verney, the presumed "last man." *Frankenstein* tells of the nefarious, furtive creation and subsequent cruel treatment of the creature (the human, non-human "monster") by his creator. "How can I describe my emotions at this *catastrophe*," reports Victor Frankenstein as he beholds his living creation for the first time.[1] Shelley, however, had a larger, societal catastrophe in mind: the consequences of the dominant patriarchal mastery that oppresses women and the more-than-human alike. Margaret Fuller, that Transcendental radical Romantic, wrote in *Summer on the Lakes* and elsewhere of the catastrophic extermination of Native Americans, the oppression of women, slaves, and prisoners, and the exploitation of the more-than-human—catastrophes wrought by patriarchal, settler-colonial industrialization, and expansionism. And Zora Neale Hurston, the gifted lyricist-anthropologist, forged radical Romantic narratives in *Their Eyes Were Watching God* that speak of catastrophic anti-Black racism, misogyny, and environmental racism (announced by a flood of biblical proportions).

Pandemics, floods, exterminations—how is a female literary artist to conjure and portray worlds ruined by catastrophes brought on or exacerbated by patriarchy? What *forms* of writing are called for, especially given patriarchal constraints on women and women writers? The forms would be nonconventional, nonpatriarchal, and have the power to move and challenge people: to reveal to them promising perspectives and ways of life that acknowledge and confront current catastrophes and avert or mitigate future ones. In a word, the forms would be feminist. Shelley, Fuller, and Hurston well understood the various ways that patriarchal culture attempted to silence or constrain women's voices. If they must write, they were to conform to genres deemed suitable for women—private journals, moralistic children's literature, domestic and sentimental novels. Our three authors painfully felt these constraints and bravely pushed back against them, creating new forms of writing and writing transgressively in such traditional genres as "the sentimental novel." At times they inhabited genres usually available only to male authors, yet they invariably unsettled gender-coded genres and ultimately created new forms of writing.[2]

Their authorship, of course, is voluminous, diverse, and resists oversimplification. The selected, central works that I focus on are richly textured, complex weaves that refuse male demands for deductive arguments warranting definitive conclusions or for unified narratives that follow a linear trajectory to deliver unambiguous judgments and resolutions. Their transgressive, feminist forms are useful vessels for marginalized voices seeking to express their difference in all its pain and beauty and power. The transgressive forms participate in radical Romantic storytelling: the crafting of multifaceted, storied landscapes as haunting sites of suffering and injustice that cry out for witness and justice. In the previous chapter, Du Bois exemplified such storytelling, emphasizing the catastrophe of anti-Black racism and the resilience and strength of Black individuals and communities; in the following chapter, we will see Leslie Marmon Silko employ the art of storytelling to bring attention to the catastrophe of anti-Indigeneity and settler colonialism and to the resilience of Indigenous peoples. In this chapter, we see a feminist art of radical Romantic storytelling, limning the catastrophe of interrelated patriarchy, racism, and environmental destruction as well as the strength of women.

Even as ecofeminist storytelling reveals the multidimensions of the catastrophic, it also offers imaginative resources for joy, resistance, and even hope. Complex, multilayered storytelling, then, is a form of radical Romantic ecofeminism. The content of their stories may in some cases be deemed "fiction" (Shelley's *Frankenstein*, for example, or Hurston's *Their Eyes Were Watching God*), but as seen in previous chapters, the distinction between fiction and nonfiction is not especially salient in radical Romanticism. Rather, a greater premium is put on the contrast between authentic and inauthentic, honest and dishonest, liberatory and oppressive. Storytelling, whether in the form of fiction or creative nonfiction, can imaginatively illuminate past and present sources of suffering and injustice, hope and resistance. Radical Romantic storytelling, however fantastic, is rooted in and speaks to the everyday.

Radical Romantic ecofeminist storytelling is a difficult art form. Among other things, it requires much research on and attentiveness to the worlds in which one is embedded—worlds of joy and loss, freedom and domination, healthy land and lands exploited. Our three feminist authors were tireless researchers. Mary Shelley studied the newest scientific advancements in chemistry, psychology, medicine, and physics, including the properties of magnetism and electricity. Margaret Fuller, the first woman permitted to conduct research at the Harvard College Library, immersed herself in the study of geography, history, literature, and especially Native American cultures. And Zora Neale Hurston—who studied at Howard, Barnard, and Columbia; won two Guggenheim Fellowships; and worked with Franz Boas, Ruth Benedict, and Margaret Mead—was a forward-looking cultural anthropologist who brought her expertise in Black folklore to every page of her novel *Their Eyes Were Watching God*. The art of these ecofeminists is grounded in critical inquiry and keen observation.

In this chapter, I focus on Shelley's and Hurston's fiction and on Fuller's creative nonfiction. "True stories well told," that is, true stories crafted "in a compelling, vivid, dramatic matter"—this is how Lee Gutkind defines the form of creative nonfiction.[3] It's an apt definition that I'd also like to apply to Shelley's and Hurston's fictional novels. For they, too, tell the truth about beauty and domination in the world, and they do so in a radical Romantic, dramatic fashion. The characters and events express *dramatic veracity*—a central aspect of the radical Romantic ecofeminist form. It tells stories in a compelling form to engage our whole self—heart and mind, affect and intellect—reminding us of things known, revealing to us things unearthed. As readers, we are reminded of the duty and joy of caring for our neighbors, whether human or more-than-human; we are exposed to patterns and instances of injustice, suffering, and loss—especially as caused by patriarchy. We are drawn into their texts, and under that pull we are compelled to respond and invited to act. Exact conclusions are not usually ready-made; we need to forge our response in our own way. As in the form of *call and response* in jazz and in many Black church services, so too the form of radical Romantic feminism issues a dramatic call and invites a response.

Having addressed the context and forms of radical Romantic ecofeminism, I now turn to its *themes*. The central themes in the works of Shelley, Fuller, and Hurston are continuous with those of radical Romanticism: social critique expressed via storied landscapes that present a tangible "face" of the oppressed; potential sources of healing and strength that emerge from an appropriate connection to place; the wild as that which unsettles repressive conventions and practices; the interdependent relation between humans and the more-than-human but also the distinctive agency of the more-than-human; the employment of the sublime and picturesque while subverting both; the cultivation of democratic relationality, inclusive of those who are otherwise ostracized or feared as "other"; resistance to patriarchal, tyrannical religion and the embrace of an earth-oriented, panentheistic spirituality; and an acknowledgment of uncertainty, despair, and wild hope.

Yet just as engagement with Du Bois expanded and transformed radical Romanticism, so too does engagement with Shelley, Fuller, and Hurston. They refashion and expand radical Romanticism, bringing to its heart critiques of dominating patriarchy as well as distinctive, life-affirming ecofeminist sensibilities and ways of being. Their struggle against patriarchy revealed the intersectional oppression of women, Black people, Native Americans, and the more-than-human. Their work often expresses Gothic grief, a dark lament over subjugated bodies and lands.

A common theme in their work is opposition to hypermasculine individuality: the arrogance of thinking that one can "go it alone," erect and solitary. Shelley critiqued such masculinity with her character Frankenstein, who perfectly embodies "the sovereign self," whereas Fuller's *Summer on the Lakes* and Hurston's *Their Eyes* vividly present such counterpractices as reciprocity, care, and mutual dependence among humans and between humans and the more-than-human. Not only did they refuse the male sovereign self, but their work also challenged anthropocentrism, dethroning humans and positioning them *among* the more-than-human rather than as conquerors. Yet this ecofeminist posthumanism also recognizes human distinctiveness (just as they recognize other forms of particularity that mark creatures and entities of all kinds). Humans experience a potential intimacy with the more-than-human that brings joy and belonging but also heartache and fear, because the ways and agents of the more-than-human are not perfectly aligned with human goals and desires.

The radical Romantic ecofeminism of our authors demonstrates a refusal of the ways and pace of white, male, extractive capitalism. This refusal has both temporal and spatial dimensions. It opposes the accelerated speed of capitalism, rushing to take and produce more. Think of Victor Frankenstein's feverish impatience, Joe Stark's—Janie's husband's—hurriedness, or Fuller's settlers' frenzied rush to occupy "free" lands. It also resists the spatial expansion of extractive capitalism, always needing new frontiers, larger mines, fresh forests, and an ever-expanding supply of laborers. All three authors challenged rapacious colonialism in its various forms, and they also suggested an alternative way of being: an ecofeminist set of practices and perspectives that place a premium on emancipatory political participation, reciprocity, justice, and the dignity of all humans and the more-than-human.

The *content* of radical Romantic ecofeminism is embodied in its *form*: a set of perspectives and ways of being that are rooted in and respond to the contexts of the often interrelated *catastrophes* of patriarchy, settler colonialism, extractive capitalism, anti-Black racism, and environmental wreckage. It would be convenient to assign a discrete catastrophe to each author, for example, patriarchy to Shelley, settler colonialism to Fuller, and anti-Black racism to Hurston. In fact, however, these catastrophes are interwoven variously in the work of each author. And to each author we now turn.

MARY SHELLEY: WOMEN AND LAND AS MONSTROUS OTHER

Shelley's dystopic, sci-fi *Frankenstein* and apocalyptic *The Last Man* are dark Romantic novels that speak powerfully to the catastrophes of our times, especially those of the oppression of women, white supremacy, and climate change. Placing Shelley in a radical Romantic interpretive framework reveals the sociopolitical implications of her work. *Frankenstein* and *The Last Man* both affirm and critique forms of humanism that lay at the heart of the Euro-American imagination. The reader is asked to consider: What is distinctive of the human, and who counts as being fully human? And even as a liberatory form of humanism is affirmed, so is a robust posthumanism, that is, a decentering of the human in an anthropocentric culture as well as a decentering of the male in an androcentric society. Additionally, Shelley's works explore the role of science, technology, and religion in modernity, including their various environmental and gendered implications. Shelley's treatment of these powerful topics establishes her as a central figure and innovator in radical Romantic ecofeminism.

In *Frankenstein*, Shelley pushes hard on the question: How porous, or rigid, is the colonial, Eurocentric boundary of what counts as human? Victor Frankenstein and his male, Euro-colonial peers exclude the creature—and the outsider's kind—from the category of humanity. Frankenstein defines and declares the creature—whom he himself created, the "Adam" of his labor (77)—a monstrous other. This exclusion from humanity causes the creature indescribable pain and moral debilitation. As we saw in chapter 2, Du Bois asked, "How does it feel to be a problem?" Mary Shelley anticipated that social, existential question. What is it like to move through life being perceived as an outsider, an "other," whose very existence is understood as a problem to be contained or expunged? Moreover, like Du Bois, Shelley added this question: What does it mean that the non-human is perceived as a problem, as an "other" to be subdued or expunged?

Shelley's aim was to make palpably clear, via radical Romantic aesthetics, the suffering and injustice of what it is to be deemed the "other," the "outsider," "the problem," especially for women and the enslaved. In *Frankenstein*, we are confronted with the creature and this question: Is it human? A test of one's humanity is one's answer to this question: Do I recognize and embrace that which is different from me? This is a version of the problem of systematic misrecognition. Is the Muslim fully human? What about the transgender person, the unhoused, the severely disabled, or the undocumented immigrant? What of women in the nineteenth century, or even today: What is their worth on the patriarchal scale? And what about the Black entrepreneur selling cigarettes on a sidewalk? Neither the enslaved African nor the Native American was human in the eyes of those who bought and sold and dispossessed them.[4]

In his "Great Books" lecture on *Frankenstein*, James Leiker poses the question, "Is the creature a human being?" and then proceeds to answer, "Probably not, according to the Romantic point of view." In Leiker's view, the Romantics would insist that the creature is soulless because its origin was a lab and not a womb. For this reason, the Romantics and the people in the novel "reject the monster [because] . . . they know he is not like us."[5] But Shelley, in my view, had a very different outlook and asked, "Why do we insist that 'he is not like us'? How do *we* need to change in order that the creature is welcomed as 'one of us'?" What would it look like, and what would be required, for patriarchal, Eurocentric societies to be transformed and marked by openness and receptivity in the face of difference and otherness? What if this openness did not stem from generosity but rather from an ongoing desire to learn and grow from otherness—other ways of being, appearing, being capable, and communicating?

This response and effort are definitory of radical Romanticism. Rousseau argued that we should be open to the idea that orangutans, or the great apes, are human. The early Wordsworth's "disability poetry"—which was criticized for its "unseemly" subject matter—sought to broaden the scope of who counts as "one of us," inclusive of "souls that appear to have no depth at all / To careless eyes."[6] And Coleridge went still further when he greeted the young ass, "I hail thee *Brother*."[7] Shelley, like her fellow radical Romantics, understood that one learns to become more fully human by opening oneself to lives that aren't traditionally or socially granted the status of being "one of us" or even of being fully human. This, of course, is a profound issue for societies that aspire to be democratic. Justice movements that pertain to women, queer people, Black people, and disabled people can be understood as progressive democratic efforts to create the kind of society that Shelley longed for, namely, a society that does not hierarchically define and rank humanity based on an elite, white male scale. The oppressive burden this scale imposes is well captured by what Lewis Gordon has called "the weight of colonial imposition: whether black woman or black man, the normative center is *white man*, not even white woman."[8]

The creature in *Frankenstein* represents an extreme form of alienation and can be considered monstrous from the start, at least from a purely physical, aesthetic point of view. He is eight feet tall, and this at a time when the average height of a male European was about five and a half feet. He was stitched together from various carcasses, mostly human but also animal parts from "slaughter-houses" (37). He had "yellow skin [that] scarcely covered the work of muscles and arteries beneath" (39). It is not a coincidence that the one person who responded kindly to the creature was blind. Shelley gives us, then, an extreme example of one who embodies what it is to be a problem. Black people, women, transgender people, undocumented people, people with disabilities—these and others are coded variously, sometimes subtly, as being "a problem" to the dominant patriarchal, white supremacist, ableist culture. Dismantle the oppressive culture and one's status-as-problem largely disappears. What dismantling would be required for the creature to no longer be perceived as a problem, as a monster? Shelley does not answer this unsettling question. Rather, she disturbs her reader with the question itself: How can you learn to embrace that which (initially) appears to you as dangerous or repulsive?

Robin Kimmerer, a Potawatomi author, addresses this challenge. On occasion, she spends her nights rescuing salamanders from being killed by cars. She notes that salamanders, unlike some "charismatic mammals," "bring us face to face with our innate xenophobia. . . . Being with salamanders gives honor to otherness, offers an antidote to the poison of xenophobia. Each time we rescue slippery, spotted beings we attest to their right to be, to live in the sovereign territory of their own lives."[9] Kimmerer is suggesting that the act of caring for and about that which initially strikes one as "slimy" is one way to begin to embrace "the other." She extends this lesson to caring for Iraqis who were deemed "other" during the U.S. invasion of Iraq. Coleridge's Ancient Mariner learns a similar lesson from the slimy water snakes.

If the creature in *Frankenstein* is largely rejected by humankind because his human identity is questioned or rejected, then it is worth asking: What identity is assigned to him? What do people think he is? His status as a problem emerges largely out of people not knowing what to make of him—perhaps, in part, because he appears to have been *made*. He is a monstrous problem because in some ways he appears to be human—walking and talking, for example—but in other ways he appears to be something else, something nonhuman. In any case, his identity is not humanhood but problemhood. The creature is a destabilizing hybrid of sorts. And as a hybrid figure, his agency is ambiguous. Helena Feder has brilliantly suggested that "the monster . . . [is] an imprint of the human fear of nonhuman agency."[10] Like the weather and other "natural forces," he appears to be amoral and beyond human control—just like the Indonesian volcano that erupted and spewed so much ash that global temperatures dropped, causing "the year without a summer" when Shelley began *Frankenstein* in 1816. The ensuing cold, stormy, wet weather—electrifying, terrifying, and not subject to human control—seeped into Shelley's text, including the climatic (and climactic) environment of the creature's birth. She created a being with the face and manners of a human and the agency and force of the nonhuman (at least in terms of the creature's height, strength, and ability to function in extreme environments). And however much the creature appears to be out of human control, that will not stop humans from attempting to subdue it.

Like the creature, women are feared, in part because there is something non-human about *their* problemhood, their creaturehood: They walk and talk (like humans) but—in the view of some misogynistic traditions—they are nonhuman in that they menstruate and give birth in the same fashion as nonhuman animals. As discussed in chapter 3, a variety of Western cultural traditions associate men with spirit, mind, and high culture, while women and the enslaved, among others, are associated with materiality, the bodily, the uncultured—with nonhuman nature. Nonhuman nature and those who are seen to embody it are feared and subject to attempted domination by patriarchal, racist cultures. Shelley's creature is the incarnation of such fear and subjugation.

Some might not be impressed with Shelley's humanism, that is, with the attempt to extend the category of human to the creature and others whose humanity is denied. Some might not deem "human" a particularly honorific category. I appreciate critiques of humanism, especially of those Eurocentric forms that exalt the white elite male as the measure of humanity and that problematically perpetuate anthropocentricism. Yet many who have yet to be treated as human or fully human often need to fight for their status as humans (for example, Black Lives Matter or the Trans Justice Initiative). Note the "fight" in these words of Susan Stryker:

> I find a deep affinity between myself as a transsexual woman and the monster in Mary Shelley's *Frankenstein*. Like the monster, I am too often perceived as less than fully human due to the means of my embodiment; like the monster's as well, my exclusion from human community fuels a deep and abiding rage in me that I, like the monster, direct against the conditions in which I must struggle to exist.[11]

Shelley sought to fight against those dehumanizing "conditions" not by jettisoning humanism but by making it more capacious. This would require the dismantlement of vicious forms of humanism, those that exclude, and the extension of the best aspects of humanism, those that honor the dignity of all humans. It would require a radically progressive cultural transformation.

"I Am Not Much Unlike to You": Posthumanism and the Sovereign Male

Shelley understood that even if humanism were extended to reject its androcentrism, it also needed to temper its anthropocentrism. Indeed, for Shelley, androcentrism and anthropocentrism are connected: Ousting white male domination over humanity goes hand in hand with ousting human domination over the more-than-human. In *Frankenstein*, Shelley critiques the male sovereign self by demonstrating its failure in the figure of Victor Frankenstein, who places himself as the sovereign center of his life and world. In so doing, he increasingly severs ties to his family, friends, colleagues, and to the natural world. He notes that as he pursues his solitary work, he is increasingly neglectful of social relations, and his eyes become "insensible to the charms of nature" (37). The very process of creating the creature indicates his alienation, working secretively and privately as the sovereign male who will give birth in monstrous isolation and self-sufficiency. He and he alone will be Creator: "A new species would bless me as its creator and source . . . would owe their being to me. . . . I could bestow animation upon lifeless matter" (36).

The more Frankenstein seeks to create life as the sovereign male, the more he is alienated from life—eventually ending up in the harsh Arctic Circle. The creature, in contrast, longs for that which Victor has deserted and desecrated. The creature may be fashioned from discrete parts, but he longs for connection and integration with humans and the more-than-human. In *Frankenstein*, then, Victor Frankenstein endeavors, disastrously, to be radically self-sufficient, isolating himself from social connections and alienating himself from the natural world as he seeks to "penetrate into the recesses of nature," showing "how she works in her hiding places" (30). The language of penetrating *her*—nature—in her hidden places is the language of domination, if not rape. And it is precisely this image of the male sovereign dominating and placing himself at the center of the more-than-human that we see in Shelley's *Frankenstein* but even more powerfully in *The Last Man*, leveraging a critique against both androcentrism and anthropocentrism.

Above all, Shelley's apocalyptic, dystopic novel *The Last Man* warns humanity that despite its efforts, it cannot achieve what Victor Frankenstein attempted:

to place the human at the center of nature and thereby control and subdue it. The setting of the novel is principally Europe in the late twenty-first century. A pandemic, which begins in Asia, sweeps across the globe and presumably kills all of humanity, except for Lionel Verney, apparently the last man. In the first of three volumes of the novel, we are introduced to the principal characters. Verney was raised in "the wilds" and was later befriended and educated by the progressively minded Adrian, the son of the former and last king of England, which has become a republic. Verney marries Idris, Adrian's sister, while Verney's sister, Perdita, marries Lord Raymond, the man who eventually becomes the head of England. Volume 2 of the novel is the start of the apocalyptic narrative: Lord Raymond, embodying Western colonialism, leads an attack on the Muslim Turks of Constantinople, unintentionally spreading across Europe the pandemic that has by then traveled from Egypt to Turkey. Whereas in volume 1 the private lives of the characters and political events in England are front and center, in the second volume the pandemic itself becomes a central character in its domination of the human dramas. In volume 3, the apocalyptic narrative eventually turns postapocalyptic as well as posthumanist as the pandemic kills off all of humanity except Verney. The more-than-human gracefully moves on without humanity, mocking any aspirations for human domination and control.

Yet even at the end of the novel, Shelley maintains a position that straddles humanism *and* posthumanism. As the now solitary Verney surveys the beauty and liveliness of a lovely evening, with the sound of songbirds and cattle, the sight of the moon and setting sun, he is struck by nature's sovereign indifference to humanity but also human relatedness to nature:

> Yes, this is the earth; there is no change—*no ruin*—no rent made in her verdurous expanse; she continues to wheel round and round, with alternate night and day, through the sky, though man is not her adorner or inhabitant. . . . *I am not much unlike to you.* Nerves, pulse, brain, joint, and flesh, of such am I composed, and ye are organized by the same laws. I have something beyond this, but I will call it a defect, not an endowment, if it leads me to misery, while ye are happy.[12]

Shelley, via her character Verney, ousts anthropocentricism, crushing the human pretension to place itself at the center of all things. Yet Verney also asserts human distinctiveness, namely, human consciousness, highlighting the human capacity to reflect on life, to assess its pains and sources of injustice, and to potentially move forward with greater awareness and care. But by acknowledging such distinctiveness, humanity is not, in Shelley's view, thereby exalted over the more-than-human.[13] Both humanism and posthumanism are affirmed, but androcentrism is challenged in either case: The lead male characters' various patriarchal aspirations all prove futile in the face of the pandemic.

Frankenstein, too, straddles both humanism and posthumanism. We have seen, for example, Shelley's attempt to expand the category *human* to embrace the creature. Yet *Frankenstein* also tames the human pretension to place itself at the center of the universe. The threatening extreme weather and the thunderous lightning, for example, check human arrogance in its aspirational control of the nonhuman world—as does the very presence of the agential hybrid creature. The only surviving member of the Frankenstein family, Victor's brother, Ernest, is encouraged by Elizabeth to become a farmer because it is "a very healthy happy life; and the least hurtful, or rather the most beneficial profession of any" (45). It is perhaps not surprising that it is a woman, Elizabeth, who proposes a vocation that—at its best—encourages a collaborative relation to the more-than-human. Anne Mellor rightfully notes that Elizabeth here "gives voice" to Shelley's own ideal of "nature as a sacred life-force in which human beings ought to participate in conscious harmony."[14]

We see here and elsewhere Shelley championing such ecofeminist ideals as care, reciprocity, and transformative justice between humans and between humans and the more-than-human. Yet in both *Frankenstein* and *The Last Man* we see not only familiarity and reciprocity between the human and the more-than-human but also dread and fear of the more-than-human. With anthropocentrism dethroned, we are left with the unnerving realization that we can neither control nature nor cuddle up to nature as our "mother" or "friend." This, too, is a message of Shelley's ecofeminism, and it is a powerful one for us today as we are confronted with climate change. As Jed Mayer astutely writes, "One of the chief difficulties of living in our ecological moment is reconciling a well-founded fear of harmful phenomena conventionally classified as 'natural' with an ethic of care toward the nonhuman, an ethic that is our best hope for reducing our impact on this planet's ecologies."[15] This "difficulty"—holding together gingerly care and fear, love and dread of the more-than-human—is at the heart of Shelley's radical Romanticism, and it would later mark the heart of that American radical Romantic, Emily Dickinson, as, for example, when she wrote these lines: "But nature is a stranger yet; /

The ones that cite her most / Have never passed her haunted house, / Nor simplified her ghost."[16]

Mary Shelley had been haunted by her own ghosts, and religion was among them. To some extent, Victor Frankenstein embodies the cold, abstract rationalism of Shelley's father, William Godwin, who became an agnostic if not an atheist. The creature, in contrast, receives a religious education via Milton's *Paradise Lost* and seems to embrace the Christianity of a benevolent Creator that bestows love and care for a world declared good. Shelley herself, at home with neither her father's lack of religion (which she associated with coldness) nor with Christianity (which she associated with the oppressive dogma and hypocrisy of organized religion), embraced a Romantic, panentheistic belief in "a larger spiritual force in the universe."[17] Her Romantic religious perspectives informed her complex posthumanist ecological view—the love and dread of the natural world—as she sought to maintain aspects of both Godwin and panentheism, that is, of a cold, indifferent world and a world infused with spirit.

Shelley employed religion to cast light on complex accounts of science, technology, and human and more-than-human relations. Religion, whether Christian or panentheistic, served to curb destructive Promethean aspirations. In *Frankenstein*, science and technology are not malicious per se; Shelley had great respect for the work of scientists. But Shelley's novel warns of the dangers of science and technology unleashed from ethical frameworks. Although Victor Frankenstein had access to personal and professional relations that could have provided him with ethical guidance for his scientific and technological endeavors, he detached the social from the scientific and thus placed himself above or outside both the human and the more-than-human world. His religious trespass—the sin of pride and narcissism—was not in the creation of the creature per se but in creating arrogantly in isolation and then in deserting the creature, giving no consideration to his well-being.[18]

This brings us back to the heart of *Frankenstein* and *The Last Man*: the ecofeminist critique of the oppressiveness of androcentrism. Victor Frankenstein, the sovereign male scientist, fails to offer the appropriate (humanist) welcome and hospitality to that which is "other," just as Lord Raymond fails to see humanity in the Muslim other. And both men fail to show the appropriate (posthumanist) care and respect—"love and fear"—for the more-than-human. To some extent, religion—Christian and panentheistic—informed Shelley's dual humanist/posthumanist perspectives. Forms of progressive Christianity supported Shelley's commitment to the dignity of all humans and hence her desire to expand humanism's reach, to expand who counts as human. Panentheism, in contrast, tended to celebrate all forms of life as infused with spirit and thereby informed Shelley's posthumanism.

Hope in the Midst of Catastrophe

Before concluding this section, I wish to briefly return to the form of Shelley's ecofeminism. The radical Romantic, ecofeminist forms that convey the catastrophic are richly textured and multilayered, resisting a simple, linear narrative with seamless unity and tidy closure. *Frankenstein*, an epistolary novel, contains stories told within stories, perspectives embedded in multifaceted scenes and landscapes. As Devon Hodges notes, "To contribute further to the novel's lack of unity, dependent upon a resolution that provides a sense of closure, Shelley directs the novel itself toward a woman reader, Mrs. Saville [the sister of Walton, the conquering sea captain searching for a passage to the North Pole], who is located both in and outside the text, and provides the narrative with an uncertain destination."[19] *The Last Man*, too, conveys catastrophe via Shelley's ecofeminist forms. Its very genre, that of apocalyptic fiction—the first of its kind—subverts the conventional narrative of the heroic male saving the world just in the nick of time. And its narrative structure, like that of *Frankenstein*, is multifaceted. Verney, the last man, writes down the apocalyptic chronicle detailing the end of the world, but with no expectation of a single living person to read it. His written record, concluded in the year 2100, mysteriously travels back in time, where it is found by an editor in 1818 as "piles of leaves" with text written on them, the work of the ancient Greek prophetess, the Cumaean Sibyl.[20] Time and space, in Shelley's framework, are as multilayered and jumbled as are the leaves of the Cumaean Sibyl—ancient leaves that convey Verney's futuristic apocalypse to its nineteenth-century editor. In both *Frankenstein* and *The Last Man*, Shelley challenged male narrative conventions by instead creating ecofeminist forms of storytelling marked by a multiplicity that unsettles unity, linearity, and closure.

Finally, both dystopic novels carry what I earlier called a dark, wild hope. In *The Last Man*'s dreary tale of human extermination, a ray of dark hope is emitted from within the framework of its mysterious origin, the prophetic leaves of the Cumaean Sibyl. Shelley's readers are graphically presented in volumes 1 and 2 with a catastrophe that, like Rob Nixon's notion of slow violence, is in the making but not yet fully realized. Perhaps if Shelley's art can wake us to the catastrophe of both androcentrism and anthropocentrism, humanity may have enough time to disrupt the otherwise steady progress toward our doom. And if hope is lodged at the start of the novel, it may also be found in its inconclusive ending: The reader cannot be certain that Verney is indeed "the last man." In the words of Hilary Strang, "Perhaps we can find . . . a perverse kind of optimism in this rigorously pessimistic novel: . . . when Lionel [Verney], carrying the works of Shakespeare, and the dog step into their little boat to sail for Africa in the novel's final moment, at least there is the possibility of more than one living, humanized creature surviving the future."[21] If there are additional survivors in other regions of the world—as in Du Bois's "The Comet"—perhaps a new, just world will come from the great catastrophe. Still, this form of hope is dark and wild, rooted in death, vulnerability, and despair. After all, the hopeful vision requires cataclysm—whether slow moving or fully formed.

Frankenstein's three male characters show some modest signs of moral growth. Victor, reflecting on his obsessive quest and self-imposed isolation, comes to understand that one must always endeavor to preserve tranquility and that "if the study to which you apply yourself has a tendency to weaken your affections, and to destroy your taste for those simple pleasures in which no alloy can possibly mix, then that study is certainty unlawful" (37). Walton, who like Victor had been obsessed with ascendency over the natural world, agrees in the end to abandon his conquest and no longer lead his crew "unwillingly to danger" (184). Victor supports this decision and encourages him to "seek happiness in tranquility, and avoid ambition, even if it be only the *apparently* innocent one of distinguishing yourself in science and discoveries" (186; emphasis added). And finally, at the end of the novel, after Victor dies from exposure to the elements, the creature—who "was benevolent and good; misery made [him] a fiend"—collapses in grief over the dead body of Victor, asking that he pardon the one "who irretrievably destroyed thee by destroying all thou lovedst" (78, 187).

Ultimately, dark, wild hope is lodged in the possibility that Shelley's powerful, ecofeminist storytelling can awaken some of her readers and bring a measure of transformative awareness, even as her three male characters, those who committed the greatest crimes, have to some degree experienced their own (albeit belated) illumination. May our own illumination not come too late, lest we become Shelley's monsters and bring great destruction to ourselves and all those around us.

MARGARET FULLER: AMERICAN RADICAL
ROMANTICISM IN ACTION

Fuller as Radical Romantic Ecofeminist

Fuller was a powerful ecofeminist storyteller. Her vocation was to wake people to the various forms of suffering and injustice caused by patriarchy, settler colonialism, racism, American imperialism, and extractive capitalism. Like radical Romantics before her, she sought, via her art in writing and lecturing, to inspire a praxis-oriented empathy directed toward transformative social and personal change. The story of her life—or, of her *lives*, to draw from the title of her biographer John Matteson's book[22]—is remarkable: Born into a patriarchal society, her early homeschool education rivaled that of elite, male private schools. When her father died, she took on the financial responsibilities of supporting her family, earning money as an innovative schoolteacher in Boston and Providence and as speaker and host to the "Conversations"—engaging, dialogical classes mostly for women for the sake of their intellectual emancipation. She became a core member of the Transcendentalists and edited their journal, *The Dial*. In it, she published a series of articles that were subsequently incorporated into the first major feminist publication in the United States, *Woman in the Nineteenth Century*, paving the way for the Seneca Falls Convention three years later in 1848. Fuller also became a front-page columnist and literary critic for the *New York Tribune*. Her praxis-oriented journalism brought attention to the unjust conditions in U.S. prisons and mental health facilities, the cruelty of slavery, and the plight of orphans and prostitutes. All the while, she was a brilliant and fierce advocate for the dignity, education, and rights of women. In 1846, she traveled to Italy as the *Tribune*'s first U.S. war correspondent, reporting on the 1848 revolutions. While there, she had a child with and married Giovanni Ossoli, an Italian revolutionary soldier. On their return trip to the United States, the family of three died in a shipwreck off Fire Island, New York. Fuller was forty years old.

In this section on Fuller, I will show how she both belongs to and expands radical Romanticism, bringing attention to her storied landscapes that reveal the subjugation of humans and the more-than-human, her radical Romantic feminism and religion, and the *form* of her ecofeminism in the context of catastrophe. Yet before my discussion of Fuller, I wish to contextualize her life and work with a brief account of the transatlantic Romanticism that helped shape her life.

In the early nineteenth century, radical Romanticism traveled across the Atlantic and took root in a U.S. culture rich with Puritanism, democratic aspirational notions of freedom and equality, a sacred—and exploitive—sense of nature, and pervasive Indigenous beliefs and practices supporting interdependent relations between people, place, and the more-than-human. Radical Romanticism was reshaped in distinctive ways by Fuller, Emerson, Thoreau, Dickinson, and Whitman, among others. By employing radical Romanticism as an interpretive framework, we can see more clearly the interrelated democratic, religious, and environmental aspects of much early- and mid-nineteenth-century American thought and literature. We can grasp, for example, the depth of Emerson's commitments to Romantic religious sensibilities (in this case, panentheistic immanence), Romantic democratic sensibilities (the freedom and progressive commitments of the self-reliant individual), and Romantic environmental sensibilities (Transcendental intimacy and "relatedness" that pervades social and natural worlds). Fuller's *Summer on the Lakes*, Emerson's *Nature*, Thoreau's *Walden*, Whitman's *Leaves of Grass*, and such poems of Dickinson as "What mystery pervades a well," "A Bird came down the Walk," and "Our little Kinsmen"—all these reflect and profoundly revise the radical Romantic inheritance.

A feature of the American revision was a distrust of European influence. Thoreau wrote, "Eastward I go only by force, but westward I go free."[23] Thoreau urged one to face Oregon, not Europe, if one sought "Nature" and "Freedom." The two were closely associated—for better, for worse. Nature, here, has no history. Of course, we know better: European Romanticism shaped North American perspectives on nature.[24] Influenced by William Wordsworth's early verse and voice, the good news that Emerson preached to the graduates at Harvard rang with inspiration from the Wordsworthian Gospel: You are a spiritual creature; divine inspiration is dynamic and available; intimate contact with the natural world can provide a source of revelation.

The early Wordsworth connected his theological, panentheistic vision of the one Life—that divinity that permeates and potentially unites all humans and the nonhuman world—with a progressive democratic politics that opposed slavery and unjust war and advocated for the dignity and rights of the disenfranchised. Emerson increasingly made a similar connection. While the United States experienced rapid urbanization and industrialization, sought to expand its borders by way of invasion in the Mexican-American War and the dispossession of Indigenous populations, and prepared to enter a bloody civil war over slavery,

Emerson's radical Romantic theological and sociocritical views coalesced in the form of "lay sermons" or essays. In these, he protested injustice in the United States and sought to mediate such unhelpful dualisms as spirit/nature and the ideal/the empirical. Ultimately, Emerson and other North American Romantics shared with British Romantics the significance of an indwelling spirit and reverence for the more-than-human world and sought to maintain an idealism (with an emphasis on the imagination) as well as a realism (with an emphasis on an empiricism of the everyday). They did not understand the natural world as dead, distant, and separate from humans. Rather, both North American and British radical Romantics posited a complex and dynamic interrelation between humans, spirit, and the natural world—not a static hierarchy.[25]

As we will see, in Fuller's *Summer on the Lakes* and various writings in the *New York Tribune*, nature and culture, empiricism and idealism, and materialism and spirituality come together in storied landscapes that bring attention to both the dignity and the oppression of women, Native Americans, and Black people, and also of prisoners, the mentally challenged, orphans, immigrants, and the impoverished. The same can be said of Thoreau's radical challenges to rapacious commercialism, militarism, slavery, and environmental exploitation. Thoreau's life and authorship are marked by an interrelated commitment to the mutual flourishing of humans and the nonhuman.[26] And finally, there is the verse and lyrical philosophy of Whitman's *Leaves of Grass*, which sings of the dignity of persons (and their sheer *diversity*) and of the complex weave of democratic culture and nature in cities and lands, in tall buildings and vast woods, in individual bodies and the body of the Earth. Nature—that is, a sensuous materialism—informs Whitman's aspirational democracy, which unites diverse citizens in the lands, seas, and air: "This is the grass that grows wherever the land is and the water is, / This the common air that bathes the globe."[27]

Of all the American inheritors of radical Romanticism, Fuller was the most forceful in putting its commitments and values into action. She was, above all, a revolutionary in thought and deed. The radical Romantic "wild" fired her imagination and allowed her to challenge oppressive conventions and institutions of all kinds. Her writings always included a profound personal element (for example, her encounters with Indigenous populations, the land, or impoverished women) as well as a deeply public aspect, advancing far-reaching social critique and reform. Her inventive connection between the personal and the public manifested her radical Romantic efforts to address her readers as "whole people," addressing the cognitive-affective nexus and endeavoring to inspire praxis-oriented witnesses.[28] Personal reflection is wed to social activism—especially concerning women's rights—in a style that seeks to further a dynamic, lively democracy as opposed to patriarchal hegemony. Like the radical Romantics before her, Fuller's art created storied landscapes that presented the "face" of the oppressed. For example, when she traveled to England as a correspondent for the *New York Tribune*, she visited textile mills in Manchester and Liverpool and coal mines in Newcastle. Her account of the mill and mine workers brought intimate attention to their lives as actual people—people marked by intellectual curiosity, deep aspirations, and challenging obstacles.[29] And while her focus was on the laborers' lives and the pollution generated by the mills and mines, she also situated the local in a larger, global context of industrialization, exploitation of workers, and social unrest.

Fuller resisted patriarchy in all its forms, including in government, religion, and extractive capitalism, aligning herself instead with a Transcendental, panentheistic spirituality that honored inclusive democratic relationality and environmental sensibilities. From a young age, she trespassed gendered boundaries, asserting her agency and moral imagination—as an educator, lecturer, activist, literary critic, and war correspondent. In place of androcentrism and anthropocentrism, Fuller championed care, reciprocity, and transformative justice between humans and between humans and the more-than-human. The substance or *content* of her creative, activist, radical Romantic ecofeminism was expressed in distinctive *forms* and addressed a distinctive *context*, namely, the catastrophes of patriarchy, expansive settler colonialism, slavery, extractive capitalism, and environmental degradation. To this content, form, and context we now turn.

The matter and manner of Fuller's ecofeminism was largely informed by the American radical Romantic religion known as Transcendentalism. Like Emerson, Fuller held the panentheistic view that there is a "unity of the world in God and the immanence of God in the world.... The soul of each individual is identical with the soul of the world, and contains, latently, all which it contains."[30] Spirit, nature, and the human are interconnected, and one must strive to realize one's indwelling Spirit by honoring the sanctity of life among humans and the more-than-human. Ultimately, one is responsible not to those with power or to social conventions and institutions but to the indwelling Spirit. And this indwelling Spirit, in Fuller's view, demanded justice, care, and respect for both humans and nonhumans. This radical Romantic panentheism supported Fuller's progressive political commitments, and hence she wrote rhetorically, "If the negro be a soul, if the woman be a soul, . . . to one Master only are they account-able," that "master" being indwelling Spirit. The social, political implications of an indwelling (nonconventional) authority are radical, at least in the hands and heart of Fuller. All institutions, all practices, all social conventions are to be scrutinized and challenged by the wild "Sun of Truth": "I would have woman lay aside all thought . . . of being taught and led by men. I would have her, like the Indian girl, dedicate herself to the Sun, the Sun of Truth, and go nowhere if his beams did not make clear the path. I would have her free from compromise, from complaisance, from helplessness, because I would have her good enough and strong enough to love one and all beings, from the fulness, not the poverty of being."[31] Whether she was fighting for the dignity and rights of women prisoners at Sing Sing, Black enslaved people, Native Americans, or the chained eagle at Niagara Falls, Fuller's radical Romantic religion taught her to see all people, indeed, all creatures, as beings worthy of love, care, and respect.

In Fuller's radical Romantic view, all people share and follow one Spirit but manifest Spirit variously. She forcefully rejected the idea that women and men and people of different races were innately different in the way of talents, virtue, disposition, or capacities. For example, she argued that women should vote not because they are naturally virtuous but simply because they are citizens with rights. She did at times employ the categories of feminine and masculine, but in her view, individuals, regardless of their gender, manifest these categories vari-ously. And hence Fuller proclaimed, "If you ask me what office [women] may fill; I reply—any. . . . Let them be sea-captains."[32] Her spiritual arguments for women's equality carried with them empirical critiques of the oppressive treatment of women in patriarchal society—for example, the lack of women's rights regarding property, children, and wages; the disregard for women's political and intellec-tual perspectives; and degrading prescriptions for how they should look and act domestically and in public. And Fuller understood the intersectional relation between the oppressive treatment of women and that of Native Americans, Afri-can Americans, and the impoverished, noting how these marginalized peoples are stripped of land, rights, and respect.

The manner or form of Fuller's activist work—which calls for simultaneous per-sonal and public transformation—is the radical Romantic, ecofeminist art of complex, multilayered storytelling. Like Shelley before her, Fuller fashioned a transgressive, feminist form of writing that refused narrow "male" forms of expression, reaching instead for a poetic prose rich in anecdote, myth, factual accounts, and fictional narratives. In her day, Fuller's writing style was deemed too convoluted, too multifarious, and not sufficiently systematic or logical.[33] In spite of this criticism, Fuller continued to forge a feminist form of expression to address the plight of the marginalized, especially women, and to further transformational change. "The conversation," for Fuller, was a mode and model of dialogical, dynamic communication, drawing in the reader to the challenges of the day and collaborating toward mutual understanding and achievement.[34] This conversational writing style expands the art of the radical Romantic storyteller, refusing the rigid distinctions between speaking and writing, poetry and prose, fiction and nonfiction.

Inherent to this conversational form is its open-endedness. Modes of freedom, not closure, are the destination. Just as the Transcendental self is always growing and changing, so too Fuller's prose invites growth and change. Indeed, her conversational, storytelling style is in some ways similar to the prose of Emerson and Thoreau, both of whom frequently turned their oral presentations at public lyceums into publications. But Fuller's feminist form pushes the conversational form still further, seeking to make a distinct space for women's public expression, as compelling as it was multilayered and faceted. The conversational form, in Fuller's view, was the means and expression of indwelling Spirit, women's rights, and a progressive democracy that valued collaborative exchange and achievement.

Fuller's Work: Summer on the Lakes *and the* New York Tribune

Fuller's ecofeminist form is fully manifested in her remarkable publication *Summer on the Lakes, in 1843,* a radical Romantic travelogue of what was at the time considered the western frontier, namely, the Great Lakes and Midwestern prairies. Fuller filled the book with critical sociopolitical commentary, ethnographic studies of both Indigenous and white populations, storied landscapes that captured the geography and life of the more-than-human, and profound personal reflection. Resisting a linear argument and unified storyline, the book is a multilayered, multifaceted text composed of poetry, lyrical and descriptive prose, dialogues, stories, ethical reflection, and detailed research conducted at Harvard. As a radical Romantic work, *Summer on the Lakes* brings together idealism and empiricism, imagination and facts, the outward and the inward, and beauty and critique—in this case, critique of patriarchy and its various expressions in manifest destiny, extractive capitalism, and the oppression of women and Native Americans.

Fuller's work, like that of Wordsworth before her and Du Bois following her, is a poignant mingling of life and death, hope and despair. This rich and tense drama of dark realities and hopeful aspiration is on full display in the very first entry of Fuller's westward journey, "Niagara, June 10, 1843." Niagara Falls—that icon of America's greatness, natural beauty, and "New World" vigor—is portrayed by Fuller in all its solemnity, corruption, and ambiguity. As one might expect, the sublime Niagara Falls is cast poetically—"a perpetual creation" and "spiritual repetition through all the spheres"—though Fuller did offer that the sight of "rapids" from the bridge to Goat Island was in fact more emotionally powerful than the falls themselves.[35] She suggested that this might be caused by her familiarity with the falls—she had been "prepared by descriptions and by paintings"; and to self-consciousness—she had "expected to be overwhelmed, to retire trembling" from the sight of the falls, but instead she "thought only of comparing the effect on [her] mind with what [she] had read and heard" (8). The robust masculine sublime, evidently, can be tamed by postcards.

For Fuller, Niagara may very well have been a symbol of America, representing failure as well as promise. The promise, in part, is to acknowledge the wondrous gift of the natural world and to strive to dwell appropriately. The failure comes into view when Fuller, sitting "on Table Rock, close to the great fall" and enjoying its grandeur, sees a man walk "close up to the fall, and, after looking at it a moment, with an air as if thinking how he could best *appropriate it to his own use*, he spat into it" (5; emphasis added). Fuller interprets this act as "a love of utility" that is indicative of the United States' extractive materialism (5). Of the sublime falls, America asks these questions: What is their use? How can they be instrumentalized? To her readers Fuller poses these counterquestions: If these lovely falls cannot be appropriately regarded but rather are deemed merely rivers of utilitarianism, what of the rest of the nation, especially the expanding West?[36] What are the chances of dwelling with thoughtful care in the lands of America, the land of promise? These were open questions for Fuller. She hoped for and endeavored to bring about a positive reply, even as she revealed formidable obstacles.

In another passage in *Summer on the Lakes*, Fuller once again moves abruptly in her storied landscape from the sublime to the morally bankrupt, from the spectacle of Niagara Falls to that of a chained, captive eagle. This symbol of the nation—the wild eagle of freedom—is dominated and made into an object of curiosity for human amusement. Those around the creature address it with "the language they seem to find most appropriate to such occasions—that of thrusts and blows" (6–7). Fuller is filled with "Byronic 'silent rages'" and, perhaps for her own solace, wondered if the eagle, as might Plotinus or Sophocles, stoically disregarded the tormentors and instead "listened to the voice of the cataract, and felt that congenial powers flowed free, and was consoled" (6, 7). Here Fuller challenges human/more-than-human dualism and interprets the eagle as a fellow sufferer deprived of freedom but perhaps not of all manner of comfort. Chained eagle, chained women, chained slaves, chained land—Fuller's storied landscapes of Niagara Falls, at the start of her journey, vividly prepare her readers for the beauty and exploitation that she would encounter in her westward expedition.

The loveliness of the western land runs deep in Fuller's text, as does a profound respect for its Indigenous populations. But that land and its people are also depicted as subjugated to an aggressive, violent American exceptionalism. Unfortunately, Fuller did not entirely escape the prejudices of her age, however much she wrestled with and against them. For example, in one report of her time at Niagara Falls, she fights against unwanted images of "naked savages stealing behind [her] with uplifted tomahawks" (4). While it may be true that "Fuller relativizes and challenges this preformed image," as Carmen Birkle argues, this "relativizing" comes only later in the book, after she encounters actual Native Americans, most notably members of the Ottawa and the Chippewa tribes (as opposed to the terrifying, racialized images of Native Americans).[37] She witnessed firsthand the dire, often fatal, effects of the United States' systematic efforts to remove Native Americans from their lands to make room for white settlers and to expand its imperial reach. Unlike the many white settlers who saw the land primarily as an expendable resource, Fuller was impressed by the way Native Americans lived sustainably, using the land but also properly caring for it. Fuller came to honor the dignity of Indigenous populations, noting their closely knit communities and their wise labor practices. And rather than describe Native Americans homogenously as "noble savages" or innocent children outside civilization, Fuller described the Indigenous people she encountered diversely, but almost always as complicated, dynamic, inventive humans who deserved respect and honor. Sometimes, to help her white readers overcome racial stereotypes, Fuller would reach for familiar, European reference points, as when she wrote of an Indigenous village, "the whole scene suggested to me a Greek splendor, a Greek sweetness" (33).

Fuller was determined to craft stories that told of the everyday and varied lives of Indigenous peoples, celebrating their cultures but also observing such internal problems as the treatment of women. While she noted Indigenous women's important roles and capabilities, she also argued that Indigenous women, like white women, suffer under oppressive patriarchy. Mostly, however, Fuller was determined to open the eyes of her readers to the courage, resilience, and dignity of Indigenous peoples, especially as they faced dispossession, loss of sovereignty, and extermination. She was highly critical of governmental and other white "plans" for Native Americans. For example, she criticized Thomas L. McKenney, the first "Superintendent of Indian Affairs" and author of *Tour to the Lakes*, for his proposed "project for organizing the Indians under a patriarchal government," and she suggested instead that if the United States let Indigenous people "act unimpeded . . . they would do far better" than if subject to "the white thinker" (144). Fuller demanded that

> every man look to himself how far this blood [the death of Native Americans] shall be required at his hands. Let the missionary, instead of preaching to the Indian, preach to the trader who ruins him. . . . Let every legislator . . . if he cannot undo the effects of past sin, try for that clear view and right sense that may save us from sinning still more deeply. And let every man and every woman, in their private dealings with the subjugated race, avoid all share in embittering, by insult or unfeeling prejudice, the captivity of Israel.
>
> (144)

In this powerful statement, Fuller exhorts business, religion, government, and private individuals to be accountable for the past and present suffering and injustice inflicted on Native Americans and to work toward their liberation.

Regrettably, Fuller seemed resigned to the demise of Native American peoples and cultures. In the face of Indigenous sorrow and death caused by racist practices, Fuller wrote, "I scarcely see how [Indigenous people] can forbear to shoot the white man where he stands," but then she immediately added, "but the power of fate is with the white man, and the Indian feels it" (71). "The power of fate" should not imply that Fuller believed in the superiority of Europeans or "the white man." She observed that if European settlers were truly Christian and civilized, the "wrongs and speedy extinction" inflicted on Native Americans never would have occurred (143). She also noted that the settler colonialist is "a halftamed pirate, and avails himself, as much as ever, of the maxim, 'Might makes right.' All that [set-tler] civilization does . . . is to cover up this with a veil of subtle evasions" (121). The tragic demise of Native Americans, then, will not be caused by a superior white culture but rather a fiendish white might. Nonetheless, Fuller was too quick to accept the "vanishing Indian" racialized paradigm.[38] She saw Indigenous tenacity and resilience firsthand; she should have known better.

Fuller's *Summer on the Lakes* has been described contradictorily as, on the one hand, a work of hope that portrays "the West" as "fertile ground to germinate the seeds of a greater, more just, open-minded, and educated America" and, on the other, a work of despair, "a type of funereal tribute" to the demise of Indig-enous people, courageous white women, and the very land itself.[39] Yet we do not need to choose between these different positions on Fuller's work—it belongs to both. While she was deeply pessimistic about the fate of Native Americans, she did hope that white settler culture would learn from its crimes and wrongdoings and treat the remaining Indigenous peoples with dignity and justice. And while she did present grim depictions of women's subjugation under patriarchy, she held that women's rights and advancement could be achieved by means of activ-ist critique and democratic education. And finally, while she did document the exploitive practices of westward expansion, detailing the settlers' disregard for both the health of the land and a sustainable interdependence between humans and the more-than-human, she also imagined healthy, ecological ways of being that could be achieved in the West, especially if settlers learned from the wise, sustainable practices manifested in Indigenous communities. In these communi-ties, Indigenous peoples worked the land but did not subject it to untrammeled domination. Fuller's ideal West was neither untouched, pristine landscapes nor territory conquered for extractive resources. Rather, she hoped for a land that was wisely cultivated and treated with respect (not unlike Wordsworth's hope for the Lake District). As Kathleen Healey aptly claims, "Fuller's ideal physical landscape is one in which humankind and nature almost merge, where there is a sense of communion between them."[40]

Monika Elbert rightfully states that "Fuller's EcoGothic vision provides us with a terrifying glimpse of an America that for Fuller can no longer exist, that has, in fact, only existed in a mythologized version of the past."[41] Her first entry on Niagara Falls signals to us her loss of faith in America's innocence and goodness. Nevertheless, *Summer on the Lakes* remains a work of hope, revealing to her read-ers the horrors of American imperialism and racism but also inspiring them to *actualize* her ecofeminist vision of progressive democratic ideals, beliefs, and sensibilities.

This vision—radical Romantic ecofeminism in action—was deepened and extended when, following the publication of *Summer on the Lakes*, Fuller joined Horace Greeley's *New York Tribune* in 1844. As a literary critic and journalist for the largest daily paper in New York City, Fuller reached a large audience with her investigative work and articles. While she wrote on various forms of structural inequality, her focus was on shaping the culture—the beliefs and practices of the democratic citizen. Her radical Romantic democratic work pushed for women's rights, the abolition of slavery, Indigenous sovereignty, antinativism, labor rights, and universal suffrage and education. This was in many ways a continuation of her earlier work as a Transcendentalist and editor of *The Dial*, except now Fuller had the opportunity to reach a larger audience with her probing critiques of and proposed reforms for America's institutions, practices, and sensibilities.[42] Contributing to a robust, inclusive, and transformed democratic culture was her aim, and that would require, among other things, a keen perspective on American culture, history, and politics.

That perspective would be deepened and broadened when Fuller moved to Italy in 1846 as a foreign correspondent for the *Tribune* and subsequently became an ally to the Italian freedom fighters. From Italy she saw more keenly, and wrote still more fiercely about, the failure of the United States to achieve democracy, especially in light of slavery, manifest destiny, the genocide of Indigenous peoples, ecological wreckage, capitalism, and materialism.[43] She also acquired a more global view of the workings of empire and patriarchy, drawing parallels between oppressed Black people and women in the United States and Italians and women under Austrian and French political control and papal domination. American exceptionalism, from abroad, no longer appeared exceptional but rather typical of transatlantic patriarchy, empire, and capitalism. As Wordsworth had been radicalized by the French Revolution, Fuller was radicalized by the 1848 Italian Revolution—a deepening of her radical Romanticism.

Early on, radical Romanticism had included such socialist projects as Coleridge's Pantisocracy and the Transcendentalist Brooks Farm. But for Fuller in Rome, socialism became a global hope and project, one that could require violent means, though education was always Fuller's preferred revolutionary agent for transformative change. As Fuller wrote in a *Tribune* article from 1849: "I believed before I came to Europe in what is called Socialism, as the inevitable sequence to the tendencies and wants of the era, but I did not think these vast changes in modes of government, education and daily life, would be effected as rapidly as I now think they will, because they must. The world can no longer stand without them." Her hope for socialism, then, was a global one. But the United States remained her home, and she never stopped working on its behalf with a "tough love," as heard in these lines written from Rome: "I see deeds of brotherhood [in revolutionary Europe]. This is what makes *my* America. . . . She [America] is not dead, but in my time she sleepeth, and the spirit of our fathers flames no more, but lies hid beneath the ashes."[44]

Fuller, true to her radical Romantic roots, sought with all her artistic and intellectual might to wake America up to *her* America, that is, to her aspirational vision of the United States as a social democracy truly inclusive of women, Black people, Native Americans, and other marginalized peoples, a democracy not wed to conquest, empire, and extractive capitalism but rather to reciprocity, economic justice, and mutual dependence between and among humans and the more-than-human. She wrote in the context of catastrophe—manifest destiny and its destruction of Native peoples and lands, slavery, the oppression of women, capitalistic materialism, and European tyranny. And from within that *context*, the *form* of her radical Romantic art was multilayered, complex, and diverse, delivering her messages of protest, critique, revolutionary reform, and dark, wild hope. And while this hope was anchored in suffering and oppression, it also moved Fuller to produce a body of work that offers her readers an ecofeminist vision of democracy in America, a vision nurtured by her radical Romantic faith—a Transcendental belief in a panentheistic Spirit that is in and of all things, endlessly moving and bringing life and beauty to a world marked by death and despair; a progressive vision calling for praxis-oriented empathy and collaborative action.

ZORA NEALE HURSTON: BLACK ECOFEMINISM AND ITS RELATION TO RADICAL ROMANTICISM

If lyrical, storied landscapes revealing topographies of pain and beauty, oppression and liberation are at the heart of radical Romanticism, then Zora Neale Hurston is a radical Romantic. And if storied landscapes that give special attention to white supremacist and patriarchal modes of the domination of the human and nonhuman is a mark of Black ecofeminism, then Hurston is a Black radical

Romantic ecofeminist. But I will not make those claims. Rather, I will state more modestly that there is a family resemblance between the art of radical Romanticism and that of Hurston's Black ecofeminism. And, more importantly, radical Romanticism is profoundly challenged and nurtured when it listens to and learns from the work of Hurston. Indeed, radical Romanticism is obliged to read, cherish, and learn from Hurston.

Hurston was an extraordinary novelist, essayist, cultural anthropologist, and ethnographer, passionately committed to studying and supporting Black culture. Anticipating such cultural anthropologists as Clifford Geertz, Hurston brought lively narrative to ethnographic studies, and anticipating such novelists as Toni Morrison and Honorée Fanonne Jeffers, Hurston brought historical and ethnographic studies to the novel. Brilliant, ahead of her time, and the winner of two Guggenheim Fellowships, Hurston later in life suffered from slander, ostracization, poverty, and illness. She died in obscurity and was buried in a segregated cemetery in an unmarked grave—a grave subsequently discovered by Alice Walker, who also resurrected Hurston's work.

In this section on Hurston, I seek to listen to and explore Hurston's storytelling—paying attention to its form, content, and context—as she sought to witness the catastrophe of interrelated patriarchy, racism, and environmental destruction as well as the resilience and strength of Black women. I pursue this aim by (1) identifying the ways and manners (the form, content, and context) of Hurston's storytelling, showing how it belongs to and contributes to a Black Romantic, ecofeminism; (2) highlighting the crucial role that religion, broadly construed, plays in her Black ecofeminism; and (3) detailing the various ways that Hurston's storytelling expresses the "ecological burden-and-beauty paradox." I begin with a brief biography of Hurston, noting various traditions that informed her life and work, and I offer a broad account of her lyrical storytelling. I then turn to her novel *Their Eyes Were Watching God*, focusing on her contributions to Black ecofeminism, highlighting her critiques of patriarchy, anti-Black racism, and exploitive approaches to the more-than-human. I show how her storytelling vividly presents powerful instances of challenge to the male sovereign self as well as to patriarchal and racist forms of anthropocentrism, dethroning humans—especially the white male—and positioning them *among* the more-than-human rather than as conquerors. Yet, as I show, Hurston's ecofeminist posthumanism also recognizes human distinctiveness, placing it among other forms of distinctiveness that mark creatures and entities of all kinds. Moreover, as we will see, humans experience an intimacy with the more-than-human that brings joy and belonging but also heartache and fear, because the ways and agents of the more-than-human are not perfectly aligned with human goals and desires.

My treatment of *Their Eyes Were Watching God* gives special attention to the role of the pear tree and the hurricane—as these powerful more-than-human entities illuminate Hurston's Black ecofeminism, particularly her complex religious views—and to their relation to the contrasting themes of beauty and hope on the one hand and catastrophe and despair on the other. I argue that Hurston articulated two, wild religions: a "pear tree religion" that is beautiful and life-affirming and a "hurricane religion" that is monstrous and ruinous. These two religions are *wild* not only in their materiality—that of the living tree and mighty winds and rains—but in their manner of being: spirited, subversive, and defiant. Yet the pear tree religion is a potentially enabling force, while the hurricane religion is a potentially ruinous one. I correlate the two religions, respectively, to what I have called Hurston's dual focus on beauty and the catastrophic, though Hurston makes it clear that the destruction that follows in the wake of "hurricane religion" is disproportionately greater for Blacks than whites because of environmental racism.

Although my focus is on Hurston, I am in conversation with scholars who have contributed broadly to Black ecofeminism, in particular with Stacy Alaimo, Sharon Patricia Holland, and Kimberly N. Ruffin. Alaimo's *Bodily Natures: Science, Environment, and the Material Self* helps theorize Hurston's depictions of the various entanglements of Black bodies and the environment; Janie's encounters with the pear tree and hurricane, for example, are embodied experiences that exemplify the material interconnectedness of the human and more-than-human.[45] Holland's *The Erotic Life of Racism* demonstrates how racism informs one's erotic experience (that is, the touch and friction of the everyday) of people and place; Janie and Nanny (a former enslaved woman) have distinct encounters with whites and Blacks and the more-than-human based on their identities as poor Black women.[46] Kimberly N. Ruffin's *Black on Earth: African American Ecological Traditions* powerfully explores how Black authors portray the more-than-human as sites of oppression and suffering as well as sites of beauty and liberation; Ruffin's "ecological burden-and-beauty paradox" is a central interpretive lens for my exploration of Hurston's Black ecofeminism.[47]

In addition to Alaimo's, Holland's, and Ruffin's providing a broad theoretical scaffolding for my approach, I have greatly benefited from the ecofeminist work on Hurston by Jennifer C. James and Sonya Posmentier. James's "A Theory of the

Bottom: Black Ecofeminism as Politics" is central to my reading of Janie as a person at "the bottom"—at the intersection of racism, patriarchy, and classism; her position at the bottom provides her with critical perspectives on social and environmental injustice and also with a profound sense of kinship with the oppressed, whether human or more-than-human.[48] Sonya Posmentier's *Cultivation and Catastrophe: The Lyric Ecology of Modern Black Literature* has a powerful chapter on the relation between Hurston's musical recordings and the connection between the hurricane and environmental racism in *Their Eyes*; although I do not pursue Posmentier's work on the musical recordings, I have profited from her account of the Jim Crow burials that link the hurricane in relation to environmental racism.[49]

Hurston and Her Affinity with Radical Romanticism

Hurston belonged to—and shaped—a variety of cultural, intellectual, and spiritual traditions. Her identity as a Black Southern woman was greatly informed by her upbringing in Eatonville, Florida, one of the first all-Black, self-governing towns in the United States. Eatonville was an important source for Hurston's collection of Black folklore as well as the setting of some of her books. Hurston's father was a Baptist minister, and in response to him and the Baptist tradition, Hurston developed both positive and critical views of Christianity. Her mother was a schoolteacher who encouraged Hurston's intellectual curiosity and love of the natural world. After earning an associate degree at Howard University, where her literary talent caught the attention of many, Hurston studied at Barnard College (where she was the sole Black student). At Barnard, Hurston was drawn to Franz Boas, given his opposition to biological racism and to European paradigms of cultural evolution and hierarchies. Boas, in turn, was drawn to Hurston's knowledge of Black American culture, her keen ethnographic observational skills, and her prodigious literary and intellectual abilities. Many people and traditions influenced Hurston, and she profoundly influenced such authors as Alice Walker, Toni Morrison, Gayl Jones, and Ralph Ellison and such traditions and modes of inquiry as Black literature, the ethnographic novel, participant-observation anthropology, religions of the African diaspora, and ecofeminism.

   Hurston's work shares many affinities with radical Romantic ecofeminism. She was a master storyteller who crafted lyrical, storied landscapes, poignantly depicting beauty and oppression, hope and despair, life and death—all in relation to both the human and the nonhuman world and the intricate relation between the two. Like Du Bois, Hurston brought art to social science research and social science research to art. For example, she was not satisfied with technical linguistic or statistical accounts of Black folklore but rather sought to convey her research in a form that expressed the literary and lyrical quality of Black folklore and spiritual traditions (including Black preaching and other poetic-spiritual forms).[50] Like Wordsworth before her, Hurston was greatly criticized for both the form and the topics of her literary work. Wordsworth revolutionized poetry by employing the matter and manner of everyday people and language; so, too, Hurston revolutionized literature by employing the matter and manner of everyday Southern Black culture and speech. She addressed, for example, women's sensuality and their quest for independence from both white and Black men, and she masterfully employed Black vernacular speech in her dialogues. This effort to represent and honor Black culture was as forward-looking as it was aggressively criticized by white and Black critics alike.

Yet, as in radical Romanticism, she also presented various sources of strength and healing that come from connection to place and cultural and spiritual traditions. This connection emphasizes the interdependent relation between humans and the more-than-human. Her depiction of human drama, for example, is richly embedded in ecological landscapes in which humans and animals are in close association. Hurston also, however, acknowledged the distinctive agency of the more-than-human. Like Shelley before her, Hurston's work embraces humanism (the dignity of human persons and a capacious understanding of who counts as human) but also posthumanism (a rejection of anthropocentrism).

Hurston rejected patriarchal, oppressive religion while, in line with the early Wordsworth, articulating an earth-oriented, panentheistic spirituality (such as that of the "pear tree" in *Their Eyes*). And like the radical Romantics, Hurston's art depicted in graphic detail the "face" of the oppressed and their suffering—especially the face of Black women in a racist, patriarchal culture. She endeavored to foster witnesses that manifested a praxis-oriented empathy; this effort to move her readers to respond is seen, for example, in the complex, story-within-a-story narrative structure of *Their Eyes*: Janie returns home under the scrutiny of its judgmental men, and she shares her story of departure and growth with her friend Pheoby. In the process, as Melissa Harris-Perry perceptively writes, "we [the readers] have heard the story, and it is our job to make politics out of it."[51]

There are, then, many affinities between Hurston and radical Romanticism. Yet, similar to the authorship of Shelley, Fuller, and Du Bois, Hurston's work potentially transforms radical Romanticism because she wrote from a perspective not found in white, male Romanticism. As a Black woman who courageously crossed gendered and racial boundaries, Hurston's work introduces profound considerations of race and gender into radical Romanticism. Like Shelley and Fuller, Hurston's feminist art of radical Romantic storytelling painted the human and environmental catastrophe of patriarchy as well as the resilience and strength of women. In *Their Eyes*, for example, Janie combats the oppression of women and increasingly gains a voice and agency that rivals all the human characters in the book. But more than Shelley and Fuller, Hurston addressed race, specifically anti-Black racism, and hence she may be considered not only an ecofeminist but a Black eco*womanist*. Melanie L. Harris has helpfully defined ecowomanist approaches as acknowledging "the importance of multidimensional womanist race-class-gender analysis regarding environmental justice issues that serve to uncover the concerns of women of color, and African and African American women in particular."[52]

While I have not claimed that Hurston was a radical Romantic, I should note that there is a tradition of Black American Romanticism that precedes Hurston. Matt Sandler notes that "in the middle decades of the nineteenth century, an independent and distinct form of Romanticism took shape among the Black writers of the U.S. abolition movement and radical Reconstruction." These Black authors "borrowed and transformed the techniques and theories of Romanticism in an effort to bring about the end of slavery and the self-conscious regeneration of Black community." Rather than confining Romanticism to a particular era of European history, these Black Romantics "understood the Civil War era as a belated iteration of Romantic revolution, and imagined their liberation as a part of an ongoing, total cultural and political transformation."[53] Frances Ellen Watkins Harper, for example, a Black woman poet and activist, drew on Romantic themes and perspectives, all the while powerfully transforming them to address the abolition of slavery and the rights of women.

It would be a mistake, however, to reduce Black American Romanticism to a form of abolitionism and women's suffrage. The content and aim of their writings, while clearly addressing pressing social justice issues of their day, also attended to more everyday aspects of Black lives and culture, seeking to honor a wide range of Black experiences. This is the case outside of North America as well. In an article titled "A Black Manifesto: Ottobah Cugoano's Radical Romanticism," Julian Whitney argues that the late-eighteenth-century, Black British writer Quobna Ottobah Cugoano demanded "to live in a world in which Black identity is appreciated more fully for its multidimensional depth beyond slavery. Cugoano's call for the radical normalization of Black experiences is what models Romanticism to embrace new horizons around a more comprehensive understanding of Black identity."[54]

While I have been stressing the importance of how authors such as Du Bois and Hurston potentially challenge and *transform* Romanticism, Whitney convincingly shows that the work for "self-definition" by Black authors such as Ottobah Cugoano reflect "some of the greatest aims *within* Romanticism, including the sustained capacity to reinvent oneself to meet the demands of a new time."[55] Surely there is a place for both arguments in the field of Romanticism, and both certainly apply to Hurston. As a Black woman whose experience informs her writing, her work does bring needed perspectives on patriarchy and anti-Black racism to a largely white, male Romanticism, however radical. On the other hand, her writing explores in the mode of Romanticism a wide range of issues and themes—beyond those of patriarchy and racism—that pertain more generally to being Black and female and even to what it means to be *human* and to experience love and beauty, loss and death. Hurston wrote powerfully about race and gender, but she refused to reduce being Black and female to being oppressed.

The Pear Tree and the Hurricane: Radical Romantic Religion in Their Eyes Were Watching God

Having provided some context for interpreting Hurston's work in relation to radical Romanticism, I now turn to her novel *Their Eyes Were Watching God*. The novel brings together history and the imagination, gender and race, love and death, and the human and the more-than-human—all conveyed in a lyrical prose that conjures rich affect and moving pathos. My account of the novel will focus on two contrasting storied landscapes: that of the pear tree and the hurricane. While others have commented on these two prominent entities—the pear tree and the hurricane—my own interpretive lens brings attention to their religious aspects and shows the attendant Black ecofeminist implications. The vision of the pear tree and the force of the hurricane will help us consider Janie's—the main protagonist's—journey to mature selfhood via spirituality and poignant encounters with the more-than-human. On this journey, Janie confronts various forms of patriarchy, anthropocentricism, and racism (including environmental racism).

At the start of the novel, Janie Crawford, the main protagonist, returns from Lake Okeechobee to Eatonville, Florida, an all-Black town where she has previously lived with her second husband, Joe Starks. Like the Romantic trope of the individual who, after experiencing various trials, returns home having achieved wisdom and personal wherewithal, Janie boldly returns to Eatonville under the suspicious eyes of the townsmen. Janie, now in her forties and having been married three times, returns with self-confidence, self-determination, and equanimity, and she tells the story of her remarkable journey to her friend Pheoby.

It's been a long journey. At age sixteen, Janie is encouraged by her grandmother to marry Logan Killicks, an older man with wealth who will supposedly protect her from being mistreated. Killicks, however, ends up treating Janie like a work mule, so Janie jumps at the opportunity to elope with Joe Starks—the eventual mayor of Eatonville. But Janie soon learns that Starks is obsessed with money and power, and he treats Janie as a decorative wife to prop up his appearance as a successful businessman. He increasingly prevents Janie from exercising her agency and from enjoying connections to the social and natural world around her. Eventually, Starks dies, and Janie falls in love with Tea Cake, a carefree younger man who, for the most part, treats Janie with dignity and respect. After they marry, they move to the fertile, deep green Florida Everglades where they work together harvesting in the fields. Except for a violent episode when a jealous Tea Cake strikes Janie—which we will return to later—they live happily together until a hurricane brings cataclysmic destruction. While attempting to save Janie from flooding waters and a rabid dog, Tea Cake is infected with rabies and becomes violent. Janie kills him in self-defense. She deeply mourns the death of Tea Cake. When she returns to Eatonville, she is comforted by his presence in the form of memories and the seeds he had been waiting to plant in their garden.

The Pear Tree

Hurston crafts a narrative of suffering and obstacles but also beauty and achievement. I will now turn to the beauty and powerful eros of the pear tree and all that it represents for Janie.

It was a spring afternoon in West Florida. Janie [at sixteen] had spent most of the day under a blossoming pear tree in the back-yard. . . . It had called her to come and gaze on a mystery. . . . It was like a flute song forgotten in another existence and remembered again. . . . It followed her through all her waking moments and caressed her in her sleep. It connected itself with other vaguely felt matters that had struck her outside observation and buried themselves in her flesh. . . .

She was stretched on her back beneath the pear tree soaking in the alto chant of the visiting bees, the gold of the sun and the panting breath of the breeze when the inaudible voice of it all came to her. She saw a dust-bearing bee sink into the sanctum of a bloom; the thousand sister-calyxes arch to meet the love embrace and the ecstatic shiver of the tree from root to tiniest branch creaming in every blossom and frothing with delight. . . . She had been summoned to behold a revelation.[56]

The pear tree is a religious vision and a powerful more-than-human guide to help Janie discern between that which brings love and life and that which brings anguish and death.[57] In this eco-storied landscape, Hurston's lyrical prose speaks of seasons and blossoms, sunshine and bees, wind and roots. The pear tree is not separate from the human world but rather calls to Janie and connects her to the more-than-human. Janie, in turn, welcomes this wild vision and character into her soul. While the pear tree is an ephemeral "mystery" and "revelation," it also immanently pervades the everyday, connecting itself with "felt matters that had struck [Janie] outside observation and buried themselves in her flesh." The pear tree religious vision, then, participates in the everyday and is enfleshed within Janie. It can be said to be pan*en*theistic, interweaving spirit, humans, and the more-than-human.

At different times in her life, Janie recollects its presence and trusts in its goodness and beauty, even as the tree helps her trust in her own goodness and beauty. When the men and political order of the day attempt to denigrate Janie, to bring her low and take away her agency—her aspirations for love and life—the pear tree bolsters her strength and creativity to forge another way: a *wild*, nonconformist way of beauty and delight. Indeed, the disruptive, nonconformist ways of the pear tree, aiding Janie in her refusal to patriarchy, among other forms of oppression, suggest the wildness of the pear tree religion. Janie's vision of the pear tree aligns itself with a radical Romantic, ecofeminist aesthetics of attention, care, and mutual dependence between and among humans and the more-than-human. Moreover, the pear tree supports Janie spiritually by reassuring her that the world for Black women is not only a place of oppression and domination but also of beauty, eros, and the sacred.

Such spiritual support has profound material outcomes. The eroticism of the pear tree—the plummeting of the bees into the "sanctum of a bloom" and the "ecstatic shiver of the tree," for example—anticipates Audre Lorde's powerful notion of women's spiritual, erotic power and its potential to transform the self and the politics of the everyday.[58] The erotic, here, is as joyful as it is demanding. It is not content with the unjust status quo but rather energetically and creatively challenges and transforms oppressive convention and patriarchal power. For Hurston's character Janie, as for Lorde, the erotic is as spiritual as it is political: It empowers and links the liberated self with liberating relationality. Hurston, via Janie, brings to radical Romantic ecofeminism a life-affirming, antipatriarchal *erotics of place*. The eroticism of the pear tree signals Janie's intimate, healthy relation with the more-than-human as well with the human. And it provides a buttress against a different kind of eroticism, namely, the everyday *eroticism of racism* that Holland describes, an eroticism that intimately touches and assaults Black women by a white world.[59]

The pear tree also provides Janie with a powerful contrasting vision to that of her Nanny and her first two husbands. Nanny, exemplifying what Alaimo refers to as the "interconnections, interchanges, and transits between human bodies and nonhuman natures," becomes alienated from the natural world because of her trauma of slavery, sexual assault, and her eventual escape from slavery through a dangerous, inhospitable swampland.[60] Nanny the former slave has a keener understanding than the young Janie of what it is to be treated as subhuman—as "de mule uh de world," as she puts it, subjugated by men both white and Black (14). In order to protect Janie from the dangers of racism and patriarchy that she herself has experienced, Nanny encourages Janie to keep a low profile, marry someone with financial means, and be satisfied with a safe but dull life in which she does not experience much agency or eroticism. Janie acquiesces to her Nanny and at the age of sixteen marries Logan Killicks, an older man of some means.

Janie's hope is that, once married, the beauty and eroticism of the pear tree will pervade her relationship with her husband. But her husband sees Janie and the natural world as resources to be exploited for profit. Unlike her husband, Janie "knew things that nobody had ever told her. For instance, the words of the trees and the wind. She often spoke to falling seeds and said, 'Ah hope you fall on soft ground,' because she had heard seeds saying that to each other as they passed" (23-24). Janie, a radical Romantic at heart, knows how to speak and listen to the more-than-human, learning from and experiencing companionship with the nonhuman.

Janie's initial, negative assessment of the prospective marriage to Killicks proves to be correct: "The vision of Logan Killicks was desecrating the pear tree" (13). So, when Joe Starks shows up in her life, Janie, now somewhat jaded (her "first dream was dead, so she became a woman" [24]), is ready to run away and marry him for the sake of a new start, even though he does not "represent sun-up and pollen and blooming trees" (28). Unfortunately, Starks turns out to be as "desecrating" as Killicks. He treats Janie as a sexualized object to adorn his life, restricting her agency, aspirations, and life-affirming engagement with the human and more-than-human. In contrast to Janie, Starks sees people and place as resources to be exploited to further his power, wealth, and status. Earlier, while under the pear tree, Janie witnesses "the ecstatic shiver of the tree from root to tiniest branch creaming in every blossom and frothing with delight," and she reflects, "So this was a marriage" (11). Given this measure of the fullness of marriage, Janie's first two marriages have surely failed.

When Starks dies, Janie shocks her community by leaving town with a younger man, Vergible Woods, known as Tea Cake. He treats her with respect, affirms her ability to make and do things, cooks meals for her, and makes her laugh. He is playful and not driven by profit or status. Early on in their relationship, Janie muses, "He could be a bee to a blossom—a pear tree blossom in the spring. . . . Spices hung about him. He was a glance from God" (101-2). His given name, Vergible Woods, intimates a deep connection with the more-than-human. Janie welcomes such a partner in her life, happy to leave behind wealth and status for Tea Cake and their new adventurous life on "the muck"—the Florida Everglades. On "the muck," they experience a gentle intimacy with each other as well as lively community with fellow workers. Janie is drawn to the wildness of the place: "Everything in the Everglades was big and new. Big Lake Okechobee, big beans, big cane, big weeds, big everything. . . . Ground so rich that everything went wild. . . . Dirt roads so rich and black that a half mile of it would have fertilized a Kansas wheat field. Wild cane on either side of the road hiding the rest of the world. People wild too" (123). Janie's new home in "the muck" is marked by the wild, that is, by a land and a people who are not subject to strict domesticity, control, and enforced conventions. For Hurston, "the muck is a wondrous and wild space, bigger than human dominion."[61] Once again, as with the appearance of the pear tree, Janie is surprised by joy and beauty. Indeed, the life, love, and geniality represented by the pear tree now have the opportunity to thrive in the muck. There, in that wild soil, Janie's ecofeminist vision takes root. She finds, and makes, a place of mutual respect and equality among and between the human and the more-than-human. Still, the muck—and the natural world more generally—is no Eden, if Eden is a place of perfect harmony. A hurricane is coming, and with it, Hurston offers a different face of nature—and of spirit—than that of the pear tree.

The Hurricane

At one point, Tea Cake becomes jealous over Janie and strikes her. They reconcile afterward. While the assault is inexcusable, structural racism has a part in it (Janie, because of her light skin, is encouraged by a Black woman—who wishes to "lighten up de race" [135]—to marry her light-skinned brother, causing the dark-skinned Tea to become angry). This violence and racism foreshadow the coming hurricane and the subsequent destruction and environmental racism.

In the culturally and ecologically diverse muck, Seminole Native Americans and animals sense the coming of the storm and wisely move to high ground.[62] But Tea Cake is dismissive, ignoring the warning from those with the most ecological knowledge, typifying the sovereign male going it alone. When the hurricane strikes with all its fury, Tea Cake and Janie leave their flimsy shelter and attempt to run on foot through it, seeking higher ground. After much struggle, "hopefully and hopelessly," they approach a high, secure bridge that offers protection, but "white people had preempted that point of elevation and there was no more room" (155, 156). Janie then falls in the rising, turbulent waters, and Tea Cake is bitten by a rabid dog in his attempt to rescue her. Later, in the aftermath of the hurricane's destruction, Tea Cake and other Black men are forced at gunpoint to bury the dead—white bodies receiving coffins and marked graves, Black bodies being thrown in open ditches (though the drowned bodies become nearly indistinguishable in color). Janie and Tea Cake eventually make their way back to the muck, but Tea Cake soon suffers from delirium and paranoia, symptoms of his rabies, and when he attacks Janie, she shoots him in self-defense.

Like the radical Romantics before her, Hurston portrays the many faces and expressions of the more-than-human world. The hurricane is nature wild and not subject to human control. Hurston had had her own experience of a massively destructive hurricane while living in the Bahamas, and she conducted extensive research on the 1928 Okeechobee Florida hurricane, in which three thousand people died, mostly Black people later buried in mass graves.[63] The hurricane, for Hurston, is a face of nature that checks human pretension and aspiration, as might the fury of God. The hurricane—again, like God—brings life to the dead and death to the living: When Tea Cake walked out into the blast of the hurricane, "he saw that the wind and water had given life to lots of things that folks thought of as dead and given death to so much that had been living things" (151–52). The hurricane moves and breathes, wielding colossal agency: "It woke up old Okechobee and the monster began to roll in his bed" (150). For a while, "the people felt uncomfortable but safe because there were the seawalls to chain the senseless monster in his bed" (150). But that changes when "the monstropolous beast had left his bed. . . . He seized hold of his dikes and ran forward until he met the quarters; uprooted them like grass and rushed on after his supposed-to-be conquerors, rolling the dikes, rolling the houses, rolling the people in the houses along with other timbers. The sea was walking the earth with a heavy heel" (153). If this were Wordsworth's one Life that "rolls through all things," the rolling is anything but gentle and harmonious.[64] Humans, the "supposed-to-be conquerors," are kicked aside as the mighty sea walks the earth. This is the face of climate change. This is the face of an indiscriminate more-than-human agency challenging human agency at its very existential core. This is the face of nature, wild.

It is also the face of a wild religion. After all, "their eyes were watching *God*," as Janie and Tea Cake stared at the dark, huddled in their cabin, listening to the winds come back with "triple fury," "their souls asking if He meant to measure their puny might against His" (151; emphasis added). Throughout her life, Hurston was captivated by religion, and it shows up, one way or another, in most of her work, including *Their Eyes Were Watching God*. Earthquakes, volcanic eruptions, and hurricanes—events outside human control—are commonly called "acts of God." The phrase may be principally a legal term, but it can also be employed as a religio-poetic term, eliding the force of nature—surely the *more*-than-human— with the *might* of God or the gods. Religions come in various kinds, but most have this in common: They decenter human power by subjecting humans to a greater power. And thus, in the face of the hurricane, Janie and Tea Cake were watching God—a wild god for a wild religion. Indeed, it is not a tame religion. Hurston's hurricane religion is as furious as it is impartial. It is Job's God in the whirlwind.

It is Kierkegaard's God of fear and trembling. It is Hurston's God of "disruptive wonderment and sacred silence."[65] This unnerving religion brings little comfort, much mystery, and dethrones humans as the center of all things. As they peer into the dark—as we search for answers and consolation in moments of agonizing uncertainty and vulnerability—they wait for God, wait for the hurricane's next move. It is easy to confuse staring into the void and waiting on God: "They seemed to be staring at the dark, but their eyes were watching God."

This wild religion is indiscriminate, not heeding social conventions or prejudice, its winds and waves transgressing racial, gendered, socioeconomic, and national borders. Still, some humans receive more protection than others from the destruction of this hurricane religion. Hurston was one of the first U.S. authors to write both empirically and lyrically—radical-Romantically—about environmental racism. Her work demonstrated, as Sonya Posmentier notes, the "continuity between environmental and human violence" as seen in "the Jim Crow burials": "Tea Cake, conscripted into labor after the storm, is instructed to bury the black dead in mass graves and the white dead in coffins (and to distinguish the bodies by their hair).... The scene of the Jim Crow burials... demonstrates the pervasiveness of Jim Crow in the white supremacy of the guards and the strength of the racist social order even after death."[66] In order to convey the robustness and violence of Jim Crow—"even after death"—Hurston, as someone with extensive social scientific training and having conducted detailed research on destructive hurricanes, could have simply provided facts and statistics; instead, she crafted poignant storied landscapes—a particular literary form—to vividly portray Janie's precarity as a Black woman facing a natural catastrophe. Janie's precarity was intensified by patriarchy (for Tea Cake refused to heed the concerns of her and others about the approaching hurricane). These forms of precarity and oppression—*abstractly* known as the effect of patriarchy and racism—are developed *concretely* in the literary form of a moving narrative that grips readers, creating an intimacy between them and Janie and potentially producing a praxis-oriented empathy.

Yet precarity and oppression are not the only contours of these storied landscapes. Resiliency and hope are there, too, and also tenderness, as when "Tea Cake touched Janie [in the midst of the hurricane] and said, 'Ah reckon you wish now you had of stayed in yo' big house 'way from such as dis, don't yuh?,'" to which Janie replies, "People don't die till dey time come nohow, don't keer where you at. Ah'm wid mah husband in uh storm, dat's all" (151). Janie and Tea Cake's marriage was not perfect, but of the three marriages, it came closest to the erotic, wild, life-affirming ways of the pear tree. Hurston created a richly layered canvas for all to behold the ugliness of environmental racism, especially as experienced by Black women, but also to regard a strength and love that persist against all odds. Unfortunately, great "odds" are still against Black women, especially as the climate catastrophes worsen.

Race, Gender, Colonialism, and Ecofeminist Dark, Wild Hope

The lyrical complexity of Hurston's authorship shares a deep affinity with radical Romanticism even as it challenges it, unsettling it with the terrible face of patriarchy and racism. The environmental and institutional racism that Hurston vividly depicted in *Their Eyes* were not harms addressed in white, Euro-American Romanticism. And the triple oppression of being poor, Black, and female was not addressed in the ecofeminism of Shelley and Fuller. Hurston, then, unsettles even progressive forms of radical Romanticism ecofeminism. Moreover, in *Their Eyes* and elsewhere, Hurston extended radical Romanticism's critique of democracy's failure to be inclusive and just. Margaret Fuller and Thoreau, for example, sought to show the ethical gap between the *aspirations* of participatory democracy and its *actual* historical record up to the present—its formal or de facto disenfranchisement based on class, gender, and race. Hurston, too, exposed this "ethical gap," but she placed race front and center. For example, employing the powerful aesthetics of *taste*, she quipped:

> I am all for tasting this democracy out. The flavor must be good. If the Occident is so intent in keeping the taste out of darker mouths that it spends all those billions and expends all those millions of lives, colored ones too, to keep it among themselves, then it must be something good. I crave to sample this gorgeous thing. So I cannot say anything different from repeal of all Jim Crow laws![67]

Additionally, Hurston's work extends radical Romanticism's critique of colonialism, as when she wrote, "The Indo-Chinese are fighting the French now in Indo-China to keep the freedom that they have enjoyed for five or six years now. The Indonesians are trying to stay free from the Dutch, and the Burmese and Malayans from the British. But American soldiers and sailors are fighting along with the French, Dutch and English to rivet these chains back on their former slaves."[68] Hurston challenged rapacious colonialism and championed an ecofeminist set of practices and perspectives that places a premium on emancipatory political participation, reciprocity, and the powerful agency of women. And in these passages just quoted, we see Hurston employing a particular *form* of ecofeminism, namely, sarcasm and scorn, to express ethical outrage and disbelief (though this is present to some extent in both Shelley and Fuller).[69] This form, and the content that it conveys, is perfectly crafted for the *context* of Hurston's art and arguments—patriarchy, anti-Black racism, and Western colonialism.

Janie refuses to stay within the narrow confines of gendered roles. As much as Nanny wants Janie to play it safe—to *be* safe—and be a "good wife," Janie insists on transgressing gendered boundaries, gaining more and more power and agency as the novel progresses. She leaves Eatonville in a pretty dress and returns in overalls to the shock of the townsmen ("What she doin' coming back here in dem overhalls? Can't she find no dress to put on?—Where's dat blue satin dress she left here in?" [2]). Domineering men repeatedly tell Janie, "Uh woman by herself is uh pitiful thing" (86), but she enjoys her independence: "This freedom feeling was fine. These men didn't represent a thing she wanted to know about" (86). Ultimately, Janie courageously and creatively becomes a woman like Hurston herself: feisty, bold, independent, and unafraid to speak in her own voice. Like the wildness of both the pear tree and hurricane religion—a wildness that surprises and that contests longstanding (often oppressive) perspectives, practices, and conventions—Janie becomes a self-confident, wild woman.

The aesthetic and ethical topography of Hurston's storied landscapes is nuanced and complex. Hurston neither flinched from disclosing domination nor reduced Black people to simply an oppressed people, as illustrated by what could be called the two wild religions in *Their Eyes*. The panentheistic pear tree religion offers a spiritual path of beauty and delight that refuses society's cruel conventions. Its life-affirming, antipatriarchal erotics guides Janie on her journey toward healthy self-love and nurturing relations with humans and the more-than-human. The hurricane religion, in contrast, is wildly fierce, frightening, and inscrutable, bringing destruction and suffering in its path to all, but especially to vulnerable Black populations subjected to environmental racism. These two religions cannot be reconciled, but they do frequently collide, dynamically mixing beauty and joy, suffering and oppression in Black lives. This was Hurston's experience of life as well as her experience of religion, broadly understood. In her own Black Baptist tradition and her subsequent study of and participation in Vodou, an African diasporic religion of the Caribbean and U.S. South, Hurston encountered the many-sidedness of religion—its powerful rituals, aesthetics, and liberatory messages as well as its oppressive patriarchy, dogmatic creeds, and fear-mongering. Although she renounced the Baptist religion in which she was raised, she continued to employ a rich, varied religious vocabulary, including Christianity, in her writings, and she maintained her own "nontraditional" religious beliefs. Among other things, this sophisticated religious vocabulary informed her complex, lyrical narratives of beauty and suffering.

Hurston's refusal to allow patriarchy and racism to monopolize her storied landscapes is also found in Du Bois's complex storied landscapes, and both authors exemplify what Kimberly Ruffin has called the "ecological burden-and-beauty paradox":

> An ecological burden is placed on those who are racialized negatively, and they therefore suffer economically and environmentally because of their degraded status. Simultaneously, however, the experience of ecological beauty results from individual and collective attitudes toward nature that undercut the experience of racism and its related evils.[70]

Hurston's ecofeminism powerfully manifests this paradox by describing Janie's painful experience of patriarchy and racism as they threaten her life and ability to have healthy relationships to the self, others, and the more-than-human; yet at the same time, Janie opens herself up to various sources of strength—for example, the love, however imperfect, of Nanny and Tea Cake, the revelation of the pear tree, and her own depth of soul—and thereby finds joy and beauty in a difficult, challenging world.

There is a dark, wild hope in the person of Janie. At the conclusion of *Their Eyes*, Janie tells her friend Pheoby, "Two things everbody's got tuh do fuh theyselves. They got tuh go tuh God, and they got tuh find out about livin' fuh theyselves" (183). Dark, wild hope abides in finding sources of strength and one's own path to a measure of joy and safety in a world of domineering Black men, racist whites, and wild hurricanes. Janie achieves just that. At the end of the novel, after having endured much oppression and pain and now mourning the death of Tea Cake, she returns home and *tastes* newness: "The place tasted fresh again" (183).

This taste of new life brings to Janie, at least for the moment, a sense of peace and of being at home—at home in her house but also in the world: "Here was peace. She pulled in her horizon like a great fish-net. Pulled it from around the waist of the world and draped it over her shoulder. So much of life in its meshes! She called in her soul to come and see" (184). Such a hopeful gesture does not deny but rather acknowledges pain and struggle and the life and beauty that Black women nonetheless achieve.

Hurston's storytelling names and challenges persistent harms and evils but also offers alternative ways of being: Black ecofeminist practices and perspectives that place a premium on emancipatory political participation, reciprocity, justice, and the dignity of all humans and the more-than-human. These alternative ways of being are discovered and learned from being at "the bottom"; as Jennifer James so movingly writes:

> If the human, the top, is what Enlightenment discourses and its offshoots have taught us it is (i.e., white, western, heteropatriarchal, capitalist able-bodied male), with all other living things at the bottom, then I submit that the bottom is where we want to be. In contact. Entangled. Undifferentiated from other life. Like Black feminism itself, Black ecofeminism is a theory of the bottom.[71]

Hurston wrote from the bottom and for the sake of the dignity of the bottom.

RADICAL ROMANTIC ECOFEMINISM:
PAST, PRESENT, AND FUTURE

In this chapter, I have sought to show how our three ecofeminists, Shelley, Fuller, and Hurston, participate in and transform radical Romanticism. I have focused on the distinctive content, form, and context of their ecofeminist writings, but I should also note their affinities with the content, form, and context of radical Romanticism more generally. The *content* of radical Romanticism engages with various socioeconomic, political, religious, and environmental issues. The *context* is the crises and catastrophes that bring harm to both the human and the more-than-human, for example, the dispossession and injustice that comes from land enclosures, the social and environmental wreckage caused by the Industrial

Revolution and extractive capitalism, and the oppression and evil inherent in slavery, racism, and patriarchy.

The *forms* of radical Romanticism—what I have called its radical aesthetics— reflect an epistemology that refuses such unhealthy dualisms as reason and emotion, culture and nature, humans and more-than-human, spirit and matter. (Rousseau, we saw, began the work of dismantling these destructive binaries.) Rather than assume there is an epistemological gulf between us and the world, the assumption is that we are intimate with the world (*pace* Cartesianism) yet also that the world is full of surprises, ready to unsettle us with the unfamiliar amid the familiar. And rather than place the highest premium on rationality, radical Romanticism emphasizes vulnerability and interdependency. A person's worth is not measured by a capacity for rationality but by simply being human, understood in the most capacious manner. This is the humanism affirmed by radical Romanticism. At the same time, however, it affirms an interdependent relationality to the more-than-human, challenging anthropocentric forms of humanism, displacing the human from the center of all things.

Naming the content, form, and context of radical Romanticism with these broad strokes is one way to define radical Romanticism and one way to limn the family resemblance between such otherwise diverse authors as Rousseau, Dorothy and William Wordsworth, Coleridge, Shelley, Fuller, Thoreau, Hurston, Du Bois, and Silko. The list of past and present authors who potentially count as radical Romantics is ongoing and dynamic. For this chapter on ecofeminism, Terry Tempest Williams is a wonderful example of a contemporary radical Romantic. She crafts her art in the context of catastrophic nuclearism, militarism, climate change, and environmental devastation. In *Refuge*, for example, her storied landscapes palpably link her family's history of breast cancer to environmental degradation caused by the reckless nuclear program of the U.S. government. Williams's art powerfully depicts people and animals pushed to the margins by government-sanctioned flooding and women suffering from breast cancer in sterile hospital wards. The result is a profound contribution to breast cancer literature and ecofeminism. In her book *The Open Space of Democracy*, we find her most explicit treatment of the three-way convergence of democracy, religion, and the environment. This convergence is seen in her notion of a "spiritual democracy" (one that she shares with Wordsworth, Whitman, and Du Bois, among others): a robust democratic culture and creed, a source of life, both real and ideal, that promotes justice and flourishing among humans and the more-than-human.

Spiritual, here, connotes the thought, skills, practices, dispositions, and emotions of diverse citizens as they pursue a distinctively democratic relation among themselves, the land, and political community. For Williams, there is a connection between democracy and interdependency.

Williams employs her art and imagination to everyday realities, giving her readers new insights into the experiences of patriarchy, war, environmental degradation, and extractive capitalism. Like other radical Romantics, we see in Williams a less "romantic" Romanticism, as she wrestles with the practical, interwoven matters of religion, politics, and the environment. Her realism of the everyday is manifested in her powerful notion of the "erotics of place," which depicts women and land not as objects to be patriarchally exploited but rather as agents with inherent dignity.[72] Not unlike Lorde's notion of the erotic, Williams's erotics of place is a form of power that seeks to free both women (and other marginalized people) and the more-than-human from oppressive patriarchal forces. Patriarchal fear of and desire for "wild" women and land are challenged by an erotics that vibrantly joins women and the more-than-human in relational respect and interdependency.

What will radical Romantic ecofeminism look like in the future? The rise of nationalistic fascism in the United States is waging a backlash and assault on four distinct yet interrelated targets: progressive advances in feminism, queer rights, civil rights, and environmentalism (broadly understood). Contemporary iterations of radical Romantic ecofeminism, such as Williams's, are robustly addressing the connections between patriarchy and harm to women and place. The future content, form, and context of radical Romantic ecofeminism is uncertain, but its foundation in such authors as Shelley, Fuller, and Hurston is as strong as it is promising.

CHAPTER 7

Leslie Marmon Silko and the Power of Indigenous Storytelling

Healing and Resistance in Defiance of Settler Colonialism

Y ou don't have anything / if you don't have the stories." With this warning, the Laguna Pueblo author Leslie Marmon Silko begins her novel *Ceremony* (1977). But Silko's warning is also a message of hope: You have everything (or at least *much*) if you have the stories—powerful, vital resources for healing, resilience, resistance, and social transformation. This chapter is largely written in the mode of listening: of attending to the stories that Silko weaves from her life and her Indigenous traditions. In the act of listening, questions are posed to us: What does it mean to "have the stories"—to have them "taking form in bone and muscle"?[1] Which stories? Whose bone and muscle? What is the connection between having the stories and having sources of life and resilience, especially in times of oppression and despair? And what might it mean to forget or neglect the stories?

In *Yellow Woman and a Beauty of the Spirit*, Silko describes how she dropped out of law school due to the savagery of the U.S. settler legal system, deciding "the only way to seek justice was through *the power of the stories*."[2] This credo may sound like hyperbole, but such judgment should be suspended until one learns what exactly the power of stories is. What if "stories" refers to the matter and manner of dynamic, emerging traditions, beliefs, rituals, and practices—replete with despair and hope, catastrophe and resilience, violence and love, and courageous solidarities and role models? Storytelling, in Silko's view, is not principally a form of entertainment but a survival skill and a practice. It is history and medicine; it is diagnostic and prognostic. Storytelling assists Indigenous populations in practical ways to cope with life's challenges. While those challenges certainly include the dispossession and oppression that have come from settler colonialism,

Indigenous storytelling as a practical praxis predates the arrival of white settlers. It is an ancient practice that has assisted with such public and private hardships as war, hunger, sickness, and heartbreak.

When Silko dropped out of law school, she already understood stories' importance—including stories that paired photographs and images with texts, looking to the Romantic author William Blake as a model. But she knew that she needed to learn more.[3] So she moved to Chinle in the Navajo Nation, taught at Diné College, and opened herself up to her Indigenous students and colleagues and to the land itself.[4] Silko, a Laguna Pueblo woman who already knew much about her family's and people's stories, allowed the stories to grow in her still more deeply as she lived and worked in Chinle with various Diné storytellers.

In *Almanac of the Dead* (1991), Silko expresses both the "high stakes" and the power of storytelling through the character Weasel Tail, a Lakota who is raised near the site of the Wounded Knee massacre. The site is haunted by the horrific event, and it informs the nature and passion of Weasel Tail's vocation as an activist and storyteller who combats unjust settler law with the power of the story—in this case, the power of poetry: "Poetry would set the people free; poetry would speak to the dreams and to the spirits, and the people would understand what they must do. . . . The [white man's] law crushed and cheated the poor whatever color they were. *'All that is left is the power of poetry.'*" For both Silko and her literary character Weasel Tail, radical change is required, and it cannot be brought about principally from working inside such settler institutions as the courts. Stories and poetry, at first blush, may seem even less productive than law in affecting revolutionary change, but that belief carries a narrow view of the power of stories and poetry to vividly depict injustice, acts of resistance, and paths toward justice. After all, in the pages of *Almanac of the Dead*, Marx is declared a great storyteller: Marx "worked feverishly to gather together a magical assembly of stories to cure the suffering and evils of the world by the retelling of the stories. Stories of depravity and cruelty were the driving force of the revolution." Here we learn not of Marx the social scientist but of "Marx, tribal man and storyteller."[5]

SILKO AS STORYTELLER

In this chapter, I aim to listen respectfully to Silko's stories and learn from them appropriately. In Silko's novel *Ceremony*, suffering, healing, and resistance are embedded in Southwestern Indigenous stories and storied landscapes. They depict such private crises as loss of identity, the trauma of war, and ruined friendships and such public crises as environmental disaster, racism, and extractive capitalism—interrelated crises produced by settler colonialism. *Ceremony*'s protagonist Tayo, a World War II veteran suffering from postwar trauma and alienation, seeks healing via a ceremonial journey through a socio-natural landscape filled with multispecies relationships and Indigenous stories and rituals. Indigenous lands and ceremonies of the Southwest become locations of healing as Tayo connects to sources of life and identity and taps into wells of communal wisdom. *Ceremony* reveals how Indigenous responses to personal pain and social injustice entail a dynamic interaction between Indigenous stories, ceremonies, land, and a nonlinear understanding of time and space that connects past, present, and future, as well as distant lands.

In Silko's novel *Almanac of the Dead*, we again find stories of suffering, healing, and resistance in both a private and public register. But this time the cast of characters and the geography are more diverse and transnational, its many protagonists including Indigenous peoples of Mexico, Black people from Africa and the diaspora, various Latin Americans, and impoverished whites in South and North America. All try to recover their stories and stolen lands and to restore health and justice to local and transnational communities by means of radical upheaval and revolution.

In both novels, past and present events and characters produce storied landscapes that speak of stolen lands, subjugated bodies, racial oppression, and broken relationships. These storied landscapes stand in opposition to the storied landscapes of settler colonialism (e.g., those settler stories that depict the white man bringing civilization and religion to the beautiful but savage New World). And in both novels, recovered stories, memories, and ceremonies work together to bring socioeconomic, ecological, and spiritual transformations. Each presents a vision of sovereignty reclaimed, cultural and personal identity reaffirmed, and land liberated from white settler colonialism.

Both *Almanac of the Dead* and *Ceremony*'s characters caution the reader again and again not to forget the stories. Why does Silko have her characters issue such incessant warnings? Without the stories, Indigenous people and their potential allies become powerless. We forget who we are, what we need to do, and where we need to go. We lose our humanity, our ability to love and grieve, to resist and create. Those who would oppress and crush life in its various forms understand the power of the stories. As Ts'eh warned in *Ceremony*, "The destroyers: they work to see how much can be lost, how much can be forgotten. They destroy the feeling people have for each other."[6] These destroyers have malicious interest in attempting to make Indigenous populations forget their stories, because the stories provide ways of life to survive, resist, and even flourish. In pursuit of this forgetting, white settler agencies and the U.S. government took Indigenous children from their families and placed them in "boarding schools." These schools attempted to achieve a genocide of Indigenous identities, disparaging Indigenous ways and beliefs, forcing children to abandon their language, culture, and religion.

Throughout the previous chapters, I have identified radical Romantic themes: storied landscapes as social critique and protest; radical aesthetics and the cultivation of praxis-oriented empathy; the everyday as the site of art, revelation, and resilience; the cognitive-affective nexus; interiority and authenticity; social realism and unromanticized nature; an interdependent relation between humans and the more-than-human; and an acknowledgment of uncertainty, despair, and dark, wild hope. All these themes and more are found in Silko's work. Yet just as engagement with Du Bois expanded and transformed radical Romanticism, bringing the catastrophe of white supremacy and anti-Black racism to the fore, and just as engagement with Shelley, Fuller, and Hurston brought ecofeminism to the fore, so now does engagement with Silko refashion and expand radical Romanticism. It grows and learns from her Indigenous ways and perspectives as she names and challenges multiple forms of settler colonialism, including displacing, poisoning, plundering, and exterminating Indigenous populations.

The interpretive lens of radical Romanticism, in turn, brings helpful attention to many aspects of Silko's work—storied landscapes, curative sources of life found in collective memory, and an intimacy between the human and more-than-human. However, it is not at all clear that Silko can or should be interpreted as a radical Romantic. While there is a strong family resemblance between Silko's craft and that of other radical Romantics, Silko's work is largely informed by a variety of intellectual and aesthetic traditions, some Euro-American (including the Romantics and transcendentalists, particularly Margaret Fuller) but especially Indigenous.[7] Silko's work in relation to radical Romanticism is excessive. She expands and transforms the tradition, but she is in no way limited by it. And insofar as radical Romanticism can claim a family resemblance with Silko's work, then Romanticism must be understood not as a circumscribed European period of the past but rather as a flexible, dynamic tradition and living practice that remains with us today, constantly being renewed and transformed. And this, of course, is one of my overall arguments: Radical Romanticism is not bound by its imagined past but instead is a developing set of beliefs, practices, and ideals.

There is, however, a still more significant challenge to interpreting Silko in the context of radical Romanticism. Such inclusion of Silko risks the *annexation* of an Indigenous author, capturing her in the conceptual nets of settler colonialism. *Assimilating* Silko into the settler "canon" would entail, among other things, subduing her far-reaching critiques of white settler culture and making her writing palatable—comforting and entertaining—to a broad, white audience. The likely readers would not be *witnesses* to Silko's stories of the oppression and resilience of Indigenous people but rather *voyeurs*—spectators entertained and fascinated by all things "native" while displaying an ineffectual sympathy.[8] Tayo's trauma in Silko's *Ceremony* may evoke a similar response to the indulgent, aesthetic gratification a voyeur may experience in reading William Wordsworth's account of the suffering of the "Female Vagrant." In contrast to voyeurism, to be a witness requires grieving and then acting on what one has seen and learned.[9]

Radical Romanticism's engagement with Silko—*my* engagement with Silko—carries the risk of cultural misappropriation, but perhaps there is a demand to take on such a risk. If engaging with Silko's authorship can be done with respect, integrity, and humility, then radical Romanticism can learn from Silko and other Indigenous authors and cultures that have suffered catastrophically but have also exhibited resilience and shown wisdom and care for the human and more-than-human. Can radical Romanticism listen to and learn from Silko's stories and become a trustworthy witness to them? Or is the gulf between them too large? Silko refers to "the boundless capacity of language that, through storytelling, brings us together, despite great distances between cultures, despite great distances in time."[10] Perhaps, then, radical Romanticism can and ought to allow itself to be questioned and challenged by the power of Silko's stories. This is the task of this chapter. At the end of the chapter, I will revisit the issue of the annexation and exploitation of Indigenous cultures. I will claim that the crucial issue is not to *call* Silko a radical Romantic but to *call on* future iterations of Romanticism to listen to and learn from Silko and other Indigenous authors. Ultimately, my own treatment of Silko can only be judged by how I write this chapter.

In the pages that follow, I focus on listening to Silko and learning how she contributes to and transforms the following radical Romantic themes: the role of art in seeking justice, awakening to everyday suffering and joy, the cultivation of praxis-oriented empathy, the healing that comes from connection to people and place, the powerful otherness and agency of the more-than-human, and the role of spirits, witches, ancestors, and other remarkable beings in narratives of oppression and resilience. However, before exploring these distinct yet related themes, I begin with a particularly powerful storied landscape in *Ceremony*, namely, the abandoned uranium mine. This storied landscape will serve as an introduction to the themes in Silko's stories while also suggesting their interwovenness.

A NUCLEAR STORIED LANDSCAPE: WITNESS TO SUFFERING AND INJUSTICE, HEALING AND RESISTANCE

Tayo, a protagonist in *Ceremony*, approaches the end of an elaborate ritual involving wild Mexican cattle, a sacred mountain, a revelatory constellation of stars, and a powerful medicine woman and medicine man—his ceremony. The ceremony has led him far across the land as he interacts with wise teachers—human, more-than-human, and spiritual beings—who assist him in his search for answers and perspectives, ways and beliefs, that will bring healing to himself and his people. This includes the easing of physical and mental suffering as well as a mending of drought-stricken lands and the brokenness caused by stolen lands, racial oppression, and extractive capitalism. Healing, here, refers to the process of recovery from trauma, both public and private.

Tayo's ceremony culminates at an abandoned uranium mine: "He had arrived at the point of convergence where the fate of all living things, and even the earth, had been laid. . . . The pattern of the ceremony was completed there."[11] Earlier in the novel, a terrible witch tells a story of—and thereby *actually conjures*—"white skinned people." (Storytelling is indeed powerful as it participates in worldmaking.) To these white-skinned people, "The world is a dead thing . . . / the trees and rivers are not alive / the mountains and stones are not alive" (135). The white world, in contrast to the Laguna Pueblo world, is not animated and vibrant, teeming with agency and spirit. Instead, "when [the white people] look / they only see objects" (135). Humans, too—especially Indigenous peoples—are seen as objects.

And since they see no life, they bring death to everything and everyone, even to themselves:

> They will take this world from ocean to ocean
> they will turn on each other
> they will destroy each other
> Up here
> in these hills
> they will find the rocks,
> rocks with veins of green and yellow and black.
> They will lay the final pattern with these rocks
> they will lay it across the world
> and explode everything.
>
> (137)

The white-skinned people do indeed find the rocks. They hire Indigenous people to do the dangerous work of digging up the once serenely positioned uranium ore. For eons, the rocks had rested in the ground, doing no harm, but when brought forth from the earth and laid in "the final pattern," the white-skinned people fashion weapons that could instantly vaporize life as we know it. In doing so, the white people become the ultimate agents of witchery, yet as I will discuss in what follows, they themselves are not the witchery.

The mining and development of the nuclear bomb is the absolute, logical extension of extractive, settler colonialism. It is the result of what Heather Davis and Zoe Todd (Métis) have called the "severing of relations between humans and the soil, between plants and animals, *between minerals and our bones.*"[12] In stark contrast to this severing of relations, Indigenous spirituality, according to Kyle Whyte of the Citizen Potawatomi Nation, "fosters accountability between humans and the environment."[13] This Indigenous spirituality calls on humans to maintain suitable and sustainable relations with the more-than-human world, with its plants and trees, insects and animals, rivers and rocks. Yes, there are appropriate and inappropriate relations with rocks: ways of approaching them, finding them, utilizing them. The nuclear pursuit of colonialism is perhaps the furthest point from Indigenous spirituality.

Silko has personally witnessed the hardship and suffering brought to her people and place as a result of nuclear colonialism.[14] She has seen the U.S.

government's and global energy companies' forcible efforts to extract uranium from Laguna Pueblo lands, among other Indigenous lands in the American Southwest, rendering Indigenous people as dispensable and Indigenous places as wastelands.[15] On Laguna Pueblo lands, three open-pit uranium mines—Jackpile, North Paguate, and South Paguate—were the largest in the United States and operated from the early 1950s until 1982. The government mined the rocks regardless of whether they were found on sacred sites. For example, Tsé Bit'a'i' (Winged Rock), or Shiprock, is a sacred site to the Diné—but evidently not to the U.S. government. Near Shiprock, the U.S. government constructed uranium mines, pursuing the credo of the Cold War nuclear arms race. Uranium was unearthed, bombs were built and stockpiled, and Tuba City—the Navajo Nation's largest community—became a central office for the Rare Metals Corporation and the Atomic Energy Commission. About 3.9 million tons of uranium were dug up from 1944 to 1986 in the Southwest.[16]

The U.S. government was the consumer, private mining companies were the producers, and Indigenous populations were the exploited laborers. Indigenous miners, in desperate need of employment, were neither provided with any protective gear nor told of known health risks. Moreover, without their knowledge or consent, they became the subjects of medical investigations on radiation exposure. Many suffered and died from lung cancer and other diseases, and their sorrow spread to family and community members.[17] When the mines shut down as the Cold War thawed, fences and other basic precautions against the dangers of nuclear debris failed to go up. To this day, abandoned uranium mines, waste dumps, and stockpiles are littered throughout the Southwest, and their toxicity threatens the Laguna Pueblo, Acoma, Zuni, Hopi, and Navajo peoples. Piles of radioactive waste and miles of open tunnels and pits deface Indigenous sites, and radioactive dust carried by desert winds contaminates Native American populations and lands. The land is so polluted that the U.S. government has sought to declare the area a "National Sacrifice Area."[18] Such a designation would permit renewed mining and the dumping of nuclear waste, exacerbating what is likely the worst case of environmental racism in the country.

Indigenous storytelling around the world has recorded and responded to the ongoing suffering caused by uranium mining. These stories have *power*: to witness the suffering, bring healing, and exact justice from governments and global energy companies for subjecting Indigenous communities to radioactive poisoning, covert medical experimentation, forcible removal, and exploitative labor practices. Silko is among the storytellers who attempt to bring witness, healing, and justice to their people's suffering.

At the abandoned uranium mine, Tayo remembers his grandmother telling him of the morning when she saw a bright "flash of light through the window.... It must have filled the whole southeast sky" (245). She wondered what it was and later reads about it in the newspaper, commenting: "Strongest thing on this earth. Biggest explosion that ever happened" (245). Shaking her head, she says to Tayo: "Now I only wonder why, grandson. Why did they make a thing like that?" (245). At the time, his answer was that he did not know, but now, near the end of his ceremony, "he knew" (245).

Why unleash darkness, despair, and death onto the entire planet? Fear, hatred, conquest, racism, greed—these are some of the destructive reasons. But ultimately, in *Ceremony*, settler colonialists performed the work of the witchery, "the fate the destroyers planned for all of them, for all living things" (246). Tayo's own ceremony brings him to "the middle of witchery's final ceremonial sand painting" (246). He now understands why the voices and faces of Japanese soldiers in World War II and those of the Laguna people had merged in his mind and dreams. He wasn't hallucinating or insane. He was seeing clearly a world in which there were no longer any boundaries: "Human beings were one clan again ... united by a circle of death" (246). The Japanese soldiers, for example, were not separate from but linked to the Laguna people by "the rocks" mined on Laguna lands as well as by their "distant," shared heritage. The Laguna and Japanese people both faced destruction by the imperial nuclear project of the United States. All along, Tayo indistinctly sensed the porosity of boundaries, as when he saw his uncle's face in that of a Japanese solider or when the Laguna and Japanese languages merged in his mind. The witchery exploited that very interconnection in order to bring about catastrophic harm.

Yet in the midst of this revelation of evil at the uranium mine, Tayo can now clearly perceive the vast interconnectedness of time and space, and with such discernment comes curative understanding as well as empowering resistance. Tayo cries tears of relief now that he sees "the pattern, the way all the stories fit together—the old stories, the war stories, their stories—to become the story that was still being told" (246). His tears are a bodily, affective response to this pivotal moment of salutary understanding—the result of an expansive, living story weaving together Tayo's personal narrative with a larger, comprehensive one. His personal story includes grappling with his mixed Laguna-white identity, experiencing the trauma of war, undergoing the incompetent treatment of white doctors, and embarking on an elaborate ceremony with the help of Betonie—the medicine man—and Ts'eh—the medicine woman and sacred being. The larger, global story includes settler colonialism, systemic racism, the annexation of Indigenous lands and culture, World War II, and the development and deployment of the nuclear bomb.

Throughout *Ceremony*, stories and events are understood not as frozen in a linear timeline or an inflexible geography but rather as interconnected in a spiraling timeframe and geography, responding to and growing in an ever-changing world and set of relationships. Stories and worlds respond to each other and are endlessly in transition. "The story," then, is always being retold: It gathers from the past, looks to the future, and responds to the present, ever-offering new knowledge, patterns, and medicine. Indeed, dynamic Indigenous stories challenge linear notions of time, for "past" ancestors and lands and "future" descendants and lands are active agents in the story. Although referring to Anishinaabe perspectives, Kyle Whyte illuminates Silko's outlook when he writes: "The spiraling narratives unfold through our interacting with, responding to and reflecting on the actual or potential actions and viewpoints of our ancestors and descendants. *They unfold as continuous dialogues.*"[19] The ruined mine reveals a complex temporality and spatiality. It is a vibrant ghost that speaks to us of what has happened in the past and how that past connects to the present and future. In the past: the operational uranium mine and atomic bombings of Hiroshima and Nagasaki; in the present: the nuclear waste dump and its toxicity; in the future: the possibility of nuclear annihilation. The ghost of the ruin connects otherwise disparate pieces of geography and time.

The "spiraling narrative" that Tayo has received is a gift and a burden. He still has one more task: "He had only to complete this night, to keep the story out of the reach of the destroyers for a few more hours, and their witchery would turn, upon itself, upon them" (247). But what does it mean to "keep the story out of the reach of the destroyers"? Tayo's task is to break the cycles of violence that the destroyers incite and feed upon. Stop the violence, and the witchery starves—at least for the time being. Tayo must break the local cycle of violence and thereby stymie the witchery and its more local destruction. Yet all is interconnected, and hence the ripples of Tayo's actions would move outward to the stars themselves (254). In Silko's Indigenous storytelling and worldmaking, personal narrative and global histories are tightly interwoven.

At the abandoned uranium mine, Tayo hides when he hears the approach of the friends who have betrayed him—Emo, Leroy, and Pinkie. By car, they arrive drunk, loud, and violent. Silko reminds us again of the connection between local events and their broad repercussions:

> The destroyers. They would be there all night, he knew it, working for drought to sear the land, to kill the livestock, to stunt the corn plants and squash . . . leaving the people more and more vulnerable to the lies; and the young people would leave, go to towns like Albuquerque and Gallup where bitterness would overwhelm them, and they would lose their hope and finally themselves in drinking.
>
> (249)

The drought, racism, poverty, homelessness, and the robbery of Indigenous land and hope—these large-scale harms are also part of the witchery that Tayo contends with as he attempts to complete the ceremony and stop his old friends' violence at the mine.

Tayo now hears his friend Harley screaming as the other men drag him from the trunk of Emo's car. Soon afterward, Harley's body is hung "upright between strands of barbed wire" (251). Emo tortures Harley, baiting Tayo to come out of hiding and confront him. As he crouches in the shadows, Tayo knows that he could kill Emo and is strongly tempted to do so. He realizes, however, that he must break the cycles of violence to stop the witchery. He must keep the curative story "out of the reach of the destroyers." If he kills Emo, the witchery prevails: A "drunk Indian war veteran" will have murdered to settle an old feud; the white doctors will say this was bound to happen; the white people will say, in faint pity, that it takes a "white man to survive in their world and that these Indians couldn't seem to make it"; and at home, on the reservation, they will blame it all on alcohol, the army, the war, and all the other ills that come from the whites, but mostly they would blame themselves (253). If Tayo kills Emo, the witchery wins again, having spun together racism, classism, settler colonialism, extractive capitalism, trauma, violence, and war into webs of personal and public lives and narratives. Tayo must defeat the story-weaving of the witchery with the story-weaving of Betonie and Ts'eh.

Strengthened by the ceremony's story and the stars joined to it, Tayo resists the temptation of violence and prevails. The ceremony is completed—"for now."

The drought will end, the rain will come, Tayo will gather and plant Ts'eh's seeds, and "the plants would grow there like the story, strong and translucent as the stars" (254). And with his eyes open, Tayo will dream: He is in his uncle Josiah's wagon, wrapped in a blanket, moving beneath Paguate Hill, with junipers blowing in the wind, his "Grandma was holding him, and [his cousin] Rocky whispered 'my brother.' They were taking him home" (254). Fully awake—perhaps more awake then ever—he dreams the truth: He is loved; he belongs to a family, a tradition, and a place. He is home. For Silko—as for Coleridge, William Wordsworth, and Mary Shelley—dreams, like stories, are not a departure from reality but inform and illuminate it. The dream is the truth: Like the junipers rooted beneath Paguate Hill, the site of the emergence of the Laguna Pueblo people, Tayo is for the first time rooted and at home.[20] His ancestors—Josiah and Rocky—are not gone but are with him. He knows who he is and who his people and traditions are. He has "crossed the river at sunrise," he is awakened, and he knows what he now must do (255). He must travel to the Laguna Pueblo *kiva*—a sacred place for ceremonies, teaching, and councils—and tell the story.

The elders sit on the wooden benches that line the long kiva, and they ask Tayo to sit on a "folding steel chair with ST. JOSEPH MISSION stenciled" on it (256). Sitting there, Tayo wonders "how far the chair had gone from the parish hall before it came to the kiva" (256). The chair, like Tayo, has traveled to the kiva from a place of racial and religious conflict and hybridity. Tayo's green eyes are a reminder to him and those around him of his mixed racial identity and the alienation that comes with it. He never knew his white father, his Laguna Pueblo mother left him when he was four, and he was mostly raised by an aunt who practiced both Roman Catholicism and Indigenous traditions—practiced both blindly and narrowly, as if they were fossilized relics, in contrast to the dynamic, vital ceremony of Ts'eh and Betonie. Yet Tayo—like the folding steel chair—is now at home on Laguna Pueblo sacred ground. It is here that he tells his story: "It took a long time to tell them the story; they stopped him frequently with questions" (257). The elders are particularly interested in the sacred woman Ts'eh, and it is later announced: "You have seen her / We will be blessed / again" (257).

Ts'eh is related to Tse'itsi'nako, the Thought-Woman who, with her sisters, creates the universe by thinking it: She "named things and / as she named them / they appeared" (1). Storytelling is a form of naming, an act of creation. But storytellers and their stories come from somewhere (except perhaps for Tse'itsi'nako, the Creator, but *that* is a different story). Storytelling is an act of creation but also an act of listening, of *receiving*. In the kiva, Tayo tells the story that he was given and that he, in his own way, creatively performed. Silko does the same: *Ceremony* begins with the narrator announcing that she is telling a story that she has received: "She [Thought-Woman, the Creator] is sitting in her room / thinking of a story now / I'm telling you the story / she is thinking" (1).

Silko is creating a story—a world of sorts. But this storied world is not an escape from the actual world. It is the real world—with its pain and injustice, its beauty and love—portrayed with exquisite clarity and power. Indeed, it is the story's profound authenticity that allows it to help one see the world clearly, as if for the first time. The familiar becomes new, strange, disturbing, yet streaked with sunrise—with hope. What was once a nondescript abandoned mine is now a place of intricate personal and public struggle, violence, racism, and geopolitical exploitation and war. This is how the storied landscape works. For non-Indigenous listeners, it names and brings to light suffering and injustice (and beauty and love) that were not understood or seen. For Indigenous listeners, it affirms and clarifies centuries of struggle and oppression, of resistance and accomplishment, and of beauty and love. In either case, the power of storytelling is rooted in the meeting place of worldfinding and worldmaking—of receptivity and imagination.

Silko's people have been exploited, their land polluted, yet they refuse the colonial settler story of their extinction.[21] They continue to remake themselves and their world despite grave hardships. Those who hear their story are likewise called upon to receive it and make something new—something that witnesses injustice, works for change, and offers some kind of dark, wild hope.

With a final chant, *Ceremony* concludes:

> Whirling darkness
> has come back on itself.
> It keeps all its witchery
> to itself . . .
> It is dead for now.
> It is dead for now.
> It is dead for now.
> It is dead for now.
> Sunrise,
> accept this offering,
> Sunrise.

(261–62)

Here, at the conclusion of the story, it is good to be reminded of how it began:

> I will tell you something about the stories,
> [he said]
> They aren't just entertainment.
> Don't be fooled.
> They are all we have, you see,
> all we have to fight off
> illness and death.
> You don't have anything
> if you don't have the stories.

(2)

SILKO'S CONTRIBUTION TO AND TRANSFORMATION OF RADICAL ROMANTICISM

As mentioned earlier, Silko left law school so she could "seek justice . . . through *the power of stories.*" I now explore that vocation—pursuing justice through the power of stories—by thinking about its contribution to and transformation of radical Romanticism. Specifically, in Silko's novels *Ceremony* and *Almanac of the Dead*, I will discuss the role and nature of art in witnessing and promoting justice; awakening to everyday suffering, oppression, resilience, and joy; cultivating praxis-oriented empathy; depicting the healing that comes from connection to people and place; highlighting the powerful otherness and agency of the more-than-human; and centering the role of spirits, witches, and other remarkable beings in narratives of oppression and resilience.

The Role and Nature of Art in Witnessing and Promoting Justice

The word creates—this is a powerful theme that runs throughout Silko's writings. In *Ceremony*, Thought-Woman and her three sisters, remarkable female deities, think and tell a story and thereby create a world. We learn more about Thought Woman and her sisters in Silko's book *Yellow Woman and a Beauty of the Spirit*:

> As the old story tells us, Tse'itsi'nako, Thought Woman, the Spider, thought
> of her three sisters, and as she thought of them, they came into being. Together

with Thought Woman, they thought of the sun and the stars and the moon. The Mother Creators imagined the earth and the oceans, the animals and the people, and the *ka'tsina* spirits that reside in the mountains. . . . As Thought Woman and her sisters thought of it, the whole universe came into being.[22]

Worldmaking by storytelling is not limited to Thought-Woman and her sisters. The dreadful witch in *Ceremony* tells a story of and thereby creates "white skinned people" who "take this world from ocean to ocean" (137). In both cases, we learn that the word is powerful: It has the capacity to conjure and participate in the act of worldmaking.

Humans, too, create, but their worldmaking is dependent on their receptivity. For humans, there is no creatio ex nihilo. Earlier, I noted how in *Ceremony* Betonie and Tayo *receive* a story from the female powers, Tse'itsi'nako and Ts'eh, and in turn participate in the female creative power to *make* something new in the world: a new ceremony and way of healing. Silko's own storytelling, of course, takes part in this generative act of receiving and creating, of worldfinding and worldmaking.

I have identified a similar logic of reception and creation in radical Romanticism. William Wordsworth, Coleridge, Mary Shelley, Emerson, and Margaret Fuller, for example, mediated or rejected the broadly conceived empiricism-idealism polarity. These Romantics understood the art of creating as a participation in the divine act of creation. But they also understood that human creation requires reception. Ultimately, their impulse was to honor a profound interconnection between worldfinding (being receptive to the world) and worldmaking (creating something new in the world). Among them there was a spectrum of emphasis—sometimes within one author's own work—between worldfinding and worldmaking. For instance, one of the stronger statements on the power of the imagination to create the world is Coleridge's "*we receive but what we give / And in our life alone does nature live.*"[23] A more dialectical or mediative statement is William Wordsworth's: "of all that we behold / From this green earth; of all the mighty world / Of eye, and ear, *both what they half-create, / And what perceive.*"[24] For radical Romantics, worldfinding and worldmaking are intimately connected. Creation requires receptivity even as receptivity requires creative attention. Radical Romantics are dedicated to the art of storytelling—the art of openness to the world (Wordsworth's "wise passiveness")—and in turn weaving something new in it.

Silko and the radical Romantics, then, share a common belief in the power of the word, a power that requires the dual act of receiving and creating. The word can bring forth life-enhancing creation, as in the case of Tse'itsi'nako, but it can also bring great suffering and destruction, as in the case of the witch who conjured "white skinned people." Words can oppress, normalizing unjust hierarchies, and exclude some and privilege others. The power of the word is not inherently emancipatory. It must be wed to ethical commitments, practices, and perspectives. For Silko and the radical Romantics, to be receptive to the world is to see and hear suffering and injustice; to create in the world is to bear witness to such suffering and injustice while also promoting liberatory commitments, practices, and perspectives. Art, here, is a form of witness and activism. For both Silko and the radical Romantics, then, art should be made in service of truth telling and social engagement, galvanizing solidarity and working toward justice and healing. However, by introducing to Romanticism the horrors of white settler colonialism, on one hand, and the life-enhancing, world-creating powers of Tse'itsi'nako and those like her, on the other, Silko extends and transforms the role of justice-seeking art in radical Romanticism.

Awakening to Everyday Suffering, Oppression, Resilience, and Joy

Silko and the radical Romantics also share a mutual commitment to pursuing art that awakens its readers to the everyday—everyday suffering and injustice, and everyday resilience and joy. The "everyday," I noted in chapter 1, is the seat of radical Romantic aesthetics. It may seem paradoxical, but radical Romantics and Silko attempt to *wake* their readers to the *commonplace*, to the familiar. Depending on the reader, this may happen in different ways. In the case of Silko's writings, a white American from the Northeast might be awakened to the everyday realities of Southwestern Indigenous populations navigating settler colonial cultures, environmental racism, and imposed boundaries—as well as of the beauty and wisdom of Indigenous peoples and lands. An Indigenous reader might be awakened to or reminded of ever-present forms of struggle and survival, grief and joy, sources of oppression and beauty. In any case, the art of Silko and the radical Romantics attempts to inform readers' perceptions of the everyday world, honing and transforming their senses so they observe with greater insight and accuracy, with more nuance and depth. Such transformation is possible when art authentically addresses the whole person, truthfully connecting the dynamic "inner" landscape of readers to the dynamic "outer" landscape of the worlds they find themselves in.[25] This, in part, is why Silko claims that "a great deal of the story is believed to be inside the listener; the storyteller's role is to draw the story out of the listeners."[26] The story appeals to the listener's experience even as the story challenges and expands it.

We see the art of waking readers to the everyday and drawing "the story out of the listeners" in Silko's powerful storied landscapes of uranium mines and nuclear weapons in *Almanac of the Dead*. We are in desperate need of such an awakening. The world has fallen strangely asleep to the threat of nuclear catastrophe and the dangerous toxicity associated with nuclear industry. Nonetheless, the threat of nuclear waste, toxicity, and annihilation—like that of climate change—is lodged inside all of us, however buried or inchoate. Wherever or whatever you might call home, the threat of colonial nuclearism is at your door, and if you live in the Southwest and you are Indigenous, colonial nuclearism *and* the poison of uranium mining are likely in your backyard. Colonial nuclearism, then, is always everywhere close to home, but for some, it is nearer still.

"Home" is the name and topic of the last chapter in *Almanac of the Dead*. When Sterling, one of *Almanac*'s protagonists, returns to the Laguna Pueblo and catches "a glimpse of the distant blue peaks of Mt. Taylor"—of Mt. Tse-pi'na, or Woman Veiled in Rain Clouds—he knows he has arrived home.[27] Of all the sacred mountains, Spider Woman first creates Mount Taylor as a home for the Laguna people. Sterling makes his way to the family sheep camp and drinks: "The taste of the water told him that he was home. 'Home.' Even thinking the word made his eyes fill with tears" (757). Like Tayo in *Ceremony*, Sterling leaves home, learns hard-won lessons about his life and the world around him, and eventually makes a redemptive return to his Indigenous home.

Why did he leave home? Many reasons, including that the "old ways" were not important or convincing to him and because he enjoyed traveling outside Laguna. But ultimately Sterling left because he had to: He was banished by the Tribal Council. White people had been raiding the Laguna Pueblo for centuries, stealing land, people, and sacred objects. When uranium was discovered near Paguate Village, mining started near "the holy place of the emergence" (34). And when a Hollywood film crew showed up to make a movie, the Tribal Council appointed Sterling to keep an eye on the film crew and make sure they didn't take or disturb things. In the meantime, a sacred stone snake suddenly appeared near the mine tailings. When the Hollywood crew filmed at the foot of the mountains near the mine tailings, they inadvertently filmed the sacred stone snake. Nonetheless, it was deemed that sacrilege had occurred still once again, and Sterling was held responsible. As punishment, the Tribal Council exiled him.

The abandoned uranium mine, the sacred stone snake, and Sterling's return home all come together at the conclusion of *Almanac*. Earlier, he is captivated by white settler culture and its magazines and their inane, gossipy news about the white world. Now, instead of looking at those magazines, he focuses on the things that he can see and touch himself, like tiny black ants gathering food. He remembers his aunt and the old people telling him that "ants were messengers to the spirits" and that the people would give the ants "food and pollen and tiny beads as gifts" (757). Sterling feeds the ants and desires to understand what the old ones understood: "the connection between human beings and ants" (758). If Sterling is to understand the connection between the uranium mine, the stone snake, and his own return home, he must learn something of the relationships between the human and the more-than-human, a more-than-human world that includes ants, ancestors, and spirits such as the stone snake. Now that he is back home, the more-than-human reaches out to Sterling, and he responds accordingly.

As part of that response, Sterling finds himself walking toward the abandoned open-pit uranium mine and the shrine of the giant stone snake: "Sterling knew the visit to the giant snake was what he must do, before anything else" (758). As he walks, he feels connected to the life around him. The Indian tea, the bee flowers, and the larks calling become sources of strength. Like such characters as Coleridge's Ancient Mariner or Silko's Tayo, Sterling *wakes up* to the complexities and sources of life around him. This awakening can be understood as a personal transformation: He grows in strength, health, and awareness. But again, like the Ancient Mariner and Tayo, this awakening also has a public, collective significance. Indeed, it can be understood as a social or political awakening and transformation. Sterling now has a greater understanding of the tiny black ants as well as of the uranium mine and its colonial nuclear logic, pain, and destruction.

Sterling's awakening also entails a newly acquired comprehension of collective Indigenous grief and protest in Laguna: "He had not understood before why the old people had cried when the U.S. government had opened the mine. . . .'Leave our Mother Earth alone,' the old folks had tried to warn, 'otherwise terrible things will happen to us all'" (759). We might wonder: "To us all"? All Laguna Pueblo people? All people in the United States? All people, animals, trees, plants, waters, and rocks in the world? "The old folks had seen the first atomic explosion—the flash brighter than any sun—followed weeks later by the bombs that had burned up a half a million Japanese" (759). The old folks saw, learned of, and remembered the massive nuclear destruction.

Sterling is now close to the Paguate mine, the largest open-pit uranium mine in the world. He "tore a cuff on his pants crawling through the barbed-wire fence that marked the mine boundaries" (760). In *Almanac* as in *Ceremony*, white settler boundaries are erected, enforced, trespassed, and broken down. Sterling moves in and out of settler boundaries, but not unscathed. This time, the tear is a reminder that he is moving from a place of home ground to a place of destruction. On the settler side of the boundary, Sterling sees "mounds of tailings thirty feet high, uranium waste blowing in the breeze, carried by the rain to springs and rivers. Here was the new work of the Destroyers; here was destruction and poison. Here was where life ended" (760). Poison, destruction, and death are on the white settler side of the boundary, but their reach is not confined. This boundary is ultimately temporary, and even now it is porous—dangerously porous. Once again, Silko traces the interconnectedness that attends nuclearism: Its lives and half-lives traverse time and space, connecting past, present, and future, as well as the local with the global. White settler boundaries, however high or secure, cannot contain uranium in wind and rain, in missiles and fallout.

Sitting among the toxic tailings is the giant snake. When Sterling first hears of the snake, he thinks it is a joke or merely an odd outcropping of sandstone. Yet there it is. "The stone snake's head was raised dramatically and its jaws were open wide" (761). Sterling is now awakened to the power and significance of the snake, Maahastryu—a protector of the Laguna people but also a spirit creature found among many Indigenous Mexican and African populations. The giant snake is Laguna and local, but it is also transglobal, honoring the distinctiveness of diverse Indigenous groups while also uniting them. Sterling now understands. The snake is looking in the direction of South and Central American Indigenous peoples and ancestors that will one day join North American Indigenous peoples and ancestors, bringing revolution and tearing down white settler U.S. borders.

The revolution will come, the borders and fences will give way, and the buffalo will return—inexorably. The correlated suffering and death of Native Americans and the American buffalo is well documented, and it is expressed powerfully by Plenty Coups, chief of the Crow Nation: "When the buffalo went away the hearts of my people fell to the ground, and they could not lift them up again. After this nothing happened. There was little singing anywhere."[28] But the buffalo and the singing *will* return, according to the Indigenous prophecy recounted in *Almanac*. Sterling recollects this prophecy as he is walking and gaining new strength during his Laguna homecoming:

> Sterling had to smile when he thought of herds of buffalo grazing among the wild asters and fields of sunflowers below the mesas. He did not care if he did not live to see the buffalo return; probably the herds would need another five hundred years to complete their comeback. What mattered was that . . . the Great Plains would again host great herds of buffalo and those human beings who knew how to survive on the annual rainfall.
>
> (758–59)

The great return of the buffalo and the liberation of Indigenous peoples may take hundreds of years, but it is unstoppable. *Almanac* is clear about this: "Marx had understood that . . . within 'history' reside relentless forces, powerful sprits, vengeful, relentlessly seeking justice. . . . The turning, the changing were inevitable. The old people had stories that said much the same, that it was only a matter of time and things European would gradually fade from the American continents" (316). The stone snake embodies a sureness of the unescapable, a solidness of endurance, and an expansive perspective on time and place: "The snake didn't care if people were believers or not; the work of the sprits and prophecies went on regardless" (762). It will be as *Almanac*'s Angelita, a Mexican-Indigenous revolutionary, says: "We are the army to retake tribal land. . . . The ancestors' spirits speak in dreams. . . . We wait for the tidal wave of history to sweep us along" (518). Sterling is now awakened to what the stone snake and Angelita understand: The oppression inflicted by settler colonialism is real but fleeting in the sacred vastness of time and space and in the holy presences of ancestors and spirits. "The earth would still be sacred. Man was too insignificant to desecrate her" (762).

Sterling's awakening and homecoming are not private feats or events. With the help of many—including agents of the more-than-human world—he is awakened to his connection to Laguna and trans-Indigenous histories, futures, and their intermingling in the present. He becomes alert to the ways of personal flourishing and meaning as well as transnational solidarity and liberation. The personal and public are mutually related to and informed by Sterling's encounter with the multifarious presence of the land, the steady southern gaze of the stone snake, and the vast timescales and spatialities posed by the uranium mine. Together, these encounters both relativize the occupation and force of white settler colonialism and reveal the enduring sacredness of the earth.

In Silko's writings, the ruined uranium mine is the image of both nuclear colonialism *and* Indigenous resistance—the quest for justice and freedom from government and global energy companies that have subjected Indigenous communities to radioactive poisoning, covert medical experimentation, exploitive labor practices, and forcible removal. What was once the fenced-off or hidden abandoned mine is now a place of intricate personal and public struggle, violence and racism, healing and hope. In this way, the imagery of the ruin in Silko's work expands and transforms even the most progressive forms of Romanticism, unsettling them by bringing alertness to the multiple catastrophic forms of settler colonialism, including the displacing, poisoning, and plundering of Indigenous populations.

I have lingered on Silko's abandoned uranium mine to help us think about the relation between her and the radical Romantics. Specifically, I am interested in how the art of both Silko and the radical Romantics seeks to wake up their readers and facilitate their becoming witnesses to suffering and injustice as well as hope and joy. Many in Wordsworth's generation had failed to grasp the hardships and oppression inflicted on impoverished and powerless populations. The same can be said of Silko's generation. For example, the catastrophic environmental racism inflicted on Indigenous populations in the Southwest is not widely known to settler populations. Moreover, while the threat of nuclear annihilation may be widely acknowledged in the abstract, it fails to *concretely* manifest itself among the public or world leaders. This, again, is in part the role of radical Romantic art: to wake us up even to things we already know but fail to appropriately register, feel, or act upon.

The Cultivation of Praxis-Oriented Empathy

Silko and the radical Romantics share a desire to cultivate in their readers a praxis-oriented empathy. In the introduction, I distinguished *praxis-oriented empathy* from *sentimental sympathy*. Praxis-oriented empathy is a form of affect that both motivates and accompanies the witnessing of social harms and the practical work of social justice and transformation. In contrast, sentimental sympathy is a form of affect that treats the reader to "deep feeling" but entails no attending, practical consequences. Sentimental sympathy must be differentiated from praxis-oriented empathy, the form of empathy that Silko and the radical Romantics endeavor to cultivate. Their work may entertain, but entertainment is not the fundamental goal. Radical Romantic aesthetics instead tangibly engages its participants in the world around them, and that tangible engagement includes a wide range of emotional, bodily, intellectual, and practical political responses.

Such radical Romantics as William Wordsworth, Mary Shelley, and Terry Tempest Williams promote practical witnessing and engagement by means of their detailed, palpable accounts of characters that suffer under various forms of oppression—as in Wordsworth's "Michael," Shelley's *Frankenstein*, or Williams's "Clan of One-Breasted Women." Silko does the same. In her art, Indigenous people are not a vague collective but individuals and communities with distinctive hands and faces, feelings and beliefs, griefs and loves. Yet unlike Wordsworth, Shelley, and even Williams, Silko gives considerably more attention to more-than-human characters—ants, snakes, and bears; ancestors, ghosts, and spirits; water, mountains, and sky. Silko's storied landscapes of the desert, for example, are teeming with multispecies life and various relations between humans and the more-than-human. For this reason, it is nearly impossible to read *Ceremony*, *Almanac*, *Storyteller*, *Yellow Woman*, *Gardens in the Dunes*, or *Turquoise Ledge* and maintain the white settler view of the Indigenous desert as desolate and ripe for extraction and sacrificial contamination.

Silko, then, like the radical Romantics, tangibly brings her readers into her stories, and this hold on her readers is potentially transformative. Yet Silko's focus and skill here is distinctively Laguna, and her relationship with readers goes deeper than that between readers and the radical Romantics. Silko tries not only to "reach" her readers but to include them in the storytelling. Bonnie TuSmith captures this notion when she writes, "When the novel [*Ceremony*] is viewed as a process rather than as a finite product it incorporates the reader into the text. The work becomes 'accessible'—a quality that, according to the author [Silko], is the foremost criterion for good literature."[29] As you might recall, Silko believes in "the boundless capacity of language that, through storytelling, brings us together, despite great distances between cultures, despite great distances in time."[30] This is not to say that Silko's white readers can necessarily or easily be "incorporated" into Silko's story-making process, but Silko's art is such that white readers are potentially drawn into her stories and altered by them as they come to acknowledge the oppression of settler culture and learn from Indigenous peoples about how to dismantle it. For attentive white readers, Silko's stories bring more dis-comfort than comfort. Yet as Emerson noted, "People wish to be settled; only as far as they are unsettled is there any hope for them."[31] To be *unsettled* is a neces-sary feature of praxis-oriented empathy.

Home, Healing, and Borders: The Curative Connection Between
People and Place

It is commonplace in settler colonialism to associate spiritual healing with Native American cultures. Native Americans, in this view, live close to nature and can thereby tap into its healing powers. Unlike white North Americans who do not live "close to Nature," presumably because they are more "advanced," Native Americans enjoy a simpler, "primitive" life. This simpler life, while deemed "other" and "lower" than white settler cultures, does have its benefits, including offering settler colo-nialism some possible antidotes to problems that come with its fast-paced, mobile way of life. Indigenous people, then, become the imagined, mirror image of alien-ated settler culture, and they can thereby provide a solution to settler alienation by offering ways to temporarily return to nature and experience its healing.

It would be unfortunate if this harmful, racist depiction of U.S. Indigenous populations were to lead us to neglect Silko's powerful accounts of the potential healing that in fact comes from individuals being reconnected appropriately to people and place, including more-than-human inhabitants and entities. Silko describes numerous, liberatory interconnections between humans, place, and the more-than-human. Such interconnections include practices and traditions that name, honor, and in some cases attempt to shape those interconnections. There are better and worse ways for humans to dwell in a place, and Silko's Laguna tra-ditions teach its people the proper relationship to "the land." When an individ-ual is disconnected from people and place, alienation and suffering are a natural result.

We have seen similar themes in the work of the radical Romantics. Individu-als, families, and communities suffer when severed from people and place, and they recover and thrive when just, sustainable connections are reestablished. The examples are plentiful: Rousseau's Julie thrives in the eco-community Clarens—an environmental, economic, and political alternative to oppressive, prevailing Euro-pean sensibilities. The inhabitants of William Wordsworth's Lake District are at home in their place—and live as "co-partner[s] with the natural world," as "sisters of nature"—but are threatened with displacement by new forms of capitalism and industry.[32] Mary Shelley's Creature strives all his life to find and create a place of belonging and suffers as he pursues this unreachable goal. Thoreau's Concord, his place of belonging to the human and the more-than-human, is threatened by a variety of oppressive market and political forces. Du Bois's Zora, "child of the swamp" and powerful female leader, creates a home and community in coopera- tion with people and place, all the while working against the weighty forces of white supremacy.[33] The theme of *alienation caused by harmful disconnection* and *heal- ing by way of liberatory connection* runs deep in radical Romanticism. Yet, once again, Silko more profoundly develops a radical Romantic theme by presenting arguably more challenging questions than that of Romantic predecessors: *How does one establish home and belonging while simultaneously experiencing the dispossession of one's land*? How are Indigenous people to build—or rebuild—homes and com- munities on lands stolen from or foreign to them?

Silko begins her essay "Landscape, History, and the Pueblo Memory" like this: "You see that after a thing is dead, it dries up. It might take weeks or years, but eventually if you touch the thing, it crumbles under your fingers. It goes back to dust." Why does Silko begin with death and dust? We all ultimately return to and rest in the land from which we draw life. To understand the cycle of dust to dust is to understand where our home is. All of us, one way or another, live among corn and rinds and bones, and to these in death we must return. Settler culture often positions itself separate from, even *against*, the land. Yet Silko notes that "the term *landscape*, as it has entered the English language, is misleading. . . . [It] does not correctly describe the relationship between the human being and his or her surroundings. This assumes the viewer is somehow *outside* or *separate from* the territory he or she surveys."[34] It is painful and dangerous to live, or attempt to live, outside or separate from the land and its sustaining traditions and practices.

These same perspectives are tangibly manifested in Silko's novel *Ceremony*. In the novel's opening, Rocky and Tayo are both U.S. soldiers far from home, fight- ing the Japanese in the Philippine jungle. Among the dead Japanese soldiers recently murdered by U.S. troops, Tayo sees his uncle Josiah—his uncle who was not in the Philippines but at home in Laguna. Rocky attempts to comfort his dis- tressed cousin: "Hey, I know you're homesick."[35] Rocky's explanation for Tayo's vision of his uncle among the dead might seem clumsy or belittling—post-traumatic stress disorder would seem a more likely account. Still, *homesickness*—to become ill by being severed from one's place of belonging—captures the more fundamental cause of Tayo's sickness. The pain and its cause are not unique to Tayo. Indigenous populations around the world suffer greatly from past and present dispossession and displacement. In some cases, such dispossession and displacement occur even when Indigenous peoples remain on their traditional lands, because the land under and around them—once their homelands—is being developed and malformed by settler colonialism. In Tayo's case, being away from home, from his Laguna people and land, leaves few resources to help him cope with the intense trauma of war and his subsequent imprisonment.

However, Tayo's cure cannot be obtained through a simple homecoming. When Tayo returns to Laguna Pueblo, having spent time being diagnosed and treated unsuccessfully at a veterans' hospital in Los Angeles, his uncle Robert greets him with, "I'm glad you are home" (32). But Tayo does not feel at home. He feels homeless: He has "the feeling that there was no place left for him" (32). Even though he is physically back in his homeland, he is not in a proper relation to it. He needs help, and not the kind of help that the white doctors had offered. His grandmother understands all this immediately: "Those white doctors haven't helped you at all," and to his aunt she says, "That boy needs a medicine man" (33). Indeed, Tayo would require the help of a medicine man, a medicine woman, and many others, both human and more-than-human. Tayo's process of healing—the ceremony—would be long and involved, "inclusive of everything" (126).

The white doctors attempted to numb Tayo's pain and restore him to the way he was—to reestablish the status quo. In contrast, the Indigenous cure that Tayo eventually embarks on is not about *restoration* but instead transformation or, to use Silko's term, *transition*. Tayo is wounded by various forms of suffering and evil: the loss of his mother, racism from some Native Americans because of his mixed-race status but especially from settler colonialists, and the trauma of military combat. Moreover, he lacks a strong sense of belonging to a set of traditions and practices to offer sources of strength. Tayo needs to be guided as he transitions from a place of homeless woundedness to a place of belonging and wholeness, where he can keenly attest to the cruelty around him, drawing on Indigenous perspectives and practices to resist forces of oppression. Understanding and resisting domination—these, too, are part of his transition and healing.

The concept of *transition* is introduced in *Ceremony* with a story of the child that was taken by a family of bears. This story, I believe, was originally told to Silko by Benjamin Barney, a Diné (Navajo) who taught with Silko at Diné College. Barney originally heard the story from his father. A boy is out with his family and becomes lost. A bear with cubs takes the boy and goes into Canyon de Chelly. Barney's father and others are told what happened, and they track the bears with the boy and find them in the canyon. Medicine men are called for, and they ceremonially remove the boy from the bear and cubs. According to Barney, the story is told to illustrate the difficulty of recovering a captured child. One cannot just grab the child and run. Special ceremonies performed by medicine women and men are required for the specific animals that took the child. A family of deer, for example, would require a different set of ceremonies than a family of bears. Also, even if the child is retrieved appropriately, the child will be altered, or as Barney put it, "the child becomes an unusual person for life."[36]

So, the child with the bears must be carefully transitioned back to the human community. This aspect of Barney's child-with-bears story is at the heart of Silko's own story in *Ceremony*:

> They couldn't just grab the child
> They couldn't simply take him back
> because he would be in between forever
> and probably he would die.
> They had to call him
> step by step the medicine man
> brought the child back. . . .
> but he wasn't quite the same
> after that
> not like the other children.

(130)

When Tayo is high up in the Chuska Mountains, he undergoes one of the many ceremonies that are part of his cure. For this particular ceremony, he is guided by the Navajo medicine man Betonie and his assistant Shush, who as a child was captured by bears and then successfully brought back. Shush makes bear prints side by side in black sand. Betonie then starts a long prayer, after which Betonie and Shush guide Tayo's "feet into the bear footprints" (143). Then Betonie begins another prayer:

> I will bring you through my hoop,
> I will bring you back.

Following my footprints
walk home
following my footprints
Come home, happily
return belonging to your home
return to long life and happiness again.

(143)

"Following my footprints, walk home" is at the heart of this ritual. To come home (and all that that means) requires taking the appropriate, curated steps. It entails transitioning skillfully. This ritual would not be the end of Tayo's cure and ceremony: The prayer concludes with, "All kinds of evil were still on him" (144). The cure and the return home are a process, a transition that involves great care. Later in the novel, when Tayo ponders other types of cures—such as when his friends try "to sink the loss in booze, and silence their grief with war stories about their courage, defending the land they had already lost"—he reflects, "There were transitions that had to be made in order to become whole again, in order to be the people our Mother would remember; transitions, like the boy walking in bear country being called back softly" (170).

Being called back softly: Such a skillful transition requires much work; for some, the work of a lifetime. "Your mother, the earth is crying for you. / Come home, children, come home" (176). What might it mean to call a people back softly? Or to call a world back softly? Who, today, has the skill of medicine people to assist with such transitions, to bring us back softly? Not to return us to past subjugations and harms but to bring us to a place of sustainable ways that promote flourishing homes of joy and justice among humans and the more-than-human. Who has such skill?

With the help of many, Tayo makes "a safe return" (116). He arrives at the kiva and is now at home on the Laguna Pueblo sacred ground. He is healed—as healed as anyone can be—and his journey brings blessings for him but also for his people: "You have seen her / We will be blessed / again" (257). Ts'eh, Betonie, Spider Woman, the spotted cattle, Josiah, grandmother, the mountain, Rocky, the ants, and rain—these are some of the agents that assisted Tayo in his ceremony, in his *being called back softly*. Like those wild spotted cattle that crossed boundary lines, Tayo defied the fences of the U.S. government and of settler private property that attempted to keep him from his sacred journey and homeland—the places and agents of his ceremony. The *refusal to accept settler colonial boundaries* is central to *Almanac* but also to *Ceremony*. Yet other boundaries are respected. The domain of the bears, Ts'eh's apricot tree, Betonie's hogan, and Thought-Woman's abode—these are some examples of spheres that are not to be trespassed on carelessly. No one has license to tread everywhere, even as all are called to engage in the process of transitioning, moving skillfully across boundaries of various kinds.[37]

Tayo's dream about being in Josiah's wagon with Rocky and grandmother comes true: "They were taking him home" (254). He transitions home. Yet presumably he will undergo future transitions or *becomings*. There is nothing static about returning home to a place and a people. Even in death, transitions continue: "You see that after a thing is dead, it dries up."

The Powerful Otherness and Agency of the More-Than-Human

In Silko's work, we are presented again and again with the palpable, powerful otherness and agency of the more-than-human: "otherness," because the more-than-human are distinctive presences and forces that cannot be reduced to anthropocentric needs, wishes, or projections, and "agency," because more-than-human beings and forces purposefully inhabit and shape the world in both individual and interdependent ways. Although "other," these nonhuman agents interact with humans, and some even have kinship relationships with human communities. "Otherness," then, signifies their relative autonomy and distinctness from humans, not a radically different ontological category or binary dualism (e.g., nature versus culture).

For some time now, a challenge for many Indigenous populations has been to establish appropriate relationships with the more-than-human while experiencing displacement or loss of sovereignty. Some Indigenous groups have been moved thousands of miles from their homeland, disconnecting them from their various more-than-human relationships. Others have remained on their homeland but have lost their sovereignty within it and are thereby thwarted from exercising stewardship and other relational practices with the more-than-human.[38]

Silko's work depicts the profound struggle and resilience of Indigenous peoples as they work to establish home and belonging under these conditions of displacement and loss of sovereignty. And that *struggle and resilience is supported by engagement with and assistance from the more-than-human*. We have seen a similar set of themes in the work of the radical Romantics, who rejected the destructive human/nature binary and brought attention to the plight of those dispossessed of their homelands via capitalistic, imperial forces. In Britain, for example, more than half the rural population was displaced between 1700 and 1850 by state-sponsored theft of lands.[39] Such displacement led to homelessness, extreme poverty, and urban squalor as well as to the criminalization of "laziness" and infirmity and the concomitant expansion of prisons and workhouses. Radical Romantics fiercely critiqued these capitalistic, imperial forms of oppression and offered alternative models that recognized the liberatory connections between people, place, and the more-than-human. Coleridge's Ancient Mariner, for instance, learns from water snakes how to cohabit peacefully with the more-than-human rather than to assault it.[40] And in his poem "To a Young Ass," Coleridge expresses kinship with the nonhuman animal as he exclaims, "I hail thee Brother."[41] William Wordsworth's "Michael," Mary Shelley's *Frankenstein*, Margaret Fuller's *Summer on the Lakes*, Henry David Thoreau's *Walden*—these radical Romantic works address the alienation that comes from disconnection from the more-than-human as well as the liberatory, healing power that the more-than-human can provide.

Once again, however, radical Romantic themes are developed still more deeply by Silko. This is in part because Silko, unlike Wordsworth or Coleridge, is a member of the oppressed group of which she writes (though Mary Shelley and Margaret Fuller's feminist critiques were informed by their experience in a patriarchal society). The deeper development of these themes is also attributable to the extremities Indigenous peoples have faced—near extermination, forcible military removal from their homelands, martial confinement to reservations, and attempted destruction of their languages and cultures. In this context of catastrophic displacement, erasure, and upheaval, Silko vividly depicts Indigenous peoples' survival and resistance as they seek to reestablish home and belonging in conjunction with the more-than-human: Tayo and Sterling require the collective effort of humans and more-than-humans. Their journey is not individualistic but with and for their people and land more generally.

In this journey toward healing and justice, the more-than-human does not loom outside humanity but rather forms a complex, interwoven tapestry of life in which humans belong. The more-than-human is plural, dynamic, multiagential, and, under the proper conditions, *supports humans in their endeavors and journeys*. In *Ceremony*, when Tayo carelessly kills flies in the kitchen, Josiah tells him of the greenbottle fly who had once intervened and saved "the people." Tayo, who now feels ashamed, is comforted by Josiah: "People make mistakes. The flies know that.

That's how the greenbottle fly first came around anyway. *To help the people* who had made some mistakes" (101–2; emphasis added). Because of the great service once given, the bottlefly and its cousins are to be remembered and treated with respect. And so Josiah hugs Tayo and tenderly instructs him: "Next time, just remember the story" (102). *Just remember the story* could serve as a subtitle to almost all of Silko's writings. And "the story," as Silko noted in *Yellow Woman*, features "the presence of elements out of the landscape, elements that directly influenced the outcome of events."[42]

In *Ceremony*, we find the following: "In a world of crickets and wind and cottonwood trees [Tayo] was almost alive again; he was visible. . . . The sickness had receded" (104). Here the more-than-human rejuvenates Tayo and makes him visible—more fully alive. But it is not simply the grandeur or beauty of the more-than-human that supports Tayo and his journey to healing. Rather, Tayo is supported by the specific presence and agency of particular more-than-human species and entities. Moreover, for Tayo to become visible, he must not only become a tangible presence among other more-than-human presences (such as the cottonwood trees), but he must also cease to be an invisible (Indigenous) man in *a white settler world* that tries to deny him agency. And this process of becoming visible is not simply located in the *setting* of the natural world but is actively supported by diverse more-than-human agents. Additionally, more-than-human agents—including those to which Euro-Americans would not ascribe agency—help protect Tayo's visibility from the settlers' destructive gaze. For example, as an army recruiter works to lure Rocky and Tayo into military service, "a big gust of wind of sand swirled around them," blowing away the recruitment pamphlets and posters and causing Tayo to cover his face (64). In the end, the recruiter is successful, but the agency of the wind has at least temporarily thwarted him and has warned Tayo to protect his face, his identity, his visibility.

So, in different ways, at different times, the more-than-human actively aids humans. In *Yellow Woman*, Silko describes the love of the Antelope People, "who agree to give up their meat and blood so that human beings will not starve."[43] Likewise, in *Ceremony* the deer give their lives to humans whom they love (51–52). In Silko's novel *Gardens in the Dunes*, snow clouds and rain clouds are ancestors that protect early-born babies and bring the water of life to the earth.[44] It is important to note that such aid and care are reciprocal and interdependent between humans and the more-than-human. The nonhuman animals care for the humans, but the humans, too, care for the nonhuman animals, honoring and respecting them and working to sustain their environment. This mutual respect, care, and upholding of responsibilities between humans and the more-than-human that Silko describes is similar to Kyle Whyte's notion of "collective continuance" among the Anishinaabe peoples:

> The qualities of relationships and responsibilities that make up collective continuance are the bonds that create interdependency between human institutions (e.g., lodges, ceremonies, offices) and ecosystems (e.g., habitats, watersheds). In this way, I am describing an ecology, that is, an ecological system, of interacting humans, nonhuman beings (animals, plants, etc.) and entities (spiritual, inanimate, etc.), and landscapes (climate regions, boreal zones, etc.) that are conceptualized and operate purposefully to facilitate a collective's (such as an Indigenous people) adaptation to changes.[45]

Collective continuance, as Whyte defines it, highlights the *interdependency* and *mutual responsibilities* between humans and the more-than-human (including "landscapes" and spiritual entities). It is a useful lens through which to view Silko's literary, aesthetic accounts of the various and complex relationships between human and such nonhuman characters as rain, dust, clouds, mountains, stars, ants, deer, and spiritual beings.

Note that the emphasis on "interdependency" and "mutual responsibilities" suggests a *diversity* of presences and agencies rather than a *monism*. The worldview found here is not that of deep ecology's "oneness" but rather a dynamic solidarity among diverse beings—a solidarity that requires constant maintenance. In *Yellow Woman*, Silko refers to the responsibility of maintenance ("the complexities of the relationship that human beings must maintain with the surrounding natural world") as well as to human distinctiveness: "being human is somehow different from all other life—animal, plant, and inanimate." Yet being aware of such distinctiveness never "[cuts] off the human from the natural world." Each species and entity is distinctive in its own way. Humans and the more-than-human, then, are intimately connected, but difference and "otherness" are respected. Humans and the Bear people, for example, may enter a beneficial alliance, but their separateness must also be honored. Ultimately, however, all things—rocks, animals, plants, and humans—do share a common origin and common destiny: "The dead become dust, and in this becoming they are once more joined with the Mother."[46]

*Spirits, Witches, and Other Remarkable Beings in Narratives of
Oppression and Resilience*

Spirits, goddess creators, ghosts, ancestors, and witches are prominent characters in Silko's writings. Such beings and presences tend to be neglected or "demythologized" by secular settler scholarship, stigmatized or demonized by settler ideological Christianity, and "spiritualized" or made otherworldly by New Age appropriation. Yet in Silko's work, ancestors, spirits, goddess creators, ghosts, and witches are a tangible, practical part of life—for better, for worse. They can bring trouble but also assistance to Indigenous populations in their struggles against settler oppression and other forms of harm.

In Euro-American scholarly environmental literature, the more-than-human typically refers to what once was referred to as "nature" when employing the human/nature binary. In this settler literature, then, the more-than-human is usually a *secular* concept. Yet for Silko, among other Indigenous authors, the more-than-human includes not only "nature" but also spirits, goddess creators, ghosts, and witches, among other beings or presences that settler cultures typically call "spiritual" or "supernatural." Yet the term "spiritual" is potentially problematic because it could suggest a nonmaterial, disembodied sphere (the "spiritual dimension") that is separate from—even above—the rest of the universe. And the term "supernatural" is potentially problematic because it could suggest a class of beings or events that operates in a fashion contrary to the ways of "the natural world," that is, the more-than-human. The stone snake in *Almanac* is distinctive and remarkable, but it does not exist in a separate spiritual world, nor does it exist contrary to the ways of the natural world—at least not the "natural world" of the Pueblo Laguna. The stone snake is one being among many in an intricate, integrated human and more-than-human world. In the following discussion, I refer to spirits, goddess creators, ghosts, and witches as "remarkable beings," stipulating that by "remarkable beings," I am referring to a broad set of diverse beings that belong to the more-than-human and human worlds.

In the United States and elsewhere, Indigenous worldviews that include remarkable beings have been and continue to be disparaged and (literally) demonized. Settler supremacist religious ideology vilifies Native American traditional beliefs as forms of idolatry, heathenism, witchcraft, and Satanic worship (all stigmatizing labels in Euro-American settler contexts). To "protect" Native American children from such primitive or dangerous beliefs, white settler governments and organizations forcibly removed children from their homes and communities and forbade them from using their Indigenous languages. Despite such suppression and oppression, U.S. Indigenous groups have been courageous and resilient, maintaining their dynamic worldviews. Indigenous populations are ever-adapting to changing circumstances, reforming their traditions and practices without forsaking them. Indeed, this is a major theme in *Ceremony*: the need to remember the stories and ceremonies and create new ones. Religious beliefs and practices among Native Americans are diverse and often syncretic, creatively mixing forms of distinctively Indigenous worldviews with forms of Christianity as well as other religions. Indigenous populations have been subjected to religious coercion by settler cultures, but these same populations have also exercised tremendous agency in forging complex, dynamic worldviews.

Silko's writings convey this rich array of religious belief and practice among Indigenous peoples (Tayo's family, for example, is associated with Laguna, Navajo, and Christian ways). And spirits, goddess creators, ghosts, and witches are salient aspects of Silko's accounts of Indigenous worldviews. As already noted, these remarkable beings are not seen as belonging to a separate spiritual dimension but as integral members of the human and the more-than-human. Like other members, they can harm humans, ignore humans, or cooperate and offer various forms of support. These forms of support are not limited to what settler culture often refers to as inner spiritual strength and insight. The support can contribute to personal strength and healing but also to social, economic, and racial justice. Indeed, in Silko's work, remarkable beings usually work to bring both personal and public healing and justice, recognizing the connection between the two. Tayo and Sterling experience personal healing as they gain political and economic understanding, and both forms of transformation are nurtured by various remarkable beings.

When viewed from the perspective of Silko's Indigenous remarkable beings and events, we gain a new sense of the vitally "spectral," remarkable dimensions of Romantic literature. Moreover, we stand to perceive in radical Romanticism the connection between personal growth and social justice and the support of this nexus by remarkable beings, presences, and events. Spirit and spirits, ghosts and witches, angels and demons, and various animated "objects" are found in radical Romanticism, particularly in Dark or Gothic radical Romanticism.[47] Today, secular scholars tend to think of the "supernatural" elements of Dark Romanticism as fictional creations fashioned for the sake of entertainment.

Scholars often assume that, with the rise of science and the (supposed) demise of religion in the age of Enlightenment, readers of Gothic Romanticism did not actually believe in spirits, witches, and ghosts, among other remarkable beings. However, such belief was prevalent, and rather than opposing science, it often complemented or was intertwined with scientific developments (Mary Shelley's *Frankenstein* being but one example).

Spirits, ghosts, demons, witches, angels, prophetic dreams, animated "inanimate" objects, deathlike trances, and haunted ruins or houses—Romantic literature is teeming with remarkable beings and events. Wordsworth's haunting poem "The Thorn" tells of a witch-like figure in a scarlet cloak who for twenty years has been wailing on a mountaintop, apparently mourning beside an infant's grave. At night, one can hear "voices of the dead," and in a pond not far from the apparent grave, one can see the shadow of "A baby and a baby's face, / And that it looks at you; / Whene'er you look on it, 'tis plain / The baby looks at you again." The self-exiled, mournful woman is subject to suspicion by the townspeople, some of whom think she killed the child. When vigilantes seek justice, with shovels in hand to dig up "the little infant's bones," the ground around the grave begins to shake, "for full fifty yards around / The grass it shook upon the ground." The vigilantism stops, but questions for the poem's readers persist: Was the cause of death stillbirth, or did the woman kill her baby? Were voices of the dead actually heard? Was the baby's face seen? And what caused the grave and earth to shake? Like the narrator, my reply is: "I cannot tell; I wish I could," "no more know, I wish I did." Wordsworth intentionally weaves mystery and uncertainty into the poem. But again, like the narrator, "I'll tell you all I know": When I read the poem from the perspective of Silko's worldview—a world that naturally contains the remarkable—"The Thorn" becomes alive with possibility, including that of ghosts, of vision and voice of the dead, and of quaking land defending the sacred.[48]

Silko's Indigenous interpretive framework enables one to view afresh the remarkable in Romanticism. Texts that once appeared to be—from a secular point of view—inoffensively deistic may now seem wildly animistic. And perhaps deism itself no longer seems quite so "inoffensive." Turning again to Wordsworth, in "Lines Composed a Few Miles Above Tintern Abbey" he writes of "a presence that disturbs" him, something

> Whose dwelling is the light of setting suns,
> And the round ocean and the living air,

And the blue sky, and in the mind of man,
A motion and a spirit, that impels
All thinking things, all objects of all thought,
And rolls through all things.[49]

A disturbing "presence," "the light of setting suns," "living air," "thinking things," and "a motion and spirit" driving and enveloping "*all things*"—this is the manner and matter of the remarkable, and it may not be so distant from the stone spirit snake in *Almanac* or Betonie's guiding stars in *Ceremony*. All things are spiritually charged; matter is not dead, but vibrant.

In *Ceremony*, *Almanac*, and other writings by Silko, there is nothing safe or tame about the remarkable. Remarkable beings must be treated with care and respect. While they may be supportive of humans, they may also be treacherous. When Tayo returns to Laguna in need of healing from traumatic war experiences, he comes to understand that the remarkable is a source of healing and rejuvenation but also of evil and destruction.

Betonie teaches Tayo that white settlers are not themselves the destructive witchery but rather are the tools of the witchery: "I tell you, we can deal with white people . . . because we invented white people; it was Indian witchery that made white people in the first place" (132). Ever since white people were conjured, they have performed the work of witchery, causing violence (human against human, human against the more-than-human), racism, extractive capitalism, and war, among other forms of evil and suffering. This internal, Indigenous account names as evil the destructive deeds of white people without calling the people evil per se. Additionally, it recognizes and honors the agency of Indigenous populations: Rather than being passive victims, they have a controlling narrative about the sources of evil in the world. Storytelling, we have seen, makes things—creates worlds, heals worlds, destroys worlds, and also offers explanations for these worlds. In *Ceremony*, a powerful Laguna story accounts for witchery, and within that story a witch tells a story that brings destruction. Tayo, we saw, must defeat the story of the witchery with the story of Betonie and Ts'eh. Such a defeat includes *naming* the destructive acts of the white settlers—killing, stealing, extracting, and polluting. But ultimately, the task is to resist the deeds of *all* who would be used by the witchery.

As readers of Silko, what are we to make of the witchery? How are we to make sense of this *remarkable* presence of destruction in the world? Silko has unflinchingly looked at evil and named its vicious deeds and willing agents, but she has not identified white people or others as evil in themselves.[50] Evil, in Silko's account, is hauntingly vital, vibrant, and shapeshifting—a dynamic power to be reckoned with. Humans, of course, are responsible and accountable for their participation in witchery. In this regard, white settler colonialism—its institutions, practices, beliefs, leaders, and accomplices—receives much treatment in Silko's authorship. Silko maintains that settler colonialism will ultimately destroy itself because it is based on the lies and violence of stolen lands, murdered populations, broken treaties, plundered lands, and, above all, *witchery*:

> If the white people never looked beyond the lie, to see that theirs was a nation built on stolen land, then they would never be able to understand how they had been used by the witchery; they would never know that they were still being manipulated by those who knew how to stir the ingredients together: white thievery and injustice boiling up the anger and hatred that would finally destroy the world.
>
> (191)

The destruction of the white settler world is not only an event to come. It has, in many ways, already arrived: Under the power of the witchery, white people have become "hollow and lifeless as a witchery clay figure . . . like a seed hoarded too long, shrunken past its time, and split open now, to expose a fragile, pale leaf stem, perfectly formed and dead" (204).

I have lingered on Silko's account of the witchery to bring attention to the power and work of the remarkable. It is precisely here, on the remarkable, that settler readers often stumble or else secularize Silko. The witchery, for example, becomes a symbol of human—specifically white—immoral institutions, individuals, and actions. But in *Ceremony*, *Almanac*, and *Yellow Woman*, among other publications, Silko is clear: There are powers and agents in the world that are *more* than human. Some of these powers and agents are what settler cultures know as plants, animals, and "inanimate" entities (e.g., rocks, water, or stars). But some are also *beyond* what settler cultures normally classify as the more-than-human, namely, spirits, goddess creators, ghosts, ancestors, and witchery—what I have been calling the remarkable. In chapters 5 and 6, I noted how secularized accounts of Wordsworth, Coleridge, and Du Bois fail to register the religion or spirituality that animates them, and the accounts thereby miss the close connections between religious, political, and environmental progressive thought. Secularized accounts of Silko hazard similar risks. The "spiritual," or the remarkable, in Silko's authorship is central to it, and it bears directly on such *material* issues as Indigenous sovereignty, land justice, resilience, and continuance. Silko, of course, is not alone as an Indigenous knowledge bearer who is subject to settler, academic secularism. Kyle Whyte skillfully writes of how settler climate scientists may draw on Indigenous knowledge to "fill in gaps" in their models that require certain local data, but these same scientists will not find acceptable or useful any traditional Indigenous knowledge that is associated with "spiritual relationships to nonhuman beings and spirits" or with "shape-shifters and ancestral spirits."[51]

The remarkable in Silko's authorship is not, of course, exclusively or primarily a destructive power. We have already seen how the remarkable—a plural category, to be sure—contributes to the healing and health of Tayo, Sterling, and their communities. Ts'eh and the stone snake are powerful, liberatory agents, as are the message-carrying ants and the beseeching bottle flies, the guiding stars, and the creator, Thought-Woman. These remarkable beings are agents of private and public well-being, justice, resistance, and transformation. They also provide profound sources of hope: Humans are interdependent and in relation with the more-than-human, including the remarkable, as they wrestle with the witchery and its agents. Tayo does not battle the witchery singlehandedly. He works with such remarkable agents as Ts'eh and her brother, such other more-than-human agents as the ants and the mountain lion, and such human agents as Betonie and grandmother. Together, they defeat the witchery, temporarily: "It is dead *for now*" (261; emphasis added). Resistance against the witchery—against the destroyers in the world—is ongoing. Each individual is called on to join with others, to make an offering to "sunrise," and to confront the witchery in all its forms. In this daily battle, the stakes are high, and the remarkable is all around. Humans must consent to work with others, in all their various forms of existence.

RADICAL ROMANTICISM'S RELATION TO SILKO

I now wish to return to the issue of the annexation and exploitation of Indigenous cultures by settler colonialism and in particular ask: Has my engagement with Silko propagated such oppression? Have I inappropriately assimilated her into settler scholarship and canons? Only my readers—especially Indigenous readers—can make that judgment. For my part, I wish to briefly restate the risk and hope of including Silko in this book. The risk is that her voice is muted and that a settler voice—my voice—is projected onto her. The hope, or promise, is that Silko's authorship deeply informs, challenges, and transforms the ways and perspectives of radical Romanticism. There are two ways of framing this hope of a just, beneficial engagement with Silko.

First, there is the minimalist way. This approach would not call Silko a radical Romantic but rather *call on* future iterations of Romanticism to listen to and learn from Silko and other Indigenous authors. The term "minimalist" should not imply that there is anything simple or straightforward about this approach. It demands that any engagement with Silko be done with such virtues as respect, integrity, and humility. In contrast to the minimalist approach, there is the maximalist: This framing would include Silko in radical Romanticism insofar as her work powerfully contributes to this ongoing tradition and way of being. It would acknowledge that in some ways the gulf between her and Romanticism is large but that in other ways it is—with sufficient sensitivity and work—bridgeable.

I believe the stakes are high for pursuing, at least, a minimalist approach. Robin Wall Kimmerer refers to the widespread call to bring Indigenous ecology "to bear on contemporary social and environmental issues. . . . Environmental leader and Onondaga Nation clan mother, the late Audrey Shenandoah, taught, 'This is why we have been able to hold on to our traditional teachings, because there would come a time when *all the world's people will need to learn it for the earth to survive.*'"[52] Kimmerer also writes of the importance of a "productive relationship" and of "complementarity" between Indigenous ecological knowledge and Western scientific ecological knowledge.[53] If Western *science* can and should engage with and learn from Indigenous traditions, knowledge, and practices, then why not Western *humanities*? Why not radical Romanticism?

What of the maximalist approach? Is it appropriate and ethical to include Silko in radical Romanticism, a living tradition and way of being? In this chapter, I have identified themes and practices that are shared by Silko and radical Romanticism—for example, storied landscapes as social critique and protest; the interdependent relation between humans and the more-than-human; the nature and role of art in witnessing injustice and seeking justice; the healing that derives from the interconnection between people and place; the powerful otherness and agency of the more-than-human; and, perhaps most importantly, *the pursuit of justice through the power of stories.* Yet we have also explored how Silko expands and transforms radical Romanticism, bringing to it powerful Laguna, Diné, and other Indigenous perspectives, ways of being, and alertness to the catastrophes of settler colonialism. Silko's relation to radical Romanticism is excessive: She broadens it even as she is not in the least limited by it. And radical Romanticism too is not bound by its past but instead moves and grows, including in its attempts to learn from Indigenous ways of knowing and being.

In my view, the crucial issue is not that Silko be included as a radical Romantic but that future iterations of Romanticism be deeply informed by her. I'm happy to defer to future generations on whether the maximalist approach is appropriate. In the meantime, if radical Romanticism is to achieve its promise as a dynamic way of life committed to sustainable, just relations among humans and between humans and the more-than-human, it must respectfully and humbly learn from those who have suffered most under the cruel subjugation of empire, white supremacy, and settler colonialism. This is both the challenge to and promise of radical Romanticism.

Conclusion

The Work and Promise of Radical Romanticism
in a World in Ruins

At the start of last chapter, I noted that Silko's warning, "You don't have anything / if you don't have the stories," is also a message of hope: You have *much* if you have the stories—powerful resources for healing and social transformation.[1] Silko's warning and hope apply not only to Indigenous cultures but also to those of greater U.S. society. What might it mean for the general population of the United States to "have the stories"? Is U.S. society, and in particular white settler cultures, lacking "the stories"? Or perhaps they have many of the wrong stories, that is, destructive ones? Have settler cultures, in the past and present, forgot, suppressed, or ignored life-enhancing stories—stories that speak of justice and care for human and more-than-human communities? Settlers were drawn to and driven by destructive stories that spoke of manifest destiny, American exceptionalism, and white male, human exceptionalism. The life-enhancing stories, however, have not died. They live in places and people, however marginally, waiting for a greater hearing to unleash their potential power.

In *The Unsettling of America*, Wendell Berry provides a sustained argument about what it is to lose the stories, that is, to sever one's identity from ethical narratives of people, history, and place. The *settlement* of America (its colonization by Europeans) caused the *unsettling* of Indigenous populations, the environment, and the identities of the settlers themselves. Elsewhere, Berry writes, "Because they belonged to no place, it was almost inevitable that [the conquerors of North America] should behave violently toward the places they came to."[2] There is, in Berry's view, a relation between the settlers' lack of connection to (and affection for) the place they sought to conquer and the massive cultural and environmental destruction they wrought. What stories did the settlers bring with them? And what are the dominant stories circulating in the settler cultures of the United States today?

The stories that I have identified in the dynamic traditions of radical Romanticism, however imperfect, are potentially liberatory, providing ethical resources for living justly among human and more-than-human communities. I have sought to identify the ways that radical Romanticism understands the *present* as a place marked by both *past* harms and resources for *future* justice. The hope and means for justice are, in part, derived from inherited sources—ancestors, traditions, practices, and the stories they convey. We have an accountability—"an ethics of entanglement"—to these past and future sources of life. As Karen Barad movingly writes, "memories/re-member-ings—are written into the flesh of the world. Our debt to those who are already dead and those who are not yet born cannot be disentangled from who we are."[3] Throughout this book, I have argued that justice, including decolonization, relies on *critically* appropriated cultural inheritances, which can be understood as a radical democratic second nature (especially for Euro-Americans). The practice of informed critique of the past and present—for the sake, in part, of a more just future—is itself a cultural inheritance. This complicated, temporal interconnection between past, present, and future in relation to harms, justice, beauty, and hope can be illustrated by the radical Romantic employment of *storied ruins*, the subject of this conclusion.

These are stories that haunt, calling out so that their prophetic voice might be heeded, their liberating power released. Radical Romantic ruins reach out from the past, wailing in the present, challenging the status quo, and crying out for renovated futurities. The work and promise of radical Romanticism is to listen to and learn from ruins, witness past and present oppression, find and make pockets of beauty and grace where possible, and engage in a praxis-oriented empathy that seeks to promote transformative justice. This conclusion will therefore attend to Wordsworth's, Du Bois's, and Silko's radical Romantic stories of ruins—ruins that witness pain and oppression but also beauty and resistance.

But the topic of ruins simultaneously necessitates the question of transformation: What might it mean to rebuild in the shadows of ruins? Such rebuilding is ongoing, undertaken in part by a new generation of radical Romantic stories. The rest of the conclusion looks forward and asks: What new stories will be told, and what renovations attempted? To address this question, we will explore new voices, for example, queer and trans authors who expand and transform radical

Romanticism with new stories of dwelling justly among fellow humans and the more-than-human. The conclusion then finishes with final reflections on the nature and role of beauty, hope, and love in a world marked by ruins.

THE WORLD IN RUINS: RUINS AS SITES OF PAIN AND INJUSTICE, HOPE AND TRANSFORMATION

For W. E. B. Du Bois and Leslie Marmon Silko, ruins are sites of haunting pain and injustice as well as liberatory hope and renovation. Both authors employed the trope of the ruin that is continuous with, but also transformative of, what I will call the Wordsworthian *prophetic ruin*. In contrast to the Wordsworthian prophetic ruin is the *picturesque ruin*. The picturesque ruin produces nostalgia for a bygone age—often an age of simplicity and spiritual wholeness, or else of grandeur and great achievement. The picturesque ruin is what many think of as the "standard" or typical Romantic ruin.[4] But there is another Romantic conception of the ruin: the prophetic ruin as a trace of past suffering and oppression and also of potential hope and social change. Against these two contrasting employments of the ruin, I discuss the ways that Du Bois and Silko subvert the picturesque ruin and radically extend and transform the prophetic ruin.

The picturesque ruin—a present fragment that evokes absence—is a real or imagined physical piece of the past that gratifies the viewer and fills them with gentle nostalgia. If you were rich in the nineteenth century and you didn't happen to have a ruin on your property, you could *build* one, gaze on it, and enjoy a congenial melancholy or nostalgia. While the picturesque ruin invites the gaze of the spectator, the prophetic ruin, in contrast, stands as a witness to past suffering and oppression, and it calls on us to share in that witnessing. The prophetic ruin remembers the past and illuminates the present and future, helping us comprehend continuity between past, present, and future pain and injustice. It has no immediate aesthetic appeal, and it is with the help of a narrator—an informed guide—that our sense and sensibility are awakened to what the ruin would disclose to us.[5]

My principal example of this alternative Romantic ruin is the early Wordsworth poem "The Ruined Cottage" (1797)—a poignantly crafted storied landscape that unearths "untold stories" of the vulnerable poor. Near the start of the poem, the young narrator is walking through a "bare wide Common."[6] This walker, however, is not enjoying Romantic, Emersonian "perfect exhilaration" but rather suffers from fatigue, tough terrain, unbearable heat, and noxious insects.[7] It is as if Wordsworth sought to signal that this will not be a particularly pleasant, picturesque poem. The poem focuses on Margaret and her once simple yet comfortable cottage. At the start of the poem, the cottage is intact—as is Margaret and her family. But when the vulnerable family is struck by callous public policy and the resulting hunger, poverty, disease, and war, Margaret sinks into despair as she loses her husband and children and eventually her own life. As Margaret experiences ruin, so does her cottage—"a ruined house, four naked walls / That stared upon each other" (32, lines 31-32). The human life and the geophysicality of the home thrive and fall together.

Armytage, an old man and friend of Margaret who tells the young narrator of these tragic events, notes that Margaret's family and those like them "cease to be, / And their place knew them not," for they are buried under suffering, death, and decay (34, lines 143-44). "No memorial [is] left" (33, line 72). Yet if one is granted the appropriate sight—or some suitable awareness—one can read or otherwise apprehend, if only partially, the memories and stories that the ruin embodies. For the ruined cottage is a geophysical site inclusive of human and more-than-human stories—stories embedded in complex temporalities, physical processes, private human lives, and such public institutions as government, class, capitalism, and the politics of war. With appropriate guidance, the ruined cottage—and ruins like it—offers us the opportunity to witness the past, memorialize it, and confront its ongoing legacies of subjugation in the present and future.

This *invitation* to serve as witness, and to grieve appropriately, is offered to the young narrator by the old man. Remarkably, the invitation is also offered to the more-than-human world: Streams, hills, and rocks are called on "to mourn" and share in human grief (33, line 75). In the poem "The First Water Is the Body," the Mojave poet Natalie Diaz tells of water that "remembers everything" and that expresses deep grief.[8] Similar to Diaz's waters, the waters in Wordsworth's poem remember Margaret and now mourn her, sharing in "one sadness" (33, line 84).

In the poem, the ruinous process of the past remains vital, haunting the present. Indeed, the narrator affirms that "the things of which" the old man spoke "seemed present" (36, lines 211-12). Margaret's ruined cottage is as much a *time machine* that takes us back in history as it is a *mirror* reflecting ruin in our present and even our future. Returning to the past and *repairing* it is not an option. The poem acknowledges the potentially unproductive work of mourning, "the impotence of grief" (43, line 500): Grief cannot revisit the past and bring comfort, at least not to those who suffered. But perhaps mourning the past may bring attention to the present. Perhaps the work of mourning *is* productive. Mourning Margaret—now that we know her story—should make a claim on how we live our lives.[9] The story, we are told, is not to be heard in "vain dalliance" (36, line 223). Rather, in the telling and listening there is some hope of "future good" and "a power to virtue friendly"—a power in a praxis-oriented empathy (36, line 226; 37, line 229). But heeding the hauntings of the ruin is work. The old man keeps returning to the ruined cottage, again and again, repeating the process of mourning, witnessing, learning of the "impotence of grief," but also moving forward with some modest power to engage with the world anew, only to return, still again, to the ruin.

How to witness the past? How to grieve? How to move forward somewhat transformed? Can these animate, geophysical ghosts disrupt our lives and inspire transformative work, having made us more familiar with unnecessary precariousness? In "The Ruined Cottage," such questions and challenges are designed to strike us, bringing a mingling of hope and despair, power and weakness, love and grief.[10]

DU BOIS'S PLANTATIONS: BUILDINGS, PEOPLE, AND SOIL IN RUIN

Du Bois is the master artist of the radical Romantic storied landscape, and among these landscapes, ruins play a prominent role. Du Boisian ruins are a dramatic geophysical nexus of the human and more-than-human, offering poignant, multifaceted accounts of the relation between white supremacy, Black Americans, and the land on which they work and dwell. Du Bois was well versed in the Romantic picturesque ruin. In *The Souls of Black Folk*, for example, Du Bois described rows of dilapidated cabins housing exploited Black laborers as "cheerless, bare, and dirty, for the most part, although here and there *the very age and decay makes the scene picturesque*."[11] Du Bois employed the trope of the picturesque ruin, yet—similar to the early Wordsworth—he inverted its pathos, inviting his readers not to delight in the ruin's aesthetic age value but rather to witness past oppression and its legacies living in the present. The ruin, in Du Bois's work, does not speak of a past wholeness, a bygone age of splendor, or an abstract, wistful register of inescapable death and decay. Rather, the ruin speaks of *specific sites* of harm and subjugation—ruined buildings, ruined soil, ruined people. These three—buildings, soil, and people in ruin—powerfully come together in Du Bois's vivid accounts of ruined slave plantations. These ruins, in Du Bois's work, do not summon nostalgia but outrage and a longing for justice.

If you would travel with Du Bois and witness the ruins of the Southern "Black Belt," then "you must come into the 'Jim Crow Car'" (78). The voyeur would be in the *whites only* train car, and perhaps gaze on occasion at the lovely countryside. The witness, in contrast, must experience the racialized, shabby Jim Crow train car and its dispirited Black riders. And, as we saw in "The Ruined Cottage," to become a witness, one needs an expert guide—a guide such as Du Bois—so that the forgotten language of the storied landscapes outside the window can begin to be understood. Additionally, the witness must also be willing to exit the train, walk the land, and meet its inhabitants for a still more intimate encounter. The voyeur, meanwhile, remains comfortably in the train.

Du Bois brought piercing attention to a ruined land. The soil is described as "thin and gray," "gloomy," "half-desolate . . . of neglect," and "run down" (79, 80, 81, 82). The buildings are "dilapidated," "moss-grown," in a state of "half ruin, or have wholly disappeared" (79, 81, 81). And the people are "discouraged," "in debt, disappointed, and embittered" (88, 89). These three forms of the ruined—soil, buildings, and people—are intricately entwined in Du Bois's storied landscapes of social and ecological devastation.

On occasion, Du Bois would juxtapose a picturesque landscape with an anti-picturesque, prophetic ruin:

I remember wheeling around a bend in the road beside a graceful bit of forest and a singing brook. A long low house faced us, with porch and flying pillars, great oaken door, and a broad lawn shining in the evening sun. But the window-panes were gone, the pillars were worm-eaten, and the moss-grown roof was falling in. Half curiously I peered through the unhinged door, and saw where, on the wall across the hall, was written in once gay letters a faded "Welcome."

(90)

The beauty of the forest and brook are starkly set against the "worm-eaten" plantation house. Du Bois often crafted artistic narratives of lands (what could be called "nature writing") not only to portray varieties of beauty but also varieties of injustice written in the land and in its ruins. In this account, the faded "Welcome" signals the reversal of that which is quintessential to the picturesque ruin, namely, the nostalgia or the longing *to return*. Du Bois carefully crafted his depictions of ruined plantations—the disruption of the picturesque ruin—to instill in his readers not a longing to be welcomed *back* (a desire to return to the plantation and all it stood for) but rather a desire to witness past transgressions and to fight against contemporary plantations and other forms of second slavery.

Du Boisian ruins tell not only of a criminal oppression in the past but also of its grip on the present and the foreseeable future:

> The whole land seems forlorn and forsaken. Here are the remnants of the vast plantations. . . . The houses lie in half ruin, or have wholly disappeared. . . . Now only the black tenant remains; *but the shadow-hand of the master's grand-nephew or cousin or creditor stretches out of the gray distance to collect the rack-rent remorselessly*, and so the land is uncared-for and poor. Only black tenants can stand such a system, and they only because they must.
>
> (81; emphasis added)

We saw a similar, complex temporality in Wordsworth's "The Ruined Cottage." There, the ghost of the ruin haunts the present and implicitly asks such rhetorical questions as: What has changed? What socioeconomic conditions for the vulnerable have improved? But in Du Boisian ruins, there is not simply an *implicit accusation* but rather an *explicit connection* between past, present, and future subjugation. Like the shadow-hand of the absentee landowner, the ruin "stretches out of the gray distance" and calls on us to witness the *continuity* of violence and hardship inflicted by white supremacy.

Du Bois, however, was not satisfied with an entirely bleak portrait of the past, present, or future. Like the complex affect and human moral drama found in "The Ruined Cottage," Du Bois described the land and its ruins as possessing a "curiously mingled hope and pain" (86). Again, then, we are struck by storied landscapes in which hope and despair, power and shackles, love and grief are held in tension. Yet unlike Wordsworth's work and white Romanticism more generally, the despair, shackles, and grief run deeper in Du Bois's work. This is because the forms of oppression—chattel slavery and its legacies—run deeper, and also because

Du Bois himself experienced daily the injustice against which he struggled, granting him an existentially and empirically informed perspective. The ghosts of the Du Boisian ruins, then, would press on us all the harder, all the more vehemently, to become witnesses to the past and present and to move forward in the work of justice and transformative change.

SILKO'S URANIUM MINES: WORLDS RUINED, WORLDS CONNECTED

In Leslie Marmon Silko's novels *Ceremony* and *Almanac of the Dead*, the site of a ruined uranium mine is where protagonists are awakened to "the big picture" and their place in it. Why, of all places, does this awakening occur at a quintessential site of white settler colonialism? The ruined mine is a place of pain and oppression wrought by nuclear colonialism, but it is also a place of hope and resilience rooted in Indigenous lands, practices, and stories. The ruined mine, in Silko's writings, reveals a complex temporality and spatiality: The past, present, and future as well as distant lands converge at the ruin. Throughout *Ceremony*, for example, stories and events are not frozen in linearity or inflexible landscapes but are rather interconnected in a spiraling timeframe and geography, responding to and growing in an ever-changing world and set of relationships. In the previous chapter, we saw this complex intermingling of temporalities and spatialities: in the *past*, the operational uranium mine in Laguna and the atomic bombings of Hiroshima and Nagasaki; in the *present*, the nuclear waste dump and its toxicity; in the *future*, the possibility of nuclear annihilation. The ghost of the ruin connects otherwise disparate pieces of geography and time.

The ruined uranium mine plays a central role not only in *Ceremony* but also in *Almanac of the Dead*. The ruined mine is the site of Sterling's awakening, and it conveys to him the suffering of his people and also their resistance, healing, and quest for justice. The vast, interweaving Laguna temporalities account for the curious, complex tone that Silko crafts at the conclusion of *Almanac*. On the one hand, the concluding chapter "Home" evokes hope as we witness Sterling's personal healing and the sacred rock snake's expectant watchfulness for revolutionary change. This hopeful mood would be straightforward if not for its being rooted in the geography of the ruined mine. The mine points to and participates in radioactive decay, otherwise known as nuclear disintegration. Like the nuclear waste it produces, settler colonialism, too, will disintegrate. Via vast, spiraling, and intertwined Indigenous perspectives on time and space, Silko intimates hope given the instability of colonial settlement. It is a powerful hope, but it is located in a ruined uranium mine and its radioactive waste and vast timeframes, and hence it is a complex hope. Indeed, we may want to call it a dark, wild hope.

A WORLD IN RUINS AND THE WORK OF RENOVATION

Some ruins are so catastrophic that it is not much of an exaggeration to speak of a *ruined world*. A "ruined world" need not refer to the entire planet but to a portion of the planet's species and entities for whom the world—*their* world—is ruined. A ruined slave plantation or a ruined village leveled by climate change—these are examples of what we might call a ruined world. So are the ruins of the more-than-human in the Chernobyl exclusion zone and the human and more-than-human ruins caused by atomic bombs dropped on Hiroshima and Nagasaki. Some ruined worlds are ancient, some are recent. And some populations experience ruined worlds, variously, time and again. The slave in the field suffered from a ruined world as did the stranded Black resident in New Orleans during Hurricane Katrina. The inhabitants of the Marshall Islands suffered from a ruined world when their home became the site of nuclear tests, and now their homes are threatened by catastrophic rising seas. There are numerous forms and causes of ruined worlds.

Wordsworth, Du Bois, and Silko are among the prophetic artists who seek to alert us to the ruins so that we might attend to them. Yet they would also teach us that *ruins are not the entire landscape*. To think of the world only as a place of ruins is to engage in cruel reductionism, and the work of Wordsworth, Du Bois, and Silko is anything but reductionistic. Their authorship includes the ruinous but also the life affirming and all those gray stretches of life between those two poles. We give too much credit to white supremacy, settler colonialism, and empire when we allow them to make us forgetful of those pockets and moments of beauty, love, and the sacred in the world. Beauty, love, and the sacred restore us, remind us that destructive mastery and control are not the only ways of being in the world, and by way of contrast, they reveal odiousness, hatred, and desecration. I have focused on the ruins, but Wordsworth, Du Bois, and Silko also teach us about beauty, love, and hope among the ruins, hence their various references to a "mingling" of hope and despair, love and grief.

Wordsworth, Du Bois, and Silko employed the ruin not to convey the general lesson of Diderot, "Everything comes to nothing, everything perishes," but to name *specific* forms of harm, suffering, and oppression.[12] Wordsworth brought attention to unjust wars and callous public policies that destroyed the lives of ordinary people in Britain. Du Bois brought attention to the inhumanity of the slave plantation and its sustained racist legacy in the United States. Silko brings attention to white settler nuclearism, its destruction of Indigenous peoples and lands, and its threat to the entire world. There is power in the *specificity* of their naming—"a power to virtue friendly." Their ruins haunt our hearts and minds with a precision designed to wake us to the world by bringing *tangible* attention to sites of oppression and sources of hope.

Of course, no depiction of a ruined world, however precisely drawn, can transport us in time and space such that we can fully fathom the existential and physical scope of the catastrophic. Slavery, the Trail of Tears, Hiroshima, climate change—these ruined worlds defy full comprehension. Nonetheless, we are all called on, each in our own limited way, to imagine the unimaginable, employing the moral imagination as a potentially transformative tool.

The moral imagination engenders the work of *renovation*, that is, *rebuilding* in the shadows of the ruin—to have learned from the ruin's lessons and history, from its ghosts. Renovating the ruined cottage would entail, among other things, rebuilding a world in which those who were once socially and economically vulnerable would enjoy secure housing, food, and employment. Renovating the ruined slave plantation would entail rebuilding a world in which systemic racism would no longer be a scourge for people of color. Renovating the ruined uranium mine would entail rebuilding a world in which Indigenous populations and their lands are no longer subject to radioactive poisoning and the world is emancipated from the threat of nuclear annihilation. Renovating ruined worlds is the work of individuals and communities, organizations and governments, in acts large and small, in the span of years and generations. Such renovation, if it comes at all, does not come quickly or easily, and the work is never completed.

The process of renovation requires knowing how to discard and how to appropriate material from the past for the sake of building the future. Renovation is never creatio ex nihilo. The very fact that the ghosts of ruins can speak and disturb us suggests that there are resources in the past that are worth repossessing—critically reappropriating. In the work of renovation, you preserve old beams and floorboards if they have beauty and use. In contrast, you do not build with that which is foul and rotten. Nonetheless, although the aim is to rebuild something sustainable, beautiful, and just, signs and traces of the history of the building site will be intentionally preserved. To learn from the ghosts of the ruins is to keep their messages alive, and that requires that the renovation not hide its work. Just as a pair of pants may be rehabilitated such that the stitches or seams of the mending are not concealed, so too renovated worlds will not hide scars.[13] Moreover, within the renovation is a place for a portion of the intact ruin, for it is good to be reminded of what prompted the ongoing, never-ending work of rebuilding. The scar must be grieved appropriately. From the start to the ever-receding finish, the ruin must be allowed to persist in the process of renovation.

We need to sit with the ruin, however uncomfortable that may be, and the difficult practice of "sitting" is surely what Wordsworth, Du Bois, and Silko had in mind. Sitting with the ruin may be the first step of renovation, but it must also be present in every step. The practice of sitting is similar to Donna Haraway's "staying with the trouble," insofar as it eschews "clearing away the present and the past in order to make futures for coming generations."[14] Yet the practice of sitting with the ruin also looks to the future, among other directions in time simultaneously. The ghosts of the ruin disturb, in part, to disrupt the unjust present status quo for the sake of reconstructing future trajectories—future *just* transitions.[15]

Dwelling with these ghosts is not easy. The ghosts in Wordsworth's writings are hard enough, but those in Du Bois's and Silko's are more difficult still. This, in part, is why the imagery of the ruin in Du Bois's and Silko's work expands and transforms even the most progressive forms of Romanticism. Their ghosts—which speak of horrific injury by white supremacy and settler colonialism—weep and howl gravely, with their ranks growing each day. Alarmingly, there are many who not only ignore or attempt to silence these ghosts but embrace their ruins with nostalgia, longing for the good old days when Black and Indigenous people were put and kept in their subservient place. This is the current danger.

Hope entails attending to the ghosts, becoming witnesses to their stories of harm and oppression, and working together to renovate our ruined world.[16] Future generations, of course, will need to tend to the ghosts of our ruins and renovations. This is inevitable. In the meantime, our world is riddled with the ruins of racism, settler colonialism, and climate change. These ruins speak of widespread catastrophic harm, especially harm to the most vulnerable. Will we wake up to the catastrophes that connect all living things? Which vibrant ghosts will we allow to disturb and haunt us, not with nostalgia for the past but with a hunger for justice, renovation, and healing?

RADICAL ROMANTIC GHOST STORIES, OLD AND NEW

The ghosts of injustice continue to haunt and inspire the dynamic, ongoing stories of radical Romanticism and the attendant work of renovation. As we saw in chapter 6, the ghosts of slavery inspired new stories created by Black Romantic authors in the mid-nineteenth century who drew from Romanticism even as they transformed it, putting it in service of abolition, reconstruction, and Black women's rights as well as honoring a range of Black experiences and forms of self-expression not limited to specific social justice issues. Just as the Black radical Romantic Frances Ellen Watkins Harper in the nineteenth century listened to the ghosts and thereby received and renovated Romanticism, so did Du Bois in the twentieth century. White radical Romantics, too, listened to the ghosts and worked for renovation. In these pages we have seen the nineteenth-century radical Romantic work of Mary Shelley, Margaret Fuller, and Thoreau, among others. That work continued in the twentieth and twenty-first centuries with such "nature writers" as Wendell Berry, Mary Oliver, Terry Tempest Williams, and Barry Lopez. By placing these so-called nature writers within the interpretive narrative of radical Romanticism, the sociopolitical dimension of their work becomes more apparent, as do the ghosts that haunt their stories—ghosts of environmental and cultural destruction, white supremacy, patriarchy, and injurious anthropocentrism.

The howling of the ghosts never stops, nor does the creation of new radical Romantic stories and renovation as long as the ghosts are heard and honored. What ghosts will be attended to as radical Romanticism moves forward? What new stories will be told and work attempted, even as one looks back on Romanticism? Thomas Berry wisely wrote, "It's all a question of story. We are in trouble just now because we do not have a good story. . . . We need a story that will educate us, a story that will heal, guide, and discipline us."[17]

Actually, we need not *a* story but a *myriad* of stories. In the final pages of this book, I turn toward new voices that speak with radical Romantic tones, contributing to a repertoire of new stories and the ongoing work of renovation. Much of this book has been *looking back* to radical Romanticism (as far back as Rousseau) for vital ethical, aesthetic, and political resources. In this conclusion, I now briefly explore how radical Romanticism is influencing the writing and activism of contemporary writers, clarifying and sharpening the radical Romantic, democratic work needed for everyday life and the catastrophes of today.

Queer and trans radical Romanticism is attending to the haunting ghosts as well as to liberatory voices and themes in past Romantic authors.[18] Andrew Elfenbein, Jean Hagstrum, Claudia Johnson, Christopher Nagle, Eve Sedgwick, Richard Sha, and Douglas Vakoch, among others, are revealing the queer and trans dimensions of Romanticism.[19] Sometimes this work reveals the explicit queerness in the texts of such authors as William Wordsworth, Samuel Coleridge, William Blake, Mary Shelley, Percy Bysshe Shelley, John Clare, Lord Byron, and John Keats; other times, attention is brought to Romantic concepts that are implicitly queer, for example, fragmentation, excess, iteration, transgression, and liminality.[20] The intersection of Romantic queer and ecology studies recognizes a more-than-human world that is neither static nor rigidly binary but rather that is dynamic, fluid, and anything but heteronormative. Work in Romantic queer ecology often starts by asking the reader to relinquish standard views of Romanticisms and to adopt, rather, a radical Romantic perspective that does not configure "nature" as the distant sublime of the male gaze or the transcendent cure—and opposing binary—to "society."

Timothy M. Griffiths's research, for example, leads to the conclusion that

> one could regard Wordsworth, among others, as a progenitor of queer ecological thought. Wordsworth, as well as other romanticists, effected this queer ecological thought through a spatial register that resisted the plotting and naming of identity and land, dominant tendencies toward reproductive futurism, and patriarchal forms of environmentalism. In this sense, queer ecology is indebted to romanticism for some of its logic, and in turn, enlivens it through new readings.[21]

Bridget Keegan is revealing an eco-queer Romanticism in such laboring-class poets as John Clare, who employed pastoral traditions not to bolster them but to subvert and queer them.[22] Colin Carman writes movingly on teaching queer ecology with the texts of John Keats, focusing on "the practice of tiptoeing in Keats's poetical works with the aim of revealing the queerly ecological implications of treading lightly across the earth." In this work, Carman expresses a central tenant of radical Romanticism, namely, that "poetry presents us with life-saving ways of making amorous promises to the earth," and he asks that we "follow in the footsteps of Keats and other ecologically alert poets of the earth by tiptoeing through the flowers and beyond, through our biosphere."[23]

Keats is not the only Romantic author that Carman turns to as a source of radical queer ecology. In *The Radical Ecology of the Shelleys: Eros and Environment*, Carman discloses how Mary Shelley and Percy Shelley jointly held that "nature and queerness are entangled." The Shelleys, in Carman's attentive interpretation, are central to what could be called a radical Romantic queer tradition, for "their writings champion the diversity of erotic *and* ecological life and combine such matters with that of political justice." The wild—a prominent theme in these pages—is not placed outside culture; rather, the Shelleys "understood nature to be an erotically charged entity that challenges such divisions as human versus non-human, civilized versus wild."[24] What Carman does for Keats and the Shelleys, Robert Azzarello does for Thoreau, showing that Thoreau's "literature makes more sense, is more *understandable* in Ricoeur's meaning of the term, through a queer-environmental theoretical conjunction." In Azzarello's detailed account of Thoreau's life and writing, we come to see how Thoreau "brilliantly demonstrates the ways in which the queer project and the environmental project are always already connected, that is to say, in which the questions and politics of human sexuality are always entwined with the questions and politics of the other-than-human world." Among other things, we learn from Azzarello that Thoreau's "sense (that is, his *meaning* and *sensation*) of eroticism, and what he specifically calls 'sensuality,' is embedded within his sense of theology and, more particularly, within his understanding of the animal-human-divine matrix."[25]

The groundbreaking work of these authors demonstrates that we are only beginning to comprehend the rich range of queer radical Romanticism. Many scholars (me included) became attuned to environmental sensibilities in Romantic texts before discovering and revealing Romantic queer and trans sensibilities. But that is changing. As Michael O'Rourke and David Collings have claimed, "If it is now possible to 'green' a text as it is to 'queer' a text, the potentialities for giving Romantic texts (prose and poetry) an ecoqueer makeover are potentially limitless."[26] George Haggerty's work on queer Gothic, Catriona Mortimer-Sandilands and Bruce Erickson's development of queer pastoral and rural space,

Jolene Zigarovich's investigation of trans legacies in *Frankenstein*, and Douglas Vakoch's edited volume *Transecology: Transgender Perspectives on Environment and Nature* reveal how radical Romanticism and queer and trans theory are linked by their attention to notions of entanglement, intimacy, fluidity, and the human and more-than-human suffering that comes from being cruelly deemed the exploitable "other."[27]

And as some are turning to the queer in past Romanticism, others may turn to the radical Romanticism in such contemporary queer persons as Derek Jarman and his queer garden. His book *Derek Jarman's Garden* could be understood as a radical Romantic queer ecological creation in the tradition of William Blake—the very tradition that was influential for Silko. In a Blakean aesthetic form, Jarman's art illustrates words and words illustrate art, together producing an entangled, storied landscape of human and the more-than-human, private and public, beauty and oppression, life and death.[28] Jarman, like past radical Romantics, is the master storyteller who is receptive to the world and, in response, creates something new in it, thereby co-creating with the world.

We need the stories—stories that listen to the howling of the ghosts, stories that contribute to the work of co-creation, of renovation. In place of dominating fixed roles, tyrannical hierarchies, and exploitive practices, radical Romanticism and queer theory jointly promote ways of justice and beauty that are marked by fluid boundaries, dynamic change, and nondomination.

What might it mean to be a radical Romantic today? What will be the legacy of twenty-first-century radical Romanticism? Which ancestors and ghosts will be attended to, and which descendants will forge still newer directions? Radical Romanticism, I have claimed, is a broad set of traditions, practices, and ways of being that is both found in the past and made anew in the present—ever dynamic, ever in motion. Some might complain that my understanding of radical Romanticism is too broad, too indeterminate. But the life and force of such liberating radical Romantic art as Wordsworth and Coleridge's *Lyrical Ballads*, Shelley's *Frankenstein*, Du Bois's *The Souls of Black Folk*, and Williams's *Refuge* is vital. Can we clamp down on such a poetic, lyrical, emancipating dynamism? Why would we want to? Could bell hooks, that keen reader of William Wordsworth and virtuoso of Romantic storied landscapes, be considered a radical Romantic? *Appalachian Elegy: Poetry and Place* and *Belonging: A Culture of Place* are but two of her powerful works that, in matter and manner, articulate such central radical Romantic themes as place and belonging in the context of racism, patriarchy, and the destruction of the environment. How about Claudia Rankine as a radical Romantic? Her *Citizen: An American Lyric* is a book of poetry that vividly and realistically portrays both everyday suffering and beauty. It is listed as nonfiction on the *New York Times* bestseller list, thereby furthering the radical Romantic challenge to the fiction/nonfiction binary. What about Carolyn Finney, one of our finest storytellers and cultural geographers? Her performances such as *The N Word: Nature Revisited* and her book *Black Faces, White Spaces: Reimagining the Relationship of African Americans to the Great Outdoors* speak of the beauty of the more-than-human, the pain of anti-Black racism, and the relation between the two. Like Du Bois before her, Finney carefully listens to the ghosts, attends to the intricacies of the present, and produces what could be called powerful radical Romantic narratives of environmental justice and environmental wonder.

Many, many more authors could be offered as belonging to or in significant ways connecting to radical Romanticism: Camille T. Dungy's *Black Nature*, Tommy Pico's *Nature Poem*, Lauret Savoy's *Trace: Memory, History, Race, and the American Landscape*, and Rebecca Solnit's *A Field Guide to Getting Lost* and *The Faraway Nearby*, for example. Renée Elizabeth Neely-Tanner's lyrical and abstract visual art in "Speculative Ecologies: The Intimate Bond of Freedom and Green" could be said to participate in the tradition of radical Romantic storied landscapes that vividly represent and narrate the ways that people of color and the more-than-human mutually flourish and suffer together. My point here is not to *claim* these artists as necessarily being radical Romantics but rather to gesture toward the open, indeterminate future of radical Romanticism and its potential, liberatory allies.[29]

BEAUTY, HOPE, AND CRAZY, WILD LOVE AMONG DEATH-ZONE RUINS

Radical Romanticism gives witness to beauty and suffering and to hope and despair. This twin witness is a powerful stance and urgent contribution. Beauty, in this tradition, is not principally pretty or sublime vistas but those pockets and occasions of tenderness, wonder, rest, healing, and love that grace our lives as we move and dwell among the human and more-than-human.[30] Suffering refers principally to what Du Bois called "the ugly," that is, unnecessary harm and oppression. Despair, here, is a dark, anguishing mood caused by an honest assessment of the ongoing iterations of unnecessary harm and oppression. And hope, as we saw in chapter 2, is a calling or cultivated disposition to continue the work for positive change despite reasonable despair and evidence that such change, while possible, may not be likely. We do not need to choose between hope and despair. We can acknowledge the uncertainty of the future but also affirm that, with hope, people are moved to join together, to work together, and thereby increase the very possibility of beneficial change.

Deborah Bird Rose wrote of the "death zone"—the zone in which "death is imminent but has not yet arrived"—and the importance of beauty therein: "The expression of our ethical lives will be visible in how we inhabit the death zone: how we call out, how we refuse to abandon others, how we refuse hardheartedness, and thus *how we embrace the precious beauty that permeates the house of life.*"[31] Embracing beauty in the face of death and despair is as salutary as it is demanding. "Hard-heartedness," though a miserable way of being, comes more easily in the ruins of the "death zone." Yet the difficult work of finding and embracing beauty is nurtured by hope and in turn nurtures hope. Beauty and hope are mutually constitutive.

Eva Beatrice Dykes understood as much. This book began with her, the first Black American woman to complete the requirements for a doctoral degree in 1921. Her Harvard dissertation was on the English poet Alexander Pope and his influence in the United States. Later, in 1942, she published *The Negro in English Romantic Thought: Or a Study in Sympathy for the Oppressed.* Her wonderful book on Romanticism, which argued that we understand Romanticism as a movement committed to "the amelioration of the condition of the lowly and oppressed," concluded with the importance of keeping "the torch of liberty burning and pass[ing] it on undimmed to those who follow." As a powerful scholar, educator, and community leader, Dykes kept that torch bright. But lest the conclusion of her book sound Pollyannaish, note that the final paragraph contained Thomas Carlyle's dire words to an American abolitionist: "The America for which you are hoping you will never see: and you will never see the whites and the blacks in the South dwelling together as equals in peace."[32] But then Dykes added this final sentence of the book: "The torch of liberty has been handed down to the twentieth century with the prophecy of Carlyle yet unfulfilled." Dykes, here, acknowledged the complicated relation between despair (an honest assessment of lack of significant progress), hope, the passing on of the torch of liberty, and the work for a better day—the very work she exemplified in her remarkable life. She did the work. She passed on the torch. Yet she never saw the America she hoped to see.

There are many great challenges—formidable powers, systems, and ways of being—that work against achieving democracy in the United States. Racism, settler colonialism, patriarchy, and neofascism are among the greatest of these. If the United States cannot address its imperial, racist, patriarchal history, if it cannot wake up and hear the voices of the wailing ghosts and honor them by attending to the present voices of the oppressed, then democracy will not be realized. Democracy, as I noted in the introduction and in chapter 1, is more than a constitution, the right to vote, or such formal institutions as Congress. It is also a shared culture, a way of being and living together. In the United States, slavery and the dispossession of Native Americans did not occur in a genuine democracy. Today, democracy in the United States remains more aspirational than actual. The promise of radical Romanticism—a movement and way of life born in revolution—is its capacity to open eyes and ears, hearts and minds to past and current subjugated peoples and to tend to them: to hear them, learn from them, work for and with them. This promise—this potential—of radical Romanticism is its greatest contribution to the democratic endeavor.

When citizens wake up, relinquish their claims to mastery, and cultivate such virtues as paying attention to the "other" outside themselves, they begin to hear the many and diverse voices in the lands and seas. To the extent that the powerless and seemingly voiceless—among humans and the more-than-human—are excluded from democratic institutions, practices, and regard, a democracy neglects its responsibility to include and consider the *entire* community. To fail to listen to and care for those who are vulnerable and seemingly mute—for whatever reason—is to fail one of the most important benchmarks of a flourishing, vital democracy.

Just imagine how our lives and institutions would change if we were to give ethical, democratic consideration to fellow, more-than-human members in our lands and seas. Would we not work and recreate, build and drive, vote and consume differently, more attentively, more justly? Concern for the more-than-human was central to radical Romanticism at its conception. Against the Industrial Revolution and its instrumental, extractive pursuits and modes of being, the Romantic revolution championed an alternative mode of being: not mastery, exploitation, and control but wonder, respect, and cooperation in relation to the more-than-human. This was and is the radical Romantic way.

Aspirational democracies need an urgent wake-up call—the very kind that radical Romanticism has sought to announce. If we are to contend with the interrelated, catastrophic social, political, and ecological challenges that confront us, we need to heed the call of humans and more-than-humans, ghosts and future descendants, that would renovate ruined worlds with the tools—the virtues—of humility, care, cooperation, and justice. What might awaken us to the call? What might enable us to become a people capable of witnessing and responding to oppression and pain among human and more-than-human communities? Surely there is no one answer, no one way. And perhaps, in the end, there will be no way. Still, in the tradition of radical Romanticism, I would recommend hope and beauty—even while, or especially while, witnessing unnecessary suffering and honoring warranted despair. Czesław Miłosz, a poet familiar with suffering and despair, wrote of the ethical, liberating power of beauty, noting that when people no longer have the capacity or inclination to determine what is good and what is evil, "Only beauty will call to them and save them / So that they will still know how to say: this is true and that is false."[33]

Here, we do not find an escape into beauty. Beauty is not a refuge from evil but rather a power to know and name it. Beauty is radical in the twofold sense of the word, rooted in the world even as it critiques it. By identifying with beauty, we are enabled to recognize "the ugly"—the ruins of life turned into ash—and to learn once again how to say: "This is true and that is false." In describing radical Romanticism, I have often employed the adjective *vivid*—authors vividly portraying richly textured ways of being (among the human and more-than-human), bringing attention to sources of life and sources of pain. Beauty is central to this tradition, because beauty vividly illuminates, by way of contrast, that which is not beautiful, that which is cruel and unjust. This is what drew Du Bois to beauty and evidently Miłosz as well. And in beauty's call to us, in its capacity to stir us and wake us up, there is the voice of hope.

In addition to beauty and hope, radical Romanticism would recommend love, especially *wild love*. Like dark, wild hope, wild love does not deny suffering and oppression but rather is a response to it. Wild love is not contingent on efficacy, that is, on its capacity to rescue or save. Like hope, it is similar to a calling or a virtue—loving wildly despite the odds and risks. Wild love is the "crazy love" that Deborah Bird Rose spoke of in her powerful essay "In the Shadow of All This Death": "Throughout the whole of the house of life, crazy love springs forth in the face of death." She explored "the practice of crazy love" by way of a grief-filled story about a caring human couple but mainly about a caring albatross couple, tending attentively to each other and to their egg that will never hatch: "The crazy love that albatross demonstrate for their mate and chick encounters the crazy love of people who are doing all they can to help them thrive. Exactly here, within the shadow of the Anthropocene, exactly here we encounter the crazy love that keeps calling others back from the edge of disaster, and staying with those who grieve in the wake of death." Crazy love is a practice shared by albatross and humans: Both respond to a call from the edge of death and despair. Again, efficacy is not the measure of or justification for such love (even if one continues to hope for efficacy). Rather, crazy, wild love is a mode of listening and acting in response to a call—to the unimaginable and overwhelming summon of despair and death:

> What is happening to other creatures in this era of mass anthropogenic death may be too large to think, too unprecedented to know how to imagine. And still we are called. For many reasons, then, we need an *ethical poetics that brings us into proximities that awaken us both to others and to ourselves, and thus to our responsibilities.* Such an ethical poetics will return us to the death zone, and to the crazy love that makes possible the refusal to abandon others.[34]

With these words, Rose brings us to the core of what I have called in these pages radical Romanticism: a dynamic tradition of "ethical poetics" offering powerful storied landscapes of "the death zone" so that we may awaken to our obligation to witness it and—despite our defensible despair—respond with a crazy, wild love. And in that witness and response, while confronting suffering and oppression among humans and the more-than-human, we experience a beauty and hope that sustains us. That is the heart and mind, the song and cry of ongoing radical Romanticism.

Acknowledgments

I t is a joy and obligation to give thanks, acknowledging the many sources of support, wisdom, and love that sustain our work and lives. However poorly and incompletely, let me attempt to name those that contributed to the making of this book.

Wendy Lochner at Columbia University Press is a brilliant editor and equally lovely human being. An author is lucky to be under Wendy's care. I am also grateful for the dedication and expert labor of production editor Michael Haskell, manuscript editor Robert Fellman, associate editor Alyssa Napier, and indexer Paula Durbin-Westby. The Press has shown me every courtesy and carries out its high calling—the publication of ideas and perspectives worthy of public consideration—responsibly and expertly. I am also indebted to Lucy Cooper-Silvis, a bright and hardworking undergraduate research assistant who has perfected the art of editing and who is herself a gifted writer. Lucy's eyes worked every page of this book, editing my prose, fixing my citations, and assembling the bibliography. Also, this book greatly benefited from the labor and insights of three anonymous readers recruited by the Press.

It is a privilege and honor to call Brown University my academic home. For me, Brown is an institution and set of relationships that fosters intellectual curiosity, ethical inquiry, interdisciplinarity, and friendship. At Brown, I have three principal academic homes: the Department of Religious Studies, the Center for Environmental Humanities, and Native American and Indigenous Studies. Colleagues in these academic units are generous and supportive, and I count them among my friends: in Religious Studies: Steve Bush, Tal Lewis, Paul Nahme, Kera Street, Dan Vaca, and Andre Willis—all close friends and colleagues in my subfield, Religion and Critical Thought; also Shahzad Bashir, Tina Creamer, Jae Han,

Susan Harvey, Nancy Khalek, Saul Olyan, Jason Protass, Hal Roth, Michael Satlow, Janine Sawada, and Nicole Vadnais; in Environmental Humanities: Amanda Anderson, Bathsheba Demuth, Macarena Gómez-Barris (coconspirator in many worthy projects), Nancy Jacobs, Brian Lander, Lukas Rieppel, Eleni Sikelianos, and Ada Smailbegovic; and in Native American and Indigenous Studies: Scott AnderBois, Geri Augusto, Kevin Escudero, Paja Faudree, Linford Fisher, Rae Gould, Amanda Lynch, Robert Preucel, and Neil Safier.

At Brown, three academic homes are not enough. Outside those academic units, I have been graced with additional close colleagues and friends: Corey Brettschneider, Janet Cooper-Nelson, Beshara Doumani, David Estlund, Alexander Gourevitch, Bonnie Honig (who reads and comments on everything I send her, usually within twenty-four hours), Juliet Hooker, Sharon Krause (comrade, coteacher, and dear friend), Charles Larmore (whose little book *The Romantic Legacy* inspired much of my own), Kevin McLaughlin, Kevin Quashie, Bernard Reginster, Melvin Rogers (whose work on Du Bois I greatly admire), Matthew Shenoda (poet and colleague par excellence), and John Tomasi.

I am also grateful for all that I have learned from students who have taken my graduate seminars on European and North American Romanticism, in particular: Brett Anders, Nicholas Andersen, Aseel Azab, Angel Calvin, Caroline Cunfer, Christopher DiBona, Nicholas Friesner, Brooke Grasberger, Scott Jackshaw, Nechama Juni, Caroline Kory, Lise Miltner, Avery Morrow, Caleb Murray, Michael Putnam, Michael Sawyer, Lauren Smith, Celia Stern, and Donnell Williamson. Also, for their astute reflections and comments on many aspects of this book, I am grateful to my co-teacher Sharon Krause and all the members of the 2019 and 2024 Brown University doctoral seminar "Thinking Democracy Ecologically." Over the years, Brown has supported my work with bright, creative undergraduate research assistants. I hope that they grasp the depth of my appreciation: Virginia Schilder, Joshua Kurtz, Luke Perrotta, Tara Sharma, Emilia Sowersby, Emma Schneider, Noah Baum, David Tapper, Ella Spungen, and Georgia Turman.

Outside Brown, colleagues and friends have contributed mightily to my life and work: Jeffrey Stout (who for over three decades has inspired and supported my work), Fannie Bialek (friend of the family and a former graduate student who always led the way—and led me—with brilliance and care), Alda Balthrop-Lewis, Jonathon Kahn (who has written the best book on Du Bois and religion), Scott Slovic (pen pal and public leader), Kyle Whyte (friend and inspiration), Carolyn

Finney (exemplar of powerful storyteller), Catriona Sandilands (friend in the north), Mark Wallace (friend since the start of my intellectual journey), Jim Wetzel (trusted colleague and friend), Kate Rigby, Emily Dumler-Winckler, Terrence Johnson (who, although I was his advisor, led me to Du Bois), Damian White, Melanie Harris, Kevin Hart, Azzurra Cox, Robert Gooding-Williams, Maggie Millner (dear family friend and bold poet), and Brent Constantz (childhood friend whose voice and light led me out of the cold and darkness to the warmth and safety of our High Sierra camp). I wish to offer special thanks to three professional organizations that have offered me opportunities to present my work, build friendships, and learn from their members: the Western Political Science Association, with its remarkable community of environmental political theorists (and much gratitude to Peter Cannavo, Gregory Koutnik, Jennifer Lawrence, John Meyer, David Schlosberg, and Christine Jill Winter); the American Academy of Religion, especially the units in Afro-American Religious History; Arts, Literature, and Religion; Ethics; Native Traditions in the Americas; Philosophy of Religion; and Religion and Ecology. I also thank the Association for the Study of Literature and Environment, surely one of the most thoughtful, humane professional organizations in the U.S. (and I am especially grateful for the wise leadership of such past presidents as Scott Slovic and Catriona Sandilands).

In addition to the above-mentioned professional organizations, I wish to mention the following institutions, organizations, and groups that have hosted presentations of my work: Haskell Indian Nations University (where Indigenous leaders exemplify wisdom, care, and resistance to oppression, a place I am grateful for and accountable to); Harvard University; Vassar College; Rhode Island School of Design; University of California, Berkeley; Yale University; Institute for the Environmental Humanities at Colby College; European Association for the Study of Literature, Culture, and the Environment; North American Society for the Study of Romanticism; Nineteenth-Century French Studies Colloquium; American Literature Association; International Society for the Study of Religion, Nature, and Culture; and at Brown University: Native American and Indigenous Studies, Center for the Study of Race and Ethnicity in America, Cogut Institute for the Humanities, Pembroke Center for Teaching and Research on Women, and Political Philosophy Workshop.

Earlier versions of portions of this book appeared as the following: "The World in Ruins: Wordsworth, Du Bois, and Silko," *Soundings: An Interdisciplinary Journal* 105, no. 4 (2022): 440-67; "Dancing on a Flaming World: Du Bois' Religiously

Inflected Poetry and Creative Fiction," *Journal of the Academy of Religion* 91 (2023): 408-29; "Romantic Nature," in *Nature and Literary Studies,* ed. Peter Remien and Scott Slovic (Cambridge University Press, 2022), 141-60; "Radical Romanticism and its Alternative Account of the Wild and Wilderness," *ISLE: Interdisciplinary Studies in Literature and Environment* 25, no. 4 (2018): 835-57; and "British Romanticism, Secularization, and the Political and Environmental Implications," *International Journal of Philosophy and Theology* 76, no. 4 (2015): 284-304.

People inform ways of being and thinking but so do places. I am grateful for the eastern slopes of the California Santa Cruz Mountains (which holds the town of Portola Valley) and for Admiralty Island in Southeast Alaska (which holds the town of Angoon): both places blessed my childhood and young adult life with beauty, learning, and a deep respect for the more-than-human. Later in life, I was shaped profoundly by the New York Hudson River Valley and the Shawangunk and Catskill Mountains (surrounding and holding Poughkeepsie). I am now nurtured by the Rhode Island Blackstone River Valley and the eastern shore of Narragansett Bay, on a peninsula separated by the Barrington River (sustaining Providence and Barrington, respectively). Portola Valley, Angoon, Poughkeepsie, Providence, and Barrington have greatly nurtured me, but— except for Angoon, Alaska—are also unceded Indigenous ancestral lands of the Muwekma Ohlone, the Munsee Lenape, the Narragansett, and the Pokanoket. Angoon, in contrast, while assailed by settler colonialism, is home to and held by the Tlingit, and they have greatly informed aspects of my life and work. I am grateful to the Angoon Tlingit community for their care and instruction during those three summers when I was a young man trying to find my way.

I wish to acknowledge two special friendships that have sustained me over the years. I have known Benjamin Barney and Paul Kane for over three decades. Ben has taught me much about Diné (Navajo) culture and ways of life, and more generally about the art of living. He has graciously instructed my students at Vassar College and Brown University, teaching them about Indigenous cultures and ecologies. He truly embodies Hózhó. Paul is my best friend (as well as a superb scholar of Romanticism and an exquisite poet). I recently published a book titled *In Search of a Course*; it is about finding a course for your life and a course for the University. Paul is the main character in the book: he is at the heart of both searches. Why? Because no one has taught me more about the "higher" in higher education—about the task and privilege of being an educator—nor about what it is to search for, or be found by, a course for your life. Both Ben and Paul have greatly informed this book.

I wish that at the start of this book project I had had the wisdom to keep an up-to-date list of all those who contributed to it. I lacked such wisdom, and even lack now the knowledge of when the project started. I suppose it started with my parents, (the late) John and Jenny Cladis, who were exemplars of courage, compassion, and resilience. I endeavor to honor them each day by striving to be like them. My siblings, Mary Worsley, Christine Billion, and George Cladis, have cared for me at every turn in my life. Our love for each other is, in part, a manifestation of the love we received from our parents. Mina, my partner, and our children, Sabine, Olive, and Luke, are my light and life: my life makes no sense without them. Mina is strength, beauty, and intelligence in motion. She inspires me, stirs me, nourishes me—me and everyone around her. Sabine, Luke, and Olive (three radical Romantics, indeed!) are bright lights in this often dark world. They bring me much hope and even more joy. This book is dedicated to them.

Notes

PREFACE; OR, HOW I CAME TO WRITE THIS BOOK AND WHAT
LIES AT ITS HEART

1. W. E. B. Du Bois, *The Souls of Black Folk*, ed. Brent Hayes Edwards (Oxford University Press, 2007), 84–85; emphasis added.
2. Du Bois, *The Souls of Black Folk*, 85.
3. Du Bois, *The Souls of Black Folk*, 86.
4. Any list of authors who potentially count as radical Romantics is ongoing and dynamic. Additionally, when I call Wordsworth and Coleridge radical Romantics, I am referring to their early life and work.
5. My notion of "spiritual democracy" is informed by what Whitman called "Religious Democracy," namely, the many and diverse cultural threads that form a complex, democratic social fabric. Walt Whitman, "Democratic Vistas," in *Whitman: Poetry and Prose*, ed. Justin Kaplan (Library of America, 1982), 977. Think of spiritual democracy as a vast assortment of cultural practices and productions that both expresses and shapes a people's democratic aspirations and aspects of their civic identity in daily life.
6. William Wordsworth, *The Prelude: 1799, 1805, 1850*, ed. Jonathan Wordsworth, M. H. Abrams, and Stephen Gill (Norton, 1979), 447, lines 166–67.
7. I especially want to acknowledge Benjamin Barney, a Diné educator who has been educating me for twenty-five years.
8. Leslie Marmon Silko, *Yellow Woman and a Beauty of the Spirit* (Simon and Schuster, 1996), 20; emphasis added.
9. Shawn Wilson, *Research Is Ceremony* (Fernwood, 2008), 59. My understanding of research as ceremony is greatly informed by this wonderful work of Shawn Wilson; he quotes his friend and colleague Lewis Cardinal: "If you talk about research as a ceremony, that's the climax of the ceremony, when it all comes together and all those connections are made. Cause that's what ceremony is about, is strengthening those connections" (89).
10. "Art can draw its weapons" is an allusion to Sarah Sentilles, *Draw Your Weapons* (Random House, 2017), a book that richly illustrates the power of art to challenge and change the world.

11. Eva Beatrice Dykes, *The Negro in English Romantic Thought, or A Study of Sympathy for the Oppressed* (Associated Publishers, 1942), vii, 154. The wonderful work of Bakary Diaby is lifting up Dykes's work and memory; see Bakary Diaby, "Black Women and/in the Shadow of Romanticism," *European Romantic Review* 30, no. 3 (2019): 252–53.

INTRODUCTION

1. William Wordsworth, *The Prelude: 1799, 1805, 1850*, ed. Jonathan Wordsworth, M. H. Abrams, and Stephen Gill (Norton, 1979), 156, lines 95–99. There are many commentaries on this passage in *The Prelude* that reference its relation to Miguel de Cervantes and a dream of Descartes; for an excellent environmental reading, see Timothy Morton, "Romantic Disaster Ecology: Blake, Shelley, Wordsworth," *Romantic Circles*, 2012, https://romantic-circles.org/index.php/praxis/disaster/praxis.2012.disaster.morton.
2. On the connection between issuing warning and hope, Octavia Butler has powerfully claimed that "the very act of trying to look ahead to discern possibilities and offer warnings is in itself an act of hope." Octavia Butler, "A Few Rules for Predicting the Future," *Essence* 31, no. 1 (2000): 165.
3. My notion of storied landscapes is informed by Leslie Marmon Silko, "Landscape, History, and the Pueblo Imagination," in *At Home on the Earth: Becoming Native to Our Place*, ed. David Landis Barnhill (University of California Press, 1999), 30–42; and by Keith Basso, *Wisdom Sits in Places: Landscape and Language Among the Western Apache* (University of New Mexico Press, 1996).
4. William Wordsworth, "Lines Written a Few Miles Above Tintern Abbey," in *William Wordsworth: The Major Works*, ed. Stephen Gill (Oxford University Press, 2008), 132, lines 11, 15; emphasis added.
5. Wordsworth, "Lines Written a Few Miles above Tintern Abbey," 134, line 120.
6. Cited in Stephen Gill, ed., *The Cambridge Companion to Wordsworth* (Cambridge University Press, 2003), xiv; emphasis added.
7. William Wordsworth, *Guide to the Lakes*, ed. Saeko Yoshikawa (Oxford University Press, 2022), 56.
8. William Wordsworth, "My Heart Leaps When I Behold," in *William Wordsworth: The Major Works*, ed. Stephen Gill (Oxford University Press, 2008), 246, line 7.
9. Robin Wall Kimmerer, "*Mishkos Kenomagwen*, the Lessons of Grass: Restoring Reciprocity with the Good Green Earth," in *Traditional Ecological Knowledge: Learning from Indigenous Practices for Environmental Sustainability*, ed. Melissa K. Nelson and Dan Shilling (Cambridge University Press, 2018), 42.
10. See, for example, Jerome J. McGann, *The Romantic Ideology: A Critical Investigation* (University of Chicago Press, 1983), 1–14.
11. See Kate Rigby, "Ecocriticism," in *Introducing Criticism in the 21st Century*, ed. Julian Wolfreys (Edinburgh University Press, 2015), 134–35.
12. Frederick Douglass, *Autobiographies*, ed. Henry Louis Gates Jr. (Library of America, 1994), 23–24.
13. Douglass, *Autobiographies*, 24.
14. This section's title is a familiar paraphrase of a statement Voltaire made, namely, "Define your terms, you will permit me again to say, or we shall never understand one

another." *The Works of Voltaire: A Contemporary Version, a Critique and Biography*, bio. by John Morley, notes by Tobias Smollett, trans. William F. Fleming (E. R. DuMont, 1901), vol. 6 (*Philosophical Dictionary*, part 4, "Miracles," section 2), 157.

15. Max Liboiron, *Pollution Is Colonialism* (Duke University Press, 2021), 6–7.
16. Walt Whitman, "Democratic Vistas," in *Whitman: Poetry and Prose*, ed. Justin Kaplan (Library of America, 1982), 977.
17. Oscar Wilde, *The Complete Works of Oscar Wilde*, ed. Ian Small, 11 vols. (Oxford University Press, 2005), 2:140; Saidiya Hartman, *Scenes of Subjection: Terror, Slavery, and Self-Making in Nineteenth-Century America* (Oxford University Press, 1997), 3–5; Xine Yao, *Disaffected* (Duke University Press, 2021), 3–5.
18. Leslie Marmon Silko, *Ceremony* (Penguin, 1986), 2.

1. RADICAL ROMANTIC AESTHETICS: WORDSWORTH AND DU BOIS

1. In chapters 4, 5, and 6, I focus on the various *forms* of radical aesthetics. In this chapter, I focus more on the aims and scope of radical aesthetics.
2. "A profoundly human project" is not meant to affirm "human exceptionalism" but rather to acknowledge a distinctive human gift and responsibility, namely, to engage in moral critique and cultivate ways of life that seek just, sustainable relations within and between the human and more-than-human worlds.
3. Percy Bysshe Shelley used the term "veil of familiarity" in his "In Defence of Poetry," in *Shelley's Poetry and Prose*, ed. Donald H. Reiman and Neil Fraistat (Norton, 2002), 533.
4. For an excellent account of what it means to broaden the scope of aesthetics, see Arnold Berleant, *The Aesthetics of Environment* (Temple University Press, 1992), 11–12, 161, 174–75.
5. William Wordsworth, "Expostulation and Reply," in *William Wordsworth: The Major Works*, ed. Stephen Gill (Oxford University Press, 2008), 130.
6. By "eco-emancipation," I refer to Sharon Krause's powerful arguments for "a new kind of political order, one that institutionalizes principled constraints on human power in relation to nonhuman beings and things, and that prevents the exploitation of nature and people." Sharon Krause, *Eco-Emancipation: An Earthly Politics of Freedom* (Princeton University Press, 2023), 9.
7. See J. K. Gibson-Graham, *A Postcapitalist Politics* (University of Minnesota Press, 2006).
8. For two excellent treatments on the history of the imagination in relation to ethics, see David Bromwich, "Moral Imagination," *Raritan* 27, no. 4 (2008): 4–33; and James Engell, *The Creative Imagination: Enlightenment to Romanticism* (Harvard University Press, 1981), esp. 3–62.
9. David Hume, *Treatise of Human Nature*, ed. David Norton and Mary Norton, 3 vols. (Clarendon, 2007), 1:273.
10. I say more about this tempered form of hope in the next chapter, where I discuss Du Bois's dark, wild hope.
11. See I. A. Richards, *Principles of Literary Criticism* (Routledge and Kegan Paul Classics, 1924), 7–13; and Pierre Bourdieu, *Distinction: A Social Critique of the Judgement of Taste* (Harvard University Press, 1984).
12. William Wordsworth, "A Guide Through the District of the Lakes," in *William Wordsworth: Selected Prose*, ed. John O. Hayden (Penguin, 1988), 46.

13.   See Paul Lukacs, "Matters of Taste," *American Scholar*, June 8, 2015, https://theamerican scholar.org/matters-of-taste/; and Paul Lukacs, *Inventing Wine* (Norton, 2012), 122.

14.   Nelly S. Hoyt and Thomas Cassirer, trans., *The Encyclopedia: Selections: Diderot, d'Alembert and a Society of Men of Letters* (Bobbs-Merrill, 1965), 336–37.

15.   Samuel Taylor Coleridge, "On the Principles of Genial Criticism," in *Coleridge's Poetry and Prose*, ed. Nicholas Halmi, Paul Magnuson, and Raimonda Modiano (Norton, 2004), 343; emphasis added.

16.   W. E. B. Du Bois, *The Souls of Black Folk*, ed. Brent Hayes Edwards (Oxford University Press, 2007), 45–52.

17.   Melvin L. Rogers, "David Walker and the Political Power of the Appeal," *Political Theory* 43, no. 2 (2015): 212; emphasis added.

18.   Lewis R. Gordon, "Fanon's Decolonial Aesthetic," in *The Aesthetic Turn in Political Thought*, ed. Nikolas Kompridis (Bloomsbury Academic, 2014), 95; emphasis in original.

19.   By "the early Wordsworth," I refer to his work in the 1790s and up to approximately 1805. There is a well-entrenched account of the trajectory of Wordsworth's poetry and political persuasion. When he was young, his poetry was original and vibrant, and his political beliefs were democratic and progressive. As he aged, his poetry became staid and his politics conservative. There is much debate about exactly when his apostasy occurred, though most agree it took place sometime between 1798 and 1806. If one is, like me, mostly interested in his early poetry and its political, religious, and environmental dimensions, then the relevance of when or whether Wordsworth committed apostasy is not entirely clear. I will say, however, that Wordsworth's transition to more conservative political and religious beliefs and practices is a long, complicated path. It is not a straight line from left to right.

20.   Alan G. Hill, ed., *The Letters of William and Dorothy Wordsworth*, 2nd ed., 8 vols. (Clarendon, 1979), 5:185; emphasis in original.

21.   William Wordsworth, *The Prelude: 1799, 1805, 1850*, ed. Jonathan Wordsworth, M. H. Abrams, and Stephen Gill (Norton, 1979), 447, lines 166–67.

22.   For helpful discussions of the sonnet, see Debbie Lee, *Slavery and the Romantic Imagination* (University of Pennsylvania Press, 2002), 203–7; Judith Page, *Wordsworth and the Cultivation of Women* (University of California Press, 1994), 67–76; Jonathan Bate, *The Song of the Earth* (Harvard University Press, 2002), 215.

23.   "Any black, mulatto, or other persons of color, of either sex." J. B. Duvergier, ed., *Collection complète des lois, décrets, ordonnances, règlements, avis du conseil-d'état* (Guyot et Scribe, 1836), 13:242.

24.   William Wordsworth, "The Banished Negroes," in *Poems, in Two Volumes, and Other Poems, 1800–1807*, ed. Jared Curtis (Cornell University Press, 1983), 161.

25.   Wordsworth, "The Banished Negroes," 161, lines 1–3; emphasis added.

26.   Wordsworth, "The Banished Negroes," 161–62, lines 3–4, 6, 9, 7–14.

27.   Wordsworth maintained this alliance throughout his life, and he cultivated strong friendships with two of the greatest abolitionists of the age, Thomas Clarkson and William Wilberforce. Early on, Wordsworth was greatly influenced by Helen Maria Williams and her long, anticolonial, abolitionist poem *Peru*. Still, as Wordsworth grew more conservative, his support for abolition became more muted by the mid-1820s. On this topic, see the

excellent article by Ronald Tetreault, "Wordsworth on Enthusiasm: A New Letter to Thomas Clarkson on the Slavery Question," *Modern Philology* 75, no. 1 (1977): 53–58.

28. Here I am largely employing the ocular metaphor "sight" to stay close to Wordsworth's own metaphorical language (to see "souls that appear to have no depth at all / To careless eyes"). More generally in this chapter, however, I have employed a variety of senses—hearing, feeling, smelling, and tasting—to express one's experience of the world, including transformative experiences.

29. Gordon, "Fanon's Decolonial Aesthetic," 96; emphasis in original.

30. See Eva Kittay, *Love's Labor: Essays on Women, Equality, and Dependency* (Routledge, 1999), 147–61; and Eva Kittay and Licia Carlson, eds., *Cognitive Disability and Its Challenge to Moral Philosophy* (Wiley-Blackwell, 2010), 1–26.

31. Bromwich, "Moral Imagination," 10.

32. William Wordsworth, "Lines Written a Few Miles Above Tintern Abbey," in *William Wordsworth: The Major Works*, ed. Stephen Gill (Oxford University Press, 2008), 134, lines 101–3; emphasis added.

33. William Wordsworth, "Essay on Morals," in *William Wordsworth: Selected Prose*, ed. John O. Hayden (Penguin, 1988), 105.

34. Edmund Burke, "To Charles-Jean-François Depont (November 1789)," in *On Empire, Liberty, and Reform: Speeches and Letters*, ed. David Bromwich (Yale University Press, 2000), 410; emphasis added.

35. Burke, "Letter to Charles-Jean-François Depont," 414.

36. Wordsworth, *The Prelude*, 402, lines 819–29.

37. Wordsworth, *The Prelude*, 402, line 817; 404, lines 860–61, 850.

38. Ralph Waldo Emerson, "Experience," in *Ralph Waldo Emerson: Essays and Poems*, ed. Harold Bloom, Paul Kane, and Joel Porte (Library of America, 1996), 492.

39. For an excellent account of the reasons for and against maintaining the notion of a "canon," see Lukacs, "Matters of Taste."

40. Paul Taylor, *Black Is Beautiful: A Philosophy of Black Aesthetics* (Wiley-Blackwell, 2016), 92.

41. Christopher M. Stampone, "Seeing Through 'the Veil' Darkly: Wordsworthian Ideals and Forms in W. E. B. Du Bois's *The Souls of Black Folk*," *Journal of Transatlantic Studies* 19 (2021): 372–86.

42. Arnold Rampersad, *The Art and Imagination of W. E. B. Du Bois* (Schocken, 1990), ix.

43. For a powerful and nuanced treatment of the strengths and limits of Du Bois's use of exemplarity, see Lawrie Balfour, *Democracy's Reconstruction: Thinking Politically with W. E. B. Du Bois* (Oxford University Press, 2011), 71–114.

44. Du Bois, *The Souls of Black Folk*, 4.

45. W. E. B. Du Bois, *A World Search for Democracy*, c. 1937, W. E. B. Du Bois Papers (MS 312), Special Collections and University Archives, University of Massachusetts Amherst Libraries.

46. Nick Bromell begins his article with this dialogue. I was unaware of *A World Search for Democracy* before I read this article. Nick Bromell, "W. E. B. Du Bois and the Enlargement of Democratic Theory," *Raritan* 30, no. 4 (2011): 140–61.

47. Joseph R. Winters, *Hope Draped in Black* (Duke University Press, 2016), 33.

48. Du Bois, *The Souls of Black Folk*, 33; emphasis added.

49.   Carole Lynn Stewart, "Civil Religion, Civil Society, and the Performative Life and Work of W. E. B. Du Bois," *Journal of Religion* 88, no. 3 (2008): 316; emphasis added.

50.   See, for example, Bernard Bell, Emily Grosholz, and James Stewart, eds., *W. E. B. Du Bois on Race and Culture: Philosophy, Politics, and Poetics* (Routledge, 1996); David Levering Lewis, *W. E. B. Du Bois: Biography of a Race* (Henry Holt, 1993); Rampersad, *The Art and Imagination of W. E. B. Du Bois*; and Stewart, "Civil Religion, Civil Society, and the Performative Life and Work of W. E. B. Du Bois," 307–30.

51.   Du Bois, *The Souls of Black Folk*, 8.

52.   Balfour, *Democracy's Reconstruction*, 7.

53.   For an excellent article on intraracial diversity in Du Bois's *The Philadelphia Negro*, see Marcus Anthony Hunter, "W. E. B. Du Bois and Black Heterogeneity: How *The Philadelphia Negro* Shaped American Sociology," *American Sociologist* 46, no. 2 (2015): 219–33.

54.   Robert W. Williams, "'The Sacred Unity in All the Diversity': The Text and a Thematic Analysis of W. E. B. Du Bois' 'The Individual and Social Conscience' (1905)," *Journal of African American Studies* 16, no. 3 (2012): 456–97. Williams has performed an invaluable service by recovering an important text by Du Bois from the convention proceedings of the 1905 Third Annual Convention of the Religious Education Association. At the Convention, Du Bois was a panelist addressing the topic "How Can We Develop in the Individual a Social Conscience?" Du Bois's text is seven paragraphs long, and it is found on pages 458–59 in William's article.

55.   Du Bois, "The Individual Social Conscience," cited in Williams, "'The Sacred Unity in All the Diversity,'" 459.

56.   Du Bois, "The Individual and Social Conscience," cited in Williams, "'The Sacred Unity in All the Diversity,'" 459; emphasis added,

57.   W. E. B. Du Bois, *The Autobiography of W. E. B. Du Bois* (International Publishers, 1968), 409–10.

58.   I am not arguing that Du Bois should be regarded only as or even primarily as a North American Romantic. I do argue, however, that radical aesthetics captures much of his aesthetic style and that he shares many characteristics with what I am calling radical Romanticism.

59.   For an excellent account of Du Bois's "troubled" relation to the land, see Michael J. Beilfuss, "Ironic Pastorals and Beautiful Swamps: W. E. B. Du Bois and the Troubled Landscapes of the American South," *Interdisciplinary Studies in Literature and Environment* 22, no. 3 (2015): 485–506.

60.   Melvin L. Rogers, "The People, Rhetoric, and Affect: On the Political Force of Du Bois' *The Souls of Black Folk*," *American Political Science Review* 106, no. 1 (2012): 199.

61.   Gordon, "Fanon's Decolonial Aesthetic," 104.

62.   See Rogers, "The People, Rhetoric, and Affect," 195.

63.   See Whitney Battle-Baptiste and Britt Rusert, eds., *Data Portraits: Visualizing Black America* (Princeton Architectural Press, 2018).

64.   Frederick Douglass, "The Color Line," *North American Review* 132, no. 295 (1881): 567–77.

65.   W. E. B. Du Bois, "Dusk of Dawn," in *Du Bois: Writings*, ed. Nathan Huggins (Library of America, 1986), 751.

66.   Du Bois, *The Souls of Black Folk*, 94, 105, 122.

67. Balfour, *Democracy's Reconstruction*, 12; emphasis in original.

68. Du Bois, *The Souls of Black Folk*, 25.

69. See Beilfuss, "Ironic Pastorals and Beautiful Swamps," 489; and Sheila Lloyd, "Du Bois and the Production of the Racial Picturesque," *Public Culture* 17, no. 2 (2005): 277–97. Lloyd, for example, writes, "in several key moments of *Souls*, Du Bois appropriates language associated with the picturesque aesthetic and produces what I am referring to as a 'racial picturesque,' in which a language of social analysis and critique is supplemented by romantic vocabulary and imagery" (277–78).

70. Melvin L. Rogers, *The Darkened Light of Faith: Race, Democracy, and Freedom in African American Political Thought* (Princeton University Press, 2023), 208; see also Rogers, "The People, Rhetoric, and Affect," 190–93, 139.

71. Gordon, "Fanon's Decolonial Aesthetic," 98, 112. I should clarify that Gordon was not referring to Du Bois but rather to Fanon.

72. W. E. B. Du Bois, "Criteria of Negro Art," in *Du Bois: Writings*, ed. Nathan Huggins (Library of America, 1986), 1000. Emphasis added. In this section I make many references to this essay, and hence I will embed the page number in the text.

73. Eric King Watts, "Cultivating a Black Public Voice: W. E. B. Du Bois and the 'Criteria of Negro Art,'" *Rhetoric & Public Affairs* 4, no. 2 (2001): 189.

74. Rogers, *The Darkened Light of Faith*, 213.

75. On Du Bois's Calvinistic background, see Rampersad, *The Art and Imagination of W. E. B. Du Bois*, 2, 4–6.

76. Emerson, "Experience," 492. For a discussion on this passage, see Mark Cladis, "Religion, Democracy, and Virtue: Emerson and the Journey's End," *Religion & Literature* 41, no. 1 (2009): 76; and for the best interpretive essay on "Experience," see Jeffrey Stout, "The Transformation of Genius Into Practical Power: A Reading of Emerson's 'Experience,'" *American Journal of Theology & Philosophy* 35, no. 1 (2014): 3–24.

77. A contemporary example of Black art wed to truth and justice are the artistic creations of the U.S. death-row prisoner Mumia Abu-Jamal. In Abu-Jamal's own words, "When we speak about art in the Black Freedom struggle, we're really speaking about the heart, the core, the essence of the Black freedom struggle because there has never been a Black freedom struggle that has not been accompanied, in some sense, by art." *Arts and the Freedom Struggle: The Works of Mumia Abu-Jamal*, ed. Anthony Bogues and Melaine Ferdinand-King, Brown University catalog, 2024, 5.

78. Arnold Berleant, among others, argues that Kant did indeed establish a firm divide between aesthetics and ethics: "The traditional view of aesthetic appreciation . . . is that a special attitude is required, one of disinterested and contemplative attention to an object for its own sake. The watchword is, of course, 'disinterested,' for Kant's legacy in making it central in appreciation has shaped the course of aesthetics over the past two centuries." Berleant, *The Aesthetics of Environment*, 161–62. For an account that complicates Kant on the relation between aesthetics and morality, see Paul Guyer, "Feeling and Freedom: Kant on Aesthetics and Morality," *Journal of Aesthetics and Art Criticism* 48, no. 2 (1990): 137–46. My aim in this chapter is not to enter debates over Kant's *Critique of Judgment* but simply to argue that Kant opened the way for aesthetics to become separate from ethics.

79. Wordsworth, "Expostulation and Reply," 130, line 24; Emerson, "Experience," 491.

80. Cited in Stephen Gill, ed., *The Cambridge Companion to Wordsworth* (Cambridge University Press, 2003), xiv. Emphasis added.

81. On the dialectical relation between affect and cognition and its social-critical power, see Sharon Krause, *Civil Passions: Moral Sentiment and Democratic Deliberation* (Princeton University Press, 2008), chap. 2; and Rogers, *The Darkened Light of Faith*, 81.

82. Wordsworth, *The Prelude*, 429–31, lines 208–15.

83. Nicholas Roe, *Wordsworth and Coleridge: The Radical Years* (Oxford University Press, 1988), 59; emphasis added.

84. Wordsworth, *The Prelude*, 521–22, lines 512, 522–28; emphasis added.

85. John Dewey, *Art as Experience* (Penguin, 2005), 3.

86. Samuel Taylor Coleridge, "Biographia Literaria," in *Samuel Taylor Coleridge: The Major Works*, ed. H. J. Jackson (Oxford University Press, 2008), 313.

87. Jacques Rancière, *The Politics of Aesthetics: The Distribution of the Sensible* (Continuum, 2004), 9. For additional work on expansive accounts of aesthetics, see Danielle Boutet, "Metaphors of the Mind," in *Carnal Knowledge*, ed. Estelle Barrett and Barbara Bolt (I. B. Tauris, 2013), 29–39; and Jondi Keane, "Æffect: Initiating Heuristic Life," in *Carnal Knowledge*, ed. Estelle Barrett and Barbara Bolt (I. B. Tauris, 2013), 41–61.

88. Rancière, *The Politics of Aesthetics*, 13.

89. I am grateful to Kevin Minister for these examples and for his excellent paper, "Public Religious Aesthetics: Theorizing the Affect and Import of Interreligious Aesthetics," presented at the 2016 annual meeting of the American Academy of Religion, San Antonio, Texas, November 19, 2016.

90. Dewey, *Art as Experience*, 142; emphasis in original.

91. I presented an early version of this chapter at the 2016 annual meeting of the American Academy of Religion. I am grateful for the helpful comments of the panel participants, Robert Davis, Kevin Martin, Kathryn Reklis, Mara Willard, and of the respondent, Tamsin Jones.

2. INTO THE WILD: ENVIRONMENTAL AND RACIAL JUSTICE IN WORDSWORTH, THOREAU, AND DU BOIS

1. In this chapter, I usually employ "the wild," "wildness," and "wilderness" as synonyms to convey not only a place but also a condition and process that brings surprise and that contests (often oppressive) practices and conventions.

2. The Grand Canyon represents much that is promising and troubling about our notions of wilderness and the wild. On the one hand, being a national park set apart from everyday human activity, it exemplifies a problematic model of pristine nature removed from human communities, especially those with limited economic means. Moreover, the Grand Canyon's Indigenous populations have been mostly dispossessed and sequestered, for the land has been almost exclusively set aside for the experience of the tourist (the exception is the roughly 850 residents of Havasupai reservation located within the park's boundaries). So, why celebrate its wilderness? Why begin this chapter with a monumental cliché? I keep thinking about the silence that the canyon imposed on the passengers

on the bus. I keep thinking about how in the midst of that conversation about how to break the spell of the wild canyon, the wild itself—or something like it—broke the conversation. It disrupted us. It brought surprise and wonder, humility and alertness—at least for a moment.

3. William Cronon, "The Trouble with Wilderness: Or, Getting Back to the Wrong Nature," *Environmental History* 1, no. 1 (1996): 7–28.

4. Michael Pollan, *Second Nature: A Gardener's Education* (Grove, 1991), 167.

5. Although they may not use the terms "wilderness" or "the wild," many contemporary theorists are bringing our attention to this condition and process that I am associating with the wild. For example, such different authors as Mark Fisher, J. K. Gibson-Graham, Catherine Keller, and Bruno Latour all invite us to be open to developing new subjectivities and ways of being receptive to alternatives in the world. Keller, for example, invites us to resist religions of control and conquest and to embrace ways of uncertainty, diversity, and surprise. Catherine Keller, *Cloud of the Impossible: Negative Theology and Planetary Entanglement* (Columbia University Press, 2015). See also Mark Fisher, *Capitalist Realism: Is There No Alternative?* (Zero, 2009); J. K. Gibson-Graham, *A Postcapitalist Politics* (University of Minnesota Press, 2006); and Bruno Latour, *Facing Gaia: Eight Lectures on the New Climatic Regime* (Polity, 2017).

6. W. E. B. Du Bois, *The Souls of Black Folk*, ed. Brent Hayes Edwards (Oxford University Press, 2007), 3.

7. For an excellent historical and conceptual account of *vulnerable, interdependent selves* as opposed to delusional *sovereign selves*, see Fannie Bialek, "Incredulity and the Realization of Vulnerability, or, How It Feels to Learn from Wounds," *Political Theology*, 2023, https://doi.org/10.1080/1462317X.2023.2185187.

8. See, for example, Jerome J. McGann, *The Romantic Ideology: A Critical Investigation* (University of Chicago Press, 1983), 90.

9. William Wordsworth, *Guide to the Lakes*, ed. Saeko Yoshikawa (Oxford University Press, 2022), 45–46. Henceforth, references to *Guide to the Lakes* will be embedded in the text.

10. This idea of "mingled wildness and cultivation" is exemplified by many North American Indigenous practices. See, for example, M. Kat Anderson, *Tending the Wild: Native American Knowledge and the Management of California's Natural Resources* (University of California Press, 2013), which demonstrates that so-called wild lands of Native Americans in the "New World" were in fact skillfully tended to, showing much care in living appropriately with the land.

11. Henry David Thoreau, "Civil Disobedience," in *Thoreau: Walden, The Maine Woods, Collected Essays and Poems*, ed. Robert Sayre and Elizabeth Witherell (Library of America, 2007), 745.

12. This is not to romanticize prisons or prisoners. Prisons are places that constrain, repress, and attempt to control the wild and are thereby dehumanizing. There is nothing wild (in my sense of the term) about prisons in themselves. But wild spirits—those that refuse to conform to unjust ways, laws, and institutions—often find themselves imprisoned (e.g., Socrates, Jesus, Susan B. Anthony, Martin Luther King Jr., and innumerable others).

13. Thoreau, "Civil Disobedience," 739.

14. Thoreau, "Civil Disobedience," 732, 737.

15.   Vassar students first brought to my attention the connections between Thoreau's wild and his walking to and out of jail. The best account of that connection—between the wild in the natural and social worlds—is Jane Bennett's remarkable book *Thoreau's Nature: Ethics, Politics, and the Wild* (Rowman & Littlefield, 2002).

16.   Henry David Thoreau, "Walking," in *Thoreau: Walden, The Maine Woods, Collected Essays and Poems,* ed. Robert Sayre and Elizabeth Witherell (Library of America, 2007), 751, 771, 775.

17.   Thoreau, "Walking," 774, 772, 765, 768, 765, 768.

18.   Thoreau, "Walking," 767.

19.   Thoreau, "Walking," 760.

20.   For a more forceful, assertive critique of Thoreau in relation to Manifest Destiny, see Richard Schneider, "Thoreau and Manifest Destiny," in *Civilizing Thoreau: Human Ecology and the Emerging Social Sciences in the Major Works* (Camden House, 2016), 177–92. For interpretations closer to my own (in which Thoreau is more of a critic than a champion of Manifest Destiny), see Alda Balthrop-Lewis, *Thoreau's Religion: Walden Woods, Social Justice, and the Politics of Asceticism* (Cambridge University Press, 2021); and Laura Dassow Walls, *Henry David Thoreau: A Life* (University of Chicago Press, 2017).

21.   Thoreau, "Walking," 781.

22.   This is not to say that Thoreau never made a distinction between something like the wild and the domestic. When he reached the peak of Katahdin, nature is described as stern, harsh, and alien; it is a wild place where humans do not belong, unlike down in the cultivated valley, where nature is gentler and accommodating. "Ktaadn," in *The Wilderness Reader*, ed. Frank Bergon (University of Nevada Press, 1980), 130. There is a dualism that is instructive and worth capturing: Perhaps there are wild places where humans do not belong or should only visit briefly and with care; for example, must settler colonialists build water-wasting megacities in dry deserts, or in the path of wild hurricanes, or on top of high summits? Yet at the end of his essay "Ktaadn," Thoreau invited us to be as amazed over the solidity and materiality of our own bodies and the wind on our cheeks as we might be in awe of standing on the surface of some star (135). Here, at the end of the essay, is the suggestion that the wildness of the summit is with us always, in some ways, as our bodies are in our contact with this planet.

23.   Thoreau, "Civil Disobedience," 739; see also 734 for Thoreau's critique of merely voting.

24.   Henry David Thoreau, *A Week on the Concord and Merrimack Rivers,* ed. H. Daniel Peck (Penguin, 1998), 246; emphasis in original.

25.   Thoreau, "Walking," 765.

26.   Michael Starkey, "Wilderness, Race, and African Americans: An Environmental History from Slavery to Jim Crow," master's thesis, University of California, Berkeley, 2005, i, https://drive.google.com/file/d/1gMdUfFtmQHi35qvLhx6PModA7vFmx6nw/view.

27.   Michael J. Beilfuss, "Ironic Pastorals and Beautiful Swamps: W. E. B. Du Bois and the Troubled Landscapes of the American South," *Interdisciplinary Studies in Literature and Environment* 22, no. 3 (2015): 488.

28.   For a superb exploration of Du Bois on "the wild" in relation to place, history, and community, see Kimberly K. Smith, "What Is Africa to Me? Wilderness in Black Thought, 1860–1930," *Environmental Ethics* 27, no. 3 (2005): 279–97; and Kimberly K. Smith,

"W. E. B. Du Bois: Racial Inequality and Alienation from Nature," in *Engaging Nature: Environmentalism and the Political Theory Canon*, ed. Peter Cannavò and Joseph H. Lane Jr. (MIT Press, 2014), 223–37.

29. Paul Outka, *Race and Nature from Transcendentalism to the Harlem Renaissance* (Palgrave, 2008), 2.

30. Michael Bennett, "Anti-Pastoralism, Frederick Douglass, and the Nature of Slavery," in *Beyond Nature Writing: Expanding the Boundaries of Ecocriticism*, ed. Karla Armbruster and Kathleen R. Wallace (University of Virginia Press, 2001), 204.

31. Camille T. Dungy, ed., *Black Nature: Four Centuries of African American Nature Poetry* (University of Georgia, 2009), xxi, xxv.

32. Du Bois, *The Souls of Black Folk*, 14, 14, 13; emphasis added.

33. Du Bois, *The Souls of Black Folk*, 129. For a powerful account of Du Bois and the Sorrow Songs, see Terrence L. Johnson, *Tragic Soul-Life: W. E. B. Du Bois and the Moral Crisis Facing American Democracy* (Oxford University Press, 2012), esp. 36–41. Johnson notes: "On the one hand, the sorrow songs articulated in detail the brutal effects of the slavery and segregation on Blacks. On the other, the songs revealed creation of beauty and hope" (38).

34. Richard Cullen Rath notes that "for Du Bois, the sorrow songs, though they were the one 'true American music,' were African, 'the voice of exile.'" Richard Cullen Rath, "Echo and Narcissus: The Afrocentric Pragmatism of W. E. B. Du Bois," *Journal of American History* 84, no. 2 (1997): 490. And Simon Gikandi claims that "Africa first entered DuBois's consciousness in the form of song, or rather the fragment of a song, which could come to stand as a synecdoche of ancestral memory." Simon Gikandi, "W. E. B. DuBois and the Identity of Africa," *Journal of African Studies* 2, no. 1 (2005), http://hdl.handle.net /2027/spo.4761563.0002.101.

35. Du Bois, *The Souls of Black Folk*, 13.

36. Jonathon S. Kahn, *Divine Discontent: The Religious Imagination of W. E. B. Du Bois* (Oxford University Press, 2011), 8.

37. See Melvin Dixon, *Ride Out the Wilderness: Geography and Identity in Afro-American Literature* (University of Illinois Press, 1987), 3; and Beilfuss, "Ironic Pastorals and Beautiful Swamps," 500.

38. See Yolanda Pierce, "The Soul of Du Bois' Black Folk," *The North Star: A Journal of African American Religious History* 7, no. 1 (2003): 2.

39. It is likely that Du Bois had read Thoreau's celebration of the swamp as "the jewel" of the land. See Beilfuss, "Ironic Pastorals and Beautiful Swamps," 496.

40. Anthony Wilson, *Shadow and Shelter: The Swamp in Southern Culture* (University Press of Mississippi, 2006), 3. See also Michael Beilfuss, who argues that "whereas the slave barons saw the swamps as a location of impurity that required the improvements of the pastoral, for Du Bois, the swamp represents a kind of purity of freedom and appropriate (and sustainable) scale when contrasted with the corruption of the Jim Crow plantation pastoral that continues to surround and encroach upon it." Beilfuss, "Ironic Pastorals and Beautiful Swamps," 501.

41. Beilfuss, "Ironic Pastorals and Beautiful Swamps," 499; emphasis added.

42. Rob Nixon, *Slow Violence and the Environmentalism of the Poor* (Harvard University Press, 2011), 137.

43.   W. E. B. Du Bois, *The Quest of the Silver Fleece*, ed. Henry Louis Gates Jr. (Oxford University Press, 2007), 2, 218.

44.   Brett Clark and John Bellamy Foster, "Land, the Color Line, and the Quest of the Golden Fleece," *Organization & Environment* 16, no. 4 (2003): 466.

45.   Du Bois, *The Quest of the Silver Fleece*, 19, 1.

46.   It would be a mistake, however, to essentialize and romanticize the swamp. Arlene Elder, for example, notes that "the Swamp represents all that is free, wild, joyful, and loving, the Plantation, all that is self-serving and exploitative," but she goes on to note that "DuBois successfully avoids the obvious trap of simplistically equating the Swamp with black life and the Plantation with white. . . . Nor does DuBois paint the Swamp mentality as all good and the Plantation view as all evil." Arlene Elder, "Swamp Versus Plantation: Symbolic Structure in W. E. B. DuBois' *The Quest of the Silver Fleece*," *Phylon* 34, no. 4 (1973): 358. While I disagree with her final claim about the Plantation not being an unqualified evil, Elder is correct to point out that the swamp is the site not only of brave characters such as Zora but also of less than admirable characters such as her mother, Elspeth. The swamp is a place of power and transformation but also of danger and despair.

47.   Du Bois, *The Quest of the Silver Fleece*, 218.

48.   Gary Lemons notes that "in writing a novel [*Quest*] in which a black woman rises to become the leader of her people, its author consciously constructed her in opposition to the existing racist and sexist myths of black womanhood." Gary Lemons, "Womanism in the Name of the 'Father': W. E. B. Du Bois and the Problematics of Race, Patriarchy, and Art," *Phylon* 49, no. 3/4 (2001): 188.

49.   Du Bois, *The Souls of Black Folk*, 80, 81, 7.

50.   For example, Boisseron claims that "anticolonialism and anti-racism cannot hold the course without an anti-anthropocentric approach to matters of power, domination, and oppression." Bénédicte Boisseron, *Afro-Dog: Blackness and the Animal Question* (Columbia University Press, 2018), 104.

51.   Du Bois, *The Souls of Black Folk*, 86. I worry about eliding two forms of violence: sexual violence against women (among others) and violence against the land. Yet it is important to note their connections as well as their differences. In various Western narratives, the natural world and women—especially women of color—need to be subdued to be made safe and useful. A classic account of this mutual oppression is found in Carolyn Merchant, *Death of Nature: Women, Ecology, and the Scientific Revolution* (HarperOne, 1990), xvi. The Potawatomi scholar Kyle Whyte (personal conversation, April 4, 2019) notes that in his tradition it is understood that as there is need for consent from sexual partners so also there is need for consent from the land.

52.   Du Bois, *The Souls of Black Folk*, 86, 88.

53.   Here is but one example of the depth of hope and resilience located in Zora's swamp and in her economic and political farm project: "In the field of the Silver Fleece all her possibilities were beginning to find expression. These new-born green things hidden far down in the swamp, begotten in want and mystery, were . . . her dream-children, and she tended them jealously; they were her Hope, and she worshipped them." Du Bois, *The Quest of the Silver Fleece*, 64.

54. Du Bois, *The Souls of Black Folk*, 84, 85.

55. Scott Hicks, "W. E. B. Du Bois, Booker T. Washington, and Richard Wright: Toward an Ecocriticism of Color," *Callaloo* 29 (2006): 210.

56. See Cronon, "The Trouble with Wilderness," 7–28; and Pollan, *Second Nature*, 167.

57. I am grateful to Anna (Fannie) Bialek for helping me think through this issue of the derogatory usage of "wild." In her correspondence to me on an earlier draft, she wrote, "black people are often 'wild' in racist literatures because they can't learn virtue; they're willful but untutored and unable to be tutored such that they can only be *tamed*, through domination."

58. For one example of a critical appropriation of the wild for the sake of combating racism, among other evils, see Jack Halberstam, "The Wild Beyond: With and for the Undercommons," introduction to *The Undercommons: Fugitive Planning and Black Study*, by Stefano Harney and Fred Moten (Minor Compositions, 2013), 5–12. I am grateful to Andre Willis for this reference.

59. Du Bois, "The Talented Tenth," in *The Souls of Black Folk*, ed. Brent Hayes Edwards (Oxford University Press, 2007), 191; emphasis added.

60. Du Bois, *The Quest of the Silver Fleece*, 202–3.

61. I learned much about Du Bois and the Niagara Movement from Amanda Hardin-Martin, "Dreaming with Du Bois: The Niagara Movement & Making Historical Black Landscapes," conference presentation, (Re)thinking Landscape: Ways of Knowing / Ways of Being Conference, Yale University, New Haven, Connecticut, September 30, 2022.

62. W. E. B. Du Bois, *Darkwater: Voices from Within the Veil*, ed. Henry Louis Gates Jr. (Oxford University Press, 2007), 110.

63. Du Bois, *Darkwater*, 111–12; emphasis added.

64. Du Bois, *The Souls of Black Folk*, 46.

65. Smith, "W. E. B. Du Bois," 228–29. Also, for an excellent article on Du Bois and Ecocriticism, see Hicks, "W. E. B. Du Bois, Booker T. Washington, and Richard Wright."

66. Jillian Forstadt, "'Make Farmers Black Again': African Americans Fight Discrimination to Own Farmland," NPR, August 25, 2020, https://www.npr.org/2020/08/25/904284865/make-farmers-black-again-african-americans-fight-discrimination-to-own-farmland.

67. Du Bois, *The Quest of the Silver Fleece*, 233, 238; emphasis added. For an extremely helpful interpretation of *The Quest of the Silver Fleece*, see Lawrence J. Oliver, "Apocalyptic and Slow Violence: The Environmental Vision of W. E. B. Du Bois's *Darkwater*," *Interdisciplinary Studies in Literature and Environment* 22, no. 3 (2015): 466–84, esp. 469–71.

68. Du Bois, *Darkwater*, 140.

69. For an excellent interpretation of "Of the Passing of the First Born" that highlights its various modes of hope and despair, see Lina L. Geriguis, "W. E. B. Du Bois's *The Souls of Black Folk*, Chapter 11," *Explicator* 68, no. 2 (2010): 111–14.

70. Du Bois, *The Souls of Black Folk*, 141; emphasis added.

71. Du Bois, *The Souls of Black Folk*, 143–44; emphasis added.

72. For example, Lee Edelman writes, "The Child has come to embody for us the telos of the social order and come to be seen as the one for whom that order is held in perpetual trust." Lee Edelman, *No Future: Queer Theory and the Death Drive* (Duke University Press, 2004), 10.

73. Ralph Waldo Emerson, "Experience," in *Ralph Waldo Emerson: Essays and Poems*, ed. Harold Bloom, Paul Kane, and Joel Porte (Library of America, 1996), 492. For a discussion on this passage, see Mark Cladis, "Religion, Democracy, and Virtue: Emerson and the Journey's End," *Religion & Literature* 41, no. 1 (2009): 76; and for the best interpretive essay on "Experience," see Jeffrey Stout, "The Transformation of Genius Into Practical Power: A Reading of Emerson's 'Experience,'" *American Journal of Theology & Philosophy* 35, no. 1 (2014): 3-24.

74. Joseph R. Winters, *Hope Draped in Black* (Duke University Press, 2016), 16. For a brilliant discussion on Du Bois and the topic of hope, see chap. 1, 31-55. Winters's work on hope has greatly informed my own view here and on many other matters as well.

75. Winters, *Hope Draped in Black*, 17.

76. For "passive nihilism," see William E. Connolly, *Facing the Planetary: Entangled Humanism and the Politics of Swarming* (Duke University Press, 2017), 9, 120, 166-68. On the notion of "moral paralysis," Robin Wall Kimmerer notes that "despair is paralysis. It robs us of agency. It blinds us to our own power and the power of the earth. Environmental despair is a poison every bit as destructive as the methylated mercury in the bottom of Onondaga Lake." Robin Wall Kimmerer, *Braiding Sweetgrass: Indigenous Wisdom, Scientific Knowledge, and the Teaching of Plants* (Milkweed Editions, 2013), 328.

77. Teresa Shewry, *Hope at Sea: Possible Ecologies in Oceanic Literature* (University of Minnesota Press, 2015), 5. Shewry is glossing Anna Lowenhaupt Tsing, *Friction: An Ethnography of Global Connection* (Princeton University Press, 2005), 269.

78. Kyle P. Whyte, "Indigenous Science (Fiction) for the Anthropocene: Ancestral Dystopias and Fantasies of Climate Change Crises," *Environment and Planning E: Nature and Space* 1, no. 1-2 (2018): 224-42.

79. The close, dialectical relation between "morning" and "mourning" is expressed by the hymn that Du Bois chose to place at the start of the chapter "Of the Dawn of Freedom," in *The Souls of Black Folk*, 15. The hymn is variously titled "My Lord, What a Morning," "My Lord, What a Mourning," and "My Lord, What a Mournin'." For an excellent discussion of this hymn and its importance to Du Bois, see Eric J. Sundquist, *To Wake the Nations: Race in the Making of American Literature* (Belknap, 1993), 497-99.

80. Lauren Berlant, *Cruel Optimism* (Duke University Press, 2011), 1, 23-24.

81. Kyle Bladow and Jennifer Ladino, eds., *Affective Ecocriticism: Emotion, Embodiment, Environment* (University of Nebraska Press, 2018), 11, 2.

82. Berlant, *Cruel Optimism*, 266. For this "reparative" interpretation, see Brian Glavey, *The Wallflower Avant-Garde: Modernism, Sexuality, and Queer Ekphrasis* (Oxford: Oxford University Press, 2015), 51.

83. Bladow and Ladino, *Affective Ecocriticism*, 3.

84. Catriona Sandilands, *Rising Tides: Reflections for Climate Changing Times* (Caitlin, 2019), 8.

85. Among other needful affective modes and sensibilities, I would include such "bad" ones as those found in Nicole Seymour's *Bad Environmentalism*, namely, irony, satire, ambivalence, irreverence, camp, anxiety, suspicion, humor, playfulness, parody, absurdism, perversity, and glee. Nicole Seymour, *Bad Environmentalism: Irony and Irreverence in the Ecological Age* (University of Minnesota Press, 2018), 4, 36, 149, 158-59.

86. This account of hope as a virtue and despair as a mood is greatly informed by Jeffrey Stout when, in conversation with Cornel West, Richard Rorty, and Stanley Hauerwas,

Stout stated that "the kind of hope I have in mind when I talk about hope is not a mood but a virtue—the mean between the vices of smug presumption and politically paralyzed despair. So let your mood be as dark as you wish. Let it be as dark as mine. The question of hope is not the question of mood, it is the question of whether we can find it within ourselves . . . to muster the moral fiber to act for justice and to make a difference." Cornel West et al., "Pragmatism and Democracy: Assessing Jeffrey Stout's *Democracy and Tradition*," ed. Jason Springs, *Journal of the American Academy of Religion* 78, no. 2 (2010): 432.

87. Macarena Gómez-Barris, *The Extractive Zone: Social Ecologies and Decolonial Perspectives* (Duke University Press, 2017), 4.

88. Gibson-Graham, *A Postcapitalist Politics*, 53–78.

89. Keller, *Cloud of the Impossible*, 266–83.

90. Kimmerer, *Braiding Sweetgrass*, 327.

91. Edelman, *No Future*, 1–30; Sarah Ensor, "Terminal Regions: Queer Eroticism at the End," in *Against Life*, ed. Alastair Hunt and Stephanie Youngblood (Northwestern University Press, 2016), 41–62.

92. Ensor, "Terminal Regions," 55.

93. Caleb Murray's dissertation project, "Feeling a Failing Climate: Tragedy, Affect, and Religious Storytelling in Literature and Film," powerfully explores the normative dimensions of dystopian films and novels. It has also greatly informed my own thinking on the relation between hope and despair in the face of climate change and other crises Caleb Murray, "Feeling a Failing Climate: Tragedy, Affect, and Religious Storytelling in Literature and Film," PhD diss., Brown University, 2023.

94. Du Bois, *Darkwater*, 131. I am grateful to Nicholas Anderson for encouraging me to mention Du Bois's own dystopian work of fiction in this regard.

95. Du Bois, *Darkwater*, 133.

3. ROUSSEAU'S GARDEN AS A WORLD IN WHICH TO LIVE

1. Robert Darnton, *The Great Cat Massacre and Other Episodes in French Cultural History* (Basic Books, 1984), 242–43, 245.

2. In this chapter, I usually employ "nature" and "the natural world" as synonyms that convey not only places but also "natural" conditions and processes. In some cases, I employ both terms in the same sentence: "the natural world" referring to the physical world and "nature" to the (so-called) innate, normative way of the world, as in the phrase "human nature." I have mostly refrained from using the term "more-than-human" so as to better engage with Rousseau's eighteenth-century context and with such terms as "state of nature," "human nature," "second nature," and "nature's garden."

3. On the association of the Black female body with animality and nature, see Shamara Shantu Riley, "Ecology Is a Sistah's Issue Too: The Politics of Emergent Afrocentric Ecowomanism," in *This Sacred Earth: Religion, Nature, Environment*, ed. Roger S. Gottlieb (Routledge, 2003), 413–15.

4. For how women and nature alike come to be seen as passive, subordinate, and that which is to be exploited, see Carolyn Merchant, *Death of Nature: Women, Ecology, and the Scientific Revolution* (HarperOne, 1990), xvi.

5. My phrase "nature as other" is similar to Donald Worster's phrase and argument "mind over matter and man over nature." Donald Worster, *Nature's Economy: A History of Ecological Ideas* (Cambridge University Press, 1994), 51. See also Jonathan Bate, who claims that "once you invent the category of the 'human,' you have to make 'nature' its Other." Jonathan Bate, *The Song of the Earth* (Harvard University Press, 2002), 35.

6. For how, in Rousseau's view, it would be impossible to return to a state of nature, see Andrew Brio, *Denaturalizing Ecological Politics: Alienation from Nature from Rousseau to the Frankfurt School and Beyond* (University of Toronto Press, 2005), 59–60.

7. See Mark Cladis, *Public Vision, Private Lives: Rousseau, Religion, and Twenty-First-Century Democracy* (Columbia University Press, 2006), 88–93.

8. For a helpful treatment on "Rousseau's most powerful normative judgment: 'Nature is good,'" see Joseph H. Lane Jr., "Jean-Jacques Rousseau: The Disentangling of Green Paradoxes," in *Engaging Nature: Environmentalism and the Political Theory Canon*, ed. Peter Cannavò and Joseph H. Lane Jr. (MIT Press, 2014), 136–37. However, Lane's claim that, for Rousseau, "man-made systems" are "*at best* imitations of 'nature'" (137) does not adequately capture Rousseau's complicated account of what it means for social conventions to work with nature and not simply imitate nature. Jonathan Bate, in his otherwise excellent book *The Song of the Earth*, supports the standard view that, for Rousseau, society negates and opposes nature and that this is the source of all our ills. Bate, *The Song of Earth*, 31. In contrast to Bate, I have argued that Rousseau's claim that "nature is good" does not necessitate the judgment "society is not good." See Cladis, *Public Vision, Private Lives*, 35–99.

9. See, for example, Macarena Gómez-Barris, *The Extractive Zone: Social Ecologies and Decolonized Perspectives* (Duke University Press, 2017), 11–12; Rob Nixon, *Slow Violence and the Environmentalism of the Poor* (Harvard University Press, 2011), 4–5; and Kyle P. Whyte, "Critical Investigations of Resilience: A Brief Introduction to Indigenous Environmental Studies & Sciences," *Dædalus, the Journal of the American Academy of Arts & Sciences* 147, no. 2 (2018): 143–45.

10. For an excellent and relatively early article that delineates the centrality of Rousseau to both environmentalism and Romanticism, see Gilbert F. LaFreniere, "Rousseau and the European Roots of Environmentalism," *Environmental History Review* 14, no. 4 (1990): 41–72.

11. See Andrew Geoffry Billing, "Rousseau's Critique of Market Society: Property and Possessive Individualism in the *Discours sur l'inégalité*," *Journal of European Studies* 48, no. 1 (2018): 3–19.

12. For more on these two paths, see Mark Cladis, "The End of the Private Life: Rousseau, Redemption, and Tragedy," *Soundings: An Interdisciplinary Journal* 84, no. 1/2 (2001): 51–77.

13. For an in-depth exploration of this "middle way," see Cladis, *Public Vision, Private Lives*, 187–213.

14. See Jean-Jacques Rousseau, *The Confessions and Correspondence, Including the Letters to Malesherbes*, trans. Christopher Kelly (University Press of New England, 1995), 343–44, 412, 509.

15. Rousseau, *The Confessions*, 343.

16. Rousseau's celebration of the Alpine landscape is not confined to *Julie*. In the *Confessions*, for example, he wrote of his "need for torrents, rocks, firs, dark woods, mountains,

steep roads to climb or descend, abysses beside me to make me afraid." Jean-Jacques Rousseau, *The Confessions*, trans. J. M. Cohen (Penguin, 1953), 167.

17. For Rousseau's "nature writing" as a form of political thought, see Joseph H. Lane Jr., "Reverie and the Return to Nature: Rousseau's Experience of Convergence," *Review of Politics* 68, no. 3 (2006): 474–99.

18. Jean-Jacques Rousseau, *Julie, or the New Heloise: Letters of Two Lovers Who Live in a Small Town at the Foot of the Alps*, trans. Philip Stewart and Jean Vaché (University Press of New England, 1997), 389. Henceforth, all references to *Julie* will be embedded in the text.

19. Jean-Jacques Rousseau, *Emile, or Education*, trans. Barbara Foxley (J. M. Dent, 1911), 228; emphasis added.

20. Ralph Waldo Emerson, "The Divinity School Address," in *Ralph Waldo Emerson: Essays and Poems*, ed. Harold Bloom, Paul Kane, and Joel Porte (Library of America, 1996), 81.

21. William Wordsworth, "Lines Written a Few Miles Above Tintern Abbey," in *William Wordsworth: The Major Works*, ed. Stephen Gill (Oxford University Press, 2008), 134, lines 99–100, 103.

22. Jean-Jacques Rousseau, *Emile, or On Education*, trans. Allan Bloom (Basic Books, 1979), 277; emphasis added.

23. Jean-Jacques Rousseau, *The Social Contract and Discourses*, trans. G. D. H. Cole, rev. J. H. Brumfitt and John C. Hall (Dent, 1988), 56.

24. Although she does not mention Rousseau, Kate Soper provides an excellent historical account of "monist" and "dualist" positions on the human relation with the rest of animality—that is, positions that emphasize continuity and those that emphasize discontinuity between humans and nonhuman animals. Kate Soper, *What Is Nature?* (Blackwell, 1995), 49–61.

25. This cohabitation model stands in sharp contrast to the mechanical model that depicts the natural world and its creatures as a machine to be ordered and controlled by "man." For more on the "mechanical model," see Merchant, *Death of Nature*, 193.

26. See Manfred Kusch, "The River and the Garden: Basic Spatial Models in *Candide* and *La Nouvelle Heloise*," *Eighteenth-Century Studies* 12, no. 1 (1978): 1–15; and Lester Crocker, "Order and Disorder in Rousseau's Social Thought," *PMLA* 94, no. 2 (1979): 247–60.

27. Kusch, "The River and the Garden," 11, 1.

28. Crocker, "Order and Disorder," 253.

29. William Wordsworth, "Expostulations and Replies," in *William Wordsworth: The Major Works*, ed. Stephen Gill (Oxford University Press, 2008), 130; and Henry David Thoreau, "Walking," in *Thoreau: Walden, The Maine Woods, Collected Essays and Poems*, ed. Robert Sayre and Elizabeth Witherell (Library of America, 2007), 751.

30. Regarding St. Preux's education in the Elysium, Zev Trachtenberg perceptively notes, "As the details of Elysium's construction are revealed, St. Preux comes to perceive more—about possibilities for human action in nature. In the first instance, Julie and Wolmar's description of their techniques demonstrates, quite literally, how human design can deploy natural processes, in ways that do not distort natural forms; this idea is, of course quite familiar today, under rubrics like design with nature and ecological engineering." Zev Trachtenberg, "Elysium," *Inhabiting the Anthropocene* [blog], December 12, 2018, https://inhabitingtheanthropocene.com/2018/12/12/elysium/.

31. Jennifer Atkinson, "Seeds of Change: The New Place of Gardens in Contemporary Uto-
     pia," *Utopian Studies* 18, no. 2 (2007): 239.

32. Susan Cross, "Revolutionary Gardens," *American Art* 25, no. 2 (2011): 30.

33. Michel de Montaigne, *The Complete Essays of Montaigne*, trans. Donald Frame (Stanford
     University Press, 1958), 139, 138.

34. For a strong argument suggesting that, for Rousseau, sexual division of labor is not based
     in "nature" or in natural dispositions and capacities but rather in politics, see Penny A.
     Weiss, "Rousseau, Antifeminism, and Woman's Nature," *Political Theory* 15, no. 1 (1987):
     81–98.

35. *The Garden*, dir. Derek Jarman (Basilisk Communications, 1990), DVD; William A. Shut-
     kin, *The Land That Could Be: Environmentalism and Democracy in the Twenty-First Century*
     (MIT Press, 2000), 143–66.

36. Shutkin, *The Land That Could Be*, 149, 146–47.

37. For a vividly presented example of "civic and environmental engagement," see the film
     The Garden, dir. Scott Hamilton Kennedy (Black Valley Films, 2008), https://www.kanopy
     .com/en/product/garden?vp=utep, a documentary that tells of an urban garden in South
     Central Los Angeles (not to be confused with Derek Jarman's film by the same name).

38. Shutkin, *The Land That Could Be*, 163.

39. For an excellent, powerful account of how Jarman's garden displays mourning, grief, and
     vulnerability—as opposed to "salvation," "cure," or "interventionism"—see Melissa Zei-
     ger, "'Modern Nature': Derek Jarman's Garden," *Humanities* 6, no. 2 (2017).

40. For their astute reflections and comments on these three political gardens, I am grate-
     ful to Professor Sharon Krause and all the members of the 2019 Brown University doc-
     toral seminar "Thinking Democracy Ecologically."

41. For the "healthy-minded" type, see William James, *The Varieties of Religious Experience: A
     Study in Human Nature* (Penguin, 1982), 104. For environmental examples of the healthy-
     minded, I am thinking of Joanna Macy's statement that "virtue is *not* required for the
     greening of the self or the emergence of the ecological self," after having quoted Arne
     Naess approvingly: Responsibility and concern "would flow naturally and easily if the
     self were widened and deepened." Joanna Macy, "The Greening of the Self," in *Dharma
     Gaia: A Harvest of Essays in Buddhism and Ecology*, ed. Allan Hunt Badiner (Parallax, 1990),
     62. Aspects of ecological health-mindedness appear occasionally in Jane Bennett's oth-
     erwise excellent book *Vibrant Matter: A Political Ecology of Things* (Duke University Press,
     2010).

42. On the environmental significance of Rousseau's critique of *amour-propre*, Austin Scott
     claims: "Rousseau's incisive social commentary on the pitfalls of society founded upon
     amour-propre resonates extremely well today. It is reasonable to assume that Rousseau
     would argue that humans have developed desires that society and the planet can never
     fully fulfill. . . . The environmental crisis is indicative of the greatest flaws of modernity:
     endless desires and wants fueled by the belief that happiness can be achieved through
     the acquisition of goods and social recognition. And, of course, the extraction and use
     of natural resources are required to fulfill this false ideal. Rousseau's criticism of mod-
     ern society is insightful even today." Austin Scott, "The 'Nature' of Rousseau: Towards
     an Understanding and Amelioration of the Human Relationship to the Environment,"

paper presented at the annual meeting of the Western Political Science Association, San Diego, March 20, 2008.

4. ROMANTICISM, RELIGION, AND PRACTICE:
POLITICAL AND ENVIRONMENTAL IMPLICATIONS

1. I presented earlier versions of some of the material in this chapter in my 2014 keynote address at Harvard Divinity School for the Ways of Knowing Graduate Conference on Religion. I am grateful to the organizers of the conference for the invitation. I learned much from many conversations in response to my lecture.

2. While it is necessary for me to identify the broad contours of what I mean by theories of secularization, I do not engage robustly with the abundant scholarship in this area. I am mainly interested in the declension and privatization aspects of these theories, which hide from view the profoundly public dimensions of radical Romanticism. A fuller account of my own engagement with theories of secularization can be found in Mark Cladis, "Religion, Secularism, and Democratic Culture," *The Good Society: The Journal of Political Economy of the Good Society* 19, no. 2 (2010): 22–29; and Mark Cladis, "Secularism and the Liberal Arts: The Good, the Bad, and the Ugly," *The Immanent Frame*, 2011, http://tif.ssrc.org/2011/01/05/the-good-the-bad-and-the-ugly/. In addition to other sources cited in the following notes, my own work on theories of secularization has greatly profited from Gil Anidjar, "Secularism," *Critical Inquiry* 33, no. 1 (2006): 52–77; Talal Asad, *Formations of the Secular: Christianity, Islam, Modernity* (Stanford University Press, 2003); Rajeev Bhargava, ed., *Secularism and Its Critics* (Oxford University Press, 1998); José Casanova, *Public Religions in the Modern World* (University of Chicago Press, 1994); Philip S. Gorski et al., eds., *The Post-Secular in Question: Religion in Contemporary Society* (New York University Press, 2012); and William E. Connolly, *Why I Am Not a Secularist* (University of Minnesota Press, 1999).

3. For my work on the political and environmental dimensions of Romantic religious thought, see Mark Cladis, "Radical Romanticism: Democracy, Religion, and the Environmental Imagination," *Soundings: An Interdisciplinary Journal* 97, no. 1 (2014): 21–49. One of the best books on the radical political dimensions of British Romanticism is Nicholas Roe, *Wordsworth and Coleridge: The Radical Years* (Oxford University Press, 1988); one of the best books on the ecological dimensions is Kate Rigby, *Topographies of the Sacred: The Poetics of Place in European Romanticism* (University of Virginia Press, 2004).

4. When I refer to the presence of tradition and practice in British Romanticism, I am not simply claiming that tradition and practice are informing Romanticism but that Romantic authors were self-consciously reflecting on the role of tradition and practice in their work and in society.

5. For excellent challenges to theories of secularization, see Saba Mahmood, "Religious Reasons and Secular Affect: An Incommensurable Divide?" in *Is Critique Secular? Blasphemy, Injury, and Free Speech*, ed. Talal Asad et al. (Fordham University Press, 2013), 58–94; Asad, *Formations of the Secular*; and Jeffrey Stout, *Democracy and Tradition* (Princeton University Press, 2004).

6.   José Casanova, among others, has identified and critiqued these two aspects of secularization theories. Casanova also identifies a third aspect, namely, the differentiation of religious and nonreligious institutions or spheres. See Casanova, *Public Religions in the Modern World*. For additional critiques of the declension and privatization view, see Peter L. Berger, ed., *The Desecularization of the World: Resurgent Religion and World Politics* (Eerdmans, 1999). Classically, declension and privatization theories were promoted, though in very different forms, by Weber and Marx.

7.   To claim that religion "cannot be separated easily or radically from other institutions" is not to ignore the legal frameworks of *laïcité*, disestablishment, or what is often referred to as "the separation of church and state." It is to claim that, even in the legal context of, say, disestablishment in the United States, religious perspectives and practices inform citizens' views on a variety of public, political issues. This claim is convincingly argued by Edwin S. Gaustad, *Proclaim Liberty Throughout All the Land: A History of Church and State in America* (Oxford University Press, 2003); and by Philip Hamburger, *Separation of Church and State* (University of Harvard Press, 2002).

8.   Peter Gay, for example, promoted this view in his *The Enlightenment: An Interpretation*, 2 vols. (Norton, 1995).

9.   Many, including Richard Rorty, have promoted this view. See, for example, Richard Rorty, *Philosophy and Social Hope* (Penguin, 1999), 169; and Richard Rorty, "Religion in the Public Square: A Reconsideration," *Journal of Religious Ethics* 31, no. 1 (2003): 142.

10.   See, for example, Richard Dawkins, "Is Science a Religion?," *The Humanist* (1997), http://www.skeptical-science.com/essays/science-religion-richard-dawkins/; and Sam Harris, *The End of Faith: Religion, Terror, and the Future of Reason* (Norton, 2005).

11.   E. D. Hirsch Jr. boldly claims, "Romanticism is a *secularized* expression of religious faith." E. D. Hirsch Jr., "The Roots of the Education Wars," in *The Great Curriculum Debate: How Should We Teach Reading and Math?*, ed. Tom Loveless (Brookings Institution Press, 2004), 17. Accounts of Romanticism playing an important role in narratives of secularism are also found in such diverse authors as Richard Rorty, "Pragmatism and Romanticism," in *Philosophy as Cultural Politics* (Cambridge University Press, 2007), 105–19; Karl Schmitt, *Political Romanticism* (MIT Press, 1986); and Charles A. Taylor, *A Secular Age* (Harvard University Press, 2007).

12.   Although M. H. Abrams's secularized account of British Romanticism has recently been challenged by such authors as J. Robert Barth, Collin Jager, Robert Ryan, and Daniel White, his interpretations continue to dominate the field. Abrams refers to "progressive secularization" as "the assimilation and reinterpretation of religious ideas, as constitutive elements in a world view founded on secular premises." M. H. Abrams, *Natural Supernaturalism: Tradition and Revolution in Romantic Literature* (Norton, 1973), 13. And although he claims that he is not advancing a "deletion and replacement" account of religion, in the end he does in fact champion a "displacement from a supernatural to a natural frame of reference" (13). Abrams's work is indicative of the many secularized accounts of British Romanticism. Martin Priestman, for example, in support of Abrams, claims "that many 'Romantic' writers use religious, 'supernatural' terminology to describe objects, experiences and ideas which they know to be purely 'natural', thus turning the language of religion against itself by directing the feelings of reverence

and attachment it has traditionally demanded towards the 'world' it has traditionally downgraded." Martin Priestman, *Romantic Atheism: Poetry and Free Thought* (Cambridge University Press, 1999), 3. Such general claims about British Romanticism and secularization correspond to claims about specific Romantic authors and texts. For example, Kenneth Johnston, writing on Wordsworth's *The Recluse*—a text that strikes me as an indisputably religious—writes, "*The Recluse* seems to have all the makings of a systematically philosophical poem: only 'God' is omitted, and that, with reference to its modernity *vis-à-vis* tradition, is very much the point." Kenneth Johnston, "Wordsworth and *The Recluse*," in *Cambridge Companion to Wordsworth*, ed. Stephen Gill (Cambridge University Press, 2003), 72.

13.   Although most British Romantic authors were influenced by various Christian traditions, they were not systematic theologians or ecclesiastical leaders engaged in church politics. Religious beliefs and practices informed their perspectives on a wide range of sociopolitical and existential issues, and their work, in turn, did much to shape the religious belief and practice in their day and beyond.

14.   See C. G. Brown, "A Revisionist Approach to Religious Change," in *Religion and Modernization*, ed. Steve Bruce (Clarendon, 1992), 31–58; and Robert Currie, Alan Gilbert, and Lee Horsley, *Churches and Churchgoers: Patterns of Church Growth in the British Isles Since 1700* (Clarendon, 1977). The latter work, in particular, is convincing for the range and detail of its data on forms of religiosity.

15.   Some claim that it is misleading to take biblical allusions or motifs as evidence of religiosity among the Romantics. Priestman, for example, writes, "At a stroke, Abrams makes impossible the simplistic move of estimating a particular poet's degree of 'religion' from a quick count of their biblical quotations." *Romantic Atheism*, 3. Fair enough. But a subtler interpretive approach would want to be attentive to the *various* ways that religious perspectives and references, including biblical allusions, inform Romantic texts. The manifestation of religion in Romantic texts is by no means limited to "biblical quotations." Rather it is, as I claimed, manifested in "robust religious traditions, themes, and images."

16.   See Robert M. Ryan, *The Romantic Reformation: Religious Politics in English Literature, 1789–1824* (Cambridge University Press, 2004), 21.

17.   Samuel Taylor Coleridge, "The Eolian Harp," in *Samuel Taylor Coleridge: The Major Works*, ed. H. J. Jackson (Oxford University Press, 2008), 27, lines 1–4. Henceforth, references to "The Eolian Harp" will be embedded in the text.

18.   See Terry Tempest Williams's account of Pan in *An Unspoken Hunger: Stories from the Field* (Vintage, 1994), 82–83.

19.   For this language, "man over nature" and "mind over matter," see Donald Worster, *Nature's Economy: A History of Ecological Ideas* (Cambridge University Press, 1994), 51.

20.   I employ Brian Barry's account of first-order impartiality. Brian Barry, *Justice as Impartiality* (Oxford University Press, 1995), 11.

21.   A similar theme is found in many of Coleridge's poems. For example, in "This Lime-Tree Bower My Prison," composed around the same time as "The Eolian Harp," Coleridge suggests that one must achieve wisdom and purity if one is to be "Awake to Love and Beauty!" and to truly see nature in that which to others appears as vacant. Samuel

Taylor Coleridge, "This Lime-Tree Bower My Prison," in *Samuel Taylor Coleridge: The Major Works*, ed. H. J. Jackson (Oxford University Press, 2008), 40, lines 59–64.

22.   For this common "pantheistic" interpretation, see Harold Bloom, *The Visionary Company: A Reading of English Romantic Poetry* (Cornell University Press, 1971), 201; and Ronald Wendling, *Coleridge's Progress to Christianity: Experience and Authority in Religious Faith* (Associated University Presses, 1995), 22, 43. For a "panentheistic" interpretation, see Mary Anne Perkins, "Religious Thinker," in *Cambridge Companion to Coleridge*, ed. Lucy Newlyn (Cambridge University Press, 2002), 190.

23.   In March 1796, Coleridge wrote: "How is it that Dr Priestley is not an atheist?–He asserts in three different Places, that God not only *does*, but *is*, every thing.–But if God *be* every Thing, every Thing is God–: which is all, the Atheists assert." Samuel Taylor Coleridge, *Collected Letters of Samuel Taylor Coleridge*, ed. Earl Leslie Griggs, 6 vols. (Clarendon, 1966), 1:192.

24.   For a fine account of atheism and British Romanticism, see Priestman, *Romantic Atheism*.

25.   Jean-Pierre Mileur refers to these lines as "a failure of imaginative nerve." Jean-Pierre Mileur, *Vision and Revision: Coleridge's Art of Immanence* (University of California Press, 1982), 40. Harold Bloom declares that "the poem collapses in a self-surrender that augurs badly for the Imagination." Bloom, *The Visionary Company*, 202. Richard Matlak remarks that the poem "verges on humiliation of the poet as seer." Richard Matlak, "Classical Argument and Romantic Persuasion in 'Tintern Abbey,'" *Studies in Romanticism* 25, no. 1 (1986): 106.

26.   I am employing William James's categories "the healthy-minded" and the "sick souls." For the healthy-minded, the world and the self are basically good and harmonious. If we experience pain and distress, we simply need to adjust our mindset. James contrasted the "healthy-minded" with the "sick souls," for whom the world and our lives within it are fundamentally flawed. All is not well, and we stand in need of a basic change or radical cure. William James, *The Varieties of Religious Experience: A Study in Human Nature* (Penguin, 1982), 77–162.

27.   Some scholars, such as Jonathan Wordsworth, claim that the early Wordsworth was a pantheist and that he shed his pantheism when he turned to Anglicanism later in life. Jonathan Wordsworth, *The Music of Humanity* (Thomas Nelson and Sons, 1969), 202. In contrast, I argue that the early Wordsworth was a pan*en*theist, not a pantheist, and, moreover, that he maintained his panentheistic views even as he became a more traditional Anglican. For support of this view, see Ryan, *The Romantic Reformation*, 94–95. And for support of the view that both Coleridge and Wordsworth were motivated by a profoundly sacramental vision and attempted to bring a one Life theology into orthodox Christianity, see J. Robert Barth, *The Symbolic Imagination: Coleridge and the Romantic Tradition* (Princeton University Press, 2016).

28.   Samuel Taylor Coleridge, "Fears in Solitude," in *Samuel Taylor Coleridge: The Major Works*, ed. H. J. Jackson (Oxford University Press, 2008), 93–94, lines 43–50. Henceforth, references to "Fears in Solitude" will be embedded in the text.

29.   Jane Bennett, *Vibrant Matter: A Political Ecology of Things* (Duke University Press, 2010), ix.

30.   Coleridge, "This Lime-Tree Bower My Prison," 38–39.

31. Samuel Taylor Coleridge, "The Rime of the Ancient Mariner," in *Samuel Taylor Coleridge: The Major Works*, ed. H. J. Jackson (Oxford University Press, 2008), 57, lines 272–87.

32. Samuel Taylor Coleridge, "To a Young Ass," in *Samuel Taylor Coleridge: The Major Works*, ed. H. J. Jackson (Oxford University Press, 2008), 10–11.

33. Samuel Taylor Coleridge, "A Moral and Political Lecture," in *Samuel Taylor Coleridge: The Major Works*, ed. H. J. Jackson (Oxford University Press, 2008), 608–9.

34. Isaiah Berlin, for example, claims that in Romanticism we find "a new and restless spirit, seeking violently to burst through old and cramping forms, a nervous preoccupation with perpetually changing inner states of consciousness." Isaiah Berlin, *The Crooked Timber of Humanity*, ed. Henry Hardy (Princeton University Press, 2013), 96. See also Tim Blanning, *The Romantic Revolution: A History* (Modern Library, 2012), 2; and Alfredo De Paz, "Innovation and Modernity," in *Literary Criticism: Romanticism*, ed. Marshall Brown (Cambridge University Press, 2000), 29–48.

35. Milan Kundera, *The Unbearable Lightness of Being* (Harper Perennial, 2009).

36. William Wordsworth, "Nuns Fret Not at Their Convent's Narrow Room," in *William Wordsworth: The Major Works*, ed. Stephen Gill (Oxford University Press, 2008), 286.

37. Ralph Waldo Emerson, "Worship," in *Ralph Waldo Emerson: Essays and Poems*, ed. Harold Bloom, Paul Kane, and Joel Porte (Library of America, 1996), 897.

38. It has become commonplace to assume that Wordsworth romanticizes the lives of such country laborers as shepherds and farmers. However, his poems often depicted in graphic detail the hardships of such laborers. Moreover, in the same year as he wrote the sonnet "Nuns Fret Not," he also wrote a series of sonnets that condemned the reintroduction of slavery by Napoleon. See "Calais" and "September 1st, 1802," in *William Wordsworth: The Major Works*, ed. Stephen Gill (Oxford University Press, 2008), 280–81, 283. He opposed, then, a variety of unjust prison cells.

39. William Wordsworth, "London," in *William Wordsworth: The Major Works*, ed. Stephen Gill (Oxford University Press, 2008), 286, line 6; William Wordsworth, "Written in London," in *William Wordsworth: The Major Works*, ed. Stephen Gill (Oxford University Press, 2008), 285, line 7.

40. Wordsworth, "Written in London," 285, lines 9–10.

41. Wordsworth, "London," 286, line 8; emphasis added.

42. Although many have argued for this view, Alasdair MacIntyre's work is perhaps the most well-known. See Alasdair MacIntyre, *After Virtue* (University of Notre Dame Press, 1984); and Alasdair MacIntyre, *Whose Justice? Which Rationality?* (University of Notre Dame Press, 1988). For the best two books that both share MacIntyre's commitment to historicism and critique MacIntyre's antiliberal (social democratic) conclusions, see Jeffrey Stout, *Flight from Authority: Religion, Morality, and the Quest for Autonomy* (University of Notre Dame Press, 1981); and especially Jeffrey Stout, *Democracy and Tradition* (Princeton University Press, 2004).

43. Michel Foucault, *Discipline and Punish: The Birth of the Prison* (Vintage, 1995), 222.

44. See Mark Cladis, "Durkheim and Foucault on Education and Punishment," in *Durkheim and Foucault: Perspectives on Education and Punishment*, ed. Mark Cladis (Berghahn, 2001).

45. For an excellent account of Wordsworth and second nature, see David Bromwich, *A Choice of Inheritance: Self and Community from Edmund Burke to Robert Frost* (Harvard

University Press, 1989), 43–78; and James Chandler, *Wordsworth's Second Nature: A Study of the Poetry and Politics* (University of Chicago Press, 1984). Unlike Chandler, I argue that Wordsworth wed a Burkean emphasis on social practice to a Rousseauian progressive vision of democracy.

46. Foucault, *Discipline and Punish*, 308.

47. Colin Jager, *The Book of God: Secularization and Design in the Romantic Era* (University of Pennsylvania Press, 2007), 213. Despite my specific disagreements with Jager, I am sympathetic with the larger purpose of his book, namely, to show how the argument from design in Romantic works challenges our standard secularized accounts of Romanticism; he also skillfully demonstrates how, among the Romantics, the secular and the religious mutually define each other.

48. Talal Asad, *Genealogies of Religion: Discipline and Reasons of Power in Christianity and Islam* (John Hopkins University Press, 1993), 207; Jager, *The Book of God*, 213.

49. Jager, *The Book of God*, 213.

50. Jager, *The Book of God*, 211–12.

51. Chandler, *Wordsworth's Second Nature*, xviii.

52. My position here is in contrast to James Chandler's view that Wordsworth forswears Rousseau in order to endorse Burke. Chandler claims that "insofar as we regard Burke's thought as the epitome of political conservatism in this period [the mid-1790s], Wordsworth's major work, his programmatic poetry of second nature, is conservative from the start." Chandler, *Wordsworth's Second Nature*, xviii. But conservative in what sense? If by "conservative" Chandler means something like self-consciously working within a historically fashioned social inheritance, within historically situated ideals, customs, beliefs, institutions, and practices, then there are good reasons to assent to the claim that "Wordsworth's major work . . . is conservative from the start." We can call this *epistemological* conservatism. But if by "conservative" Chandler means *political* conservatism, namely, self-consciously promoting the privilege of the wealthy and elite classes, established social hierarchies, and the disenfranchisement of the commoners, then there are good reasons to disagree with Chandler's claim. Chandler tends to conflate these two distinct forms of "conservatism." I suspect that Chandler, like Burke, would think of a progressive *democratic second nature* as an oxymoron. In Chandler's view, if Wordsworth accepts Burke's epistemological conservatism (or what could be called his philosophical anthropology), then he must necessarily accept his political views as well, thereby renouncing his earlier commitment to Rousseauian democratic perspectives.

53. Later in life, Wordsworth maintained an emphasis on second nature but abandoned much of his early radicalism, though he still retained important lessons and perspectives from his republican days. He remained, for example, a critic of unbridled capitalism and modern ways of commerce and manufacturing that were devastating communities, personal dignity, and the environment.

54. William Wordsworth, *The Prelude: 1799, 1805, 1850*, ed. Jonathan Wordsworth, M. H. Abrams, and Stephen Gill (Norton, 1979), 406, lines 889–90; 438, lines 24–26; and 440, line 57; emphasis added.

55. I am borrowing language here from Aldo Leopold's "Land Ethic." He claimed "a thing is right when it tends to preserve the integrity, stability, and beauty of the biotic

community." Aldo Leopold, *A Sand County Almanac and Sketches Here and There* (Oxford University Press, 1987), 224–25.

5. DANCING ON A FLAMING WORLD: DU BOIS'S POETRY AND CREATIVE FICTION

1. See, for example, David Levering Lewis, *W. E. B. Du Bois: The Fight for Equality and the American Century* (Henry Holt, 2000), 19, 175.
2. Jonathon S. Kahn, *Divine Discontent: The Religious Imagination of W. E. B. Du Bois* (Oxford University Press, 2011), 5.
3. Herbert Aptheker, ed., *Creative Writings by W. E. B Du Bois: A Pageant, Poems, Short Stories, and Playlets* (Kraus-Thomson, 1985), xii.
4. W. E. B. Du Bois, *The Souls of Black Folk*, ed. Brent Hayes Edwards (Oxford University Press, 2007), 14.
5. Du Bois, *The Souls of Black Folk,* 134.
6. Kahn, *Divine Discontent*, 13.
7. I'm not the first to do this. Russell Goodman, for example, interprets the thought of "James and Dewey as a perpetuation in philosophy of the original Romantic enterprise." Russell Goodman, *American Philosophy and the Romantic Tradition* (Cambridge University Press, 1990), 129. Relatedly, Ulf Schulenberg claims that Romanticism is "an important phase of a development that culminates in (neo)pragmatism." Ulf Schulenberg, *Romanticism and Pragmatism: Richard Rorty and the Idea of a Poeticized Culture* (Palgrave MacMillan, 2015), 5.
8. Allison Blackmond Laskey, "Of Forms and Flow: Movement Through Structure in *Darkwater*'s Composition," *New Centennial Review* 15, no. 2 (2015): 107–18.
9. Here Du Bois joins Emerson, Dewey, and Jeffrey Stout in their belief that the cultivation of progressive democratic forms and practices (ways of life) are essential to liberatory aims, including the very practice of social critique. For the best treatment of this topic, see Jeffrey Stout, *Flight from Authority: Religion, Morality, and the Quest for Autonomy* (University of Notre Dame Press, 1981); and especially Jeffrey Stout, *Democracy and Tradition* (Princeton University Press, 2004).
10. W. E. B. Du Bois, *Dusk of Dawn*, ed. Henry Louis Gates Jr. (Oxford University Press, 2007), 111.
11. By "creative fictional pieces," I refer to the poetry and short stories. However, I am uneasy with referring globally to Du Bois's poetry as "fictional," because his poetry often depicts real or actual events, sorrows, and oppression.
12. For example, Octavia Butler, *Parable of the Sower* (Grand Central, 2019); Louise Erdrich, *Future Home of the Living God* (Harper Perennial, 2017); and Carmen Maria Machado, *Her Body and Other Parties* (Graywolf, 2017).
13. W. E. B. Du Bois, *Darkwater: Voices from Within the Veil*, ed. Henry Louis Gates Jr. (Oxford University Press, 2007), xli. Henceforth, all references to *Darkwater* will be embedded in the text.
14. Arnold Rampersad claims that "the essential debate in 'A Litany of Atlanta' is not between a man and a distant God, but within the speaker himself. . . . He finds himself

wavering between the rival forces of radical anger and divine reason, between human despair and sublime faith." Arnold Rampersad, *The Art and Imagination of W. E. B. Du Bois* (Schocken, 1990), 105. Although I take the debate "between a man and a distant God" to be central to the poem, I appreciate Rampersad's bringing attention to the equally important internal struggle within Du Bois.

15. In an excellent article on Du Bois's short stories in *Darkwater*, Hee-Jung Serenity Joo refers to the conclusions of Du Bois's stories as intentional "failures": "I look at moments in his *Darkwater* stories in which he could easily resolve the instances of social injustice he depicts but chooses not to, resulting in the world staying the same or going back to how it was. These narrative failures are . . . scathing critiques of the historical specificities of his time. Moreover, I regard these moments of narrative failure as ones of political resistance, a rejection of ideas of social development rooted in capitalist trajectories." Hee-Jung Serenity Joo, "Racial Impossibility and Critical Failure in W. E. B. Du Bois's *Darkwater*," *Science Fiction Studies* 46, no. 1 (2019): 106.

16. As Thomas Meagher puts it: "In lynching blacks (as occurs in 'Jesus Christ in Texas') they are lynching the divine." Thomas Meagher, "*Darkwater*'s Existentialist Socialism," *Socialism and Democracy* 32, no. 3 (2018): 95.

17. On a personal note, to forbid this "mighty beauty" would be to deprive me of the greatest beauty in my life—my partner and our three children.

18. Frederick Douglass, *Autobiographies*, ed. Henry Louis Gates Jr. (Library of America, 1994), 23.

19. Du Bois, *The Souls of Black Folk*, 7.

20. Samuel Taylor Coleridge, "The Eolian Harp," in *Samuel Taylor Coleridge: The Major Works*, ed. H. J. Jackson (Oxford University Press, 2008), 28–29, lines 26 and 48.

21. Ulysses G. Weatherly, "The First Universal Races Congress," *American Journal of Sociology* 17, no. 3 (1911): 315–16.

22. Du Bois, *Dusk of Dawn*, 74–75.

23. To claim that Du Bois "belongs" to radical Romanticism is not to claim that he only or mainly belongs to this tradition. The influences on him were various, and many will want to make a case for Du Bois belonging to other traditions. This is to be expected for any powerful thinker and artist.

6. ECOFEMINISM AND THE EXPANSION AND TRANSFORMATION OF RADICAL ROMANTICISM

1. Mary Shelley, *Frankenstein, or the Modern Prometheus: The 1818 Text*, ed. Marilyn Butler (Oxford University Press, 2008), 39; emphasis added. Henceforth, references to *Frankenstein* will be embedded in the text.

2. For helpful work on both the constraints on and new forms of women's authorship in the nineteenth century, see Jane Duran, "Margaret Fuller and Transcendental Feminism," *The Pluralist* 5, no. 1 (2010): 65–72; Sandra M. Gustafson, "Choosing a Medium: Margaret Fuller and the Forms of Sentiment," *American Quarterly* 47, no. 1 (1995): 34–65; Annette Kolodny, "Inventing a Feminist Discourse: Rhetoric and Resistance in Margaret Fuller's *Woman in the Nineteenth Century*," *New Literary History* 25, no. 2 (1994): 355–82;

Samantha Webb, "Reading the End of the World: The Last Man, History, and the Agency of Romantic Authorship," in *Mary Shelley in Her Times*, ed. Betty T. Bennett and Stuart Curran (Johns Hopkins University Press, 2000), 119–33; Olivia Zolciak, "Sublimating an Apocalypse: An Exploration of Anxiety, Authorship, and Feminist Theory in Mary Shelley's *The Last Man*," *American Journal of Economics and Sociology* 77, no. 5 (2018): 1243–76.

3. Lee Gutkind, *You Can't Make This Stuff Up: The Complete Guide to Writing Creative Nonfiction* (Lifelong Books, 2012), 6; cited in Michael Putnam, "Reverence the Stones: The Ethics of Environmental Attention," PhD diss., Brown University, forthcoming.

4. Such public issues always have a personal face, as when, in my case, white Rhode Islanders ask me, "*Where* do your kids"—my biracial children—"come from?" This question of place, with its assumption that my children are not from here, that they are outsiders, is a question about identity and belonging. "Where do they come from?" is in fact their *answer* to the question: "Are they one of us? Do they belong?" along with the implied answer, "No" or "Not entirely." And the more the exclusionary group identifies itself as being definitory of humanity, the more the excluded are dehumanized.

5. James Leiker, "Great Books: *Frankenstein* by Mary Shelley," October 11, 2018, YouTube video, 38:25, https://youtu.be/Za5K_Q7Arc8.

6. William Wordsworth, *The Prelude: 1799, 1805, 1850*, ed. Jonathan Wordsworth, M. H. Abrams, and Stephen Gill (Norton, 1979), 447, lines 166–67.

7. Samuel Taylor Coleridge, "To a Young Ass," in *Samuel Taylor Coleridge: The Major Works*, ed. H. J. Jackson (Oxford University Press, 2008), 10, line 26; emphasis added.

8. Lewis Gordon, "Fanon's Decolonial Aesthetic," in *The Aesthetic Turn in Political Thought*, ed. Nikolas Kompridis (Bloomsbury Academic, 2014), 96.

9. Robin Wall Kimmerer, *Braiding Sweetgrass: Indigenous Wisdom, Scientific Knowledge, and the Teachings of Plants* (Milkweed Editions, 2013), 358.

10. Helena Feder, *Ecocriticism and the Idea of Culture: Biology and the Bildungsroman* (Routledge, 2014), 65.

11. Susan Stryker, "My Words to Victor Frankenstein Above the Village of Chamounix," in *The Transgender Studies Reader*, ed. Susan Stryker and Stephen Whittle (Routledge, 2006), 245.

12. Mary Shelley, *The Last Man*, ed. Morton D. Paley (Oxford University Press, 1998), 459; emphasis added.

13. For an excellent argument for why human distinctiveness, but not dominating human exceptionalism, needs to be affirmed, see Sharon Krause, *Eco-Emancipation: An Earthly Politics of Freedom* (Princeton University Press, 2023), 16–18, 29–51. In particular, Krause argues convincingly that "human beings do have some distinctive capacities not shared by most other parts of nature, and this distinctiveness is significant insofar as it makes us subject to ethical and political accountability in special ways. But to acknowledge this distinctiveness is a far cry from insisting on a strict, hierarchical divide between human beings and everything else on Earth, one that could justify unchecked human power and exploitation in relation to nature" (16–17).

14. Anne K. Mellor, *Mary Shelley: Her Life, Her Fiction, Her Monsters* (Methuen, 1988), 124.

15. Jed Mayer, "The Weird Ecologies of Mary Shelley's *Frankenstein*," *Science Fiction Studies* 45, no. 2 (2018): 235. Mayer writes about *Frankenstein*, but the claim is even more apt for *The Last Man*.

16. Emily Dickinson, "What mystery pervades a well!," in *The Complete Poems of Emily Dickinson*, ed. Thomas H. Johnson (Little, Brown, 1960), 599–600.

17. Marilyn Gaull, "Radical Imaginings: Mary Shelley's 'The Last Man,'" *The Wordsworth Circle* 26, no. 3 (1995): 149. See also Jennifer L. Airey, "Domesticity," the final chapter in *Religion Around Mary Shelley* (Pennsylvania State University Press, 2019), for Shelley's religion of "interpersonal love."

18. As noted by Sheldon Krimsky in a footnote to the MIT version of *Frankenstein*, "Scientists' responsibility must be engaged before their creations are unleashed." Mary Shelley, *Frankenstein: Annotated for Scientists, Engineers, and Creators of All Kinds*, ed. David H. Guston, Ed Finn, and Jason Scott Robert (MIT Press, 2017), 73n4.

19. Devon Hodges, "*Frankenstein* and the Feminine Subversion of the Novel," *Tulsa Studies in Women's Literature* 2, no. 2 (1983): 158.

20. Shelley, *The Last Man*, 5. For a wonderful account of Shelley's literary framework for *The Last Man*, see Webb, "Reading the End of the World," 119–33.

21. Hilary Strang, "Common Life, Animal Life, Equality: *The Last Man*," *English Literary History* 78, no. 2 (2011): 427–28.

22. John Matteson, *The Lives of Margaret Fuller: A Biography* (Norton, 2012).

23. Henry David Thoreau, "Walking," in *Thoreau: Walden, The Maine Woods, Collected Essays and Poems*, ed. Robert Sayre and Elizabeth Witherell (Library of America, 2007), 760.

24. See Barbara L. Packer's "Romanticism," in *The Oxford Handbook of Transcendentalism*, ed. Joel Myerson, Sandra Harbert Petrulions, and Laura Dassow Walls (Oxford University Press, 2012), 84–101.

25. On the "Romantic triad"—nature, spirit, humanity—see Samantha Harvey's wonderful account in her *Transatlantic Transcendentalism: Coleridge, Emerson, and Nature* (Edinburgh University Press, 2013), 14–21.

26. See Alda Balthrop-Lewis, *Thoreau's Religion: Walden Woods, Social Justice, and the Politics of Asceticism* (Cambridge University Press, 2021), for the best account we have of the connection between Thoreau's social justice and ecological commitments.

27. Walt Whitman, "Song of Myself," in *Whitman: Poetry and Prose*, ed. Justin Kaplan (Library of America, 1982), section 17, p. 204.

28. On the connection between the public and private in Fuller's work, see Carmen Birkle, "Travelogues of Independence: Margaret Fuller and Henry David Thoreau," *Amerikastudien / American Studies* 48, no. 4 (2003): 499.

29. Margaret Fuller, *"These Sad but Glorious Days": Dispatches from Europe, 1846–1850*, ed. Larry J. Reynolds and Susan Belasco Smith (Yale University Press, 1991). For a helpful account of Fuller's visit to these factories and mills, see Amber Shaw, "'Like the Incense of a Bad Heart': The Ethics of Industry in Sophia Hawthorne's and Margaret Fuller's English Travelogues," *Nathaniel Hawthorne Review* 41, no. 1 (2015): 75–95.

30. H. C. Goddard, "Unitarianism and Transcendentalism," in *American Transcendentalism: An Anthology of Criticism*, ed. Brian M. Barbour (Notre Dame University Press, 1973), 161.

31. Margaret Fuller, *Woman in the Nineteenth Century* (Norton, 1998), 20, 71.

32. Margaret Fuller, *Woman in the Nineteenth Century*, 102. On the same page she commented, "Some little girls like to saw wood, others to use carpenters' tools. Where these tastes are indulged, cheerfulness and good humor are promoted. Where they are forbidden, because 'such things are not proper for girls,' they grow sullen and mischievous."

33. For negative responses to Fuller's writing style, see Kolodny, "Inventing a Feminist Discourse," 356–58.

34. As noted earlier, Fuller hosted and led "Conversational" classes for women; the few times men were invited, the collaborative ethos collapsed into male grandstanding. For an excellent article on Fuller's writing style, see Gustafson, "Choosing a Medium: Margaret Fuller and the Forms of Sentiment," esp. 44 and 55 for her conversational style.

35. Margaret Fuller, *Summer on the Lakes, in 1843* (University of Illinois Press, 1991), 3, 4. Henceforth, references to *Summer on the Lakes* will be embedded in the text.

36. As Kathleen Healey writes, "Most Americans cannot see the Falls except as a commodity, something that has a use. The aesthetic beauty of the Falls, their sublimity, and the power of God they revealed to some Americans, are lost on the majority of Americans who look only for what they can gain from the natural world." Kathleen Healey, "'The Mighty Meaning of the Scene': Feminine Landscapes and the Future of America in Margaret Fuller's *Summer on the Lakes, in 1843*," *Humanities* 8, no. 31 (2019): 12.

37. Birkle, "Travelogues of Independence," 505.

38. On the "vanishing Indian," see Christina Zwarg, "Footnoting the Sublime: Margaret Fuller on Black Hawk's Trail," *American Literary History* 5, no. 4 (1993): 616–42; and Serena Mocci, "Addressing Racial Conflict in Antebellum America: Women and Native Americans in Lydia Maria Child's and Margaret Fuller's Literary Works," *Journal of American History and Politics* 3, no. 1 (2020): 1–16. Unlike my account, Mocci does claim that Fuller held "that the Native Americans were doomed to extinction before the advance of the superior white race" (6).

39. These two contrary views are found in the following two excellent articles: Healey, "'The Mighty Meaning of the Scene,'" 1–2; and Monika Elbert, "Haunting Transcendentalist Landscapes: EcoGothic Politics in Margaret Fuller's *Summer on the Lakes*," *Text Matters* 6, no. 6 (2016): 71.

40. Healey, "'The Mighty Meaning of the Scene,'" 7.

41. Elbert, "Haunting Transcendentalist Landscapes," 71.

42. Adam-Max Tuchinsky convincingly argues that Fuller's work at the *Tribune* was an extension of various Transcendentalist efforts to critique American antidemocratic capitalism and that as Brook Farm "critiqued the hegemony of competitive capitalism. . . . [It was] an attempt to embed Emersonian principles into a communal practice. . . . The same might be said of Margaret Fuller's journalism." Adam-Max Tuchinsky, "'Her Cause Against Herself': Margaret Fuller, Emersonian Democracy, and the Nineteenth-Century Public Intellectual," *American Nineteenth Century History* 5, no. 1 (2004): 73.

43. For example, Fuller always supported abolitionism, but that support became all the stronger in Italy, from where she wrote: "How it pleases me here to think of the Abolitionists! . . . [Their cause is] worth living and dying for[,] to free a great nation from such a terrible blot, such a threatening plague." Fuller, *These Sad but Glorious Days*," 166).

44. Fuller, *These Sad but Glorious Days*," 320, 230.

45. Stacy Alaimo, *Bodily Natures: Environment, and the Material Self* (Indiana University Press, 2010).

46. Sharon Patricia Holland, *The Erotic Life of Racism* (Duke University Press, 2012).

47. Kimberly N. Ruffin, *Black on Earth: African American Ecological Traditions* (University of Georgia Press, 2010).

48. Jennifer C. James, "A Theory of the Bottom: Black Ecofeminism as Politics," *Resilience: A Journal of the Environmental Humanities* 10, no. 1–2 (2022/2023): 46–52.

49. Sonya Posmentier, *Cultivation and Catastrophe: The Lyric Ecology of Modern Black Literature* (Johns Hopkins University Press, 2017).

50. In a wonderful article, Jenny Hyest, quoting from a letter and publication of Hurston's, states powerfully and succinctly: "In her writings, a leader of prayers is a 'prayer-artist,' a preacher is 'a poet and an actor of a very high order,' a singer of spirituals is 'trying to express himself through song,' and the 'religious service' itself 'is a conscious art expression.'" Jenny Hyest, "'Born with God in the House': Feminist Vision and Religious Revision in the Works of Zora Neale Hurston," *Legacy* 35, no. 1 (2018): 30.

51. Melissa Harris-Perry, *Sister Citizen: Shame, Stereotypes, and Black Women in America* (Yale University Press, 2013), 23.

52. Melanie L. Harris, "Ecowomanism: Black Women, Religion, and the Environment," *The Black Scholar* 46, no. 3 (2016): 33.

53. Matt Sandler, *The Black Romantic Revolution: Abolitionist Poets at the End of Slavery* (Verso, 2020), 14–15.

54. Julian S. Whitney, "A Black Manifesto: Ottobah Cugoano's Radical Romanticism," *Studies in Romanticism* 61, no. 1 (2022): 48.

55. Whitney, "A Black Manifesto," 49; emphasis added.

56. Zora Neale Hurston, *Their Eyes Were Watching God* (Harper and Row, 1990), 10–11. Henceforth, references to *Their Eyes* will be embedded in the text.

57. Gurleen Grewal aptly describes the tree as "a vision of Life that becomes a blueprint for the soul's quest." Gurleen Grewal, "Beholding 'A Great Tree in Leaf': Eros, Nature and the Visionary in *Their Eyes Were Watching God*," in *"The Inside Light": Collected Essays on Zora Neale Hurston*, ed. Deborah Plant (Praeger, 2010), 104.

58. Audre Lorde, "Uses of the Erotic: The Erotic as Power," in *Sister Outsider: Essays and Speeches by Audre Lorde* (Crossing, 2007), 60–65.

59. Holland, *The Erotic Life of Racism*, 6.

60. Alaimo, *Bodily Natures*, 2.

61. John Claborn, *Civil Rights and the Environment in African-American Literature, 1895–1941* (Bloomsbury Academic, 2018), 126.

62. As John Claborn rightly claims, the "interspecies solidarity and collectivity that constitutes backwaters ecology [of the muck] are key notions in . . . *Their Eyes Were Watching God*." Claborn, *Civil Rights and the Environment in African-American Literature*, 126.

63. Susan Scott Parrish, "Zora Neale Hurston and the Environmental Ethic of Risk," in *American Studies, Ecocriticism, and Citizenship: Thinking and Acting in the Local and Global Commons*, ed. Joni Adamson and Kimberly N. Ruffin (Routledge, 2013), 31.

64. William Wordsworth, "Lines Written a Few Miles Above Tintern Abbey," in *William Wordsworth: The Major Works*, ed. Stephen Gill (Oxford University Press, 2008), 134, line 103.

65. Marcus Harvey, "'Hard Skies' and Bottomless Questions: Zora Neale Hurston's *Their Eyes Were Watching God* and Epistemological 'Opacity' in Black Religious Experience," *Journal of Africana Religions* 4, no. 2 (2016): 186–214.

66. Posmentier, *Cultivation and Catastrophe*, 165.

67. Zora Neale Hurston, "Crazy for This Democracy," in *Available Means: An Anthology of Women's Rhetoric(s)*, ed. Joy Ritchie and Kate Ronald (University of Pittsburgh Press, 2001), 251.

68. Hurston, "Crazy for This Democracy," 249.

69. See Joy Ritchie and Kate Ronald's introductory comments to Hurston, "Crazy for This Democracy," 248.

70. Ruffin, *Black on Earth*, 2–3

71. James, "A Theory of the Bottom," 50.

72. Terry Tempest Williams, "Yellowstone: An Erotics of Place," in *An Unspoken Hunger: Stories from the Field* (Vintage, 1994), 81–87. I call my use here of "erotics of place" a *critical* employment, because although I find the term powerful, I also acknowledge that in "Yellowstone: An Erotics of Place" Williams failed to recognize the extent to which National Parks such as Yellowstone are monuments of displacement and colonization of Indigenous populations.

7. LESLIE MARMON SILKO AND THE POWER OF INDIGENOUS STORYTELLING: HEALING AND RESISTANCE IN DEFIANCE OF SETTLER COLONIALISM

1. Leslie Marmon Silko, *Ceremony* (Penguin, 1986), 2, 226.

2. Leslie Marmon Silko, *Yellow Woman and a Beauty of the Spirit* (Simon and Schuster, 1996), 20; emphasis added.

3. See Silko, *Yellow Woman and a Beauty of the Spirit*, 20; see also Leslie Marmon Silko, "Leslie Marmon Silko Saw It Coming," interview by Ismail Ibrahim, *New Yorker*, April 16, 2023, https://www.newyorker.com/culture/the-new-yorker-interview/leslie-marmon -silko-saw-it-coming.

4. Silko, *Yellow Woman and a Beauty of the Spirit*, 20–21.

5. Leslie Marmon Silko, *Almanac of the Dead* (Penguin, 1992), 713–14, 316, 520; emphasis added.

6. Silko, *Ceremony*, 229.

7. For Silko's high esteem for American Transcendentalism and Margaret Fuller, see Ellen L. Arnold, ed., *Conversations with Leslie Marmon Silko* (University Press of Mississippi, 2000), 179–80, where she says, "I loved Margaret Fuller for years and years. She's a great hero of mine," and she claims that American Transcendentalism has been informed by Indigenous peoples and the land itself, which follows old Indigenous prophecies that "purely European way of looking at this place and relationships" will change.

8. I have in mind here Saidiya Hartman's distinction between witness and voyeurism. Saidiya Hartman, *Scenes of Subjection: Terror, Slavery, and Self-Making in Nineteenth-Century America* (Oxford University Press, 1997), 3–4.

9. While I find the analytical distinction between voyeur and witness to be helpful, it is rarely clear-cut in the lives of actual people.

10.   Silko, *Yellow Woman and a Beauty of the Spirit*, 59.

11.   Silko, *Ceremony*, 246. Henceforth, references to *Ceremony* will be embedded in the text.

12.   Heather Davis and Zoe Todd, "On the Importance of a Date, or Decolonizing the Anthropocene," *ACME* 16, no. 4 (2017): 770. Emphasis added.

13.   Kyle P. Whyte, "Critical Investigations of Resilience: A Brief Introduction to Indigenous Environmental Studies & Sciences," *Dædalus, the Journal of the American Academy of Arts & Sciences* 147, no. 2 (2018): 141.

14.   For the term, "nuclear colonialism," see Valerie Kuletz, "Invisible Spaces, Violent Places: Cold War Nuclear and Militarized Landscapes," in *Violent Environments*, ed. Nancy Lee Peluso and Michael Watts (Cornell University Press, 2001), 240–43; and Isabel Lockhart, "Intimacies of the Atom: On Rocks and Decolonization in the Work of Leslie Marmon Silko," *American Quarterly* 72, no. 3 (2020): 679–80.

15.   For the term, "wasteland," see Traci B. Voyles, *Wastelanding: Legacies of Uranium Mining in Navajo Country* (University of Minnesota Press, 2015), 1–26.

16.   July Pasternak, "A Peril That Dwelt Among the Navajos," *Los Angeles Times*, November 9, 2006.

17.   Doug Brugge, Timothy Benally, and Esther Yazzie-Lewis, eds., *The Navajo People and Uranium Mining* (University of New Mexico Press, 2006), xvii–xviii, 3–5, 89–115.

18.   Rebecca Tillett, "Reality Consumed by Realty: The Ecological Costs of 'Development' in Leslie Marmon Silko's *Almanac of the Dead*," *European Journal of American Culture* 24, no. 2 (2005): 153.

19.   Kyle P. Whyte, "Indigenous Science (Fiction) for the Anthropocene: Ancestral Dystopias and Fantasies of Climate Change Crises," *Environment and Planning E: Nature and Space* 1, no. 1-2 (2018): 229; emphasis added.

20.   On the significance of Paguate Hill, see Leslie Marmon Silko, "Landscape, History, and the Pueblo Imagination," in *At Home on the Earth: Becoming Native to Our Place*, ed. David Landis Barnhill (University of California Press, 1999), 38.

21.   For an excellent account of Silko's decolonial practices, including resistance in the face of radioactive toxicity, see Lockhart, "Intimacies of the Atom." In particular, see 680 and 693, where, for example, she writes: "Silko resists narratives that reproduce an impression of Indigenous homelands as toxically, tragically doomed, and that perpetuate the colonial tethering of Indigenous peoples to extinction" (693).

22.   Silko, *Yellow Woman and a Beauty of the Spirit*, 64.

23.   Samuel Taylor Coleridge, "Dejection: An Ode," in *Samuel Taylor Coleridge: The Major Works*, ed. H. J. Jackson (Oxford University Press, 2008), 115, lines 47–78; emphasis added.

24.   William Wordsworth, "Lines Written a Few Miles Above Tintern Abbey," in *William Wordsworth: The Major Works*, ed. Stephen Gill (Oxford University Press, 2008), 134, lines 105–8; emphasis added.

25.   For this language of inner and outer landscape and the relation between the two, see Barry Lopez, "Landscape and Narrative," in *Crossing Open Ground* (Vintage, 1988), 64–65.

26.   Silko, *Yellow Woman and a Beauty of the Spirit*, 50.

27.   Silko, *Almanac*, 756. Henceforth, references to *Almanac of the Dead* will be embedded in the text.

28. Jonathan Lear, *Radical Hope: Ethics in the Face of Cultural Devastation* (Harvard University Press, 2006), 2.

29. Bonnie TuSmith, *All My Relatives: Community in Contemporary Ethnic American Literatures* (University of Michigan Press, 1994), 123.

30. Silko, *Yellow Woman and a Beauty of the Spirit*, 59.

31. Ralph Waldo Emerson, "Circles," in *Emerson: Essays and Poems*, ed. Harold Bloom, Paul Kane, and Joel Porte (Library of America, 1996), 413.

32. William Wordsworth, *Guide to the Lakes*, ed. Saeko Yoshikawa (Oxford University Press, 2022), 54, 56.

33. W. E. B. Du Bois, *The Quest of the Silver Fleece*, ed. Henry Louis Gates Jr. (Oxford University Press, 2007), 19.

34. Silko, "Landscape, History, and the Pueblo Memory," 30, 32.

35. Silko, *Ceremony*, 8. Henceforth, references to *Ceremony* will be embedded in the text.

36. Benjamin Barney related his father's story to me via email on May 30, 2021, and we also discussed it soon after that date. I am grateful to Benjamin Barney for this story and for so much more. Ben has graced my life for more than two decades, and he is one of my principal educators on the Diné and other Indigenous peoples.

37. There are various ways to learn the lesson that "no one has license to tread everywhere." My colleague Paul Kane and I once traveled to the Southwest to study with two Indigenous educators, Lorain Fox Davis (Cree and Blackfeet) and Benjamin Barney (Diné). Shortly after we entered the Navajo Nation, when traveling to meet Mr. Barney, we encountered a twister—a dust devil—at a Thriftway gas station. The twister came directly for us. We began walking toward the gas station entrance, quickening our pace and finally broke into a sprint as the twister rushed upon us. Once inside the store's entrance, with the twister at our heels, we were unable to close the door. There was something of an explosion as an outside trashcan erupted, spewing paper, dirt, bottles, and cans in every direction, inside and outside, and the dust—it was everywhere. When it finally settled and our eyes cleared, we met the firm gazes of the two Navajo women behind the counter. Their eyes seemed to hold both amusement and exasperation. Here were two white guys chased into their store by a cloud of dust and garbage. In no uncertain terms, the land had let us know that we did not belong there. I am not suggesting that we should have stayed home instead of visiting the Navajo Nation. But we had received a forceful reminder that we were short-term visitors in a foreign land and that *we should not feel at home*. We might have come to believe, at some level, that we had earned the spiritual right to travel self-assuredly among the Diné. Yet within five minutes of our arrival in the Navajo Nation, we were quickly—and categorically—set straight.

38. For treatment on the topic of attempts to thwart Indigenous stewardship, see Kyle P. Whyte, "Indigenous Experience, Environmental Justice and Settler Colonialism," in *Nature and Experience: Phenomenology and the Environment*, ed. Bryan E. Bannon (Rowman & Littlefield, 2016), 165–67.

39. Leigh Shaw-Taylor, "Parliamentary Enclosure and the Emergence of an English Agricultural Proletariat," *Journal of Economic History* 61, no. 3 (2001): 642.

40. Samuel Taylor Coleridge, "The Rime of the Ancient Mariner," in *Samuel Taylor Coleridge: The Major Works*, ed. H. J. Jackson (Oxford University Press, 2008), 57, lines 272–87.

41.   Samuel Taylor Coleridge, "To a Young Ass," in *Samuel Taylor Coleridge: The Major Works*, ed. H. J. Jackson (Oxford University Press, 2008), 10, lines 26–28.

42.   Silko, *Yellow Woman and a Beauty of the Spirit*, 44.

43.   Silko, *Yellow Woman and a Beauty of the Spirit*, 26.

44.   Leslie Marmon Silko, *Gardens in the Dunes* (Simon and Schuster, 1999), 348, 49.

45.   Kyle P. Whyte, "Settler Colonialism, Ecology, and Environmental Injustice," *Environment and Society: Advances in Research* 9 (2018): 133–34.

46.   Silko, *Yellow Woman and a Beauty of the Spirit*, 37, 27.

47.   Earlier scholarship tended to differentiate Romanticism from Gothicism, but more contemporary work understands Gothic literature as a subset of Romanticism, sometimes called Dark or Gothic Romanticism. See, for example, Angela Wright and Dale Townshend, eds., *Romantic Gothic: An Edinburgh Companion* (Edinburgh University Press, 2015); and Jerrold E. Hogle, "The Gothic-Romantic Nexus: Wordsworth, Coleridge, *Splice* and *The Ring*," *The Wordsworth Circle* 43, no. 3 (2012): 159–65.

48.   William Wordsworth, "The Thorn," in *William Wordsworth: The Major Works*, ed. Stephen Gill (Oxford University Press, 2008), 64, line 174; 65, lines 228–31, 234, 238–39; 62, line 89; 63, line 155; 62, line 114. To name just a few other examples of what I am calling the remarkable in radical Romanticism: in Wordsworth, the wood spirit in "Nutting," and in Coleridge, the skeleton-ship and ghosts in "The Rime of the Ancient Mariner," the witches and ghosts in "Christabel," and the "waning moon . . . haunted / By woman wailing for her demon-lover!" in "Kubla Khan." In *Samuel Taylor Coleridge: The Major Works*, ed. H. J. Jackson (Oxford University Press, 2008), 103, lines 15–16.

49.   Wordsworth, "Lines Composed a Few Miles Above Tintern Abbey," 134, lines 95, 98–103.

50.   I should note that in *Almanac* the destroyers are the Gunadeeyahs, and they appear to be closely associated with white Europeans ("the Gunadeeyahs had called for their white [European] brethren to join them" [760]).

51.   Kyle P. Whyte, "What Do Indigenous Knowledges Do for Indigenous Peoples?," in *Traditional Ecological Knowledge: Learning from Indigenous Practices for Environmental Sustainability*, ed. Melissa K. Nelson and Dan Shilling (Cambridge University Press, 2018), 63–64.

52.   Robin Wall Kimmerer, "*Mishkos Kenomagwen*, the Lessons of Grass: Restoring Reciprocity with the Good Green Earth," in *Traditional Ecological Knowledge: Learning from Indigenous Practices for Environmental Sustainability*, ed. Melissa K. Nelson and Dan Shilling (Cambridge University Press, 2018), 42. Emphasis added.

53.   See, for example, Kimmerer, "*Mishkos Kenomagwen*, the Lessons of Grass," 49.

CONCLUSION: THE WORK AND PROMISE OF RADICAL ROMANTICISM IN A WORLD IN RUINS

1.   Leslie Marmon Silko, *Ceremony* (Penguin, 1986), 2.

2.   Wendell Berry, *The Art of the Commonplace: The Agrarian Essays of Wendell Berry*, ed. Norman Wirzba (Counterpoint, 2002), 11.

3.   Karen Barad, "Nature's Queer Performativity," *Qui Parle* 19, no. 2 (2011): 150.

4. What I am calling the picturesque ruin is commonly associated with Romanticism. The-odore Ziolkowski, for example, claims that the "fragment and ruin trigger a sense of longing for completion, for fulfillment, that characterizes Romanticism." Theodore Ziolkowski, "Ruminations on Ruins: Classical Versus Romantic," *German Quarterly* 89, no. 3 (2016): 274. Similarly, Andreas Huyssen writes that "nostalgia is never very far when we talk about authenticity or romantic ruins." Andreas Huyssen, "Authentic Ruins: Products of Modernity," in *Ruins of Modernity*, ed. Julia Hell and Andreas Schönle (Duke University Press, 2010), 21.

5. As a heuristic device, I have stipulated the picturesque and prophetic ruin dichoto-mously. However, I should note that a Romantic ruin with aesthetic appeal and that conjures nostalgia may also have a prophetic dimension.

6. William Wordsworth, "The Ruined Cottage," in *William Wordsworth: The Major Works*, ed. Stephen Gill (Oxford University Press, 2008), 31, line 19. Henceforth, references to "The Ruined Cottage" will be embedded in the text.

7. Ralph Waldo Emerson, "Nature," in *Emerson: Essays and Poems*, ed. Harold Bloom, Paul Kane, and Joel Porte (Library of America, 1996), 10.

8. Natalie Diaz, *Postcolonial Love Poem* (Graywolf, 2020), 50.

9. For my account of the new conclusion that Wordsworth added to the poem, which includes what appears to be a callous response by the old man, see Mark Cladis, "The World in Ruins: Wordsworth, Du Bois, and Silko," *Soundings: An Interdisciplinary Journal* 105, no. 4 (2022): 444–45.

10. A similar set of challenges and minglings of affect are posed by the early Wordsworth's heartbreaking poem "Michael"—another site of the prophetic ruin. See Cladis, "The World in Ruins," 445–46.

11. W. E. B. Du Bois, *The Souls of Black Folk*, ed. Brent Hayes Edwards (Oxford University Press, 2007), 88; emphasis added. Henceforth, references to *Souls* will be embedded in the text.

12. Denis Diderot, *Diderot on Art*, trans. John Goodman, 2 vols. (Yale University Press, 1995), 2:198.

13. This language of preserving the stitches and seams was offered to me by Sharon Krause, my colleague at Brown University.

14. Donna J. Haraway, *Staying with the Trouble* (Duke University Press, 2016), 1.

15. For a definition of "just transitions," see "Just Transition: A Framework for Change," Cli-mate Justice Alliance, https://climatejusticealliance.org/just-transition/.

16. For a moving and excellent account of how the lens of the ecological, Romantic Gothic can be employed to attend to the ghosts and ruins of the catastrophic Bhopal 1984 trag-edy in India, see Pramod K. Nayar, *Bhopal's Ecological Gothic: Disaster, Precarity, and the Biopolitical Uncanny* (Lexington, 2017).

17. Thomas Berry, *The Dream of the Earth* (Sierra Club Books, 1988), 123–24.

18. I recognize the complicated history of the word "queer" and note that its reclamation is not accepted by all. I employ the word "queer" in a nonpejorative fashion refer to those who do not identify as cisgender or heterosexual.

19. See Andrew Elfenbein, *Romantic Genius: The Prehistory of a Homosexual Role* (Columbia University Press, 1999); Jean Hagstrum, *The Romantic Body: Love and Sexuality in Keats, Wordsworth, and Blake* (University of Tennessee Press, 1985); Claudia Johnson, *Equivocal*

Beings: Politics, Gender, and Sentimentality in the 1790s (University of Chicago Press, 1995); Christopher C. Nagle, *Sexuality and the Culture of Sensibility in the British Romantic Era* (Palgrave Macmillan, 2007); Eve Kosofsky Sedgwick, *Between Men: English Literature and Male Homosocial Desire* (Columbia University Press, 1985); Richard Sha, *Perverse Romanticism: Aesthetics and Sexuality in Britain, 1750–1832* (Johns Hopkins University Press, 2009); and Douglas A. Vakoch, ed., *Transecology: Transgender Perspectives on Environment and Nature* (Routledge, 2022).

20.   For an excellent if somewhat dated overview of queer Romanticism, see Michael O'Rourke and David Collings, "Introduction: Queer Romanticisms: Past, Present, and Future," *Romanticism on the Net* 36–37 (2004).

21.   Timothy M. Griffiths, " 'O'er Pathless Rocks': Wordsworth, Landscape Aesthetics, and Queer Ecology," *Interdisciplinary Studies in Literature and Environment* 22, no. 2 (2015): 299–300.

22.   Bridget Keegan, "Romantic Labouring-Class Pastoral as Eco-Queer Camp," *Romanticism on the Net* 36–37 (2004).

23.   Colin Carman, "Tiptoeing Through Keats: Teaching Queer Ecology in the Anthropocene," *Romantic Circles*, 2020, https://romantic-circles.org/praxis/anthropocene/praxis.2020.anthropocene.carman.html.

24.   Colin Carman, *The Radical Ecology of the Shelleys: Eros and Environment* (Routledge, 2020), 1, 19, 5; emphasis in original.

25.   Robert Azzarello, *Queer Environmentality: Ecology, Evolution, and Sexuality in American Literature* (Routledge, 2016), 28, 4, 48; emphasis in original.

26.   O'Rourke and Collings, "Introduction: Queer Romanticisms."

27.   Keegan, "Romantic Labouring-Class Pastoral as Eco-Queer Camp"; George Haggerty, "The Horrors of Catholicism: Religion and Sexuality in Gothic Fiction," *Romanticism on the Net* 36–37 (2004); Catriona Mortimer-Sandilands and Bruce Erickson, *Queer Ecologies: Sex, Nature, Politics, Desire* (Indiana University Press, 2010); Jolene Zigarovich, "The Trans Legacy of Frankenstein," *Science Fiction Studies* 45, no. 2 (2018): 260–72; and Vakoch, *Transecology*.

28.   Derek Jarman, *Derek Jarman's Garden* (Thames & Hudson, 2018).

29.   And I am not alone in *reclaiming* Romanticism—to allude to the title of Kate Rigby's marvelous book—and imagining its future. There are contemporary scholars offering powerful, nuanced accounts of Romanticism as a dynamic movement, showing both its past limits and strengths and envisioning its liberatory resources for today's challenges. Kate Rigby, *Reclaiming Romanticism: Towards an Ecopoetics of Decolonization* (Bloomsbury Academic, 2021); Kate Rigby, *Topographies of the Sacred: The Poetics of Place in European Romanticism* (University of Virginia Press, 2004); Jonathan Bate, *Radical Wordsworth: The Poet Who Changed the World* (Yale University Press, 2020); Jonathan Bate, *The Song of the Earth* (Harvard University Press, 2002); Mark Lussier and Bruce Matsunaga, eds., *Engaged Romanticism: Romanticism as Praxis* (Cambridge Scholars Publishing, 2008); James McKusick, *Green Writing: Romanticism and Ecology* (Palgrave, 2010); and Hephzibah Roskelly and Kate Ronald, *Reason to Believe: Romanticism, Pragmatism, and the Teaching of Writing* (State University of New York Press, 1998)—these, among others, are both revealing and creating radical Romanticism.

30. To claim that "beauty, in this tradition, is not principally pretty or sublime vistas" is not to deny the potential solace of the more-than-human. The Wordsworths, Mary Shelley, Zora Neale Hurston, Du Bois, Terry Tempest Williams, and Carolyn Finney (among many others) acknowledge the respite and succor that the beauty of the more-than-human can offer. That some have more access to this form of beauty is an instance of profound injustice.

31. Deborah Bird Rose, "In the Shadow of All This Death," in *Animal Death*, ed. Jay Johnston and Fiona Probyn-Rapsey (Sydney University Press, 2013), 4. Emphasis added.

32. Eva Beatrice Dykes, *The Negro in English Romantic Thought, or A Study of Sympathy for the Oppressed* (Associated Publishers, 1942), 12, 155.

33. Czesław Miłosz, "One More Day," in *New and Collected Poems, 1931–2001* (Ecco, 2001), 419.

34. Deborah Bird Rose, "In the Shadow of All This Death," 5, 10, 12; emphasis added.

Bibliography

Abrams, M. H. *Natural Supernaturalism: Tradition and Revolution in Romantic Literature*. Norton, 1973.

Abu-Jamal, Mumia. *Arts and the Freedom Struggle: The Works of Mumia Abu-Jamal*. Ed. Anthony Bogues and Melaine Ferdinand-King. Brown University catalogue, 2024.

Airey, Jennifer L. *Religion Around Mary Shelley*. Pennsylvania State University Press, 2019.

Alaimo, Stacy. *Bodily Natures: Environment, and the Material Self*. Indiana University Press.

Anderson, M. Kat. *Tending the Wild: Native American Knowledge and the Management of California's Natural Resources*. University of California Press, 2013.

Anidjar, Gil. "Secularism." *Critical Inquiry* 33, no. 1 (2006): 52–77.

Aptheker, Herbert, ed. *Creative Writings by W. E. B. Du Bois: A Pageant, Poems, Short Stories, and Playlets*. Kraus-Thomson, 1985.

Arnold, Ellen L., ed. *Conversations with Leslie Marmon Silko*. University Press of Mississippi, 2000.

Asad, Talal. *Formations of the Secular: Christianity, Islam, Modernity*. Stanford University Press, 2003.

—. *Genealogies of Religion: Discipline and Reasons of Power in Christianity and Islam*. Johns Hopkins University Press, 1993.

Atkinson, Jennifer. "Seeds of Change: The New Place of Gardens in Contemporary Utopia." *Utopian Studies* 18, no. 2 (2007): 237–60.

Azzarello, Robert. *Queer Environmentality: Ecology, Evolution, and Sexuality in American Literature*. Routledge, 2016.

Balfour, Lawrie. *Democracy's Reconstruction: Thinking Politically with W. E. B. Du Bois*. Oxford University Press, 2011.

Balthrop-Lewis, Alda. *Thoreau's Religion: Walden Woods, Social Justice, and the Politics of Asceticism*. Cambridge University Press, 2021.

Barad, Karen. "Nature's Queer Performativity." *Qui Parle* 19, no. 2 (2011): 121–58.

Barry, Brian. *Justice as Impartiality*. Oxford University Press, 1995.

Barth, J. Robert. *The Symbolic Imagination: Coleridge and the Romantic Tradition*. Princeton University Press, 2016.

Basso, Keith. *Wisdom Sits in Places: Landscape and Language Among the Western Apache*. University of New Mexico Press, 1996.

Bate, Jonathan. *Radical Wordsworth: The Poet Who Changed the World*. Yale University Press, 2020.

—. *The Song of the Earth.* Harvard University Press, 2002.

Battle-Baptiste, Whitney, and Britt Rusert, eds. *Data Portraits: Visualizing Black America.* Princeton Architectural Press, 2018.

Beilfuss, Michael J. "Ironic Pastorals and Beautiful Swamps: W. E. B. Du Bois and the Troubled Landscapes of the American South." *Interdisciplinary Studies in Literature and Environment* 22, no. 3 (2015): 485–506.

Bell, Bernard, Emily Grosholz, and James Stewart, eds. *W. E. B. Du Bois on Race and Culture: Philosophy, Politics, and Poetics.* Routledge, 1996.

Bennett, Jane. *Thoreau's Nature: Ethics, Politics, and the Wild.* Rowman & Littlefield, 2002.

—. *Vibrant Matter: A Political Ecology of Things.* Duke University Press, 2010.

Bennett, Michael. "Anti-Pastoralism, Frederick Douglass, and the Nature of Slavery." In *Beyond Nature Writing: Expanding the Boundaries of Ecocriticism,* ed. Karla Armbruster and Kathleen R. Wallace, 195–210. University of Virginia Press, 2001.

Berger, Peter L., ed. *The Desecularization of the World: Resurgent Religion and World Politics.* Eerdmans, 1999.

Berlant, Lauren. *Cruel Optimism.* Duke University Press, 2011.

Berleant, Arnold. *The Aesthetics of Environment.* Temple University Press, 1992.

Berlin, Isaiah. *The Crooked Timber of Humanity.* Ed. Henry Hardy. Princeton University Press, 2013.

Berry, Thomas. *The Dream of the Earth.* Sierra Club Books, 1988.

Berry, Wendell. *The Art of the Commonplace: The Agrarian Essays of Wendell Berry.* Ed. Norman Wirzba. Counterpoint, 2002.

Bhargava, Rajeev, ed. *Secularism and Its Critics.* Oxford University Press, 1998.

Bialek, Fannie. "Incredulity and the Realization of Vulnerability, or, How It Feels to Learn from Wounds." *Political Theology* (2023), http://doi.org/10.1080/1462317X.2023.2185187.

Billing, Andrew Geoffry. "Rousseau's Critique of Market Society: Property and Possessive Individualism in the *Discours sur l'inégalité.*" *Journal of European Studies* 48, no. 1 (2018): 3–19.

Birkle, Carmen. "Travelogues of Independence: Margaret Fuller and Henry David Thoreau." *Amerikastudien / American Studies* 48, no. 4 (2003): 497–512.

Bladow, Kyle, and Jennifer Ladino, eds. *Affective Ecocriticism: Emotion, Embodiment, Environment.* University of Nebraska Press, 2018.

Blanning, Tim. *The Romantic Revolution: A History.* Modern Library, 2012.

Bloom, Harold. *The Visionary Company: A Reading of English Romantic Poetry.* Cornell University Press, 1971.

Boisseron, Bénédicte. *Afro-Dog: Blackness and the Animal Question.* Columbia University Press, 2018.

Bourdieu, Pierre. *Distinction: A Social Critique of the Judgement of Taste.* Harvard University Press, 1984.

Boutet, Danielle. "Metaphors of the Mind." In *Carnal Knowledge,* ed. Estelle Barrett and Barbara Bolt, 29–39. I. B. Tauris, 2013.

Brio, Andrew. *Denaturalizing Ecological Politics: Alienation from Nature from Rousseau to the Frankfurt School and Beyond.* University of Toronto Press, 2005.

Bromell, Nick. "W. E. B. Du Bois and the Enlargement of Democratic Theory." *Raritan* 30, no. 4 (2011): 140–61.

Bromwich, David. *A Choice of Inheritance: Self and Community from Edmund Burke to Robert Frost.* Harvard University Press, 1989.

—. "Moral Imagination." *Raritan* 27, no. 4 (2008): 4–33.

Brown, C. G. "A Revisionist Approach to Religious Change." In *Religion and Modernization*, ed. Steve Bruce, 31–58. Clarendon, 1992.

Brugge, Doug, Timothy Benally, and Esther Yazzie-Lewis, eds. *The Navajo People and Uranium Mining.* University of New Mexico Press, 2006.

Burke, Edmund. "To Charles-Jean-François Depont (November 1789)." In *On Empire, Liberty, and Reform: Speeches and Letters*, ed. David Bromwich, 401–14. Yale University Press, 2000.

Butler, Octavia. "A Few Rules for Predicting the Future." *Essence Magazine* 31, no. 1 (2000): 165–66, 264.

—. *Parable of the Sower.* Grand Central, 2019.

Carman, Colin. *The Radical Ecology of the Shelleys: Eros and Environment.* Routledge, 2020.

—. "Tiptoeing Through Keats: Teaching Queer Ecology in the Anthropocene." *Romantic Circles*, 2020, https://romantic-circles.org/praxis/anthropocene/praxis.2020.anthropocene .carman.html.

Casanova, José. *Public Religions in the Modern World.* University of Chicago Press, 1994.

Chandler, James. *Wordsworth's Second Nature: A Study of the Poetry and Politics.* University of Chicago Press, 1984.

Claborn, John. *Civil Rights and the Environment in African-American Literature, 1895–1941.* Bloomsbury Academic, 2018.

Cladis, Mark. "Durkheim and Foucault on Education and Punishment." In *Durkheim and Foucault: Perspectives on Education and Punishment*, ed. Mark Cladis, 3–18. Berghahn, 2001.

—. "The End of the Private Life: Rousseau, Redemption, and Tragedy." *Soundings: An Interdisciplinary Journal* 84, no. 1/2 (2001): 51–77.

—. *Public Vision, Private Lives: Rousseau, Religion, and Twenty-First-Century Democracy.* Columbia University Press, 2006.

—. "Radical Romanticism: Democracy, Religion, and the Environmental Imagination." *Soundings: An Interdisciplinary Journal* 97, no. 1 (2014): 21–49.

—. "Religion, Democracy, and Virtue: Emerson and the Journey's End." *Religion & Literature* 41, no. 1 (2009): 49–82.

—. "Religion, Secularism, and Democratic Culture." *The Good Society: The Journal of Political Economy of the Good Society* 19, no. 2 (2010): 22–29.

—. "Secularism and the Liberal Arts: The Good, the Bad, and the Ugly." *The Immanent Frame*, 2011, http://tif.ssrc.org/2011/01/05/the-good-the-bad-and-the-ugly/.

—. "The World in Ruins: Wordsworth, Du Bois, and Silko." *Soundings: An Interdisciplinary Journal* 105, no. 4 (2022): 440–67.

Clark, Brett, and John Bellamy Foster. "Land, the Color Line, and the Quest of the Golden Fleece." *Organization & Environment* 16, no. 4 (2003): 459–69.

Climate Justice Alliance. "Just Transition: A Framework for Change." https://climatejusticealliance .org/just-transition/.

Coleridge, Samuel Taylor. *Coleridge's Poetry and Prose.* Ed. Nicholas Halmi, Paul Magnuson, and Raimonda Modiano. Norton, 2004.

——. *Collected Letters of Samuel Taylor Coleridge.* Vol. 1: *1785–1800.* Ed. Earl Leslie Griggs. Clarendon, 1966.

——. *Samuel Taylor Coleridge: The Major Works.* Ed. H. J. Jackson. Oxford University Press, 2008.

Connolly, William E. *Facing the Planetary: Entangled Humanism and the Politics of Swarming.* Duke University Press, 2017.

——. *Why I Am Not a Secularist.* University of Minnesota Press, 1999.

Crocker, Lester. "Order and Disorder in Rousseau's Social Thought." *PMLA* 94, no. 2 (1979): 247–60.

Cronon, William. "The Trouble with Wilderness: Or, Getting Back to the Wrong Nature." *Environmental History* 1, no. 1 (1996): 7–28.

Cross, Susan. "Revolutionary Gardens." *American Art* 25, no. 2 (2011): 30–33.

Currie, Robert, Alan Gilbert, and Lee Horsley. *Churches and Churchgoers: Patterns of Church Growth in the British Isles Since 1700.* Clarendon, 1977.

Darnton, Robert. *The Great Cat Massacre and Other Episodes in French Cultural History.* Basic Books, 1984.

Davis, Heather, and Zoe Todd. "On the Importance of a Date, or Decolonizing the Anthropocene." *ACME* 16, no. 4 (2017): 761–80.

Dawkins, Richard. "Is Science a Religion?" *The Humanist* (1997), http://www.skeptical-science .com/essays/science-religion-richard-dawkins/.

Dewey, John. *Art as Experience.* Penguin, 2005.

Diaby, Bakary. "Black Women and/in the Shadow of Romanticism." *European Romantic Review* 30, no. 3 (2019): 249–54.

Diaz, Natalie. *Postcolonial Love Poem.* Graywolf, 2020.

Dickinson, Emily. *The Complete Poems of Emily Dickinson.* Ed. Thomas H. Johnson. Little, Brown, 1960.

Diderot, Denis. *Diderot on Art.* Vol. 2: *The Salon of 1767.* Trans. John Goodman. Yale University Press, 1995.

Dixon, Melvin. *Ride Out the Wilderness: Geography and Identity in Afro-American Literature.* University of Illinois Press, 1987.

Douglass, Frederick. *Autobiographies.* Ed. Henry Louis Gates Jr. Library of America, 1994.

——. "The Color Line." *North American Review* 132, no. 295 (1881): 567–77.

Du Bois, W. E. B. *The Autobiography of W. E. B. Du Bois.* International Publishers, 1968.

——. *Darkwater: Voices from Within the Veil.* Ed. Henry Louis Gates Jr. Oxford University Press, 2007.

——. *Du Bois: Writings.* Ed. Nathan Huggins. Library of America, 1986.

——. *Dusk of Dawn.* Ed. Henry Louis Gates Jr. Oxford University Press, 2007.

——. *The Quest Of The Silver Fleece.* Ed. Henry Louis Gates Jr. Oxford University Press, 2007.

——. *The Souls of Black Folk.* Ed. Brent Hayes Edwards. Oxford University Press, 2007.

——. *A World Search for Democracy,* c. 1937. W. E. B. Du Bois Papers (MS 312), Special Collections and University Archives, University of Massachusetts Amherst Libraries.

Dungy, Camille T., ed. *Black Nature: Four Centuries of African American Nature Poetry.* University of Georgia, 2009.

Duran, Jane. "Margaret Fuller and Transcendental Feminism." *Pluralist* 5, no. 1 (2010): 65–72.

Duvergier, J. B., ed. *Collection complète des lois, décrets, ordonnances, règlements, avis du conseil-d'état.* Vol. 13. Guyot et Scribe, 1836.

Dykes, Eva Beatrice. *The Negro in English Romantic Thought, or A Study of Sympathy for the Oppressed.* Associated Publishers, 1942.

Edelman, Lee. *No Future: Queer Theory and the Death Drive.* Duke University Press, 2004.

Elbert, Monika. "Haunting Transcendentalist Landscapes: EcoGothic Politics in Margaret Fuller's *Summer on the Lakes.*" *Text Matters* 6, no. 6 (2016): 53–73.

Elder, Arlene A. "Swamp Versus Plantation: Symbolic Structure in W. E. B. DuBois' *The Quest of the Silver Fleece.*" *Phylon* 34, no. 4 (1973): 358–67.

Elfenbein, Andrew. *Romantic Genius: The Prehistory of a Homosexual Role.* Columbia University Press, 1999.

Emerson, Ralph Waldo. *Ralph Waldo Emerson: Essays and Poems.* Ed. Harold Bloom, Paul Kane, and Joel Porte. Library of America, 1996.

Engell, James. *The Creative Imagination: Enlightenment to Romanticism.* Harvard University Press, 1981.

Ensor, Sarah. "Terminal Regions: Queer Eroticism at the End." In *Against Life*, ed. Alastair Hunt and Stephanie Youngblood, 41–62. Northwestern University Press, 2016.

Erdrich, Louise. *Future Home of the Living God.* Harper Perennial, 2017.

Feder, Helena. *Ecocriticism and the Idea of Culture: Biology and the Bildungsroman.* Routledge, 2014.

Fisher, Mark. *Capitalist Realism: Is There No Alternative?* Zero Books, 2009.

Forstadt, Jillian. "'Make Farmers Black Again': African Americans Fight Discrimination to Own Farmland." *NPR*, August 25, 2020, https://www.npr.org/2020/08/25/904284865/make-farmers-black-again-african-americans-fight-discrimination-to-own-farmland.

Foucault, Michel. *Discipline and Punish: The Birth of the Prison.* Vintage, 1995.

Fuller, Margaret. *Summer on the Lakes, in 1843.* University of Illinois Press, 1991.

——. *"These Sad but Glorious Days": Dispatches from Europe, 1846–1850.* Ed. Larry J. Reynolds and Susan Belasco Smith. Yale University Press, 1991.

——. *Woman in the Nineteenth Century.* Norton, 1998.

Gaull, Marilyn. "Radical Imaginings: Mary Shelley's 'The Last Man.'" *The Wordsworth Circle* 26, no. 3 (1995): 147–52.

Gaustad, Edwin S. *Proclaim Liberty Throughout All the Land: A History of Church and State in America.* Oxford University Press, 2003.

Gay, Peter. *The Enlightenment: An Interpretation.* Norton, 1995.

Geriguis, Lina L. "W. E. B. Du Bois's *The Souls of Black Folk*, Chapter 11." *Explicator* 68, no. 2 (2010): 111–14.

Gibson-Graham, J. K. *A Postcapitalist Politics.* University of Minnesota Press, 2006.

Gikandi, Simon. "W. E. B. DuBois and the Identity of Africa." *Journal of African Studies* 2, no. 1 (2005), http://hdl.handle.net/2027/spo.4761563.0002.101.

Gill, Stephen, ed. *The Cambridge Companion to Wordsworth.* Cambridge University Press, 2003.

Glavey, Brian. *The Wallflower Avant-Garde: Modernism, Sexuality, and Queer Ekphrasis.* Oxford University Press, 2015.

Goddard, H. C. "Unitarianism and Transcendentalism." In *American Transcendentalism: An Anthology of Criticism*, ed. Brian M. Barbour, 159–77. Notre Dame University Press, 1973.

Gómez-Barris, Macarena. *The Extractive Zone: Social Ecologies and Decolonial Perspectives.* Duke University Press, 2017.

Goodman, Russell B. *American Philosophy and the Romantic Tradition.* Cambridge University Press, 1990.

Gordon, Lewis R. "Fanon's Decolonial Aesthetic." In *The Aesthetic Turn in Political Thought,* ed. Nikolas Kompridis, 91–112. Bloomsbury Academic, 2014.

Gorski, Philip S., David Kim, John Torpey, and Jonathan VanAntwerpen, eds. *The Post-Secular in Question: Religion in Contemporary Society.* New York University Press, 2012.

Grewal, Gurleen. "Beholding 'A Great Tree in Leaf': Eros, Nature, and the Visionary in *Their Eyes Were Watching God.*" In *"The Inside Light": New Critical Essays on Zora Neale Hurston,* ed. Deborah G. Plant, 103–12. Praeger, 2010.

Griffiths, Timothy M. "'O'er Pathless Rocks': Wordsworth, Landscape Aesthetics, and Queer Ecology." *Interdisciplinary Studies in Literature and Environment* 22, no. 2 (2015): 284–302.

Gustafson, Sandra M. "Choosing a Medium: Margaret Fuller and the Forms of Sentiment." *American Quarterly* 47, no. 1 (1995): 34–65.

Gutkind, Lee. *You Can't Make This Stuff Up: The Complete Guide to Writing Creative Nonfiction.* Lifelong Books, 2012.

Guyer, Paul. "Feeling and Freedom: Kant on Aesthetics and Morality." *Journal of Aesthetics and Art Criticism* 48, no. 2 (1990): 137–46.

Haggerty, George. "The Horrors of Catholicism: Religion and Sexuality in Gothic Fiction." *Romanticism on the Net* 36–37 (2004).

Hagstrum, Jean H. *The Romantic Body: Love and Sexuality in Keats, Wordsworth, and Blake.* University of Tennessee Press, 1985.

Halberstam, Jack. "The Wild Beyond: With and for the Undercommons." Introduction to *The Undercommons: Fugitive Planning & Black Study,* by Stefano Harney and Fred Moten, 5–12. Minor Compositions, 2013.

Hamburger, Philip. *Separation of Church and State.* University of Harvard Press, 2002.

Haraway, Donna J. *Staying with the Trouble.* Duke University Press, 2016.

Hardin-Martin, Amanda. "Dreaming with Du Bois: The Niagara Movement & Making Historical Black Landscapes." Conference presentation at the (Re)thinking Landscape: Ways of Knowing / Ways of Being Conference, Yale University, New Haven, CT, September 30, 2022.

Harris, Melanie L. "Ecowomanism: Black Women, Religion, and the Environment." *Black Scholar* 46, no. 3 (2016): 27–39.

Harris, Sam. *The End of Faith: Religion, Terror, and the Future of Reason.* Norton, 2005.

Harris-Perry, Melissa. *Sister Citizen: Shame, Stereotypes, and Black Women in America.* Yale University Press, 2013.

Hartman, Saidiya. *Scenes of Subjection: Terror, Slavery, and Self-Making in Nineteenth-Century America.* Oxford University Press, 1997.

Harvey, Marcus. "'Hard Skies' and Bottomless Questions: Zora Neale Hurston's *Their Eyes Were Watching God* and Epistemological 'Opacity' in Black Religious Experience." *Journal of Africana Religions* 4, no. 2 (2016): 186–214.

Harvey, Samantha. *Transatlantic Transcendentalism: Coleridge, Emerson, and Nature.* Edinburgh University Press, 2013.

Healey, Kathleen. "'The Mighty Meaning of the Scene': Feminine Landscapes and the Future of America in Margaret Fuller's *Summer on the Lakes, in 1843*." *Humanities* 8, no. 31 (2019): 1–16.

Hicks, Scott. "W. E. B. Du Bois, Booker T. Washington, and Richard Wright: Toward an Eco-criticism of Color." *Callaloo* 29, no. 1 (2006): 202–22.

Hill, Alan G., ed. *The Letters of William and Dorothy Wordsworth.* 2nd ed. Vol. 5: *The Later Years: Part II: 1829–34.* Clarendon, 1979.

Hirsch, E. D., Jr. "The Roots of the Education Wars." In *The Great Curriculum Debate: How Should We Teach Reading and Math?*, ed. Thomas Loveless, 13–24. Brookings Institution Press, 2004.

Hodges, Devon. "*Frankenstein* and the Feminine Subversion of the Novel." *Tulsa Studies in Women's Literature* 2, no. 2 (1983): 155–64.

Hogle, Jerrold E. "The Gothic-Romantic Nexus: Wordsworth, Coleridge, *Splice*, and *The Ring*." *The Wordsworth Circle* 43, no. 3 (2012): 159–65.

Holland, Sharon Patricia. *The Erotic Life of Racism.* Duke University Press, 2012.

Hoyt, Nelly S., and Thomas Cassirer, trans. *The Encyclopedia: Selections: Diderot, d'Alembert, and a Society of Men of Letters.* Bobbs-Merrill, 1965.

Hume, David. *Treatise of Human Nature.* Vol. 1: *Texts.* Ed. David Norton and Mary Norton. Clarendon, 2007.

Hunter, Marcus Anthony. "W. E. B. Du Bois and Black Heterogeneity: How *The Philadelphia Negro* Shaped American Sociology." *American Sociologist* 46, no. 2 (2015): 219–33.

Hurston, Zora Neale. "Crazy for This Democracy." In *Available Means: An Anthology of Women's Rhetoric(s)*, ed. Joy Ritchie and Kate Ronald, 248–51. University of Pittsburgh Press, 2001.

——. *Their Eyes Were Watching God.* Harper and Row, 1990.

Huyssen, Andreas. "Authentic Ruins: Products of Modernity." In *Ruins of Modernity*, ed. Julia Hell and Andreas Schönle, 17–28. Duke University Press, 2010.

Hyest, Jenny. "'Born with God in the House': Feminist Vision and Religious Revision in the Works of Zora Neale Hurston." *Legacy* 35, no. 1 (2018): 25–47.

Jager, Colin. *The Book of God: Secularization and Design in the Romantic Era.* University of Pennsylvania Press, 2007.

James, Jennifer C. "A Theory of the Bottom: Black Ecofeminism as Politics." *Resilience: A Journal of the Environmental Humanities* 10, no. 1–2 (2022/2023): 46–52.

James, William. *The Varieties of Religious Experience: A Study in Human Nature.* Penguin, 1982.

Jarman, Derek. *Derek Jarman's Garden.* Thames & Hudson, 2018.

——, dir. *The Garden.* Basilisk Communications, 1990. DVD.

Johnson, Claudia. *Equivocal Beings: Politics, Gender, and Sentimentality in the 1790s.* University of Chicago Press, 1995.

Johnson, Terrence L. *Tragic Soul-Life: W. E. B. Du Bois and the Moral Crisis Facing American Democracy.* Oxford University Press, 2012.

Johnston, Kenneth R. "Wordsworth and *The Recluse*." In *Cambridge Companion to Wordsworth*, ed. Stephen Gill, 70–89. Cambridge University Press, 2003.

Joo, Hee-Jung Serenity. "Racial Impossibility and Critical Failure in W. E. B. Du Bois's *Darkwater*." *Science Fiction Studies* 46, no. 1 (2019): 106–26.

Kahn, Jonathon S. *Divine Discontent: The Religious Imagination of W. E. B. Du Bois.* Oxford University Press, 2011.

Keane, Jondi. "Æffect: Initiating Heuristic Life." In *Carnal Knowledge*, ed. Estelle Barrett and Barbara Bolt, 41–61. I. B. Tauris, 2013.

Keegan, Bridget. "Romantic Labouring-Class Pastoral as Eco-Queer Camp." *Romanticism on the Net* 36–37 (2004).

Keller, Catherine. *Cloud of the Impossible: Negative Theology and Planetary Entanglement.* Columbia University Press, 2015.

Kennedy, Scott Hamilton, dir. *The Garden.* Black Valley Films, 2008, https://www.kanopy.com /en/product/garden?vp=utep.

Kimmerer, Robin Wall. *Braiding Sweetgrass: Indigenous Wisdom, Scientific Knowledge, and the Teachings of Plants.* Milkweed Editions, 2013.

——. "*Mishkos Kenomagwen*, the Lessons of Grass: Restoring Reciprocity with the Good Green Earth." In *Traditional Ecological Knowledge: Learning from Indigenous Practices for Environmental Sustainability*, ed. Melissa K. Nelson and Dan Shilling, 27–56. Cambridge University Press, 2018.

Kittay, Eva. *Love's Labor: Essays on Women, Equality and Dependency.* Routledge, 1999.

Kittay, Eva, and Licia Carlson, eds. *Cognitive Disability and Its Challenge to Moral Philosophy.* Wiley-Blackwell, 2010.

Kolodny, Annette. "Inventing a Feminist Discourse: Rhetoric and Resistance in Margaret Fuller's *Woman in the Nineteenth Century*." *New Literary History* 25, no. 2 (1994): 355–82.

Krause, Sharon. *Civil Passions: Moral Sentiment and Democratic Deliberation.* Princeton University Press, 2008.

——. *Eco-Emancipation: An Earthly Politics of Freedom.* Princeton University Press, 2023.

Kuletz, Valerie. "Invisible Spaces, Violent Places: Cold War Nuclear and Militarized Landscapes." In *Violent Environments*, ed. Nancy Lee Peluso and Michael Watts, 237–60. Cornell University Press, 2001.

Kundera, Milan. *The Unbearable Lightness of Being.* Harper Perennial, 2009.

Kusch, Manfred. "The River and the Garden: Basic Spatial Models in *Candide* and *La Nouvelle Heloise*." *Eighteenth-Century Studies* 12, no. 1 (1978): 1–15.

LaFreniere, Gilbert F. "Rousseau and the European Roots of Environmentalism." *Environmental History Review* 14, no. 4 (1990): 41–72.

Lane, Joseph H., Jr. "Jean-Jacques Rousseau: The Disentangling of Green Paradoxes." In *Engaging Nature: Environmentalism and the Political Theory Canon*, ed. Peter Cannavò and Joseph H. Lane Jr., 133–52. MIT Press, 2014.

——. "Reverie and the Return to Nature: Rousseau's Experience of Convergence." *Review of Politics* 68, no. 3 (2006): 474–99.

Laskey, Allison Blackmond. "Of Forms and Flow: Movement Through Structure in *Darkwater's* Composition." *New Centennial Review* 15, no. 2 (2015): 107–18.

Latour, Bruno. *Facing Gaia: Eight Lectures on the New Climatic Regime.* Polity, 2017.

Lear, Jonathan. *Radical Hope: Ethics in the Face of Cultural Devastation.* Harvard University Press, 2006.

Lee, Debbie. *Slavery and the Romantic Imagination.* University of Pennsylvania Press, 2002.

Leiker, James. "Great Books: *Frankenstein* by Mary Shelley." YouTube video, October 11, 2018, https://youtu.be/Za5K_Q7Arc8.

Lemons, Gary L. "Womanism in the Name of the 'Father': W. E. B. Du Bois and the Problematics of Race, Patriarchy, and Art." *Phylon* 49, no. 3/4 (2001): 185–202.

Leopold, Aldo. *A Sand County Almanac and Sketches Here and There.* Oxford University Press, 1987.

Lewis, David Levering. *W. E. B. Du Bois: Biography of a Race.* Henry Holt, 1993.

——. *W. E. B. Du Bois: The Fight for Equality and the American Century.* Henry Holt, 2000.

Liboiron, Max. *Pollution Is Colonialism.* Duke University Press, 2021.

Lloyd, Sheila. "Du Bois and the Production of the Racial Picturesque." *Public Culture* 17, no. 2 (2005): 277–97.

Lockhart, Isabel. "Intimacies of the Atom: On Rocks and Decolonization in the Work of Leslie Marmon Silko." *American Quarterly* 72, no. 3 (2020): 675–96.

Lopez, Barry. *Crossing Open Ground.* Vintage, 1988.

Lorde, Audre. *Sister Outsider: Essays and Speeches by Audre Lorde.* Crossing, 2007.

Lukacs, Paul. *Inventing Wine.* Norton, 2012.

——. "Matters of Taste." *The American Scholar*, June 8, 2015, https://theamericanscholar.org/matters-of-taste/.

Lussier, Mark, and Bruce Matsunaga, eds. *Engaged Romanticism: Romanticism as Praxis.* Cambridge Scholars, 2008.

Machado, Carmen Maria. *Her Body and Other Parties.* Graywolf, 2017.

MacIntyre, Alasdair. *After Virtue.* University of Notre Dame Press, 1984.

——. *Whose Justice? Which Rationality?* University of Notre Dame Press, 1988.

Macy, Joanna. "The Greening of the Self." In *Dharma Gaia: A Harvest of Essays in Buddhism and Ecology,* ed. Allan Hunt Badiner, 53–63. Parallax, 1990.

Mahmood, Saba. "Religious Reasons and Secular Affect: An Incommensurable Divide?" In *Is Critique Secular? Blasphemy, Injury, and Free Speech,* ed. Talal Asad, Wendy Brown, Judith Butler, and Saba Mahmood, 58–94. Fordham University Press, 2013.

Matlak, Richard E. "Classical Argument and Romantic Persuasion in 'Tintern Abbey.'" *Studies in Romanticism* 25, no. 1 (1986): 97–129.

Matteson, John. *The Lives of Margaret Fuller: A Biography.* Norton, 2012.

Mayer, Jed. "The Weird Ecologies of Mary Shelley's *Frankenstein.*" *Science Fiction Studies* 45, no. 2 (2018): 229–43.

McGann, Jerome J. *The Romantic Ideology: A Critical Investigation.* University of Chicago Press, 1983.

McKusick, James. *Green Writing: Romanticism and Ecology.* Palgrave Macmillan, 2010.

Meagher, Thomas. "*Darkwater*'s Existentialist Socialism." *Socialism and Democracy* 32, no. 3 (2018): 81–104.

Mellor, Anne K. *Mary Shelley: Her Life, Her Fiction, Her Monsters.* Methuen, 1988.

Merchant, Carolyn. *Death of Nature: Women, Ecology, and the Scientific Revolution.* HarperOne, 1990.

Mileur, Jean-Pierre. *Vision and Revision: Coleridge's Art of Immanence.* University of California Press, 1982.

Miłosz, Czesław. *New and Collected Poems, 1931–2001.* Ecco, 2001.

Minister, Kevin. "Public Religious Aesthetics: Theorizing the Affect and Import of Interreligious Aesthetics." Paper presented at the 2016 annual meeting of the American Academy of Religion, San Antonio, TX, November 19, 2016.

Mocci, Serena. "Addressing Racial Conflict in Antebellum America: Women and Native Americans in Lydia Maria Child's and Margaret Fuller's Literary Works." *Journal of American History and Politics* 3, no. 1 (2020): 1–16.

Montaigne, Michel de. *The Complete Essays of Montaigne.* Trans. Donald Frame. Stanford University Press, 1958.

Mortimer-Sandilands, Catriona, and Bruce Erickson. *Queer Ecologies: Sex, Nature, Politics, Desire.* Indiana University Press, 2010.

Morton, Timothy. "Romantic Disaster Ecology: Blake, Shelley, Wordsworth." *Romantic Circles*, 2012, https://romantic-circles.org/index.php/praxis/disaster/praxis.2012.disaster.morton.

Murray, Caleb. "Feeling a Failing Climate: Tragedy, Affect, and Religious Storytelling in Literature and Film." PhD diss., Brown University, 2023.

Nagle, Christopher C. *Sexuality and the Culture of Sensibility in the British Romantic Era.* Palgrave Macmillan, 2007.

Nayar, Pramod K. *Bhopal's Ecological Gothic: Disaster, Precarity, and the Biopolitical Uncanny.* Lexington, 2017.

Nixon, Rob. *Slow Violence and the Environmentalism of the Poor.* Harvard University Press, 2011.

Oliver, Lawrence J. "Apocalyptic and Slow Violence: The Environmental Vision of W. E. B. Du Bois's *Darkwater.*" *Interdisciplinary Studies in Literature and Environment* 22, no. 3 (2015): 466–84.

O'Rourke, Michael, and David Collings. "Introduction: Queer Romanticisms: Past, Present, and Future." *Romanticism on the Net* 36–37 (2004).

Outka, Paul. *Race and Nature from Transcendentalism to the Harlem Renaissance.* Palgrave, 2008.

Packer, Barbara L. "Romanticism." In *The Oxford Handbook of Transcendentalism,* ed. Joel Myerson, Sandra Harbert Petrulions, and Laura Dassow Walls, 84–101. Oxford University Press, 2012.

Page, Judith. *Wordsworth and the Cultivation of Women.* University of California Press, 1994.

Parrish, Susan Scott. "Zora Neale Hurston and the Environmental Ethic of Risk." In *American Studies, Ecocriticism, and Citizenship: Thinking and Acting in the Local and Global Commons,* ed. Joni Adamson and Kimberly N. Ruffin, 21–36. Routledge, 2013.

Pasternak, July. "A Peril That Dwelt Among the Navajos." *Los Angeles Times,* November 9, 2006.

Paz, Alfredo de. "Innovation and Modernity." In *Literary Criticism: Romanticism,* ed. Marshall Brown, 29–48. Cambridge University Press, 2000.

Perkins, Mary Anne. "Religious Thinker." In *Cambridge Companion to Coleridge,* ed. Lucy Newlyn, 187–200. Cambridge University Press, 2002.

Pierce, Yolanda. "The Soul of Du Bois' Black Folk." *The North Star: A Journal of African American Religious History* 7, no. 1 (2003): 1–4.

Pollan, Michael. *Second Nature: A Gardener's Education.* Grove, 1991.

Posmentier, Sonya. *Cultivation and Catastrophe: The Lyric Ecology of Modern Black Literature.* Johns Hopkins University Press, 2017.

Priestman, Martin. *Romantic Atheism: Poetry and Free Thought.* Cambridge University Press, 1999.

Putnam, Michael. "Reverence the Stones: The Ethics of Environmental Attention." PhD diss., Brown University, forthcoming.

Rampersad, Arnold. *The Art and Imagination of W. E. B. Du Bois.* Schocken, 1990.

Rancière, Jacques. *The Politics of Aesthetics: The Distribution of the Sensible.* Continuum, 2004.

Rath, Richard Cullen. "Echo and Narcissus: The Afrocentric Pragmatism of W. E. B. Du Bois." *Journal of American History* 84, no. 2 (1997): 461–95.

Richards, I. A. *Principles of Literary Criticism.* Routledge and Kegan Paul Classics, 1924.

Rigby, Kate. "Ecocriticism." In *Introducing Criticism in the 21st Century*, ed. Julian Wolfreys, 122–54. Edinburgh University Press, 2015.

——. *Reclaiming Romanticism: Towards an Ecopoetics of Decolonization*. Bloomsbury Academic, 2021.

——. *Topographies of the Sacred: The Poetics of Place in European Romanticism*. University of Virginia Press, 2004.

Riley, Shamara Shantu. "Ecology Is a Sistah's Issue Too: The Politics of Emergent Afrocentric Ecowomanism." In *This Sacred Earth: Religion, Nature, Environment*, ed. Roger S. Gottlieb, 412–27. Routledge, 2003.

Roe, Nicholas. *Wordsworth and Coleridge: The Radical Years*. Oxford University Press, 1988.

Rogers, Melvin L. *The Darkened Light of Faith: Race, Democracy, and Freedom in African American Political Thought*. Princeton University Press, 2023.

——. "David Walker and the Political Power of the Appeal." *Political Theory* 43, no. 2 (2015): 208–33.

——. "The People, Rhetoric, and Affect: On the Political Force of Du Bois' *The Souls of Black Folk*." *American Political Science Review* 106, no. 1 (2012): 188–203.

Rorty, Richard. *Philosophy and Social Hope*. Penguin, 1999.

——. *Philosophy as Cultural Politics*. Cambridge University Press, 2007.

——. "Religion in the Public Square: A Reconsideration." *Journal of Religious Ethics* 31, no. 1 (2003): 141–49.

Rose, Deborah Bird. "In the Shadow of All This Death." In *Animal Death*, ed. Jay Johnston and Fiona Probyn-Rapsey, 1–20. Sydney University Press, 2013.

Roskelly, Hephzibah, and Kate Ronald. *Reason to Believe: Romanticism, Pragmatism, and the Teaching of Writing*. State University of New York Press, 1998.

Rousseau, Jean-Jacques. *The Confessions*. Trans. J. M. Cohen. Penguin, 1953.

——. *The Confessions and Correspondence, Including the Letters to Malesherbes*. Trans. Christopher Kelly. University Press of New England, 1995.

——. *Emile, or Education*. Trans. Barbara Foxley. J. M. Dent, 1911.

——. *Emile, or On Education*. Trans. Allan Bloom. Basic Books, 1979.

——. *Julie, or the New Heloise: Letters of Two Lovers Who Live in a Small Town at the Foot of the Alps*. Trans. Philip Stewart and Jean Vaché. University Press of New England, 1997.

——. *The Social Contract and Discourses*. Trans. G. D. H. Cole, rev. J. H. Brumfitt and John C. Hall. Dent, 1988.

Ruffin, Kimberly N. *Black on Earth: African American Ecoliterary Traditions*. University of Georgia Press, 2010.

Ryan, Robert M. *The Romantic Reformation: Religious Politics in English Literature, 1789–1824*. Cambridge University Press, 2004.

Sandilands, Catriona. *Rising Tides: Reflections for Climate Changing Times*. Caitlin, 2019.

Sandler, Matt. *The Black Romantic Revolution: Abolitionist Poets at the End of Slavery*. Verso, 2020.

Schmitt, Carl. *Political Romanticism*. MIT Press, 1986.

Schneider, Richard. *Civilizing Thoreau: Human Ecology and the Emerging Social Sciences in the Major Works*. Camden House, 2016.

Schulenberg, Ulf. *Romanticism and Pragmatism: Richard Rorty and the Idea of a Poeticized Culture*. Palgrave Macmillan, 2015.

Scott, Austin. "The 'Nature' of Rousseau: Towards an Understanding and Amelioration of the Human Relationship to the Environment." Paper presented at the annual meeting of the Western Political Science Association, San Diego, CA, March 20, 2008.

Sedgwick, Eve Kosofsky. *Between Men: English Literature and Male Homosocial Desire.* Columbia University Press, 1985.

Sentilles, Sarah. *Draw Your Weapons.* Random House, 2017.

Seymour, Nicole. *Bad Environmentalism: Irony and Irreverence in the Ecological Age.* University of Minnesota Press, 2018.

Sha, Richard. *Perverse Romanticism: Aesthetics and Sexuality in Britain, 1750–1832.* Johns Hopkins University Press, 2009.

Shaw, Amber. "'Like the Incense of a Bad Heart': The Ethics of Industry in Sophia Hawthorne's and Margaret Fuller's English Travelogues." *Nathaniel Hawthorne Review* 41, no. 1 (2015): 75–95.

Shaw-Taylor, Leigh. "Parliamentary Enclosure and the Emergence of an English Agricultural Proletariat." *Journal of Economic History* 61, no. 3 (2001): 640–62.

Shelley, Mary. *Frankenstein, or the Modern Prometheus: The 1818 Text.* Ed. Marilyn Butler. Oxford University Press, 2008.

——. *Frankenstein: Annotated for Scientists, Engineers, and Creators of All Kinds.* Ed. David H. Guston, Ed Finn, and Jason Scott Robert. MIT Press, 2017.

——. *The Last Man.* Ed. Morton D. Paley. Oxford University Press, 1998.

Shelley, Percy Bysshe. *Shelley's Poetry and Prose.* Ed. Donald H. Reiman and Neil Fraistat. Norton, 2002.

Shewry, Teresa. *Hope at Sea: Possible Ecologies in Oceanic Literature.* University of Minnesota Press, 2015.

Shutkin, William A. *The Land That Could Be: Environmentalism and Democracy in the Twenty-First Century.* MIT Press, 2000.

Silko, Leslie Marmon. *Almanac of the Dead.* Penguin, 1992.

——. *Ceremony.* Penguin, 1986.

——. *Gardens in the Dunes.* Simon and Schuster, 1999.

——. "Landscape, History, and the Pueblo Imagination." In *At Home on the Earth: Becoming Native to Our Place,* ed. David Landis Barnhill, 30–42. University of California Press, 1999.

——. "Leslie Marmon Silko Saw It Coming." Interview by Ismail Ibrahim. *New Yorker,* April 16, 2023, https://www.newyorker.com/culture/the-new-yorker-interview/leslie-marmon-silko -saw-it-coming.

——. *Yellow Woman and a Beauty of the Spirit.* Simon and Schuster, 1996.

Smith, Kimberly K. "W. E. B. Du Bois: Racial Inequality and Alienation from Nature." In *Engaging Nature: Environmentalism and the Political Theory Canon,* ed. Peter Cannavò and Joseph H. Lane Jr., 223–37. MIT Press, 2014.

——. "What Is Africa to Me? Wilderness in Black Thought, 1860–1930." *Environmental Ethics* 27, no. 3 (2005): 279–97.

Soper, Kate. *What Is Nature?* Blackwell, 1995.

Stampone, Christopher M. "Seeing Through 'the Veil' Darkly: Wordsworthian Ideals and Forms in W. E. B. Du Bois's *The Souls of Black Folk.*" *Journal of Transatlantic Studies* 19 (2021): 372–86.

Starkey, Michael. "Wilderness, Race, and African Americans: An Environmental History from Slavery to Jim Crow." Master's thesis, University of California, Berkeley, 2005, https://drive .google.com/file/d/1gMdUfFtmQHi35qvLhx6PModA7vFmx6nw/view.

Stewart, Carole Lynne. "Civil Religion, Civil Society, and the Performative Life and Work of W. E. B. Du Bois." *Journal of Religion* 88, no. 3 (2008): 307-30.

Stout, Jeffrey. *Democracy and Tradition*. Princeton University Press, 2004.

—. *Flight from Authority: Religion, Morality, and the Quest for Autonomy*. University of Notre Dame Press, 1981.

—. "The Transformation of Genius into Practical Power: A Reading of Emerson's 'Experience.'" *American Journal of Theology & Philosophy* 35, no. 1 (2014): 3-24.

Strang, Hilary. "Common Life, Animal Life, Equality: *The Last Man*." *English Literary History* 78, no. 2 (2011): 409-31.

Stryker, Susan. "My Words to Victor Frankenstein Above the Village of Chamounix." In *The Transgender Studies Reader*, ed. Susan Stryker and Stephen Whittle, 244-56. Routledge, 2006.

Sundquist, Eric J. *To Wake the Nations: Race in the Making of American Literature*. Belknap, 1993.

Taylor, Charles A. *A Secular Age*. Harvard University Press, 2007.

Taylor, Paul. *Black Is Beautiful: A Philosophy of Black Aesthetics*. Wiley-Blackwell, 2016.

Tetreault, Ronald. "Wordsworth on Enthusiasm: A New Letter to Thomas Clarkson on the Slavery Question." *Modern Philology* 75, no. 1 (1977): 53-58.

Thoreau, Henry David. "Ktaadn." In *The Wilderness Reader*, ed. Frank Bergon, 123-35. University of Nevada Press, 1980.

—. *Thoreau: Walden, The Maine Woods, Collected Essays and Poems*. Ed. Robert Sayre and Elizabeth Witherell. Library of America, 2007.

—. *A Week on the Concord and Merrimack Rivers*. Ed. H. Daniel Peck. Penguin, 1998.

Tillett, Rebecca. "Reality Consumed by Realty: The Ecological Costs of 'Development' in Leslie Marmon Silko's *Almanac of the Dead*." *European Journal of American Culture* 24, no. 2 (2005): 153-69.

Trachtenberg, Zev. "Elysium." *Inhabiting the Anthropocene* (blog), December 12, 2018, https://inhabitingtheanthropocene.com/2018/12/12/elysium/.

Tsing, Anna Lowenhaupt. *Friction: An Ethnography of Global Connection*. Princeton University Press, 2005.

Tuchinsky, Adam-Max. "'Her Cause Against Herself': Margaret Fuller, Emersonian Democracy, and the Nineteenth-Century Public Intellectual." *American Nineteenth Century History* 5, no. 1 (2004): 66-99.

TuSmith, Bonnie. *All My Relatives: Community in Contemporary Ethnic American Literatures*. University of Michigan Press, 1994.

Vakoch, Douglas A., ed. *Transecology: Transgender Perspectives on Environment and Nature*. Routledge, 2022.

Voyles, Traci B. *Wastelanding: Legacies of Uranium Mining in Navajo Country*. University of Minnesota Press, 2015.

Walls, Laura Dassow. *Henry David Thoreau: A Life*. University of Chicago Press, 2017.

Watts, Eric King. "Cultivating a Black Public Voice: W. E. B. Du Bois and the 'Criteria of Negro Art.'" *Rhetoric & Public Affairs* 4, no. 2 (2001): 181-201.

Weatherly, Ulysses G. "The First Universal Races Congress." *American Journal of Sociology* 17, no. 3 (1911): 315-28.

Webb, Samantha. "Reading the End of the World: The Last Man, History, and the Agency of Romantic Authorship." In *Mary Shelley in Her Times*, ed. Betty T. Bennett and Stuart Curran, 119-33. Johns Hopkins University Press, 2000.

Weiss, Penny A. "Rousseau, Antifeminism, and Woman's Nature." *Political Theory* 15, no. 1 (1987): 81-98.

Wendling, Ronald. *Coleridge's Progress to Christianity: Experience and Authority in Religious Faith.* Associated University Presses, 1995.

West, Cornel, Richard Rorty, Stanley Hauerwas, and Jeffrey Stout. "Pragmatism and Democracy: Assessing Jeffrey Stout's *Democracy and Tradition*." Ed. Jason Springs. *Journal of the American Academy of Religion* 78, no. 2 (2010): 413-48.

Whitman, Walt. *Whitman: Poetry and Prose.* Ed. Justin Kaplan. Library of America, 1982.

Whitney, Julian S. "A Black Manifesto: Ottobah Cugoano's Radical Romanticism." *Studies in Romanticism* 61, no. 1 (2022): 47-56.

Whyte, Kyle P. "Critical Investigations of Resilience: A Brief Introduction to Indigenous Environmental Studies & Sciences." *Dædalus, the Journal of the American Academy of Arts & Sciences* 147, no. 2 (2018): 136-47.

——. "Indigenous Experience, Environmental Justice and Settler Colonialism." In *Nature and Experience: Phenomenology and the Environment*, ed. Bryan E. Bannon, 157-73. Rowman & Littlefield, 2016.

——. "Indigenous Science (Fiction) for the Anthropocene: Ancestral Dystopias and Fantasies of Climate Change Crises." *Environment and Planning E: Nature and Space* 1, no. 1-2 (2018): 224-42.

——. "Settler Colonialism, Ecology, and Environmental Injustice." *Environment and Society: Advances in Research* 9 (2018): 125-44.

——. "What Do Indigenous Knowledges Do for Indigenous Peoples?" In *Traditional Ecological Knowledge: Learning from Indigenous Practices for Environmental Sustainability*, ed. Melissa K. Nelson and Dan Shilling, 57-81. Cambridge University Press, 2018.

Wilde, Oscar. *The Complete Works of Oscar Wilde.* Vol. 2: *De Profundis; "Epistola: In Carcere et Vinculis."* Ed. Ian Small. Oxford University Press, 2005.

Williams, Robert W. "'The Sacred Unity in All the Diversity': The Text and a Thematic Analysis of W. E. B. Du Bois' 'The Individual and Social Conscience' (1905)." *Journal of African American Studies* 16, no. 3 (2012): 456-97.

Williams, Terry Tempest. *An Unspoken Hunger: Stories from the Field.* Vintage, 1994.

Wilson, Anthony. *Shadow and Shelter: The Swamp in Southern Culture.* University Press of Mississippi, 2006.

Wilson, Shawn. *Research Is Ceremony.* Fernwood, 2008.

Winters, Joseph R. *Hope Draped in Black.* Duke University Press, 2016.

Wordsworth, Jonathan. *The Music of Humanity.* Thomas Nelson and Sons, 1969.

Wordsworth, William. *Guide to the Lakes.* Ed. Saeko Yoshikawa. Oxford University Press, 2022.

——. *Poems, in Two Volumes, and Other Poems, 1800-1807.* Ed. Jared Curtis. Cornell University Press, 1983.

——. *The Prelude: 1799, 1805, 1850.* Ed. Jonathan Wordsworth, M. H. Abrams, and Stephen Gill. Norton, 1979.

——. *William Wordsworth: The Major Works.* Ed. Stephen Gill. Oxford University Press, 2008.

——. *William Wordsworth: Selected Prose.* Ed. John O. Hayden. Penguin, 1988.

Worster, Donald. *Nature's Economy: A History of Ecological Ideas.* Cambridge University Press, 1994.

Wright, Angela, and Dale Townshend, ed. *Romantic Gothic: An Edinburgh Companion.* Edinburgh University Press, 2015.

Yao, Xine. *Disaffected.* Duke University Press, 2021.

Zeiger, Melissa. "'Modern Nature': Derek Jarman's Garden." *Humanities* 6, no. 2 (2017).

Zigarovich, Jolene. "The Trans Legacy of Frankenstein." *Science Fiction Studies* 45, no. 2 (2018): 260–72.

Ziolkowski, Theodore. "Ruminations on Ruins: Classical Versus Romantic." *German Quarterly* 89, no. 3 (2016): 265–81.

Zolciak, Olivia. "Sublimating an Apocalypse: An Exploration of Anxiety, Authorship, and Feminist Theory in Mary Shelley's *The Last Man.*" *American Journal of Economics and Sociology* 77, no. 5 (2018): 1243–276.

Zwarg, Christina. "Footnoting the Sublime: Margaret Fuller on Black Hawk's Trail." *American Literary History* 5, no. 4 (1993): 616–42.

Index

354   *Index*

Rose, Deborah Bird, 277, 279–80

Rousseau, Jean-Jacques, 8, 19, 91, 128; Alpine landscape in imagination of, 92, 95, 97–99, 302, 303n16; *amour-propre*, 94, 113, 304n42; commitment to "the people," 138; as early protoenvironmentalist, 94; on human relation to a variety of lands, 99; industrialization critiqued by, 92–93; middle way, 96; "nature as other" model challenged by, 94, 302n8; rationality, view of, 100–101; religious aesthetic of, 98–101; Wordsworth, influence on, 137–38; *Works: Considerations on the Government of Poland*, 97; *Discourse on the Origin of Inequality*, 101; *Emile*, 98, 99–100, 108, 146; *The Materialism of the Wise*, 97; *The Reveries of the Solitary Walker*, 97; *Second Discourse*, 101; *The Social Contract*, 95, 96, 98. *See also Julie; or, The New Heloise* (Rousseau)

Roxbury, Massachusetts garden, 110–12

Ruffin, Kimberly N., 204, 218

"Ruined Cottage, The" (Wordsworth), xv, 5, 59, 80, 263–65, 266, 267, 321n9

ruins: beauty, hope, and love among, 276–80; in Du Bois, 265–68; ghosts of, 265, 267–68, 270–76; picturesque, xiv–xv, 263, 265–67, 321n4, 321n5; prophetic, xiv–xv, 263–64, 266–67, 321n5; rebuilding in shadow of, 22, 245, 262, 269–73, 275, 279; "ruined world," 269–72; as sites of pain and injustice, hope and transformation, 263–65; "sitting" within, 271; "staying with the trouble," 270; stories of, 22, 262–64; in Wordsworth, xv, 5, 59, 80, 263–65. *See also* catastrophe; nuclear colonialism

Sandilands, Catriona, 89

Sandler, Matt, 207

second nature: corruption of, 160; emphasis on tradition, practice, form, and place, 138; as formative process, 136–37, 140

second nature, democratic, 37, 40, 262; and more-than-human world, 142–43; and praxis-oriented empathy, 16–17; role of

place and taste in, 139–40; Rousseau's view, 94, 108; and wildness/wilderness, 65–66, 71; and women, 108; Wordsworth's view, 132, 136–41, 310n52. *See also* nature; spiritual democracy

"second-sight," of Black people, 42, 50–51

secularization, 114–15, 305n2; attributed to Wordsworth's sonnet, 134–35; darker side to, 116; disrupted by radical Romanticism, 115; Nature portrayed as replacement for religion, 129; standard theories of religion and Romanticism, 12, 115–17, 127, 129, 133, 142–43, 306n11. *See also* religion

secular traditions, 61

self-interest, 26

self-reliance, 70, 141–42, 192

Seneca Falls Convention, 191

settler colonialism, 20–23, 199–200; boundaries imposed by, 237, 240, 248–49; catastrophe produced by, 223–24; forgetting as strategy of, 225, 269; stereotypes of Indigenous spirituality, 244; stories of, 261–62; swamp as site of resistance to, 77–78. *See also* colonialism; nuclear colonialism

Shelley, Mary Wollstonecraft, 8, 109, 175, 180–90, 274; climate in, 183–84, 187; "dark, wild hope" in, 190; dual humanist/posthumanist perspectives, 188–89; moral imagination solicited from reader, 27–28; nature, view of, 187; religion in, 188; as researcher, 178; wilderness, view of, 64–65. *See also Frankenstein* (Shelley); *The Last Man* (Shelley)

Shelley, Percy, 274

Shewry, Teresa, 88

Shutkin, William, 110–12

silence, 63, 99–100, 294–95n2; as agency, 33; of catastrophe, 165–66; of God, 150–51; of the wild, 119–20

Silko, Leslie Marmon, xv, xviii–xix, 3, 9, 18, 140, 178, 222–60; awakening to everyday suffering, oppression, resilience, and joy in,

United States Department of Agriculture
(USDA), 84
Unsettling of America, The (Berry), 261
utopian thought, 107, 110–12, 167–68

vision, 4, 291n28; in Du Bois, 46–47; ethical,
14, 39; hypervisibility, 32, 46, 165; public,
117–19
Voltaire, 29

Walker, Alice, 203
Walker, David, 30, 39, 81
"Walking" (Thoreau), 70, 71, 83
Watts, Eric, 53–54
west, as symbolic direction, 71
white people: as agents of witchery, 228,
230–32; objectification of world, 227–28;
readers of Indigenous literature, 243–44;
white nationalism, 88, 221; whiteness as
ownership of the earth, 172; white
privilege, 49, 53. *See also* settler
colonialism
white supremacy: Black responses to, 147;
Christianity of, 76; continuity of, 215,
267–68; counteracted in *The Quest*, 8, 78;
countered in "The Prayers of God,"
154–59; durability of, 152; as ownership of
earth, 172; Southern, 77; and taste, 28–29
Whitman, Walt, 16, 192, 193, 287n5
Whitney, Julian, 208
Whyte, Kyle, 228, 231, 298n51
Wilberforce, William, 118, 290n27
wild, the (wildness, wilderness), 8, 61, 62–91,
211–12, 295n5; "acts of God," 214; of
Africa, 75–76, 297n34; alternative
accounts of, 18–19, 64–66; as alternative
to patriarchy, 64–65, 78–79; art and
theory as participants in, 63; Black
mother as, 172; and citizenship, 69–70,
72; as "close to home," 66, 70; as
condition and process, 62–66, 71; critique
of, 18, 74; depicted as distant or removed
from everyday experience, 64; dialectical
process with, 72; in Du Bois, 18–19, 73–91;
embraced by vulnerable, interdependent

selves, 65; as erotically charged entity,
274; Euro-American views of, 74, 80, 93;
and hope, 71, 80, 87–89; "the muck" as,
212–13, 316n62; need for, 80–84; and
Niagara Movement, 81–82; "pear tree
religion" and "hurricane religion," 204,
218–19; as place, 64–65; prison as, 69;
racism associated with, 80–81, 299n57; as
rebellious state of being, 65; and
resistance, 8, 70–80, 87–89, 106–7; and
second nature, 65–66, 71; silence of,
119–20; and Sorrow Songs, 75; subversive
culture as, 106; swamps, 71, 74, 76–80,
85–86; Thoreau's views, 69–73;
transgression of gendered boundaries,
217; wilderness of failure and terminality,
111; Wordsworth's views, 65–69. *See also*
storied landscapes
Wilde, Oscar, 17
Williams, Terry Tempest, 317n72; *Works:*
"Clan of One-Breasted Women," 243; *The
Open Space of Democracy*, 220; *Refuge*,
220–21
Wilson, Anthony, 77
Winters, Joseph, 41, 87
wise, materialism of, 97–98
"wise passiveness," 25, 57, 106, 139, 236
witnessing, xii, 2, 57; expert guide needed,
264, 266; to nuclear colonialism, 228–29;
of prophetic ruins, 264–65; role and
nature of art in, 235–37; voyeurism
versus, xii, 17, 226, 266
Wittgenstein, Ludwig, 140
Woman in the Nineteenth Century, 191
women, Black, 298nn50, 51; Du Bois on
oppression of, 171–72; triple oppression
of, 52
women, in general: associated with nature,
93–94, 298n51; and ecofeminism, 108–10;
erotic power of, 211; gender reversals in
Rousseau, 104–5; Indigenous, 199; as
monstrous other, 180–90; problemhood
of, 184; and way of the eco-mountain
community, 96; wilderness as alternative
to patriarchal structures, 64–65, 78–79

GPSR Authorized Representative: Easy Access System Europe, Mustamäe tee
50, 10621 Tallinn, Estonia, gpsr.requests@easproject.com

www.ingramcontent.com/pod-product-compliance
Lightning Source LLC
Chambersburg PA
CBHW022133020426
42334CB00015B/871